Mysticism
and the
Early South
German–Austrian
Anabaptist
Movement
1525–1531

Mysticism and the Early South German–Austrian Anabaptist Movement 1525–1531

Werner O.Packull

WIPF & STOCK · Eugene, Oregon

Wipf and Stock Publishers
199 W 8th Ave, Suite 3
Eugene, OR 97401

Mysticism and the Early South German - Austrian Anabaptist Movement 1525 - 1531
By Packull, Werner O.
Copyright©1977 Herald Press
ISBN 13: 9781532666995
Publication date 12/03/2008
Previously published by Herald Press, 1977

To my wife, Karin
(daughter of Lili [Rolfs] † 1975 and Erich Fiebig),
and to our children,
Christine and Reinhold,
in gratitude and affection.

CONTENTS

ACKNOWLEDGMENTS

I wish to express my appreciation for the assistance rendered to me in the course of this study by the following: Dr. Kenneth Davis, for first arousing my interest in Anabaptist studies while I was one of his students at the University of Waterloo, for his many suggestions regarding the book, and especially for his encouragements during the rather stormy first two years of my teaching career; all my colleagues in the History Department of the University of Waterloo; graduate students Dennis Martin and John Braun; Dr. Walter Klaassen, for patiently listening to some of my less realistic ideas, and for making the Anabaptist Collection at Conrad Grebel College accessible to me; Mr. Nelson P. Springer, Curator of Mennonite Historical Library, Goshen, Indiana, for his personal interest in my research, and for making numerous items from the John Horsch and Rare Book collections available.

I also thank the many helpful persons I met while researching in the Bibliotheek der Vereenigde Doopsgezinde Gemeente te Amsterdam, Generallandesarchiv Karlsruhe, Stadtarchiv Worms, Stadtarchiv Nürnberg, Stadtarchiv and Stadtbibliothek Augsburg and Mennonitische Forschungsstelle Weierhof; Dr. Gottfried Seebass for unselfishly making his groundbreaking work on Hans Hut in as-yet unpublished manuscript form available to me, when my own work was still in an early stage, also for suggestions and corrections he offered after reading my dissertation; Dr. Hans-Jürgen Goertz for his extremely helpful references to literature I had originally ignored, his other suggestions and corrections regarding the manuscript; Canada Council for providing the financial assistance that made this work possible; Mrs. Gerlinde Borth for typing this "stuff" at least three times; and all the staff and faculty at Renison College and my students for making the two years when this work was in the process of being written such a memorable occasion. Above all, I thank my petite wife for her unwavering faith in her husband's scholarly and literary competence, for the countless ways in which she furthered my scholarly progress while selflessly assuming extra family responsibilities.

And, finally, I acknowledge my indebtedness, to Dr. James Stayer, my former supervisor at Queen's University. Professor Stayer's excellent graduate seminar on the Reformation in 1970-71 provided the background for my research. It would constitute a long list to enumerate all the acts of kindness with which he furthered my work. All the material and information which he believed pertinent was passed on to me. His many stylistic and interpretative suggestions pervade the better portions of the book, and were it not for the weaker sections, Dr. Stayer should appear as its coauthor.

Werner O. Packull
Department of History
University of Waterloo
Waterloo, Ontario

INTRODUCTION

The special merit of Werner Packull's work is that he delineates more clearly than any previous scholar the theological and spiritual differences between South German and Swiss Anabaptists by a thorough examination of the dominant medieval mystical influence in the thought of Denck and Hut and the latter's immediate South German Anabaptist followers. Indeed, Packull decides that South German Anabaptism derives more from medieval mysticism than from the reformation. Packull is convincing in his demonstration of this thesis both because of his meticulous care in reading the primary sources and also because he examines and refutes the arguments of those who would place the Protestant influence as the primary one. He is at his best when he isolates and explains particular ideas of the medieval mystics and demonstrates their influence on Denck and Hut.

In pursuit of his thesis Packull expands and elaborates the earlier suggestions of Kiwiet (*Pilgram Marbeck, Ein Führer in der Täuferbewegung.* Kassel: Oncken, 1957.) and Williams (*The Radical Reformation.* Philadelphia: Westminster, 1962), both of whom postulated a discrete Anabaptism in South Germany as against that of Switzerland; and he draws on the more recent and still unpublished work of Gottfried Seebass (*Müntzer's Erbe. Werk, Leben und Theologie des Hans Hut*), especially on Seebass' selection of writings which he ascribes to Hut.

Packull's second major thesis is that the earliest form of South German Anabaptism was transitional both sociologically and theologically. Here Packull is convincing although less surprising because the point is rather more obvious and because he directed his research more toward the religious backgrounds of Denck and Hut than to those changes in South German Anabaptism brought by a more direct encounter with the Swiss Brethren. The effect of Packull's work is to underline the point that there were indeed strains of Anabaptism which were not as clearly biblicist in emphasis as the one in Zurich. His work makes the phenomenon of early Anabaptism more complex, less uniform, but historically more accurate, more in line with the realities of the religious ferment of the 1520s among German-speaking people.

Not every doctoral dissertation deserves to be published. Studies in Anabaptist and Mennonite History has published six of them, and is pleased to be able to add the seventh because of its excellence. Since

Mennonite historians have been the principal opponents of a mysticism-spiritualism motif in Anabaptism in recent decades, in deference to a more dominant biblicist strain, it is appropriate that a Mennonite series publish the work of Packull.

The Mennonite Historical Society wishes to thank Cornelius J. Dyck of the Institute of Mennonite Studies for his editorial supervision and skillful guidance of this work through the details of the publication process, and his assistant, Mrs. Rachel Friesen, for her help in copy editing. The Canada Council again deserves the warm thanks of the scholarly community for providing a publication subsidy on the basis of which the book can be marketed at a more reasonable price.

Werner Packull, assistant professor of history at Renison College, Waterloo, wrote an earlier version of this work as a doctoral dissertation at Queen's University, Kingston, Ontario, under the professorial supervision of James Stayer, whose influence in bringing the volume to press is gratefully acknowledged.

John S. Oyer
Goshen, Indiana

ABBREVIATIONS

ARG	*Archiv für Reformationsgeschichte*
BQ	*Baptist Quarterly*
CH	*Church History*
LCC: SAW	Williams, George, and Mergal, Angel (eds.), *Spiritual and Anabaptist Writers*
MB	*Mennonitische Blätter*
ME	*The Mennonite Encyclopedia*
MGB	*Mennonitische Geschichtsblätter*
ML	*Mennonitisches Lexikon*
MQR	*Mennonite Quarterly Review*
TA: Baden und Pfalz	Krebs, Manfred (ed.), *Baden und Pfalz*
TA: Bayern, I	Schornbaum, Karl (ed.), *Markgraftum Brandenburg: Bayern,* Part I
TA: Bayern, II	Schornbaum, Karl (ed.), *Markgraftum Brandenburg: Bayern,* Part II
TA: Denck	Baring, Georg, and Fellmann, Walter (eds.), *Hans Denck: Schriften*
TA: Elsass, I	Krebs, Manfred, and Rott, Georg (eds.), *Elsass,* Part I: *Stadt Strassburg, 1522-1532*
TA: Elsass, II	Krebs, Manfred, and Rott, Georg (eds.), *Elsass,* Part II: *Stadt Strassburg, 1533-1535*
TA: Glaubenszeugnisse, I	Müller, Lydia (ed.), *Glaubenszeugnisse oberdeutscher Taufgesinnter,* Vol. I
TA: Hubmaier	Westin, Gunnar, and Bergsten, Torsten (eds.), *Balthasar Hubmaier: Schriften*
TA: Oesterreich, I	Mecenseffy, Grete (ed.), *Oesterreich,* Part I
TA: Oesterreich, II	Mecenseffy, Grete (ed.), *Oesterreich,* Part II
TA: Ostschweiz	Fast, Heinold (ed.), *Ostschweiz*
TA: Württemberg	Bossert, Gustav, Sr., and Bossert, Gustav, Jr. (eds.), *Herzogtum Württemberg*
TSK	*Theologische Studien und Kritiken*
TZ	*Theologische Zeitschrift*
ZBKG	*Zeitschrift für Bayerische Kirchengeschichte*
ZHVSN: Augsburg	Roth, Friedrich (ed.), "Zur Geschichte der Wiedertäufer in Oberschwaben": Part III: "Der Höhepunkt der Bewegung in Augsburg und der

	Niedergang im Jahre 1528." *Zeitschrift des historischen Vereins für Schwaben und Neuburg,* XXVIII
ZHVSN: Hut	Meyer, Christian (ed.), "Zur Geschichte der Wiedertäufer in Oberschwaben": Part I: "Die Anfänge des Wiedertäufertums in Augsburg." *Zeitschrift des historischen Vereins für Schwaben und Neuburg,* I
ZHVSN: Langenmantel	Roth, Friedrich (ed.), "Zur Geschichte der Wiedertäufer in Oberschwaben": Part II: "Zur Lebensgeschichte Eitelhans Langenmantels von Augsburg." *Zeitschrift des historischen Vereins für Schwaben und Neuburg,* XXVII
ZKG	*Zeitschrift für Kirchengeschichte*
ZST	*Zeitschrift für Systematische Theologie*
Zwingliana	*Beiträge zur Geschichte Zwinglis, der Reformation und des Protestantismus in der Schweiz*

1

A MEDIEVAL POINT OF DEPARTURE

An analysis of the relationship of medieval mysticism to early South German Anabaptist theology contains a complex of interpretive problems. Inextricably interwoven are the questions of the relationship between (1) the Reformation and mysticism (e.g., the young Luther versus the old),[1] (2) Müntzer and Luther, (3) Müntzer and South German Anabaptism, and (4) of South German Anabaptism to the Reformed and Swiss Anabaptist movements. Part of the same problem is the relationship of mysticism and spiritualism and of both to humanism. Consequently the question of whether the South German Anabaptists should be regarded as radical children of the Reformers—the "left wing of the Reformation"—or spiritual heirs of a medieval legacy is also reopened. Neither the mystical tradition nor the Anabaptist movement were monolithic historical entities.

Some of these issues became apparent during the Holl-Troeltsch controversy. Karl Holl, whose perspective coincided with that of Luther, tended to see all Anabaptists as *Schwärmer* and disciples of Müntzer. As a *Geistesgeschichtler* allegedly interested primarily in historical connections, he warned that Anabaptism could not be conceived of apart from mysticism, and he believed somewhat generously that Luther was the mediating source of mysticism for his "wayward followers."[2] Against Holl, Ernst Troeltsch underlined the differences between the mystical church view of the Spiritualists and the sect-type ecclesiology of the Anabaptists. For Troeltsch both were legitimate social manifestations of the "Christian idea" existing beside the dominant "church type" represented in Catholicism and the major

Reformers.[3] He, therefore, cleared the way for a more appreciative approach to deviants from the church model, and made possible a clear separation of Anabaptist sectarians from spiritual enthusiasts.[4] It was hardly accidental that his view spelled progress for scholars descended from or sympathetic to the Anabaptist or free-church tradition. The Troeltsch thesis became an inextricable part of the "revisionist" school, which proved to be particularly productive in generating typologies of Reformation radicalism with varying degrees of relevance to the historical context. Anabaptism became *de facto* separatist and sectarian in the minds of a generation of church historians.[5]

Pioneering research on the Swiss Anabaptists primarily preoccupied with political ethic or congregation building appeared to favour Troeltsch's thesis. Zürich replaced Zwickau as the birthplace of Anabaptism. The lines between *Schwärmer* or Spiritualist and Anabaptist were drawn more clearly in keeping with Troeltsch's distinction between mysticism and sect. The Schleitheim Confession with its strong biblicism became accepted as theologically normative for "main stream evangelical Anabaptism." Consequently the Anabaptists were generally conceived of as the radical children of the Reformation (specifically, the Reformation of Zwingli).[6]

In spite of its initial fruitfulness in helping to distinguish between Spiritualists and Anabaptists, however, the Troeltsch thesis contained certain inherent weaknesses.[7] From his liberal sociological perspective, Troeltsch saw both the sect and mysticism as general Protestant manifestations.[8] The acceptance of this assumption prejudiced any serious effort to seek historical connections between Anabaptism and sources other than the Reformers—an attitude congenial to the climate of Reformation renaissance in vogue during the fifties. This tendency was encouraged by the exaggerated efforts of nineteenth-century historians to find direct historical connections between Anabaptism and an underground medieval church or a succession of historical sects.[9] Mennonite reluctance to see their forebears implicated in any kind of spirituality that would compromise their assumed Protestant "evangelical biblicism and fideism" further contributed to the mentality which refused to look beyond the Reformation and the Bible for possible antecedents of Anabaptism.[10]

Recent scholarship, without denying the achievements of what we have labelled above as the revisionist school, has recognized some of its weaknesses. The historical discussion of Anabaptist origins has gone well beyond the limited Zwickau or Zürich debate of Holl and

Troeltsch.[11] It has now been recognized that the Swiss Brethren emerged as a peaceful, confessional movement only after a painful process of gestation,[12] and it has become part of a scholarly consensus that Anabaptism in Switzerland, at least in its conception, was not exclusively separatist and sectarian. The same social and economic impulses that inspired local peasant unrest fueled the religious dissent of the early Anabaptists.[13] Past attempts to conceive of Anabaptism as sealed off from any influence of Müntzer have become less convincing even for Swiss Anabaptism, and for the German branches of Anabaptism they have become untenable.

Meanwhile a certain "protestantized" form of a "medieval lay, ascetic spirituality" has been rediscovered as part of the Anabaptist vision.[14] Research on Balthasar Hubmaier has uncovered his indebtedness to scholastic nominalism.[15] Müntzer scholarship itself has come to recognize the importance of medieval mysticism for Müntzer.[16] It appears, therefore, legitimate to break with the time-honoured lateral approach of outlining the theological views of Anabaptist leaders with reference to the major Reformers. Given the main focus of this book on the early South German Anabaptist protest movement, whose strong indebtedness to mystical theology has long been recognized, an analysis of the main tenets of medieval mysticism is a necessity as a point of departure.

Because of its introductory nature to the main body of this work, the discussion undertaken here cannot navigate the whole ocean of ink spilt by and about the mystics. It aims by touching upon the writings of Meister Eckhardt, John Tauler, and the *Theologia Deutsch* to plumb medieval German mysticism in its deepest, most concentrated form and to lay bare the cardinal themes of the tradition which influenced early South German Anabaptist theology. This type of mysticism has often been contrasted with the less speculative, more devotional Latin mysticism of a St. Bonaventura and St. Bernard of Clairvaux. According to this distinction the Germanic tradition has been classified as "essentialistic, transformational, and theocentric," concerned with the intellectual contemplation of God (*visio Dei*), who in turn was defined as "truth."

The theological framework of the German mystics, often members of the Dominican Order, was supposedly Thomist in orientation containing a strong dose of Dionysian Neoplatonism. By contrast, the Latin mystics, who were more often than not of the Cistercian or Franciscan orders, have been described as "affective, penitential, and Christocentric," concerned with volitional conformity to the will of God, while God was defined as "good."[17] This Franciscan tradition proved particularly productive as an agent of cross-fertilization with German mysticism during the fifteenth century when many of the Latin texts were translated into German.[18] A veritable Bonaventura renaissance spread through the Tyrol and Upper Bavaria,[19] an area from which some of the later Anabaptist leaders were to emerge. Hence it would be wrong to think of the two traditions as mutually exclusive. Although the mystics disagreed on the mode of the *unio mystica*, which was perceived from different metaphysical presuppositions, they had more in common with one another than either had with pure scholasticism, particularly its late medieval nominalist variety. For while nominalism reduced God's relation to His creation and man to the covenantal—to willed agreements and conventions—the mystics affirmed

> that God and man share a common nature and are really connected. This is highlighted on the anthropological level by the weight placed on the *synteresis voluntatis et rationis* and/or *Seelengrund;* in the area of soteriology it is set forth in the principle equally widespread . . . [that] likeness (similitude) is the *sine qua non* for saving knowledge and relationship.[20]

German and Latin mysticism were not two separated entities existing side by side. At least by the fifteenth century they had become intertwined in various degrees of complexity. In particular, the influential *Theologia Deutsch* can be seen as a merger of the two streams.[21]

Meister Eckhardt was the fountainhead of German mysticism. He was one of the first Central Europeans to give theoretical expression to medieval mystical aspirations. His contribution to the medieval intellectual landscape was sufficiently original (or unorthodox) to draw upon him the suspicions and eventual condemnation of the contemporary theological establishment. From a religious studies approach or from a psychological point of view the mystical experience described by Eckhardt may be viewed as transcendental, that is, as something transcending ordinary sense perception. However, expressed theologically, the chief theme of Eckhardt's mysticism was a strong emphasis on the immanence of the divine in man. The theological focus rested on the connection between the human and divine in the human soul.[22] This emphasis corresponded to the general medieval ethos, which was strongly impressed with the immediacy of the supernatural, and to the widespread religious mood which sought fulfillment in direct contact and union with God.

Basic to an understanding of Eckhardt was his explanation of the Trinity in terms of a Neoplatonic emanation theory of creation. Creation itself was conceived as a trinitarian process.[23]The first step in this process was the birth of the *logos* or Son. The Father, becoming self-conscious by introspection and reflection, brought about the spontaneous generation of a subject-object relationship within the Godhead. Thus, the Son (*logos*), the object or mirror in which the Father recognized Himself and comprehended Himself, was born. The medium which carried filial recognition and sponsored love between the object and subject in the Godhead was the Holy Spirit.[24] Creation, which thus began through a division in the Godhead, was nothing but a duplication and externalization of divine thought in material dimensions of space and time. It becomes at once obvious that in this framework Eckhardt, in harmony with John 1, would stress Christ as the transhistorical *logos*. In His capacity as the divine Word (reason and understanding) He was the *Urbild* and mover of creation. That is to say, He represented both Architect and living blueprint in an ongoing process. In this context Eckhardt's explanation of creation can be described as Christocentric.[25]

Just as the *logos* was crucial to the process of genesis, so His role was crucial in man's salvation. Salvation was a reversal of the creation process, a bringing back together of all diversity into unity through the *unio mystica*. Longing for unity and return to oneness for Eckhardt appeared to be a natural law built into all creatures.[26] But it was a direct possibility for man only, for he alone was the direct image of God, that is to say, man was a replica of the eternal Son. For as there was one Son in eternity, so many were born in time. Through his higher powers lodged in the soul, man was directly connected with the Divine. In fact, some of Eckhardt's bolder statements suggest that the "nobler (rational) powers of the soul" were identical with the indwelling logos.[27] The problem for man was to recognize the divine in him. This could be achieved only by turning inward. The senses communicated only external and, therefore, secondary reality, but reason, the noblest power of the soul, could clasp naked divinity.[28] Eckhardt blended medieval theory of knowledge and scholastic anthropology to support his explanation of mystical experience. Knowledge of an object presupposed equality or sameness with that object. "As the masters say, to be (*sein*) and to have knowledge of (*Erkenntnis*) are one and the same thing (*durchaus Eines*)."[29] To achieve saving knowledge of the Divine, therefore, implied divinity on

man's part and humanity on God's part. The *logos* as the universal pro-
totype and archetype provided the crucial link both as an anthropological resource and as the revelatory image of the Father to man. For it
logically followed that only the Son, being equal to the Father, could reveal the Father to man in mystical union. Mystical union thus ontologi-
cally perceived implied the deifying transformation of man. This
process was nothing else than the inverted *"filiato generatio."*[30]

A strong emphasis on what later would be considered sanctification
was a direct corollary of Eckhardt's *via mystica.* Man's responsibility
was to cooperate with the divine in him, that is to say, to subject all
externals including his body to the powers of the soul. For only in total
detachment (*Gelassenheit*) from all creatureliness could the "inner
Word" be apprehended.

> For whoever would like to hear God's Word, must be com-
> pletely detached (*gelassen*). Precisely that which hears, is the same
> as that which is being heard in the eternal Word. Everything which
> the eternal Father teaches, that is His being, His nature, and His
> goodness, He reveals to us in His only begotten Son, teaching us
> that we are the same Son.[31]

Thus it is Christ, the preincarnate *logos*, who becomes the central
link between God and man. The *logos* through His participation in divinity as well as His immanence in man makes union between man and
God feasible.[32]

Eckhardt's cardinal axiom of divine immanence continued to be
the central theme of the mystical tradition and carried with it certain
implications for future dissenters. Obviously the possibility of
unmediated contact with God implicitly undermined all authority relating to objective externals. It undermined the mediating role of the
medieval church and its sacramentalism. Indeed, Eckhardt warned
against false confidence in the sacraments. These could be a hindrance
if the believer remained preoccupied with the outer and sensual. Those
who sought God only through outer aids, in certain physical locations,
and so on, would never know of Him in truth.[33] The emphasis on the
true inner reality contained also certain hermeneutical implications. It
appears that Eckhardt, like most of his medieval contemporaries, accepted Augustine's distinction between *signum* and *res* and the com-
patible *Signifikationshermeneutik.* In practice he favoured the allegorical method of scriptural interpretation which was better suited to
grasping the real spiritual meaning. A literal interpretation would lean

too heavily on the creaturely letter.[34] Later, opposition against the Reformation principle of *sola scriptura* would be launched from similar assumptions.

Similarly, the emphasis on the indwelling universal *logos* carried implicit Christological implications. The uniqueness of the historical or incarnate Word was minimized in favour of the cosmic *logos* present in every man. The redemptive role of the incarnate Christ could not be crucial in Eckhardt's system. The righteousness of the *viator* attained in union with the Divine could not be an alien righteousness. In fact, the depravity of man, a necessity in any system stressing man's need for redemption, was diluted in Eckhardt's writings. The concept of the fall of man and resulting original sin underwent a drastic transformation of meaning when the attempt was made to harmonize it with the emanation theory of creation. In keeping with the strong matter-spirit dichotomy, the Fall itself became almost synonymous with the act of creation, and original sin with creatureliness. Eckhardt indicated a preference for such topics as the nobility of man rather than man the sinner. Not surprisingly, therefore, one will search in vain for the deeper questions of human depravity which later occupied the Reformers. On the other hand, the Neoplatonic matter-spirit dichotomy forced the conclusion that all preoccupation with externals and material things hindered man's communion with the Divine. Man's sinfulness, then, grew out of his plight of having been created in part as a material being. His salvation, according to the *theologia mystica* of Eckhardt, involved a gradual disengagement from externals climaxing in union with the Divine. Man was called upon to participate actively with the Divine in him.[35]

Although there was only one Meister Eckhardt, all later mystics in the German tradition were directly or indirectly influenced by him, including Tauler and the unknown author of the *Theologia Deutsch*.[36] Like Eckhardt, these influential popularizers of the *via mystica* supported their explanation of the mystical experience by an appeal to divine immanence. By adjusting mysticism to the common man, they watered down speculative aspects of Eckhardt's thought, thereby broadening the influence of mysticism.[37] To the relief of church historians sympathetic to him, Tauler also tipped the balance in favour of the orthodox Christian tradition.[38] Tauler did not place the same importance as Eckhardt on the role of reason. His claims about the powers of the soul were more restrained, his description of the mode of union between the human and Divine more qualified.[39] His greater apprecia-

tion of original sin and human depravity, suggesting an Augustinian influence,[40] meant a more serious approach to the problem of evil. Hence
Tauler emphasized the preparatory cleansing struggle necessary before
the human and Divine could join in harmonious union. Evil and sin
were to be overcome through suffering—purgation from all creatureliness. While this process did not exclude outer hardships—sickness,
persecution, and the like—Tauler appears to have thought of it primarily in terms of inward trials, "cruel fighting, and strange dread, and
unheard of distress, which none can understand but he who has felt
them."[41] Thus was added to the German mystical tradition the all-im-
portant theme of "cross mysticism."

From this point of view the passion of the human Christ, which
moved the medieval mind to sympathetic pity, became primarily the
cosmological symbol of the suffering experienced by every viator on the
"inner cross," which was the cleansing prerequisite for ultimate union
with the Divine. For if Christ suffered to be perfected, so must "every
friend of God."[42] In suffering man was brought into conformity with the
human Christ, and only through conformity with the human Christ was
union with the divine *logos* achieved. Thus Tauler laid the foundation
for that stream within the *imitatio* tradition which stressed discipleship
with a focus on the passion of Christ as a necessary element of piety.[43]

This tendency towards the practical life was further accentuated in
the *Theologia Deutsch*. As a concession to scholastic orthodoxy of a
Thomist or nominalist variety, the author described the nature of
mystical union as one of wills.[44] With the attention shifted to human volition, obedience to the divine will was pushed into the foreground. And
although the tendency to internalize the life of Christ and the concept of
the *logos* is by no means lost,[45] the historical (incarnate) Christ assumed
greater significance as the exemplar of obedience. In the *Theologia* we
therefore find a mixture of the German and Latin mystical motifs. The
spiritualized internalized role of Christ as the universal connection
between the human and Divine and the gradual transformational
understanding of justification, culminating in the *unio mystica* are
complemented by an appeal to follow Christ's historical example of
obedience to the divine will. "He who will follow Him, must take up the
cross, and the cross is nothing else than the Christ-life, for that is a bitter
cross to all nature. . . ."[46] Thus the *Theologia* incorporated strong ascetic
and moralistic ethical overtones.

The relationship of the mystical legacy to late medieval scholasticism, as well as the cardinal theological insights of the Reformers,

specifically Luther, now needs to be examined. It has been argued that
Tauler and the *Theologia* by their focus on the experience of an inner
cross in humility and obedience—*resignatio*—foreshadowed Reformation *sola gratia* insights. In contrast to the *facere quod in se est* of scholasticism the mystics appeared to give decided prominence to God's role
in the work of redemption. According to this distinction between
mysticism and scholasticism the mystics taught a *sola gratia iustitia
passiva* and limited the immanence of God to a *capacitas passiva* in the
soul. The soul contained the possibility to know and love God, but this
did not mean that natural man without grace was able to love and know
God.[47] By internalizing and individualizing all relations with God the
mystics became precursors of Luther's personalized approach to religious authority.[48]

This reading of the mystics, however, ignored the typically
medieval anthropological assumptions found in their writings. No clear-
cut distinction existed between the natural and supernatural activity in
man,[49] precisely because God was immanent in the soul—or, anthropo-
logically speaking, because man possessed in his inner being (*Seelengrund*) the potential to participate in the supernatural and divine. And
even the *Theologia* which distinguished between the "eternal will" and
the "created will" argued that the eternal was immanent so that "the
will in the creature which we call a created will, is as truly God's as the
Eternal Will, and is not a property of the creature."[50] And it is clear that
neither the author of the *Theologia* nor Tauler conceived of the process
of justification via the *unio mystica* as an experience in which man
remained totally passive. Salvation was possible through the *cooperatio*
between the human and divine activity in the soul.[51]

> For God Himself can never make a man virtuous, good, or
> blessed, so long as he is outside of his soul; that is, so long as he casts
> about outwardly with his senses and reason, and does not withdraw
> into himself and learn to know his own life, who and what he is.[52]

The ambivalence between the natural and supernatural, human
and divine activity in the order of salvation, may be traced to a new
theological *potentia ordinata* forged by the mystical theologians. The
divinely ordained, dynamic order presupposed the Neoplatonic creation
process and medieval anthropology, but omitted the mediating role of
the sacramental system and the church. From a purely nominalist
perspective which included the sacramental system and the church as

part of God's preordained order of grace, it appeared, therefore, that the mystics with their focus on unmediated contact with God in the soul appealed to the *potentia Dei absoluta*. Or that on the basis of a unique receptacle for God in the soul—the inalienable and irrepressible *synteresis voluntatis et rationis* or Seelengrund—the mystics assumed a *potentia hominis absoluta*.[53] For unlike the mystics who, irrespective of their disagreements about the mode of union, affirmed that God and man shared a common nature and were really connected, the nominalists insisted that God's relation to the world and man was after all not dependent on real connections, but on covenantal, willed agreements and conventions. The nominalist *potentia ordinata* was reliable because of God's fidelity to His promises and because of the trustworthiness of God's Word behind the "system." The nominalists, therefore, unlike the mystics, did not cling to the principle that "likeness (similitude) is the *sine qua non* for saving knowledge and relationships." [54] For them the synteresis became primarily an enabling resource orientated toward the ordained ethical activity in the way of salvation. The believer's saving relation to God was primarily circumscribed by the "Pelagian historical covenant" or an "oath-conditioned, 'fair bargain' policy in the order of salvation." God had bound Himself historically to respect and respond to man's activity—*facere quod in se est*.

To the extent that the divergent philosophical assumptions of nominalism and mysticism were brought together in the late medieval context, it appears that the mystical theologians placed greater emphasis on a natural rather than a historical covenant. Final authoritative "texts" were found in the soul and "the experiences which have occurred in the history and tradition of the heart,"[55] rather than the doctrinal statements of the church. The mystical *viator* found his relation to God embraced in "a natural creational 'covenant' " which in keeping with the general Neoplatonic understanding of the creation process presupposed a "commitment" by God *sola gratia*, to be present in His creation via the *logos*. By virtue of his creation and on the basis of divine immanence, man possessed the inalienable possibility of salvation. God had bound Himself to increase His divine presence in man as man cooperated in weeding out the creaturely.[56]

> For in what measure we put off the creature, in the same measure are we able to receive the Creator; neither more nor less. For if mine eye is to see any thing it must be purified, or become purified, from all other things; for if heat and light are to enter cold and darkness must needs depart; it cannot be otherwise.[57]

The mystical *potentia ordinata*, therefore, retained synergistic overtones. If salvation was viewed as possible because of the creational and continuous commitment of God, then the whole order of salvation was indeed *sola gratia Dei*. For creation itself was the product of God's goodness. Within the order of salvation, however, the *viator* was called upon to cooperate with God. Thus the mystics could maintain that salvation was all of grace without surrendering free will.

Since the aim was reunion with the Divine, but union between opposites an impossibility, union was achieved by man ascending into the Divine and the Divine descending into man. Again the *logos* provided the connection in this process which could be alternately described as man's spiritual rebirth (regeneration) or the birth of God's Son, the inner Word, in the soul. The historical incarnation was thereby given a universal application repeated in every true *viator*. This internalized understanding of incarnation later reappeared in South German Anabaptism.

Within this framework justification could only be conceived of as a gradual deification process in which the mystic ascended by progressive stages.[58] Justification and sanctification were inseparably one and the same movement.[59] A necessary corollary was a Catholic conception of grace as an enabling power subsistent within the human being,[60] making possible the gradual immobilization of the self-affirming and creaturely, seeking activity in man.[61] And all this was inconceivable apart from medieval anthropology which functioned on the assumption of gradualness—the more of a sinner, the less of a saint, the less the sinfulness, the greater the righteousness.

Early South German Anabaptist soteriology and theology were to show strong similarities in all essentials to the mystical tradition. On the contrary, no similar statement can be made about the magisterial Reformers. Whatever his indebtedness to nominalism and mysticism, Luther's crucial understanding of justification by faith alone dynamited the basic axioms of both traditions. His central theological insight that the justified man was *simul iustus et peccator* was an impossibility from a mystical perspective. It has even been argued that Tauler and Gerson were Luther's "earliest major conscious opponents."[62] His definition of the *homo spiritualis* as the man of faith as early as 1516 fundamentally threatened the entire medieval system. [63] These claims may exaggerate Luther's reformed theological consciousness for 1516. For Luther willingly utilized mystical vocabulary after 1516 to argue against traditional assumptions concerning the nature of sin, grace, and sacramentalism. Moreover Luther's perception of the externalness of the "righteousness of God" may in fact have been influenced by mystical conclusions.[64]

Nevertheless, Luther did eventually reject mystical and scholastic anthropology in favour of the *totus homo peccator*, making it a foregone conclusion that his answer to the quest for righteousness before God would fall outside the unio mystica tradition. The shortcomings of the forensic or imputative theories as attempts to circumscribe Luther's understanding of justification notwithstanding, it is clear that his Reformation insights on justification centered around the *aliena iustitia* of Christ, an idea which "lies outside the doctrinal system of mysticism."[65] Luther's *propter Christum* referred to the historical *Christus incarnatus* as against the mystical transhistorical *verbum incarnatum*. Luther's cross theology accentuated the historical uniqueness of Christ's redemptive work. His Christocentricism, in turn, stressed the righteousness of the justified sinner before God through faith in God's promises rather than through any real connection between God and man via the *logos*.[66]

Luther's insistence on the externalness of grace is inseparable from his rejection of the general medieval conception of grace as a *habitus*. Similarly his acceptance of faith bound to the Word of God as the means of grace can be understood only within the context of his rejection of the traditional hermeneutic of signification. For him the Christian teaching of both grace and faith had been perverted by metaphysical anthropological speculations. For Luther, faith was bound to and by the Word of God. Christ was the incarnate Word. The Word was external, confronting man in Christ, in the Scriptures, and in the sacraments. Man's existence before God was qualified in hearing or not hearing the Word (*Wortgeschehen*). The Word revealed both man's true sinful status before God and the grace and righteousness of God. The Word alone worked the sinner's reconciliation before God. This emphasis on the historically active external Word differed from the traditionally accepted role of the outer Word as a mere pointer (sign) to the inner unspoken, unspeakable Word experienced in the soul. The hermeneutical implications moved Luther into opposition not only to the scholastic and mystical traditions but also to many of his contemporaries.

We conclude that the cardinal emphasis on the Word of God as understood by Luther is not found in the mystical tradition. Neither is Luther's crucial understanding of law and gospel or promise part of the mystical tradition. In spite of the focus on the suffering Christ in cross mysticism, the emphasis was not the *solus Christus* of the Reformers but a "cross in me" emphasis. For the entire mystical and imitatio tradition, the cross remained symbolic of suffering to be experienced internally in conformity with Christ or accepted in discipleship. It was not the vicarious and historical intervention of God on behalf of man that it was for the Reformers.[67] It would, therefore, appear historically fallacious to read cross mysticism forward into Luther or Luther's "cross theology" back into the mysticism of Tauler and the *Theologia Deutsch*.[68] In fact, when viewed from the perspective of the mystical tradition, even the early Martin Luther could at best qualify only as a wayward follower of the mystics. In contrast to many members of the so-called left wing of the Reformation, Luther's understanding of justification proved to be a much more radical break with both the medieval scholastic and mystical traditions.

If in the case of Luther, his central doctrine of justification can be shown to have constituted a major break with medieval mystical anthropology and soteriology, this was not true of Thomas Müntzer. As with the entire mystical tradition Müntzer's basic assumption was that of the immanence of God in the human soul (*Abgrund der Seele*).[69] God was not far; man needed only to turn inward to the common ground for union with the Divine. "There man is being taught alone by God . . . and not by any creature."[70]

The theological significance of Müntzer lay precisely in the fact that he sought to answer the problems raised by Luther from the medieval mystical perspective.[71] Luther's formulation of justification carried not only a different understanding of reconciliation but it also raised the question of final authority. As was noted above, for Luther the latter lay in the promises of the Word of God which he closely allied to the Scriptures.

Against Luther, Müntzer reiterated the mystical emphasis on the transhistorical inner Word. The Reformation idea of a "fixed word of God" historically given and contained in Scripture—although in need of illumination by the Spirit—was foreign to the mystical tradition and to Müntzer.[72] The Scriptures communicating through the senses belonged to the creaturely and could not communicate faith. At best, they gave witness (*Zeugnis*) to the mystical experience in which the inner Word was active in faith-bringing revelation. The outer Scriptures, therefore, appear in Müntzer's polemics against the "scribes in Wittenberg" as the death-bringing letter. Even though the viator literally swallowed a hundred thousand Bibles, through the senses, the letter could not communicate the Word of God nor true living faith.[73]

> Those who eat their way through the invented faith . . . they
> see that the Word, where the true faith connects (*angehenckt*), is
> not a hundred thousand miles from them, but they see that it swells
> up (*quillt*) in the bottom of the heart. They become aware that it
> proceeds (*abgeht*) from the living God. It is here that God writes the
> true Scripture, not with ink but with His living finger, to which the
> outer Bible rightly gives witness. And there is also no surer witness
> to demonstrate the truthfulness of the Scriptures than the living
> speech of God, where the Father addresses the Son in the heart of
> man. This Scripture all the elect can read.[74]

As with Tauler and Eckhardt before him, trinitarian speculations
played a significant role in Müntzer's understanding of the creation
process as creative dialogue. In the mystical experience of reunion the
trinitarian movement was repeated in man.[75] For Müntzer the inner
Word, which was the Father addressing the Son in the soul, appears to
have been interchangeable with the movement of the Spirit. The result
was the addition of certain spiritualistic overtones to his mysticism. Consequently, it is possible to interpret Müntzer as a Spiritualist. However,
if mysticism and spiritualism are contrasted in the conventional way,
that is, spiritualism assuming a fixed gulf between man and the Divine
which can only be bridged by the Spirit, while mysticism assumes a
unity of the two, then Müntzer was neither one nor the other.[76] He
assumed a position between mysticism and spiritualism.[77] But, as we
noted earlier, the borders between the natural and divine spheres touching each other in the human soul were left undefined in the mystical
tradition. Müntzer, perhaps influenced by the Reformation controversy
with regard to merit, clearly reserved the original movement in man to
the Spirit.

Addressing himself to Luther's crucial doctrine of faith, he sought
to bring the mystical framework into play against Luther who was
"stealing" faith from the Scriptures.

> The godless softlings know no other reason why the Scriptures
> ought to be accepted or rejected except that they have been ac-
> cepted of old and by many. Such ape-like reasons (*affen-
> schmaltzische weyss*) the Jews, Turks and all peoples can give as
> basis for their faith.[78]

Against Luther, for whom faith was communicated through the
preached Word of God (*fides ex auditu*), Müntzer favoured the mystical

explanation pinpointing its arrival in the soul. Since for him false faith originated in externals, he declared it the first task of the inner Word to dismantle all belief communicated through externals. Only after the *viator* discovered his unbelief could true faith begin.[79] Once living faith had been born in the soul, it could be confirmed as true faith by comparing it with the scriptural record, which gave witness to the experience of other true believers.[80]

Thus Müntzer's greater pneumatological stress was at once a concession to the Reformation doctrine of *sola gratia*, while at the same time directed against Luther's *sola fide* and *sola scriptura*. The Spirit first awakened the *viator*, making him aware of and punishing his unbelief.[81] But Müntzer did not intend to make the Spirit's working conditional on divinely predestined decrees.[82] Like all the mystics he assumed that purification was a gradual process which necessitated human and divine *cooperatio*. He implicitly accepted the mystical anthropology[83] and explicitly rejected Luther's all too humble opinions about human nature.[84]

Müntzer's understanding of justification also proved to be genuinely pre-Reformation. It was literally conceived of as a deification process leading through the preparatory inner cross to the *unio mystica*. Justification was one and the same movement of cleansing from and punishment of sin. Each *viator* had to bear his own cross and must/should not, like Luther, assume that Christ suffered for him.[85] Suffering was the means of purification, and Müntzer insisted over and over again that the "bitter Christ" had to be experienced first before the "sweet Christ" would bring comfort.[86] Müntzer, therefore, turned cross mysticism into the normative way of salvation, and in this regard formulated most of the theological currency to be used by early South German Anabaptists.

But Müntzer was more than a mystical theologian. He was also an "apocalyptic crusader."[87] According to his understanding of biblical prophecy and church history, the kingdom of God, which in Daniel was described as the stone "cut out without hands," had begun rolling during the days of the apostles. It had been held back in the next generation through inequities and corruption which infiltrated the church. However, the day of reckoning had come. The kingdom was about to be established—the stone about to turn into the mountain filling the whole earth. Here the apocalyptical and mystical themes in Müntzer's thought were blended into a revolutionary ideology. Only those who had experienced the inner cross and obeyed the inner Word were fit instruments for God's programme which envisaged the punishment of the

wicked.[88] A social and political order responsible for keeping men preoccupied, either through riches or through extreme poverty, with the
outer creaturely order forfeited its right to existence. Thus Müntzer
forged mysticism and apocalypticism into a critical view of the social
and political establishment.[89]

Müntzer's apocalypticism shows traces of the excitement of the first
years of the Reformation. Luther himself was smitten by end-time fever.
He hastened his translation of Daniel "so that everyone might read and
comprehend the prophecy of Daniel before the end of the world."[90]
Natural phenomena and personal ills were interpreted as omens of the
last days. The Reichstag in Augsburg appeared to him as "the last
trumpet call" before the judgment would fall on Europe.[91] Some of his
followers outdid their master.[92] In the early stages of the Reformation,
supporters began to acclaim him as the promised Elijah. Medieval prophecies were brought to bear to strengthen the cause of the Reformation.[93]

However, it appears that Müntzer's own apocalypticism drew both
on Taborite chiliasm and on the medieval Joachimite tradition, rather
than upon Luther directly. Joachimism experienced a revival in the
fifteenth and sixteenth centuries.[94] Between 1516 and 1527 a group of
secret admirers began to edit and publish Joachim's works.[95] One of the
by-products was the pseudo-Joachimist *Super Hieremiam* read by
Müntzer.[96]

The contribution of Joachimism to Müntzer's thought was, at best,
tenuous and should not be exaggerated.[97] However, the significance of
his interest in medieval apocalypticism should not be ignored. The Joachimite tradition kept alive by the third order of Franciscans was admirably suited for its role as a vehicle of protest against the religious establishment.[98] Popular mystical and apocalyptical tendencies often
combined to reinforce their mutual anti-institutional bent. Traces of
medieval apocalypticism reappearing among South German Anabaptists warrant a background summary of that tradition.[99]

Medieval apocalyptical speculations including Joachimism owed
their basic contours to St. Augustine. Augustine had superimposed the
six-day creation process on general history. He distinguished five ages
up to the birth of Christ.[100] The sixth age encompassed the duration of
the new covenant and Christ's church. There remained the seventh age,
the world Sabbath. Did the great Sabbath fall into history or outside it?
Augustine explicitly distinguished the seventh from the "eternal eighth
day." Thus the Sabbath would fall into history. Was it a historical

millennium? Yes and no. Augustine allegorized the millennium into a mystical kingdom present in the sixth day.[101] Thus, his view of history by itself was apocalyptically inconsequential.[102]

This was not true, however, when Augustine's sevenfold patterns became cross-pollinated with Joachim's view of history. Like Eckhardt's formulation about the *via mystica,* Joachim's insights into history depended largely on trinitarian speculations.[103] Superimposed upon Augustine's six divisions Joachim distinguished three basic historical stages of spiritual progress. These were the age of the Father succeeded by that of the Son and finally by that of the Spirit. Chronologically, the three stages were not sharply divided. The second and third periods overlapped with the stage that preceded them. Thus, the age of the Son was literally conceived in the womb of the old dispensation, marking a mediating or transitional stage to the purely spiritual third stage. In this gradualist scheme Christ marked no sudden break with the Jewish past, but embodied a progressive developmental factor (*Entwicklungsfaktor*)[104] in man's history of salvation.

Significantly, the beginning of the second age had been marked by the appearance of the prophetic gift. The latter was personified by Elijah. Another Elijah was expected to announce the beginning of the spiritual stage. Peter Olivi, a disciple of Joachim, later complicated matters by adding the concept of three advents of Christ. Christ had first come in the flesh, second in the spirit of evangelical reform, and would finally come in judgment. In the original scheme St. Francis himself had marked Christ's second advent.[105] Later, one of Hut's disciples was questioned as to why he believed in three Christs.[106]

When the blessed principle of threefold and sevenfold divisions (3x7) was applied further to each of the three ages, the historical patterns became so intricate that without the special portion of the Spirit granted to Joachim the mystery of history might never have been unlocked. Crucial periods in history were reached during transitional stages from the sixth to the seventh division. New epochs were literally born through great tribulation. The Maccabean period in Jewish history, which served as the prime example, marked the end of the age of the Father. Hence that fondness of Joachim's followers for apocryphal texts stemming from this period, a tendency also evident among some early Anabaptists influenced by Hut.[107]

The tribulations arising between different stages again unwound according to a sevenfold pattern. Joachim had here taken his clue from the Book of the Seven Seals of Revelation 5:1. It was to be the major source for Hut's apocalyptic speculations also. According to Joachimist theory, the most crucial point of all would be reached at the end of the Augustinian sixth age, which also marked the end of the sixth epoch of the second dispensation. When this was reached, the sixth seal of the Book of Seven Seals would be opened and the church would suffer the seven persecutions which symbolized the world's history in microcosm.[108]

Thus Joachim and his followers accepted Augustine's contention that the world was in its sixth day. Like Augustine they believed that the seventh day, as distinct from the eighth eternal day, would fall into history. Moreover, with Augustine they spiritualized the Sabbath, loosely identified with the age of the Spirit, and maintained that it was conceived in the age of the Son. However, in doing so, they also implicitly suggested that the Sabbath was to be chronologically consequential. It was not completed in the age of the Son—the area of institutionalized Christianity—but would supersede it. Thus, ironically, although awaiting a spiritual kingdom which was to grow out of the hearts of men, Joachim and his later followers—many of whom lacked the master's deeper understanding of the numerical symbols—opened the way to expectations of a literal historical millennium.

In the pages which follow, we presupposed that the early Reformation radicals had deeper insights into the mystical and apocalyptical ideas of the past than into their evangelical free-church future. The implicit synergism that pervaded South German Anabaptism, the moralism that emerged later, the dualistic or tripartite anthropology which opened the possibility that man could "become righteous" rather than merely be "accounted righteous," the Christology which focused both on the transhistorical *logos* (the inner Word) and the human Jesus, who was to be imitated both in suffering and conduct, the stress on the insufficiencies of the outer Word—these are all so very unLutheran that they could better be accounted for as medieval vestiges than as a radicalization of the Reformation. In the original dissent of the South German Anabaptists from institutionalized Catholicism and confessionalized Protestantism we find the echoes of the mystical appeal to the immanence of God. They thus linked up with a tradition running through Müntzer and the *Theologia Deutsch* to Tauler and Eckhardt. South German Anabaptists, we maintain, took their theological starting point not from the Reformers but from a popularized medieval mystical tradition.

2

HANS DENCK:
THE ECUMENICAL ANABAPTIST

Hans Denck has been variously rediscovered as the "Schleiermacher of the Reformation," a "rationalist and Pietist in one person," and therefore, "neither one nor the other,"[1] a forerunner of an "undogmatic Christianity,"[2] or "ethical moral action Christianity,"[3] and as a typical product of the German *Volksgeist*.[4] What endeared this pivotal figure of early South German Anabaptism to nineteenth-century liberal theologians made him suspect in the eyes of traditional dogmatists. For different reasons, both sides recognized Denck's affinity to other sixteenth-century Spiritualists. None could escape the appeal of his erudition and personality.

A new problem was injected when Anabaptist scholars began to adopt Troeltsch's distinction between sectarians and Spiritualists. Studies on the Swiss Brethren had contributed the doctrinal content to Troeltsch's sectarian form. The Schleitheim Confession, if not normative, became typical of true Anabaptism in the minds of many historians. Denck appeared not to fit the biblicist, congregationalist Anabaptist model, which was oriented to discipleship. His individualistic mystical bent set him apart. He was a "*Halbtäufer*"; he was not "representative."[5]

However, this interpretation raised new problems. Denck's significance for the beginning of South German Anabaptism could not be denied. His repeated contacts with Hans Hut, the most significant baptiser among early South German Anabaptists, are well established. It was Denck who baptised Hut during May 1526 in Augsburg.[6] In the framework of those scholars who strained to incorporate South German Anabaptism, its peculiarities notwithstanding, within the boundaries of a monolithic evangelical Anabaptism, even the unrepresentative Denck was now a welcome apostolic link to join Hut and those Anabaptists influenced by him to the pure stream flowing from Zurich origins.[7]

For scholars willing to give up the normativeness of Swiss Anabaptists, Denck became after all a "typical representative of the free-church movement," and a "founding father" of South German Anabaptism. According to this thesis South German Anabaptism founded by Denck and continued by Pilgram Marpeck was different from its Swiss progenitor. Swiss Anabaptists broke with Zwingli over church polity on the basis of *sola scriptura*. The German Anabaptists argued with the Lutherans concerning the way of salvation on the basis of *sola fide*. Thus the spiritualist tendencies of Denck were real enough to set him apart from the more literalist Swiss Brethren, but did not warrant retroactive suspicions of his Anabaptist credentials.[8]

But a pluralistic approach to Anabaptist "essence" carried implications involving the "sinister" influence of the "Revolutionary Spiritualist," Thomas Müntzer (to use the terminology of George Williams' classification).[9] For those accustomed to thinking of Anabaptism as a living expression of the Sermon on the Mount ethic, Denck, the pacifist, could have little in common with Müntzer, the revolutionary. In contrast those who believed that all sixteenth-century Spiritualists, if not dependent on Müntzer, were influenced by him, stressed Denck's intellectual relatedness to Müntzer.[10] Whatever the virtues of the respective claims and counterclaims, it should be clear that they can be weighed and evaluated only after we gain some understanding of the historical Denck.

Like the historical Jesus, Denck remains an illusive but impressive personality. His own career as a dissenter began in Nuremberg.[11] Even before his arrival in that city during September of 1523, he had been exposed to humanistic and mystical influences in Basel.[12] In Nuremberg he was drawn into a circle of would-be Reformers, drinking from these same springs. In 1512 and again in 1516 Johann Staupitz preached to large crowds in Nuremberg. An examination of Staupitz' popular sermons from that period reveals similarities to Müntzer's cross mysticism and a strong emphasis on the inner Word.[13] A small group of mystical humanists first welcomed the ideas of the Reformers.[14] From this circle Andreas Osiander later emerged as the major champion of the Lutheran party.[15] Early in 1524 a more radical faction made its appearance. In

May of that year a peasant and a linen weaver led public demonstrations demanding a more radical reformation course from the city council.[16] One month later Denck was in difficulties with the authorities for the first time. He had on his own initiative forbidden his students to assist in church ceremonials.[17] It is possible that Denck at this stage began to identify with the emerging radical party in the controversy about the Lord's Supper. The Seebald School to which he had been appointed as headmaster on the recommendation of Oecolampadius remained a pro-Zwinglian island in regard to the Lord's Supper long after Denck's departure.[18]

At any rate, Denck's earlier exposure to mysticism disposed him favourably towards the "Carlstadt-Müntzer tendency" which spread to Nuremberg in the summer and fall of 1524.[19] The Lutheran party soon had reason to complain that Carlstadt's views on the sacraments were all too favourably received in the city.[20] Laymen now turned authors. An interesting phenomenon was the individualist painter Hans Greiffenberger, who launched a series of pamphlets in 1523-24.[21] It is not easy to classify Greiffenberger. An analysis of his writings would suggest that theologically he could be identified with Luther. He was finally exiled from Nuremberg in August 1526 because he exercised his priestly right as head of a household and administered the Lord's Supper to his wife.[22] Of a different caliber were the ideas of Martin Reinhardt,[23] Andreas Carlstadt, Heinrich Pfeiffer, Thomas Müntzer, and Simon Haferitz, all circulating among the radicals in the fall of 1524. A sermon by Haferitz, the assistant of Müntzer in Allstedt, provides some insights into the quasi-mystical ideas current in this group.[24] Haferitz' tract first received attention in the nineteenth century, but its significance in relation to Denck and South German Anabaptism has not been examined in subsequent literature.[25]

A brief survey of the sermon indicates striking similarities between Haferitz' and Müntzer's concerns. Haferitz asserted his sympathy for the poor and railed against the "false soft preachers" who wanted to fill the poor and meek with "books and dead letters," thus "carrying water into the well" instead of permitting the living water "to spring forth of itself" in the soul. The result was a "phony, invented faith" by which a man built only on what the Scriptures said, without having experienced the birth of true faith in his heart. The latter was the product of the Holy Ghost, while the Lutheran demand simply to believe the Scriptures was "the sin against the Holy Ghost"; for the Bible was only intended as a witness to the experience of the inner Word.

Oh, what a miserable faith would that have been, if the pious wisemen should have built only upon the tender scribes at Jerusalem, . . . [as to] where Christ should be born. Yes, they were not satisfied by words of Scripture, . . . but wanted to see the inner word, which the Holy Spirit had already awakened with high desire in their hearts. . . . The holy Christian faith does not begin unless man has given leave to all his lusts of the flesh and the spirit, yes, also the lusts which he has relating to the gifts of God—as the Holy Scripture, good words and good works.[26]

Like Müntzer and many of the South German Anabaptists after him, Haferitz rejected the *aliena iustitia* taught by the Reformers. The passion of Christ was primarily conceived existentially, rather than historically. Like Christ's birth, it was to be repeated in and experienced by every believer. Most interesting of all, Haferitz suggested that where the right Christianity is restored through the living word all "usury, oppression, and scraping" would cease, and no one would be permitted to "assault, shoot or draw a knife or sword."[27] Was this to be the norm for a future order?

Haferitz' sermon may have been brought to Nuremberg by Hans Hut, who according to his own confession stayed with Denck in 1524.[28] In October of that year Hut and Pfeiffer brought Müntzer's manuscript, the *Special Exposé*, to Nuremberg.[29] Five hundred copies were printed on Hans Hergott's press, and one hundred sent on to Augsburg[30] before the city council confiscated the rest.[31] Pfeiffer himself appears to have carried two of his own manuscripts with him. These were examined and condemned by Osiander. According to Osiander, in one Pfeiffer failed to distinguish between law and gospel, and in the other he advocated that false teachers should be put to death in keeping with Old Testament practice. Osiander also accused Pfeiffer of minimizing the importance of Scripture and thereby becoming a *Schwärmer* and agitator (*Rumorer*).[32] On October 29, Pfeiffer was expelled and moved on to nearby Erlangen from whence he retained contact with the "godless painters." Surprisingly, Hut, who had been detained, was treated with great leniency. On November 2 he was reimbursed for the four hundred confiscated copies of the *Special Exposé* and then released. Four journeymen had printed the manuscript during the absence of their master, Hergott.[33]

Perhaps the leniency shown to Hut encouraged Müntzer to enter Nuremberg in person early in December of that year. His intention, as a later letter to his friend Christoph Meinhard indicates, was to publish another of his manuscripts, a polemic against Luther entitled A *Highly Justified Apology*.[34] He therefore proceeded with caution and secrecy, rejecting the requests of many sympathizers to preach openly.[35] Whether Denck was among those who encouraged him to preach is not clear.[36] The only thing that is clear is that Müntzer shortly thereafter contacted Denck's personal friend and patron Oecolampadius in Basel,[37] and that Denck in turn was implicated in the trial of the godless painters, who were accused of studying and proselytising for Müntzer's and Carlstadt's ideas.

As early as November 10 the city council had reprimanded Hans Greiffenberger for some scandalous paintings and unorthodox views.[38] A few weeks later the godless painters, three students of Albrecht Dürer—Barthel Beheim, Sebald Beheim, and Jörg Benz—were put on trial. Their declaration amazed not only contemporaries, but has astonished more recent scholars. One historian has been tempted to "see in them pioneers of the 'Death of God Theology' " or forerunners of logical positivism engaging in rational probing of "nonverifiable theological statements." More soberly, he suspected that they must have been "blind drunk."[39] They denied not only the divinity of Christ but also questioned the existence of God as then conceived.

One of the trio, Sebald Beheim, implicated Denck as being part of their circle.[40] On January 10, 1525, Denck was brought before the council and then turned over for examination to the Lutheran ministers led by Andreas Osiander. Denck proved himself an agile defendant. He was, therefore, asked to give a written statement of his beliefs on (1) Scripture, (2) sin, (3) the righteousness of God, (4) law and gospel, (5) baptism, and (6) the Lord's Supper. The trial of the godless painters was recessed until Denck's views could be examined, a clear indication that in the minds of the authorities Denck's cause was connected to theirs.[41] Denck himself closed his confession pleading that he and his "imprisoned brethren, whom I love in truth," might be judged fairly.[42] The authorities, accepting the recommendations of the Lutheran pastors, found Denck's reply under the circumstances unreassuring and unacceptable. He was expelled together with his "brethren," the painters.[43] This, then, is the historical context in which Denck's Nuremberg confession must be examined.[44] In Nuremberg he was undeniably in contact with and part of that faction which, employing ideas of Müntzer and Carlstadt, drew upon mystical sources to combat and criticize the Lutheran Reformation.[45]

Denck's movements after his expulsion from Nuremberg remain

problematic. According to one contemporary source, he received an invitation to teach in Mühlhausen, where Müntzer's and Pfeiffer's followers had taken control.[46] Unfortunately, we can no longer ascertain whether he accepted the invitation, or even whether he received it. It must, therefore, also remain conjecture as to whether the schoolmaster with whom Pfeiffer intended to flee to Switzerland in May 1525 was Denck.[47] Denck was shortly thereafter imprisoned in Schwyz for his negative view on pedobaptism.[48] Later he surfaced near St. Gall.[49] Here he maintained contact with Anabaptists associated with Hans Krüsi. These Anabaptists were not yet meek pacifist evangelicals. Some expressed inclinations to defend their views with the sword.[50]

Denck's relationship to the goings-on among Anabaptists and Reformers in St. Gall is no longer clear. However, we can assume that his conversion to Anabaptism was probably a lengthy process. From reports of the two St. Gall Reformers, Joachim Vadian and Johannes Kessler, we are told that his theological development was not at all in the direction of the magisterial Reformers. Among other things he now allegedly taught universalism.[51]

Historians have been divided as to the validity of the Reformers' accusations of doctrinal heterodoxy against Denck. Those sympathetic have registered increasing scepticism about the logic of the charges.[52] The general approach of these scholars has been to view Denck's universalism as a myth ascribable to "slanderous rumours," and to see Denck as a victim of the bad anti-Anabaptist press. Denck could not have been interested, they argue, in speculations about the life hereafter implicit in universalism. After all, like all Anabaptists, his concern was with "the life of a Christian in the present."[53] At most, he expressed the general belief that the kingdom of darkness would be overcome. Besides, universalism was impossible for one who cherished free will and human responsibility. Therefore, "in order to convict Denck of Universalism one must cite passages where he actually declares that eventually Satan too will be saved."[54] Such passages, however, are hard to come by, in particular if one approaches Denck's writings from a post-Reformation perspective. The task is less difficult and more rewarding if Denck's teachings are examined from the mystical point of view. Our concern here is primarily the historical Denck. The testimonies of his contemporaries cannot, therefore, be ignored. The question of his universalism is all the more crucial, since it figures prominently among the charges against later followers of Hut.[55] How such diametrically opposed concepts as the redemption of all things and

Hut's revengeful apocalypticism could be combined baffles the historical imagination,[56] but provides an interesting insight into the eclectic nature of much of early South German Anabaptist thought.

Among those registering disapproval of Denck's teachings on the subject of universal salvation was the Anabaptist leader Balthasar Hubmaier. The two met during May/June of 1526 in Augsburg.[57] According to a secondhand report Hubmaier disapproved of Denck's low opinion of the Scriptures, and censured him for holding the "errors of Origen."[58] The differences which surfaced in Augsburg between the more scholastic Hubmaier and the mystical Denck could have been more fundamental than historians have hitherto been willing to recognize.

Rumours that Denck was disseminating the doctrines of Origen soon reached the major Reformer of Augsburg, Urbanus Rhegius. According to Rhegius, when he confronted Denck with the rumours, Denck at first denied them, but then in tears admitted that he could not conceive of an eternal punishment. He supported his contention with references to God's mercy which did not wish the sinner's death. Rhegius then arranged a discussion before his associates, hoping to convince Denck of his error. When Rhegius cornered Denck with scriptural texts incompatible with universal salvation, Denck is said to have brought forth "a fantasy" about "how God was one, and that in that same oneness all disunited things might be united."[59] Denck then agreed to defend this position in a public disputation. However, he left Augsburg before the announced debate could take place.[60]

If Rhegius' report is trustworthy, then Denck's universalism rested on assumptions which conceived of salvation as reunion and return to oneness on a cosmic scale. When Justus Menius later attacked the universalism held by Anabaptists whom he believed to be followers of Denck, he gave the following popularized version of the return of all things to their origin. After the millennium Christ would return all power to the Father terminating His own redemptive ministry. Together with His brothers in the covenant He would be raptured to eternal bliss. Those left behind would be less fortunate and their return to God more painful. Together with Satan and his angels they would be consumed by God who is defined as the eternal fire. Thus the unrepentant sinners and demons would at last find salvation by being reunited with God through fire. If Menius' information was accurate, then Denck taught the apokatastasis, an idea shared by his most notable convert to the Anabaptist cause, Hans Hut.[61] Obviously, either Menius or his source of information had combined Hut's apocalyptical expectations of divine punishment with Denck's belief of universal redemption.

The charges of universalism followed Denck through Strassburg and Landau on his way to Worms.[62] It is possible that news of his views preceded him from Augsburg and prejudiced the minds of his contemporaries against him. Fortunately for the historian a rather objective account of his convictions on the subject has been preserved in a letter from Nikolaus Thomae (Sigelsbach) to Oecolampadius.[63] Thomae, who witnessed Denck's disputation with the Jews at Landau and engaged Denck in personal discussion, retained good relations with Anabaptists as late as 1529, referring to them as "god-fearing and brave people."[64] Later he himself became suspect of being a Schwenckfeldian. Since Schwenckfeld thought more highly of Denck than of any other Anabaptist leader, the testimony of Thomae cannot be written off as another attempt to discredit Denck.

The letter dated April 1, 1527, largely confirms the charges made by Vadian, Kessler, Hubmaier, Rhegius, Bucer, Johann Bader, Cochleaus, and Menius. Denck had thrown Thomae into consternation by citing passages such as Jeremiah 3:5, which indicated that God's wrath did not endure forever and which seemed to imply that the godless would be saved. Thomae listed thirteen other passages apparenty utilized by Denck to argue for universalism and requested Oecolampadius to give his interpretation of these texts.[65] However, at the heart of the argument had been not biblical authority but Denck's speculation about the nature of God. Denck argued that the essence of God was love and that His teachings could not contradict His essence.

Christ, Himself a manifestation of divine love, had taught us to love our enemies. If God did otherwise He contradicted His revelation in Christ. To punish anyone eternally could not be interpreted as an exercise of love. When Thomae countered by citing the words of Christ in Matthew 25:41, that some would be condemned into eternal fire, Denck's reply had been that Scripture could not be taken literally. Here, as "often in other places," Scripture addressed itself in a "misleading way" (*verkehrter Weise*) to the godless. Its real meaning was to bring the godless to repentance. God no more punished out of vengeance than any good father. His purpose was correction. Thomae then asked Denck why he still admonished people to die to self and the creaturely, since they would all be saved anyhow. Denck replied that he would rather die one death than suffer through a thousand. Thomae then queried when the restoration of all things would take place. Denck, without denying this apocalyptic concept as such, cautioned that only the Father knew the time.[66] Therefore, unless we assume that Thomae and other contemporaries of Denck passed their time engaged in imaginary dialogue, and invented arguments with which to frame Denck, we must conclude that the historical Denck did hold to universalism, even though he did not commit his ideas on the subject to print.

Denck's universalism rested on assumptions which in the final analysis grew from Neoplatonic mystical and humanistic roots. What was crucial was Denck's understanding of evil and God's way of dealing with it. Denck did not consider evil as objective reality. Both evil and sin lacked independent existence.[67] Both were a necessary by-product of the creation process, resulting from the Neoplatonic spirit-matter dichotomy and the nature of physical existence *per se*.[68] Evil and sin were the deprivation of the divine presence, parasitic in relation to the good, but necessary if goodness and mercy were to be actualized. For goodness was the overcoming of its opposite. As he said in one of his published writings:

> Had He never created, then He would never have been recognized, except by Himself, which was not enough for His glory. Had He prevented the existence of sin, then there would have been no mercy, because it would not have had a counterpart into which it could have reached, or which would have needed it.[69]

In Denck's system, unlike the predestinarianism of the Reformation, God could never be held responsible for evil and sin since they lacked independent existence and were a mere by-product—an indirect result of God's positive purpose in creation.[70] On the other hand, Denck could endorse free will without rejecting universalism, which was implicit in his conviction that evil and sin would ultimately be overcome, and explicit in his view that all divine punishment served a corrective purpose.

> If sin would not be overcome then God would not be omnipotent, [and] would have eternally to see His enemy beside Him and against Him; yes, His enemy would be equally powerful.[71]

> . . . the father who loves his child punishes it so long, until it agrees to do what it should have done before it sinned.[72]

Denck's focus was, therefore, not so much on the relation of sin to human nature—original sin—as on the didactic nature of evil, and the corrective and purifying quality of all punishment. It was God's purpose that man should overcome evil and achieve the stature intended for him.[73] Man was not left resourceless. He could overcome sin and evil in cooperation with the divine presence in him. Here the mystical immanence thrust made its reappearance making an either-or approach on predestination and free will unnecessary.[74] Those unwilling to cooperate with God would ultimately become willing through the suffering which resistance brought upon them. No punishment was, therefore, final or eternal, and Denck logically extended this understanding of punishment to the concept of hell. Hell was but a transitional purgatorial state to which he gave an internalized interpretation.[75] As Sebastian Franck, one of his sympathetic contemporaries, explained:

> The hell into which the godless are placed he [Denck] holds to be the torment of the conscience which will not be outside man but within him, and which begins when man is shown his sin and unbelief. . . . Not that he has to remain there and that there is no grace in hell. . . .[76]

Thus the combined testimony of Denck's contemporaries indicates that Denck taught universalism. An analysis of his writings does not prove the contrary; rather does it provide a context in which the rumours about Denck appear entirely plausible. From his perspective free will and universalism were not opposites. As on other issues, Denck was both well behind and ahead of his time in his understanding of evil. His mystical presuppositions did not permit the same appreciation of human depravity as in Luther.[77] On the other hand, his conception of evil as nonbeing no doubt prevented him from seeing objective manifestations of the demonic loitering on eavestroughs as Luther did. The absence of passages in Denck's writings in which he "actually declares that Satan too will be saved" is partially explained by this fact. Unlike the magisterial Reformers, Denck could not conceive of the devil as a personal entity. With regard to universalism, then, the accounts of contemporaries, not all of them hostile, illuminate and give a more radical twist to Denck's ideas than one might assume if one were to approach his writings in a vacuum or from the perspective of evangelicalism.

If the historical Denck was a universalist, then we are probably not far from the mark to see a relationship between his universalism and his plea for tolerance.[78] Denck was one of the few ecumenical spirits of the Reformation willing to engage in dialogue with Jews. And according to

Nikolaus Thomae, Denck on such occasions brought forth all kinds of interesting insights.[79] Although the major discussion appears to have centered on the law, we suspect that ideas were also exchanged about the Trinity—an unavoidable topic in Christian-Jewish dialogue.[80]

When Denck and Ludwig Hätzer translated the Old Testament prophets in Worms, they obtained the expert aid of Jewish rabbis. In their first edition of the *Wormser Propheten* they tacitly acknowledged the Jewish aid, recognizing that it would not satisfy everyone.[81] Their expectation was justified. Luther, who did not share the ecumenical vision of Denck, saw the Jewish participation as the major flaw in the *Wormser Propheten*. He indicated that the Jewish influence worked to the detriment of a proper appreciation of Christ.[82] Bullinger, who was particularly gifted in utilizing rumours to discredit his opponents, later scornfully labelled Hätzer and Denck the two "rabbis" among the Anabaptists.[83] However, that all this was based upon something more than slanderous rumour is substantiated from unexpected quarters. Oswald Leber, the faithful companion of Augustin Bader, later emerged from the Worms Anabaptist circle, having studied Hebrew under Jewish rabbis in that city. Leber's exposure to Jewish apocalypticism was to produce unexpected results in Bader's fantastic schemes.[84]

In the light of such evidence it comes as a surprise that scholars dealing specifically with the *Wormser Propheten*, while arguing at great length about its merits in relation to Luther's translation, have never attempted to trace a possible Jewish influence on the work of Denck and Hätzer.[85] This is not the place to undertake such a task. However, we suggest that a meeting place for Denck and the Jewish rabbis may have existed in their mutual exposure to mysticism and humanism. Since the thirteenth century a strong Jewish mystical tradition had existed in Germany. Like its Christian counterpart it was indebted to the Neoplatonic emanation theory.[86] Similar to the tradition derived from Eckhardt and Tauler, Jewish mysticism centered on the immanence theme.[87] Not surprisingly, others before Denck discovered a close relationship between Jewish mysticism and the truths of the Christian faith. Interest in the mystical Jewish *Cabala* had spread from the Neoplatonic humanist circles around Pico in late fifteenth-century Italy to the German groups led by Denck's great contemporary, Johann Reuchlin, a fellow humanist and Hebraist.[88] It would, therefore, appear not at all farfetched to see a connection between Denck's attitude towards Jews and his universalism. And just as the mystical assumptions of reunion inspired by Neoplatonism provided a key for his belief in universal redemption, so they provided a stimulus for his ecumenical interests.

Whatever the net results of Denck's dialogue with Jewish rabbis, Denck discovered that dialogue with theologians of like faith was not always profitable. As noted earlier, the Lutherans in Nuremberg found his understanding of Scripture as witness to the inner Word wanting. The Reformers in Augsburg, including his Anabaptist brother, Hubmaier, registered similar concern and Martin Bucer in Strassburg charged that Denck did not want to be bound to Scripture.[89] Yet Bucer, when setting forth his own view of Scripture, carefully avoided a simple equation of the Word of God with Scripture. In fact, Bucer's own position appears to have been based on interdependence of outer Scripture with inner, spiritual illumination, in other words upon the sort of synthesis attributed to Denck by sympathetic historians.[90]

Bucer's charges were seconded by Johann Bader, who conversed with Denck in Landau. Bader related how he had been favourably predisposed to Anabaptist practice by studying one of their pamphlets, *Of the Christian Baptism*.[91] In fact, he appears to have been a confidant of Melchior Rinck, participating as a sponsor at Rinck's adult baptism.[92] Then came Denck and prejudiced Bader against the Anabaptist cause by his un-Reformation stance on Scripture.[93] According to Bader, Denck's views echoed those expressed earlier by Müntzer on the subject.[94] Bader wrote that if Denck had been primarily interested in guarding against a flat equation of the Word of God with Scripture, he could have agreed with him.

> But my baptist brother does not leave it at that, but gives people to understand that the man who has the Spirit no longer has need of the Scriptures and need not believe the same. But much rather his spirit, and what the same reveals and gives to understand, that is true, even if it be not contained in the Scriptures. He gives as example the revelation of John, saying that the apostle, too, could not substantiate [his revelation] with Scriptures.[95]

Bader then related how he reminded Denck of the dangers of emphasizing direct revelation. He cited the example of a certain Anabaptist from Bentfeld who, contrary to all scriptural injunctions, had set 1533 as the date for the end of the world.[96] However, instead of condemning claims to special revelation, Denck cautiously defended their possibility. What might remain hidden to the godless, the Spirit could reveal to a believer, and such a man might speak the truth. He could, therefore, not condemn him as a liar.[97]

Did Bader and the other contemporary critics grievously misunderstand or purposely misrepresent Denck's position? This appears to be the impression of scholars who assure us that Denck and the magisterial Reformers agreed in principle, differing only in emphasis, with regard to Scripture. Thus, when Denck drew up a list of contradictions from Scripture, "his point in so doing was not to argue that Scripture should not be authoritative, but rather to point out that in order to reconcile seemingly contradictory understandings, there must be deeper personal penetration of what the texts are all about."[98]

No doubt this was part of Denck's intent, but why were his astute opponents unable to recognize that he intended no more than to guard against a mechanical interpretation of the letter? And how is one to explain Bucer's and Wolfgang Capito's different attitude toward Sattler? Capito wrote a lengthy letter to comfort the "beloved brethren and sisters" in Horb and signed the letter "a faithful brother and fellow (*mitgenoss*) of your hope in the Lord, whose name God knows."[99] Capito's attitude to Denck was different. He had earlier expressed doubts as to Denck's orthodoxy.[100] Bucer assured his readers twice that he had not detected the Denckian heresy in Sattler, and that Sattler was theologically sound with the exception of baptism.[101] Denck, on the other hand, had never courted the friendship of Sattler, and Hätzer, who was Denck's trusted colabourer in Worms, expressed rather low opinions about the Anabaptists of Swiss derivation, as represented by Sattler.[102]

The differences between Denck and Swiss Anabaptism as represented by Sattler cannot be ignored, and the protest of the Reformers against Denck cannot be avoided in any historical assessment of his thought. Moreover, it is only fair to assume that the disagreements which emerged during the debates did not spring from the "open Bible," but originated in the presuppositions of the respective protagonists. Denck's clash with his contemporaries must be viewed in the larger context of his religious pronouncements.

The first theologically significant statement from Denck's own pen was the Nuremberg confession of January 1525. In it are found in concentrated form the themes expounded in his other writings.[103] This subtle statement showed striking similarities to the mystical assumptions delineated by Müntzer and his helper Haferitz. Denck began with an anthropological pronouncement which set him apart from his Reformation opponents. Beside a sinful nature which he carefully defined as "inborn weakness" (*angeborne armutseligkayt*), he found in

himself a resource which resisted his inclinations to evil.[104] In his subsequent writings Denck labelled this soteriologically significant
resource variously "the Word, the Lamb, divine light," and the "divine
power" which was active in man without external medium (*in alle mit-
tel*).[105] Thus, like the mystics he assumed a real connection between the
human and divine.

This anthropological resource, the divine in man, became the
springboard for Denck's rejection of external authority with regard to
matters of faith.[106] An incipient dualism supported his view of man.[107]
Matter and spirit were opposites, but man was partaker of both. His
lower nature remained welded to physical, transient things, while his
nobler, spiritual powers connected immediately to divine-spiritual
reality. A *logos* theology provided the under-carriage for this anthropology. The preincarnate Word was active in the world and in the
human soul.[108]

> But what [God] works . . . that He does through the Word,
> which in the beginning through His Spirit was born from Him or
> has flowed out of Him; this Word does not cease to be active as long
> as a time or place remains.[109]

Denck's thought was Christocentric in the same sense as was that of
the mystics. In his Christology, which supported his anthropology, the
focus remained on the *verbum incarnatum* as against the *Christus incarnatus* of the Reformers.[110] The Word, originally active in the genesis
of physical reality, remained the real connection between man and God.

> For the Word of God surely addresses everyone clearly: the
> dumb, the deaf, the blind; yea, unreasoning animals; indeed, leaf
> and grass, stone and wood, heaven and earth, and all that is therein,
> in order that they might hear and do His will.[111]

As Denck's contemporaries noticed, the mystical focus on the
preincarnate Word influenced Denck's appreciation of the historical
Christ. The human Jesus became primarily the great pedagogue and
example. His sacrificial and redemptive work on the cross was
relativized while attention shifted to His life and teachings.[112] Denck
himself recognized a problem arising out of his position. He asked: "If,
then, the Word is thus in all people, what need had it of the humanity of
Jesus of Nazareth?"[113] He answered that, while the inner Word provided the necessary means for "deification," the historical Jesus served

as an outer witness to the ethical and moral conduct required of the believer. "The Word, however, had to become man in Jesus for this reason: that people both in spirit and in the flesh, from within and without, behind and before, and in all places might have testimony."[114] The historical Jesus was, therefore, primarily a model, a signpost to all those seeking a proper relationship with God. Raising the question whether Christ's work had been vicarious and sufficient for His followers, Denck answered subtly that it had been sufficient by showing the way to be followed.

> Yes, He has given satisfaction for the whole world, and has pre-pared the way, which no man might find, so that one might walk on it and come to life. Whoever does not walk in it, he does not come to the life and the way will be useless for him. He fulfilled the Law, not that He wanted to exempt us from it, but because He wanted to give us an example to follow Him.[115]

That Denck was unwilling or unable to endorse the Reformation understanding of *solus Christus* was made clear when, like Müntzer before him and Hut and his followers after him, he attacked the Lutherans for seeking God's redemptive work only in the flesh of the historical Christ, instead of experiencing it in and on themselves.[116]

By internalizing the life of Christ and emphasizing the believer's need of conformity and imitation, Denck countered not only the Reformation's understanding of Christ's historical redemptive role, but threatened to separate the two natures of Christ. The divine and human natures remained unfused beside each other, but with regard to the historical Christ, the emphasis was on His humanity. The difference between the believer and Christ became one of degree and not of essence. Because of the divine immanence through the Word, real contact between man and God had never been lost, only ignored. Unlike the average person, Christ had lived in harmony and consciousness of the divine presence in Him.

Such a focus could blur the differences between the historical Jesus and ordinary humans. Christ was unique inasmuch as He never left union with the Divine. He had lived in total obedience to God and was, therefore, the perfect illustration to be imitated.[117] From this point of view, it was merely a small step to the denial of Jesus' divinity in the traditional sense. True, He was a son of God but so were all men to a lesser degree by virtue of the indwelling *logos*. Some disciples of Denck appear to have undertaken this extension of his logic,[118] which led to a denial of the traditional understanding of the Trinity. This may have been the basis of the complaints circulating about the radicals in Nuremberg and repeated by Capito with regard to Denck. It was a position at which Hätzer had arrived by 1528 when he relegated the historical Christ to the role of a prophet.[119] Later the Anabaptists in the area exposed to Denck's influence had difficulties accepting the traditional formulation of the Trinity.[120] Moreover, during the Nicolsburg disputation, Hubmaier accused the unsuspecting Hut of denying Christ's divinity and honouring Him only as a prophet. Hut at his trial denied these charges.[121] Yet Hubmaier in his last account refused to drop that accusation, warning that an unholy ecumenical concern was at the heart of this error.[122] Perhaps such a statement could have been expected from a man who in his early career had been instrumental in driving the Jews from Regensburg. However, it marks more than an insight into Hubmaier's anti-Semitism, if it is considered with relation to Denck. Yet it is unlikely that Denck intended such a radical interpretation of his Christology. He showed greater interest for the *nova lex Christi* than for speculations about Christ's nature. This becomes plain in his discussion in *On True Love*. Here God is defined not as "the truth" but in the Latin mystical tradition as "the good" and as "love."

> This love is God, who cannot make Himself, even though He has made all things, who cannot break Himself, even though He will break all things. Therefore, He is from eternity to eternity immovable, He who has to love Himself so much, inasmuch as He is good, that He conceives out of Himself, and gives birth to Himself forever and ever, . . . This love could not be comprehended by flesh and blood if God had not especially demonstrated it in some people, whom one calls godly people and children of God, because they show a resemblance to God as their spiritual Father. . . . Therefore, it was the pleasure of the eternal love that the human being in whom the love would be most perfectly demonstrated would be called a Saviour of His people . . . . But He who is the most perfect in this love, He is a predecessor of all those who shall be saved. . . .[123]

Denck's views could therefore be seen as following the "affective" mystical tradition with its concern for conformity to the will of God. The mode of union was love, which Denck carefully defined as "a spiritual power through which one is united, or desires to become united."[124] Love assumed ontological qualities as the divine spark present in all men but having its source in God Himself. Thus Denck drew his inspiration clearly from a pre-Reformation *Weltanschauung*. The immanence theme of the mystical tradition provided the foundation of his most basic anthropological and Christological presuppositions. In fact, all his thought revolved around the real connection between the human and divine in the soul—the theme of immanence.

Both the voluntaristic and moral thrusts of Denck's thought are inseparable from the larger mystical framework. His stress on the moral accountability of man and his pertinent critique of the Lutherans on this subject grew more out of mystical presuppositions than out of an existential disillusionment with Reformation morals. From the mystical perspective he could reject both the predestinarian and Pelagian positions. Free will in the Pelagian sense was "open human pride" which made no concession to the fear of God and believed it could do whatever it pleased. The other extreme was "a malicious humility and prudence" which "does not want to be anything in itself," leaving it all to God.[125]

Denck obviously believed that salvation necessitated *cooperatio* between the human and divine. Cooperation was possible because of the immanence of God through His Word, which "shines in the hearts of all men who come into this world, because it is there from the beginning and gives men free power. . . ."[126] Nevertheless, from the Reformers' perspective, Denck was unable to overcome the latent synergism inherent in the mystical tradition. For there remained in his position that ambivalence about the real connection between the human and divine. No clear demarcation existed between the natural and supernatural resource in man.[127]

If Denck could not agree to the Lutheran stance on human depravity, it is not surprising that he could not accept the Lutheran interpretation of justification as *gratis propter Christum* through the *via iustitia aliena* of Christ. In orthodox mystical fashion justification implied a regenerated *iustitia propria*. Luther's formula of justification by faith alone seemed to him to advocate a fictitious righteousness.[128] The formula—"justified but always a sinner"—had to be alien to a mind which conceived of salvation as a gradual deification process in man.[129] Justification was not the restoration of fellowship with God through an imparted righteousness, but a literal becoming righteous. However, unlike Müntzer, who stressed the preparatory inner cleansing stage, Denck in humanistic fashion concentrated on moral and ethical conduct, which was to accompany the inner transformation. This was brought about through the gradual immobilization of the creaturely-seeking activity of man's will. The pre-Reformation *homo spiritualis* was a prerequisite to this view.

Thus, paradoxically, Denck, who did not share the same appreciation of the general sinfulness of human nature with the Reformers, accentuated the need for high ethical conduct and holy living.[130] From a perspective of eighteenth- and nineteenth-century "evangelicalism" it appears that his was a greater concern for "sanctification." However, it would be inadequate to explain the differences between Denck and the Reformers solely in terms of varying emphases on justification and sanctification. Denck's views on this subject must be judged in their overall context.

Correspondingly, Denck's understanding of faith and grace was not that of Luther. Although the mystics by internalizing religion had implicitly overcome sacramentalism, which insisted on external means of grace manipulated by the church, they retained the basic medieval outlook which conceived of grace as a spiritual medicine necessary to strengthen the ethical powers of man in his battle with evil. Grace was, therefore, not primarily an attitude of God towards the sinner. It was the divine Word itself effecting a transformation in the sinner and enabling him to imitate Christ's holy example.[131] In this system regeneration and discipleship were logical corollaries of the birth of the Son in the soul. The life of Christ provided the norm to be followed, the inner Word the enabling grace. Similarly, faith was neither a human exercise nor an irresistible gift bestowed on man. It was born in the twilight zone where the human and the Divine met.[132] But, as in nominalist thought, it remained one of the human virtues oriented to obedience to God's law, hence to the achievement of proper conduct.

From Denck's perspective it was, therefore, superfluous to debate about God's foreknowledge, "about which absolutely nothing has been ordered or revealed . . . whether it be before or after our sin."[133] Man's concern should be with the revealed law of God. Both Denck's understanding of the law and of Scripture have to be seen in the above context. At his trial in Nuremberg he had been asked to give his understanding of the righteousness of God, the law, and the gospel. Denck replied:

> The righteousness of God is God Himself. . . . Righteousness works through the Word, which was from the beginning, and is divided into two, law and gospel, by reason of the two offices which Christ, the King of righteousness, exercises, namely to kill the unbelieving and to quicken the believing.[134]

This condensed description of law and gospel, which on the surface appeared to embrace Luther's dialectic, was, however, mystically and existentially understood as the dual work of Christ in the *viator*. Denck's later writings indicate that the Lutheran dialectic, which saw the gospel as the liberating answer to human unrighteousness, was foreign to him. The law was not made without effect in Christ, but fulfilled by Him and to be fulfilled by all the members of His body.[135] Since love fulfilled the law, and love was mediated through Christ,[136] Christ literally fulfilled the law in His members by imbuing them with the necessary love. Denck's position was, therefore, a consistent *solus Christus* position, but again through the indwelling, not the historical Christ.[137]

Denck believed that his understanding of the law avoided both Pelagian works righteousness and the antinomian tendencies of the Reformers. Luther had misunderstood the function of the law as primarily condemnatory and revelatory of man's sinful condition. Not so Denck. To plead the impossibility of its demands was a refusal to accept Christ as having come into one's flesh, and to speak of Christ as if He were ten thousand miles away. Like Müntzer, therefore, Denck refused to endorse the Lutheran law-gospel dichotomy.[138]

This is further substantiated by Denck's tendency to internalize the law. Denck refused to distinguish between Old Testament and New Testament law, seeing the *nova lex Christi* as the unchanging essence of the transhistorical law of God. This essence had been revealed to Adam in paradise, namely that man ought not to love anything outside God.[139] Moses merely interpreted the universal law given into the hearts of all men.[140] Christ added nothing new, except that He was able to reveal love more completely as the fulfillment of the law.[141] His superiority to Moses rested not on a superior message but on His relation to the law. He was not only an interpreter, but the instigator (*Urheber*) of the law. "Christ has . . . not only spoken or written the divine Law outwardly like Moses, but speaks and writes it from the beginning of the world until its end in men's hearts."[142] The internalization of the law contained certain spiritualistic tendencies. Denck could at times refer to the whole Scripture as the outer law, particularly when he distinguished between letter and spirit. The relationship between the external historical manifestations of the law and the true inner universal law was analogous to the relationship between the Scriptures and the Word of God.[143]

The transhistorical understanding of the law was supplemented by Denck's acceptance of a "natural law" and a witness to this law in creation. His understanding of God's self-revelation assumed not only the divine immanence in man but in all creation. All created things were oriented toward their origin—their Creator. Thus the order of creation contained its own law, at once divine and natural. But the principles governing creation could only be grasped through the mystical inward gaze. However, since every man could perceive the divine law in him, Denck could also speak consistently of a natural law present in all men.[144]

> No man has the power to do good from himself but from God, who has still left him His Word in the heart—the law of nature— and through it we can through Christ, if we [but]follow it [the inner law], make God again into a friend through something which is God's own. The opposite happens when we let the mustard seed choke under the thorns; that is, if we will not let the Word of God born with us break out [from under] the fleshly lusts, we make God into our enemy.[145]

Two forms of witness existed for Denck. The higher of these was the personal revelation possible because of the direct connection with God. Here unmediated revelation of the *raison d'être* of existence was granted in oneness with the Divine. All things were revealed as having their being from and in God. The purpose and destiny of the divinely created order was unveiled—to be reunited with its Creator. The external witness of nature was of a lesser order because visible physical reality was a witness of opposites. In visible reality the invisible assumed paradoxical, special, temporal limitations turning into its opposite. All physical reality was, therefore, an inverted witness of invisible being, a witness of the part about the whole.[146] As Denck explained, the basic unity of all things and their relatedness to God "might not be grasped, thought, observed or recognized, except from and through the One even perhaps in its opposite."[147] Thus the outer witness was in true mystical fashion given at best a supporting role to true inner revelation.

We are now in a position to evaluate Denck's understanding of the role of Scripture. It was almost analogous to his view of natural and divine law. As noted earlier Hubmaier, Osiander, Bucer, and Johann Bader had all been critical of Denck's view of Scripture. In his Nuremberg confession Denck indicated that he could not endorse the Lutheran position on the Word of God and the Scriptures. He also instinctively rejected the Lutheran correlation between the heard word and faith. He believed that the Lutherans were advocating a creedal faith which gave mental assent to certain dogmatic propositions. This kind of

faith, while it verbally punished human sinfulness, was unable to overcome and cure it. In contrast, true faith was existentially born when the
internal Christ was conceived in the heart.[148] To seek God's revelation in
Scriptures without waiting for the experience of the inner Word and
true faith born in the soul turned Bible study into an act of idolatry.

> Yes, whoever does not want to await the revelation from God,
> but ventures on his own upon the work which belongs to the Spirit
> of God alone, he surely makes out of God's secret, contained in
> Scripture, a dissolute abomination and applies the grace of our God
> to lasciviousness. . . .[149]

Like Müntzer, Haferitz, and the mystics before him, Denck argued
that Scripture itself was only a *Zeugnis* to the inner Word. For Scripture
was a record of true experiences with God. That Denck was not primarily striving for a balanced hermeneutic without the pitfalls of a
wooden biblicism is clear from the context. He asserted, like Hans
Bünderlin and Christian Entfelder after him, that a biblicist mentality
had been responsible for the sectarian divisions which set in soon after
the passing of the apostles.[150] Denck clearly aimed against the *sola scriptura* position assumed by Osiander and the Lutheran Reformers. Since
he had not yet experienced the inner Word to the extent that he could
claim to have proper understanding of the Scriptures, all dialogue on
the basis of scriptural authority had become meaningless. This was
clearly how the Reformers understood Denck when they reported:
"This Denck, however, and his companions neither want to know nor
hear the Scripture, except alone for the sake of witness."[151]

That Denck opposed the Reformers in principle and not merely
through different interpretations of biblical texts becomes clear from his
subsequent writings. If anything, his statements after he left Nuremberg, at least until his recantation, became more radical in their
anti-Reformation orientation.

> He who has not the Spirit and presumes to find Him in the
> Scripture, he seeks light and finds darkness, seeks life and finds
> empty death, not only in the Old Testament, but also in the New;
> that is the reason that the most learned are always the most irritated
> by the truth, because they think that their understanding, which
> they have selected so cleverly and tenderly from the Holy Scripture,
> could not fail them. . . . Whoever has the truth in the truth, he can
> account for it without any Scripture. That the scribes could never
> do, because they did not receive the truth from the truth [directly],

but stole it only from the witness of the truth. But those who have this in their heart . . . to them is the written law everywhere annulled.[152]

Furthermore, if the Word of God was to be revealed only in Scripture, then God would "long remain unknown," for "whoever does not perceive God from God Himself, has never perceived Him."[153] And, like the mystics and Müntzer before and Hut and his followers after him, Denck spoke of the "key of David" which was necessary to unlock the Scriptures.[154] The point that Denck wanted to make with his collection of biblical contradictions was that the Bible could not be accepted as an objective authority.[155] The contradictions were overcome by those with proper understanding and perception of the whole. This was granted through the inner Word. Denck, like his more spiritualistic followers, Entfelder and Bünderlin, hinted that a literalist attitude, which grasped parts rather than the whole, was responsible for the proliferation of sects and a cantankerous spirit.[156]

Denck was here consciously labouring in a mystical tradition with an emphasis on the inner Word. This tradition made it a foregone conclusion that he would end in opposition to the Reformation's stance on Scripture. First, by stressing the transhistorical and general nature of revelation, he universalized revelation and undermined the value of and need for a special revelation. Then by stressing the spirit over the letter, and the unmediated, immediate inner Word against the written *Zeugnis*, he personalized revelation.[157] This view of revelation ran counter to the Reformers' understanding of scriptural authority. It placed Denck on common ground with Müntzer[158] and his own spiritualistic followers, Bünderlin and Entfelder.

That Denck and the Reformers disagreed on principle can be confirmed from the indirect evidence of Denck's impact on his colleagues Hätzer and Jacob Kautz in Worms.[159] Under the influence of Denck, Hätzer shed his earlier "massive biblicism," and began to find contradictions in the canon. We are told that a greater change than in Hätzer's view on Scripture is hardly imaginable.[160] Hätzer's writings at once took on mystical overtones which echoed Müntzer. He now heard the "living voice," which he believed was present in every man from his mother's womb and which he alternately described as the "key of David," the "divine seed," and the "preaching of the lamb of God" in man. The Lutheran position was attacked as "wisdom of the scribes (*Schriftgelehrsamkeit*), rape of the Spirit (*Vergewaltigung des Geistes*) sophistry and blatant deception (*gleissende Verführung*)." Faith, he insisted, preceded scriptural knowledge and had to be learned in the depths of the soul *(Abgrund der Seele).* Cross mysticism with a new emphasis on suffering became an essential element of Hätzer's writings. The whole life of the believer was now conceived as one of suffering.[161] Hätzer's Christology shifted in the direction of the *imitatio* tradition and a *philosophia Christi.* Christ became a great teacher and the ideal mystic.[162] The Reformation's principles of *sola fide* and *solus Christus* were now ridiculed as cheap grace and devilish inventions.[163]

Hätzer's movement towards spiritualism under Denck's tutoring was by no means an isolated historical phenomenon. Denck's activity in Worms left a similar impact on Kautz, although Kautz' evolution to extreme spiritualism was completed well after Denck's death. Kautz, who in 1529 was still willing to suffer imprisonment for his Anabaptist convictions, by 1532 had become disillusioned and described his earlier flirtations with Anabaptism as due to "fleshly enthusiasm."[164] Through his contacts with Denck and Hätzer, he had become part of the early South German Anabaptist movement which drew heavily on the mystical tradition and showed strong spiritualistic tendencies. This becomes obvious from an analysis of Kautz' "articles," which he prepared for a debate with the Lutheran ministers in Worms.[165]

Historians sympathetic to Denck have consistently tried to distance Denck from Kautz' seven articles.[166] However, if Denck did not actually formulate their wording, he certainly agreed with them in principle, and he must be regarded as their spiritual father.[167] The chronicler of Worms, Friedrich Zorn, informs us that the original copy, nailed to the church door, began: "Jacob Kautz, minister at Worms, with his brothers Hätzer, Denck and Rinck. . . ."[168] Another source tells us that Kautz defended the theses publicly with the help of two supporters.[169]

The theses represented an unmistakable frontal attack on Reformation principles. The first article relegated the outer Word to the role of a mere witness (*nur eyn gezeugnuss oder anzeygung dess innern*).[170] The other articles developed the inner-outer principle set forth in the first thesis. The inner Word alone had the potential to communicate grace. The rejection of the objective divine presence in the sacraments was a logical consequence. Like the Scriptures and the preached word, the sacraments were merely an outer witness to an inner occurrence. The living Word was active *in* man.[171] The main thrust came in the last two articles. They constitute an assault on the crucial Reformation insight of justification by faith and Luther's theology of the cross.

According to Kautz, the significance of Calvary lay in its exemplary nature. The lesson to be imitated was Christ's inner obedience, the end aimed at was union of the human will with the divine will. The soteriological principle of the Reformers' *sola fide* and *solus Christus* was rejected for the mystical *cooperatio* and *imitatio*.[172] To put it bluntly, Kautz, Denck, and Hätzer defended what recent scholars, rediscovering the Anabaptist vision, characterized as "discipleship." However, the formulation at Worms clearly did not grow out of a radicalization of Reformation principles, but was annunciated in opposition to them. The new ethical moralism championed by Kautz grew out of pre-Reformation mystical assumptions.[173]

The reaction to Kautz' seven articles substantiates the interpretation above. Catholics were most upset by the third and fourth articles which denied the objective validity of the sacraments of baptism and the Eucharist.[174] Interestingly, Cochleaus, who replied in print on June 17, 1527,[175] credited Kautz' conception of the inner Word with being closer to the truth than the Lutheran understanding of the Word of God.[176] However, he could not quite comprehend what implications were intended with regard to Christ's suffering.[177]

Most enlightening was Martin Bucer's response.[178] Bucer, who himself in the view of a modern Lutheran academic lacked accurate comprehension of the "Lutheran dialectic between law and grace,"[179] had no difficulty in detecting Denck as the real force behind the "Wormser articles."[180] He concentrated on the authority of Scripture and Christ's redemptive role as being under attack.[181] He believed that Kautz, following Denck, who in turn is described as a follower of Müntzer, reduced the role of Christ to that of a mere teacher and exemplar. He argued that Kautz thereby reopened the door to personal merit and bootstrap salvation.[182] He further detected a conception of sin alien to the Reformation anthropology. For Kautz and Denck, original sin did not eclipse the total human being. Both to do evil and to do good remained a possibility for fallen man.[183] This point had been debated by Bucer and Denck in Strassburg. Bucer claimed that he had reminded Denck of the Pauline view of human sinfulness, but that Denck had brushed Paul aside.[184] Thus Bucer in replying to Kautz' articles judged that the soteriological tenets of Kautz' and Denck's teaching came in a harmonious package which rested on assumptions not shared by the magisterial Reformers. From his perspective the *imitatio* emphasis represented a step backward to anthropocentric religiosity.

All this would strongly suggest that the differences between Denck and the Reformers were real and, as Bucer's response to Kautz' articles illustrates, primarily theological in nature.[185] Denck and the Reformers began from fundamentally different assumptions. To relegate their disagreement to unfortunate misunderstandings or to differences of emphasis amounts to a historical misjudgment of the theological acumen of the parties involved. An evaluation of Denck's writings must take into account his running debate with the magisterial Reformation.

It is within this larger historical and intellectual framework that the problem about Denck's relationship to the beginnings of South German Anabaptism must be solved. How was it that one who sought religious tolerance and engaged in ecumenical dialogue contributed to dissent? One can only infer that Denck's vision of what was essential to Christian belief was in conflict with the tendencies and climate created by the Reformation. Since his Reformed and Lutheran counterplayers did not share Denck's theological assumptions his courage to differ had to result in separation. However, it does not follow that he aimed at establishing a separatist or sectarian movement. For him the *communio sanctorum* was a logical extension of his mystical individualistic piety. The *Gemeinde*, as conceived by the Swiss Brethren and the later Hutterites and Pilgramites, was not central to his theology. Perhaps it was not accidental that his peculiarly Anabaptist statements are all found within the latter part of his *On True Love*,[186] the authenticity of which was seriously questioned by Denck's first biographer, and the disparate nature of which has remained a problem in present historiography.[187]

Moreover, even these statements lack the clear-cut precision of a Schleitheim Confession and are "not entirely free from paradox."[188] The mystical tendency to internalize religious experience carried within it the latent tendency to reject all external authority. It was particularly suited to support resistance against external coercion in matters of faith. On the other hand, it provided the basis for an ecumenical vision which looked beyond disagreements over ceremonies and dogma to Christlike conduct and a proper inner disposition. This is illustrated in his views on baptism and the Lord's Supper. Denck consistently stressed the greater significance of the inner spiritual experience.[189] And he declared himself ready to suspend outer baptism and the Lord's Supper if they should offend his neighbour and create division.[190]

However, Denck's mystical tendencies clashed with the events and trends unleashed by the Reformation. He did not live the life of a hermit. Denck's controversial *Recantation* must, too, have originated from the clash of his basic mysticism with the Reformation environment. The open hostility and published attacks against him by the Reformers could not fail to leave some effect on him.[191] The development of sectarian tendencies in the evolving Anabaptist movement raised new problems. Denck's encounter with followers of Hut at the Martyrs' Synod may have added to his disillusionment. Returning to Basel, Denck sent an apologetic letter to his old friend Oecolampadius in which he admitted that he had erred in doctrine. He also conceded to a more Pauline theology.

> In as much as I value that zeal to live rightly, which I truly know and daily experience in myself more and more, it is after all not sufficient for one to carry the Christian name, without that recognition which Paul demands in his letters. I do not deny that in questions of dogma I have erred at times and can still err, that I even expressed myself at times in such a way that I wish I had rather been quiet.[192]

Understandably Oecolampadius, who had been the recipient of all sorts of reports of Denck's heterodoxy, treated Denck's last statement as a recantation and concession to Reformation orthodoxy. However, the letter indicated Denck's reluctance to surrender his mystical assumptions and internalizing tendencies.

> I am of a totally different persuasion from those who tie the kingdom of God all too much to ceremonies and elements of this time, whoever they may be, even though I cannot deny that for a time I did so [also].[193]

Was Denck referring to his involvement with Anabaptism or to his Roman Catholic youth? An examination of his *Recantation* would suggest the former.

A focus on the essentials of Denck's theology derived from the mystical axiom of immanence leaves the impression that Denck's *Recantation* was not a recantation. He reasserted his mystical presuppositions and at most made an honest attempt to compromise with Reformation principles.[194] The Scriptures were exalted as the highest earthly treasure, but not equal to the Word of God, which is described as "eternal, living, powerful" and free from all "elements of this world." Through its inner activity in men it alone could reach those unable to read the written word or not privileged to hear the preached word. With regard to the sufficiency of Christ Denck reiterated that it was not enough to rely on the merit of Christ, but that true righteousness had to be a *iustitia propria*. He also repeated his stands on faith, free will, and good works. The cosmological Christ was confirmed as the ground of being (*Ursprung*) and enabling resource in man.[195]

If, on the other hand, the focus is on the elements of Denck's thought which were specifically Anabaptist, then his *Recantation* does indeed document his disillusionment with his Anabaptist past,[196] or at least with the new turn which Anabaptism was taking. Like his spiritualistic followers, Bünderlin and Entfelder, he went on record as being against separation and sects. He had separated himself from others only out of fear of persecution and because he did not want to be coerced into beliefs against his conscience.[197] The establishment of primitivist brotherhoods apparently had not been his foremost concern. Outer ceremonies, he believed, should be treated as *adiaphora* and should not become bones of contention. True, he reaffirmed his conviction that pedobaptism was unscriptural, but he warned that no one ought to initiate a new mode of baptism without a specific divine commission. As for himself, he indicated that he was willing to suspend baptising "eternally," if he did not receive a contrary command from God.[198]

There can be little doubt that in Denck early South German Anabaptism found one of its noblest representatives. However, he was better equipped to sponsor dissent within and exodus from the established churches than to become the founding father of another church—even a free church. He was, therefore, also representative of much that remained transitional about the earliest phase of Anabaptism. Intuitively he reacted against the institutionalizing and dogmatic tendency of the Reformers, as well as against the Anabaptists when they began to manifest similar inclinations. His theological pronouncements can be viewed as instinctive, defensive reflexes against what he perceived to be wrong priorities and directions in Reformation thought. Those reflexes were, however, grounded in mystical assumptions about the relationship between God, creation, and man. All aspects of his thought that we have touched upon, whether they be his universalism, anthropology, Christology, or his teachings about revelation, Word of God, Scripture, law, or love, revealed Denck's reckoning with the immanence of God. It was this pivotal idea that reinforced his more tolerant and ecumenical spirit. Unfortunately for Denck he proved to be an ecumenical Anabaptist out of season.

3

HANS HUT:
THE FOILED REVOLUTIONARY

A. Hans Hut, Hans Denck, and Thomas Müntzer

Hans Hut has long been recognized as one of the more important early Anabaptist leaders. While he lacked the intellectual sophistication of Denck, he compensated for it with missionary zeal. Making more converts in South Germany than any other leader, Hut had contacts extending from Central Germany into Austria and Moravia. In terms of influence his significance for the early Anabaptist movement was certainly equal to that of Conrad Grebel.[1]

It is well documented that Hut's contact with Thomas Müntzer was more than casual, although Hut sought to convey at his trial that their relationship was only casual. On September 9, 1524, Müntzer, who had fled from Allstedt to Mülhausen, was temporarily exiled from that city together with his colleague Pfeiffer. Carrying a red cross and a naked sword ceremoniously before them, the two revolutionaries led their faithful followers to a nearby public house. There they all solemnly signed their names to a list of the "eternal covenant." Among the signatories was one Hans of Bibra, who has in recent Anabaptist literature been identified with Hut.[2]

A few weeks later, when Müntzer and Pfeiffer were exiled a second time from Mühlhausen, Müntzer stopped in Bibra and entrusted Hut with his manuscript of the *Special Exposé*.[3] As we noted earlier, in October 1524, Hut, accompanied by Pfeiffer, brought the manuscript to Nuremberg. Here he made contact with Denck and contributed to the radicalization of the local situation.[4] Later, during the eventful days of the peasants' revolt, Hut, who had been arrested by distrustful peasants, was freed by Müntzer's personal intervention. He was with Müntzer at Frankenhausen until "the shooting became too thick."[5] On his return to Bibra in May 1525 he joined Jörg Haug, who had been elected as spiritual leader by the rebellious peasants in that region. Haug invited Hut to share his opinions on pedobaptism, the peasants' defeat, and so on, from the open pulpit. At that point Hut still advocated the killing of the *Obrigkeit* to clear the world for the triumph of Christ's kingdom. Haug, himself never an Anabaptist in the true sense of the word, belonged to the thought world of Müntzer. Hut later helped to publish new editions of his pamphlet of 1524, thus assuring Haug a niche in Anabaptist literature.[6]

Thus Hut's historical contacts with Müntzer have been a well established fact. But how did this relate to his career as an Anabaptist? Anabaptist scholars with little sympathy for Müntzer have interpreted Hut's baptism by Denck as a regenerative experience, initiating a transvaluation of all of the values Hut inherited from Müntzer. His baptism was assumed to mean a conversion to an Anabaptist movement complete with a separatist ecclesiology and with a new emphasis on discipleship and brotherhood. For rebaptism was "necessarily practised only in connection with a separated brotherhood."[7] By recovering a somewhat idealistic vision of Anabaptism and postulating a complete movement born in the "heart of the Swiss Reformation," this historiographical standpoint could assume that Hut was literally "won for the Anabaptist movement."[8] Through Denck and indirectly through Hubmaier, Hut received from the Swiss the basic insight of suffering discipleship and separated brotherhood. Thereafter, the "centrality of the church in Hut's writings and life is striking."[9]

Support for the conversion emphasis came from the editor of Hut's confessions, and, admittedly, from Hut himself. Allegedly Hut, taught by Denck and Hätzer, left the more radical sociopolitical ideas of Müntzer, and from then on "his teachings . . . were the noblest and most conciliatory" found in Anabaptism at this early stage.[10] However, these comments were based on the limited area of Hut's political ethic. They do not justify applying to Hut the typological and theological connotations of the sectarian model.[11]

Hut himself, when asked about his relation to Müntzer's revolutionary activity, confessed to have been "taught differently" since he knew Müntzer.[12] However, the reference was explicitly to Hut's view of the peasants' role in God's eschatological economy. With hindsight, Hut knew that the peasants had failed because they sought their own rather than God's honour.[13] Müntzer had come to a similar conclusion after the fiasco at Frankenhausen. Are we to argue a great conversion experience at this point in Müntzer's life?

Hut's own statements concerning his baptism do not support the theory of his conversion to a movement patterned on the Swiss Anabaptist model. Hut recalled his conversation of more than a year earlier with three artisans, possibly disciples of Storch or Müntzer. This dispute awakened his interest in rebaptism (*widertauff*). He first sought answers in Wittenberg but did not find them.[14] Finally it was the report of one Casper Ferber, "how some brothers in the Inntal (in the Tyrol) had been baptized and now lived Christian lives," which moved Hut to request baptism from Denck.[15] That Denck, by the act of baptism, did not necessarily communicate any distinctly Swiss values to Hut, becomes clear from the fact that Hut later opposed Swiss attitudes when they began to infiltrate among his own followers. He dissented from their views on the sword and oath and from what to him appeared to be legalistic concerns with dress.[16] Furthermore, Hut's mode of baptism was not that used by the Swiss, nor that used by Hubmaier. Hut preferred the eschatologically significant sign of the cross on the forehead.[17]

We conclude that Hut's baptism by Denck did not constitute a break with his Müntzerian past. On the contrary, an analysis of his ideas indicates a strong dependence on Müntzer.[18] Hut, even as an Anabaptist, was but a foiled revolutionary. His theological and eschatological framework appears to have been complete before his baptism. As for Müntzer so for him, religious and social concerns were inextricably interwoven, even after the peasants' defeat. True, Hut undertook a readjustment of his general apocalyptic expectations. But this did not constitute a shift from social to religious concerns. It reflected the changed circumstances but not a grand religious conversion with theologically revolutionary implications.

The question of Denck's relation to Hut remains more problematic. Denck's own relationship to Müntzer and early Swiss Anabaptism is part of the problem. Scholars accepting a conversion of Denck via Hubmaier, and in turn a conversion of Hut to the Anabaptism represented by Denck, all recognized Denck's influence on Hut.[19] Ironically, scholars arguing for an influence of Müntzer on Denck seconded the thesis of strong similarities between Denck and Hut for the opposite reason, in that they saw in Denck a conveyor of Müntzer's theology.[20] More recently, the theory of Hut's conversion has been reversed and his indebtedness to Müntzer reaffirmed.[21] Hut's eschatological mode of baptism has been seen to be fundamentally distinct from the practice of the Swiss Brethren and Hubmaier. Certainly Hubmaier's protest that his baptism was as far removed from Hut's "as heaven and hell, orient and occident, Christ and Belial" has become more credible.[22]

But what of the fact that Hut had been baptised by Denck? For scholars who accepted the traditional assumption that Denck himself had been baptised by affusion by Hubmaier,[23] the only conclusion possible was that Hut developed his peculiar mode of baptism independently of Denck.[24] For it was assumed that Denck in turn had baptised Hut in a Hubmaierian fashion.[25] This conclusion appeared to be supported by recent research on Denck which concentrated on differences between Denck and Müntzer.[26] If a strong differentiation between Denck and Müntzer were accepted, a clearer distinction between Denck and Hut had to be a logical consequence[27]—because studies on Hut have argued his indebtedness to Müntzer.

Unfortunately, the assumption that Hubmaier baptised Denck was an unwarranted inference from a dubious source.[28] We cannot assume that Denck baptised by affusion, the mode used by Hubmaier. We are simply uninformed as to how, when, where, and by whom Denck was baptised, if he was baptised at all. In fact, it is not impossible that he baptised Hut with a sign on the forehead. Denck was certainly familiar with Hut's supporting texts. In a copy of the *Wormser Propheten* found on an Anabaptist deacon the following significant passages had been underlined:

> Ezekiel 36: "I will sprinkle you with pure clean water, from which you will become clean."
> Ezekiel 11: "All those who have the sign on them, you shall not touch."
> Ezekiel 9: "Go and mark them with a sign on the forehead."[29]

The low eschatological content in his published works notwithstanding, Denck, as noted earlier, did not deny the possibility of special revelation regarding future events.[30] And if a passage in the commentary on Micah, attributed to Denck, was indeed reflective of his view, then he was not a consistent follower of Origen with regard to eschatology. For in that passage the author characteristically refused to commit himself to a purely spiritualized expectation of the kingdom. He wrote: "Neither do I resist totally those who seek something temporal in

Christ's kingdom, because the prophets say much about it—here I wish to avoid further disagreement."[31] Moreover, he often ended his writings with allusions to a coming punishment of the godless.[32]

It is also possible that Denck, for whom outer formalities were not all that significant, simply patterned his mode of baptism on traditional rites without any deeper apocalyptical intent. His colleague, Hätzer, was capable of baptising without the use of water. We are here merely arguing that Hut possibly copied his mode of baptism from Denck. That he later developed his own peculiar eschatological interpretation of this mode is not at issue. There was apparently nothing in Denck's historical act preventing that development.[33] On the theoretical side Denck's view of baptism as an inner covenant with God was not in conflict with Hut's understanding of the subject.[34]

Within our context, then, the similarities between Denck and Hut are again put into central focus. Both drew heavily on a popular mystical tradition and this made them spiritual cousins of Müntzer. Both Denck and Hut were first-generation Anabaptists and to a certain extent both remained transitional figures. This, however, does not constitute a denial of all differences. For Denck, with his humanistic and scholarly interests, apocalyptical expectations were not as significant as for Hut, the foiled revolutionary. While Denck stressed the theme of love and the *nova lex Christi* in his writings, Hut, who here came closer to Müntzer, continued to speak of suffering in terms of cross mysticism and of divine judgment in an apocalyptical context. And yet the theological and soteriological differences between Hut, Denck, and Müntzer were differences of degree,[35] and, in comparison with the presuppositional differences which separated all three from the Reformers, they were not fundamental.

B. Hans Hut's Theology of Protest

In this analysis of Hut's theology the writer was able to profit greatly from Gottfried Seebass' ground-breaking research of the sources. While none of his corrections of and additions to the primary materials have been revolutionary, their total effect has been to increase substantially our knowledge of Hut.[36] Hut's own writings, as well as the anonymous sources associated with the movement influenced by him, suggest that the early South German and Austrian Anabaptists were directly indebted to the medieval mystical and apocalyptical traditions. This is perhaps best illustrated by Hut's fondness for the trinitarian pattern.

For Hut, as for Denck and Müntzer, mystical reunion between man

and God was the cardinal soteriological and theological axiom.[37] Like
Bünderlin and Entfelder later, he conceived of the Trinity primarily as a
threefold activity present in creation and revealing itself to man in the
mystical experience. In this theology of analogy the Father was revealed
as "omnipotence" and "power," the Son as "righteousness" and
"severity," and the Holy Spirit as "mercy" and "goodness."[38] True
knowledge of God came through the personal experience of the trinitarian movement.[39] Divine revelation could, therefore, be experienced
first as the revelation of God as omnipotent Creator. This was a universal
revelation but, on its own, inadequate. The second movement, the justice or "severity" of the Son as the inner cross, had to be experienced
before the third, the encounter with the merciful Spirit, was possible.
Thus the confession which declared its faith in the Father, Son, and
Holy Ghost was to be existentially entered into by the viator.[40] The
genuineness of the experience could be verified from Scripture.[41] Thus
Hut depersonalized the Trinity into a threefold creative-redemptive-
revelatory activity.

It is possible that the mystical understanding of God's trinitarian
activity was reinforced by a Joachimite philosophy of history. The
Father was particularly active during the stage which preceded the giving of the law, the Son during the age of law, and the Spirit during the
last stage. The third stage, which was to be ushered in by severe
persecution of the true children of God, was to be the age when all were
taught directly by the Spirit.[42]

Thus three stages similar to those of the Joachimite tradition corresponded historically to the trinitarian revelation outlined above. The
witness of the omnipotent Father was the witness in all creatures, the
witness of the severe Son that in the law or Scripture, and the witness of
the goodness of the Spirit found in the exemplary lives of the believers.
The witness of the Son was central, literally constituting the medium
through which the viator needed to pass from knowledge of God's omnipotence to knowledge of divine goodness and mercy. Although each had
its special period in history, the three witnesses had been active together
since the beginning of the world. In the last age, when the Spirit would
impart God's will directly to the hearts of men,[43] dreams and visions
would be legitimate vehicles of revelation.[44] Hut's pneumatology was,
therefore, as much derived from his view of history as from his
mysticism.

Interestingly, in this scheme the Son revealed not the good news of
forgiveness, but represented a message of severity—suffering and

punishment. Here a mixture of motifs from the traditions of imitatio and cross mysticism reappeared. Like Müntzer and Denck before him, Hut did not accept Luther's formulation of justification as a *iustitia aliena,* namely *gratis propter Christum.* True righteousness was attained only in the experience of the bitter Christ.[45] The Word had to be conceived and become flesh in the viator as it had in Mary.

> The Word has to be conceived in him with a pure heart through the Holy Spirit, and has to become flesh in him. . . . That happens through great fear and trembling . . . just as with Mary, when she heard the will of God from the angel.[46]

It is clear that Hut thought of the Word not as covenantal promises of God, but in the mystical fashion as the connection between man and God. To experience the Word was literally to experience that regeneration through which a man emptied himself of the creaturely in spiritual rebirth. This mystical understanding of the internal Word was complemented by an appeal to Christ, the historical "example." Like Müntzer, Hut focused on the passion of Christ, rather than on the *nova lex Christi.* True righteousness was attainable only in conformity with Christ in His suffering.

> . . . and whosoever does not want to follow these footsteps and this way, and has not carried the cross of Christ, or does not want to carry it, he does not have or recognize the Son, and whoever has not the Son, he does not have or recognize the Father, and can also not be illuminated through the goodness of the Holy Spirit. . . .[47]

Hut believed that Christ's conception, birth, passion, and resurrection were to be repeated in every true follower of Jesus.[48] In the undated letter in which he made allusions to his difficulties with Hubmaier in Nicolsburg,[49] he exhorted his readers not only to conceive the Word as Mary had done, but also to give birth to it and die with it in order to participate in its resurrection.[50] This peculiar internalized recapitulation of the four stages of Jesus' earthly mission differed from the traditional focus on Christ's birth, passion, resurrection, and ascension. Together with the "gospel of all creatures" it became a distinguishing mark of Hut's influence on the early South German Anabaptist movement.[51]

Hut's controversial gospel of all creatures was, among other things, a deliberate projection of Müntzer's cross mysticism onto a cosmic scale.[52] The creatures, like the Scriptures, gave witness that redemption necessitated purgation through suffering.[53]

> The whole world with all creatures is a book in which one sees everything as a work which can be read in the written book. For all the elect, from the beginning of the world until Moses, have studied in the book of all creatures and . . . perceived the understanding [sense], which has been written into their hearts naturally through the Spirit of God, since the whole Law has been described with creaturely works.[54]

Moses, by way of the law and ceremonies, gave an outer exposition of this gospel. The New Testament in describing the suffering Son repeated it. Both creation and the Scriptures, Old and New Testaments, therefore, contained the same gospel.[55]

The gospel of all creatures, containing as it did echoes of a natural theology, involved more than an ignorant reading of the Latin genitive for the dative case. Hut's choice of the genitive was a conscious act.[56] It could be utilized against a clerical monopoly on God's revelation. This becomes obvious in Hut's outbursts against the "tender, worldly, voluptuous scribes" and "brother soft-life" in his "den of thieves and murderers" at Wittenberg.[57] Against the scribes, who gave inflated importance to the written word, Hut's gospel of all creatures held out the possibility of direct knowledge of God attainable even by the poor and illiterate.[58]

It remains controversial to what extent Hut was dependent on Müntzer in developing this important concept. Some scholars believe that in his theoretical assumptions as well as in his polemical purpose Hut was in agreement with Müntzer.[59] The gospel of all creatures was certainly not a peculiarly evangelical Anabaptist concept. In fact, it has been argued that it stood too near the world of late medieval mysticism to have enduring value for the Anabaptist movement, which was to develop "its own authentic ethos."[60]

The gospel of all creatures incorporated the medieval assumption of a hierarchical chain of being. God had structured creation so that the lower orders found their fulfillment in submission to the rule of the higher. The animals must serve man; man must serve God. Hut supported this understanding of an ordained hierarchy in creation by an exposition of Genesis 1:28, in which man was admonished to "subdue" and "have dominion" over "every living thing." Thus the creatures found their true fulfillment only by submitting to man. Submission and obedience meant suffering.[61] However, Hut did not utilize this concept to construct his political ethic; apparently the vertical order had no horizontal implications for relations between human beings. Instead he applied it to the realm of revelation. Thus the divine order implanted in nature demonstrated the principle of redemptive and restorative suffering. Creation not only mirrored the omnipotence of the Creator, but revealed His redemptive activity.

But is it really possible to harmonize the idea of a revelation in nature with the mystical maxim that true knowledge of God is accessible only in the inner recesses of the soul? The mystics were preoccupied with the anthropological immanence of God, and any revelation mediated through externals and the senses was looked upon as inferior, if not false and perverted. Knowledge of God or of the order of being, which regulated man's relation to the Divine, could only be learned in the salvation process itself. This was the context in which those familiar with the *Theologia Deutsch* expounded Genesis 1:28. The order mentioned there was not only an order of obedience (*Gehorsamsordnung*) but also an order of being (*Seinsordnung*). Only in the mystical experience of reunion between the human and divine was the original relationship of obedience signified in the order of Genesis 1:28 made possible and achieved.[62]

It appears that Müntzer understood both the order of God and the witness of the creatures in a mystical sense. When he wrote about order (*Ordnung*) he referred primarily to the order governing man's relation to God. The creatures gave not an autonomous witness, but one which became meaningful only when the proper inner relationship between man and God had been restored.[63]

It was Hut's achievement that he gave the external witness of the creatures a greater autonomous role. Whether Hut was here influenced by a more scholastic tradition is not clear, for at the same time he stressed that the witness in nature was not merely the conventional witness to God's glory, but a witness of the crucified Son and of the cathartic quality of suffering. It is possible that Hut here elaborated or added to concepts he had heard not only from Müntzer but also from Denck.[64]

Denck, like Müntzer, had retained the mystical priority of the inner witness. In one passage he wrote that the creatures were sent to preach to man's "derision but not his detriment" because he did not heed the lamb speaking in the heart.[65] What was unique in Hut was the bringing together of the concept of the gospel preached by the creatures and Christ's Great Commission recorded in Mark 16:15, 16 (albeit in the wrong grammatical context). Hut combined a sequential literalism of preach, believe, and baptise with an ungrammatical exposition of what was to be preached—the gospel of all creatures. It appears that in this exposition Hut combined medieval allegorical imagination with a Reformation literalism. Müntzer, who had cited the Great Commission in his *Prague Manifesto*, had shown greater concern for the deeper meaning of the text and polemicized against those who were preoccupied with the literal sequence.[66] Thus, at least in this regard, Hut appears not to have been directly indebted to Müntzer.

Similarly, the insistence on making faith a prerequisite to outer baptism was not a logical consequence of Müntzer's teachings. If anything, Hut here came closer to Denck, who as early as January 1525 had utilized Mark 16:16 against the pedobaptist position of the Lutherans in Nuremberg, and who in other places insisted that proper teaching should precede baptism.[67] In all probability, however, Hut had also been exposed to Carlstadt's and possibly to Hubmaier's influence. As a result, his own interpretation of the subject combined at times incompatible elements from the ideas of his contemporaries.[68] Hut did not follow the *Theologia Deutsch* and the mystics with the consistency of a Denck or Müntzer.

This point is perhaps best illustrated by reference to Hut's understanding of faith. Like Müntzer, he distinguished between an untried, imperfect, untested, preliminary faith, which came through hearing, and the real justifying faith born in the agony of inner purification.

> Their teaching, as one hears, is nothing else than to believe, and reaches no further; because they do not tell through which medium one may get to [faith] . . . for where the order of God's secrets is not heeded properly there is vain error. . . . Therefore, my beloved brethren in the Lord, you must learn God's judgments concerning His commandments and words yourselves and be informed of them directly by God. . . .[69]
> But that takes time and does not happen fast, as our scribes say, who persuade the poor people saying believe, believe, yes, yes.[70]

Only the faith born in the cathartic mystical experience of the cross—an experience which was itself the justifying process—was true justifying faith.[71] Like Müntzer, Hut claimed that such belief as had been communicated through externals had first to be overcome by unbelief. True faith born in the mystical experience of the cross would then appear and distinguish itself from the false or invented faith.[72] Hut then asked the rhetorical question: "Where then is the outer word and belief?"[73] It appears he attempted to remain on the ground of sola fide without accepting Luther's close correlation between the outer Word and justifying faith. The mystical explanation of how true faith was born provided an alternative.

Yet Hut could not eliminate the role of the outer witness. In contrast to Müntzer, who totally rejected the "phony faith," Hut had a complicated and ambivalent attitude towards it. After all, he considered himself to have been especially commissioned to preach the gospel of all creatures and, according to Mark 16:16, to baptise those who believed. Accordingly, Hut made allowance for a preliminary function of the outer witness. An interim righteousness was imputed to the believer on account of a prevenient faith, which came through hearing the external witness. Effective righteousness accompanied the tried faith, generated in the mystical experience of the cross.

> The faith originating in hearing preceded justification, after which the tried faith begins. . . . The outer word reaches unto justification, in justification the word and faith disappear for [the viator]. . . . In this fashion it happens to all pious, elect people. The seed must first die in every one before it brings forth fruit, and must be enclosed in unbelief before God appears in His mercy.[74]
> But the untried faith reaches no further than to righteousness. There it must be prepared and justified. But the whole world fears justification like the devil and wants to pay for it with the invented faith and does not want, after all, to come to justification.[75]

This formulation was directed against the Lutherans, who allegedly fell back on God's omnipotence to argue that justifying faith sprang directly from the external witness.

> Then they say: well my dear, to God all things are possible through His omnipotence. Answer, yes, God is omnipotent and can do all things, but He does not do all things, but orders all things in His omnipotence according to measure, number and weight.[76]

The Lutherans were, in Hut's eyes (just as he in theirs), seeking to short-circuit God's normal order of grace and salvation. That order required that something physical and external should precede the spiritual inner process.[77] Paradoxically, Hut's stress on the priority of an outer witness, which might have appeared to support the Lutherans' position, was turned against them. His outer witness in preaching, unlike theirs, was an appeal to turn away from externals such as Scripture to the true inner witness. Thus, although Hut conceded a functional role to the external Word as part of the divinely ordained order of grace and salvation, he polemicized against the Lutherans for turning the external Word into an idol. In the final analysis, this suggests that Hut's mystical presuppositions were dominant enough to prevent him from accepting Luther's position on faith without qualifications; but Hut was too eclectic a thinker, too influenced by the various currents of his time, to be simply "Müntzer's heir." Rather, he marks the beginning of a diffusion and dilution of the German mystical tradition which accelerated in South German Anabaptism.

Hut's indebtedness to the mystical tradition can be further illustrated by his view of Scripture. Scripture, as a witness to divine revelation, testified to the activity of omnipotence in sustaining the creatures, of righteousness in purging man from all creatureliness, and of goodness in leading the viator to perfection.[78] Thus Hut's understanding of God's trinitarian revelation provided a key to proper understanding of the Scriptures. To the uninitiated into the inner secrets of God's threefold activity the Scriptures remained a sealed book.

> Where this order is not taken heed of and the three parts not applied everywhere as a structuring principle, there it is impossible to treat the Scriptures without error or offence to the truth.[79]

To underscore his point Hut, like Denck, cited contradictory passages from Scripture.[80] It was logically inherent in his mystical position that only those who had experienced the suffering Son became partakers of the Spirit and therewith received the key to unlock the meaning of the Scriptures. Hut could, therefore, accentuate the letter-spirit dichotomy when confronted by an appeal to Scripture. He could also insist on a literal interpretation, if it was the meaning the Spirit intended.[81] Historians have, therefore, found evidence—depending on their own perspectives—to support both a spiritualist and a biblicist tendency in Hut.[82] So did Hut's followers. And yet it remains undeniable that both Hut and his Reformation opponents considered themselves opposed to each other not only with regard to certain scriptural interpretations, but also with regard to the principle of scriptural authority. This antagonism becomes explicable only when Hut's larger mystical frame of reference is taken into account.

One of his differences with the Reformers grew out of Hut's more mystical understanding of the Word of God, which drew implicitly on a logos theology. Like Müntzer and Denck, Hut appealed to the mystical inner Word against Luther's stress upon the authority of the preached and written Word of God.

> Therefore, whoever wants to use Scripture with proper honour
> and not attribute to it more than is its own and becoming to it, he
> must distinguish it [Scripture] from the inner Word of the heart. . . .
> The eternal Word is not written on paper or tables, is also not
> spoken or preached, but a man is alone assured of it by God in
> solitariness in the bottom of the soul; and [it] is written into the
> heart of flesh through the finger of God.[83]

Both the preached word and the written Word belonged to the outer
witness, and both Old and New Testament fell under the leveling category of letter.

> . . . everything which one may read in books, which one hears or
> sees in the creatures or of other men, is not the living Word of God,
> but only a letter and duplicated sign or witness [*zeugknus*] of the in-
> ner and eternal or living Word . . . just as a sign before a tavern wit-
> nesses to the wine in the cellar, but the sign is not the wine.[84]

Hut, like Müntzer and Denck, could, therefore, polemicize against
the preachers who "deceived the people," convincing them that the
preached and printed word was the real Word of God. Since it was not, it
brought no fruit, no improvement.[85] The inner Word, on the other
hand, was more than sound, and more than secondhand witness. It was
both the medium and the substance of the revelation of God to man and
as such served more than a merely intellectual, instructive function. It
was "an eternal and omnipotent power of God, the same in men as in
God, and capable of all things."[86]

Hut's polemical use of the inner Word against the Lutherans,
which appears so obviously to echo familiar mystical assumptions,
makes it even more difficult to assess Hut's insistence upon a revelation
in the creatures. Just as the relationship between the preliminary and
justifying faith, the outer and inner Word, remains ambivalent, so the
gospel of all creatures was never logically synchronized with Hut's
otherwise mystically oriented theology. When polemicizing against the
Lutherans he found it convenient to appeal to a universal witness personally verified in man's inner experience of reorientation. That
reorientation necessitated the believer's suffering as the creatures
testified. Thus Hut ascribed to the outer witness—the revelation in the
creatures—merely a preliminary function which pointed to and needed
verification in the mystical self-disclosure of God. It appears Hut either
ignored or remained oblivious of the latent contradiction between his
insistence on the autonomous external witness of the outer word and the
revelation of all creatures and his mystical appeal to the inner

experience and verification of that witness. Thus one can but conclude that the mystical legacy that influenced Müntzer and Denck was diluted and diffused by the eclectic nature of much of Hut's thought.

Hut's emphasis on suffering as the means of cleansing did not harmonize with Luther's teachings on justification. From a Reformation point of view, Hut undercut the vicarious nature of Christ's suffering.[87] Suffering itself became "the medium and the justice" through which justification was obtained. This maxim was expressed most forcefully in one of Hut's letters.

> Suffering is the medium on account of which the Lord justifies His own. This happens through penitence and bitterness. . . . Therefore I say . . . there is no other way, we must step into the footpath of Christ.[88]

Yet at his trial Hut maintained that he had not subtracted from the sufficiency of Christ's merit, nor ascribed any inherent merit to the sufferer.[89]

How is this statement to be harmonized with Hut's other pronouncements on the subject? The mystical tradition again provides the key. It was a foregone conclusion that his mystical presuppositions would make it impossible for Hut to embrace the Lutheran understanding of justification. It was equally true that a Lutheran could not appreciate the consistency of Hut's mystical theology. Hut could claim to remain Christocentric in his soteriology by emphasizing the union of the viator with Christ. "The whole Christ must suffer in all His members and not as our scribes preach Christ, . . . as if Christ, the head, had carried it all out and performed it all."[90] From this vantage point Hut could call the believer's suffering Christ's suffering, and Christ's merit the believer's merit.

> Everything that such persons suffer is all called Christ's suffering and not ours, because we are in Christ one body in many members, united and allied in the bond of love. Wherefore . . . Christ accepts such persons as His own body . . . because Christ's suffering must be fulfilled in every member. . . . For just as Christ, the lamb, has been slain from the beginning of the world, so also is He still crucified until the end of the world, that the body of Christ be perfected according to the length, width, depth and height in the love of Christ.[91]

Since Hut's eschatological expectations, as we will see, forecast external suffering for God's faithful, he no longer advocated a purely internalized cross mysticism. In this regard he bridged the gap from Müntzer to the later theology of martyrdom of the Anabaptists. His emphasis on following in Christ's footsteps helped to blur the line between himself, Denck, and the Swiss Brethren.[92]

Thus we can conclude that in spite of his preoccupation with Reformation topics and the undeniable influence of the contemporary debates on him, Hut intuitively remained closer to the thought world of the late medieval mystics. The voluntaristic thrust of his thought further substantiates the conclusion reached above. Although he nowhere developed an explicit anthropology, it is evident that he did not accept Luther's pessimistic view of man. With Müntzer, Denck, and the other dissenters against the main Reformation he shared the late medieval tendency to minimize the effect of original sin.[93] Although he carefully avoided the semi-Pelagian consequences inherent in late medieval theology, his emphasis on the mystical experience of the cross, which required resignation from all creaturely attachments, should on no account lead to the conclusion that he, like Luther, taught a *iustitia passiva*.[94] The overall framework of Hut's system did not permit predestinarianism, a logical prerequisite to Luther's *iustitia passiva* and *sola gratia*. Like the mystics, Hut subscribed to the principle of *cooperatio* with regard to salvation.

But again, his views were not devoid of ambivalence. This is perhaps best illustrated by Hut's baptismal theology. Reminiscent of Denck, Hut saw baptism as a dual covenant between the viator and God and the viator and his fellow travellers.[95] At the same time, he conceived of baptism as an internal process of which the outer was a mere sign. The inner essence was more significant than the outer sign. But the relation between inner and outer was complicated by Hut. On the one hand he accepted the outer sign as symbolic of the initiation process of salvation; on the other hand, he appeared to have seen it as symbolic of the entire salvation process.[96] Inner baptism was nothing less than cathartic purification. In this sense man did not baptise himself, but submitted to the inner baptism of suffering. However, Hut explicitly stated that inner baptism followed outer baptism, and that outer baptism was a voluntary acceptance of the covenantal sign (*ein bunt . . . der verwilligung*).[97] Thus baptism was not a testimonial service witnessing to conversion, regeneration, or justification, but something preceding it and pointing forward to it. However, as we noticed, on other occasions Hut argued that baptism, according to Mark 16:16, followed faith and was a testimonial to one's fellowmen of that faith. Thus, as in his understanding of justification in which the believer chose to suffer God's will, Hut's baptismal theology retained synergistic elements. He advocated a passive submission to the divine will, while at the same time embracing baptism as a sign of a freely-willed covenant.

The medieval undercurrent in Hut's thought can also be seen as reflected in his hermeneutical fondness for allegory and number symbols. Particularly the numbers three, four, and seven appear to have been very significant for him. God revealed Himself in a threefold way. The work in the viator, as we noticed earlier, went through four stages—conception, birth, death, and resurrection—analogous to stages in Christ's historical career. The Scripture remained a "sevenfold sealed book for the scribes," who refused to suffer the work of God in them.[98]

Jörg Haug had earlier drawn attention to the importance of the number seven in Scripture and related it to the mystical experience of the viator:

> A Christian life has steps and degrees until it becomes perfect. It has also time, numbers and measure. . . . A faithful reader often finds number, order and measure in the Scriptures, and this is especially demonstrated by the number seven. . . . This number points always to the perfect, since it is always at rest and can go no higher. Thus a person comes through the seven spirits to the perfection of the united Spirit, in trouble and great tribulation. When a person comes to the seventh degree of blessedness, there the Spirit rests upon him, and he is conformed to Christ, whence all the witness of the Scripture drives [him], and [beyond which it] can point no further. Therefore, the beginning of the Christian life stands in the fear of God, and it goes from one [stage] to the other until he [the viator] has been tested to the utmost through all seven [stages] and conformed to Christ, that means to hold the true Sabbath when the Spirit of God rests.[99]

In the confessions of his Salzburg followers Hut was said to be in possession of the book with the seven seals, which God had sent to the prophet Daniel but which would not be revealed until the day of the Lord.[100] Hut denied any knowledge of a book given to Daniel, but suggested that his followers meant his exposition of the seven seals in the Apocalypse.[101] His reference was, no doubt, to the "concordance of the seven judgments" in which he sought to give a summary of the whole Bible under seven headings.[102] These headings have long been familiar as the so-called "seven judgments" (*Sieben Urteile*) in Anabaptist sources. [103] Hut and his followers were repeatedly questioned about their meaning. [104] It appears that he considered them to be part of his special commission granted by direct revelation, [105] and the only correct interpretation of biblical prophecy. [106] They were:

(1) The covenant of God (the gospel about Christ, faith, and baptism)
(2) The body of Christ (about the Lord's Supper)
(3) About the end of the world
(4) About the future and about the judgment (about the judgment and the future of the Lord)
(5) About the resurrection (about the resurrection of the dead)
(6) About the kingdom of God
(7) About the eternal judgment (about the pain of the damned) [107]

The first two judgments summarized Hut's teachings on the sacraments—baptism and the Lord's Supper—while the last five dealt with his eschatology. Although Hut's views of baptism and the Lord's Supper cannot be separated from his eschatology, it was primarily his eschatology contained in the last five judgments which worried the authorities and caused dissent even within his own camp. [108]

It is possible that the last four judgments were originally intended as subheadings and an elaboration of the third judgment. During his trial he repeated twice that the third judgment—about the end of the world—was divided into four parts:

(1) About the judgment over the house of God
(2) About the judgment of the world
(3) About the future
(4) About the resurrection [109]

This would harmonize with Hut's fondness for the trinitarian division since the major judgments would be three. And it would be consistent with his predilection for threefold and sevenfold patterns.

Curiously, Hut's concordance of the seven judgments makes reference under the very first heading of "the covenant of God" to those who will "hold the Lord's Sabbath." [110] The intended meaning within that specific context is no longer clear. However, one of Hut's earliest disciples, when questioned about the seven judgments, gave a rather interesting explanation of the Sabbath which fits into the context of Hut's apocalypticism.

[As] Christ had laboured six days, and [then] celebrated the
seventh, so God's Word had been persecuted six times and now for
the seventh time, [but] it would be brought into rest through the
Anabaptists after they experience the same [persecution] and have
punished the sins and eradicated the *Obrigkeit*.[111]

This follower, accordingly, indicated that Hut thought in terms of the
Sabbath as the seventh stage of world history. Like the Joachimists
before him, Hut focused on the seven seals in the Apocalypse for his
understanding of the last seven years. Similar fragments of the medieval
apocalyptical tradition, as we will see, reappeared in Leonhart
Schiemer.

Other allusions in Hut's writings indicate strong similarities
between his own ideas and Jörg Haug's. Hut's favourite salutation to his
readers—"I wish you the pure fear of God as the beginning of godly
wisdom"[112]—was the major theme of Haug's tract.[113] For according to
Haug the "spirit of fear" was the first of the "seven gifts of the Spirit."
The spirit of fear had to penetrate the spirit of the viator until the "right
light—the sun of righteousness"—would rise in him and "enlightening
his darkness" lift him out of his unbelief, thus making him a partaker of
the second gift—God's wisdom.[114]

Justus Menius, who wrote specifically against Anabaptists supposedly among the adherents of Denck, claimed that the concept of the
sevenfold gift of the Spirit was crucial to the Anabaptist practice of rebaptism.

Before they baptize the newcomer or, to speak after their
fashion, seal him with the covenantal sign, they tell him about the
seven bad spirits with which he is possessed; he has to confess first
that he possesses the same and then renounce them. After he has
renounced the seven bad spirits, then they tell him of the seven
good spirits, which he should receive and retain. When the
newcomer is ready to do the same, then they give him the
covenantal sign or baptism. The seven bad spirits are these: fear of
man, human wisdom, human understanding, human skill, human
counsel, human strength and human blessedness. Against them
they counterpose the seven good spirits as follows: fear of God,
God's wisdom, God's understanding, God's skill, God's counsel,
God's strength and God's blessedness.[115]

The reception of the gifts of the Spirit was usually associated with the
practice of *Firmung* (later confirmation), which makes it probable that
Menius' description was based on information coming out of Hut's

rather than Denck's following. For it was Hut who seems to have evolved his mode of baptism as a confirmation and eschatological symbol.[116] As we will see later, Menius' description of Anabaptist eschatology also fitted well with the ideas held by Hut and his followers. Of course, it is also possible that Menius, perhaps familiar with Haug's teachings, superimposed these on Anabaptist practice. Even so, it is clear that Hut absorbed much of Haug's system, or that both fed on the same medieval sources. Hut's use of the number seven in biblical exegesis was certainly not accidental.[117]

We can now return to the seven judgments. Hut's *Of the Mystery of Baptism* was nothing less than an exposition of the first of the seven judgments necessary to understand Scripture.[118] And it is very probable that he intended this tract to be the first part of a larger treatise. He himself announced his intentions:

> I am therefore moved out of Christian love and brotherly faithfulness to record the judgments which are necessary to the beginning of the Christian life, to the degree that God gives grace, as a witness to all brothers and sisters in the Lord . . . and not at all for the sake of the worldly lustful people, because such judgments would be incomprehensible to them, too biting, perverse, heretical, despised and condemned . . . such a high and impossible thing it is for a fleshly man to comprehend God's judgments in truth, when they are not, together with all [their] parts, composed into a proper order. Therefore we want at first to deal with the judgment of baptism—the beginning of the Christian life.[119]

Hut's view of baptism, as we noted earlier, implied the voluntary acceptance of a dual covenant. From his treatise, *Of the Mystery of Baptism,* we can now sketch in more fully his covenantal theology. He did not conceive of baptism as newly instituted by Christ, nor did he distinguish between the baptism of John and of Christ. True inner baptism was the divinely ordained cleansing process, which had been in effect since Adam. The drowning of the godless by the Great Deluge and the drowning of Pharaoh and the Egyptians in the Red Sea were cited by Hut as symbolic of inner baptism.[120] The covenant of which outer baptism was but a sign embraced both Old and New Testament saints. This set Hut apart from the Swiss Brethren and later South German Anabaptists, who distinguished between two covenants as historically identical with the two Testaments.[121] Hut's understanding of the dual (inner and outer) covenant in fact was closer to that of Müntzer, Denck, and the later Spiritualists, Entfelder and Bünderlin.[122] It should, therefore, be obvious that Hut could not have derived a two-kingdom concept, which distinguished the kingdom of Christ and the kingdom of this world, from his covenantal theology. Such a teaching would have presupposed a historical distinction between the Old and New Testaments, which was alien to Hut's thought. In fact, it has been argued that the essentials of a two-kingdom theory were lacking in Hut, and that with regard to his views of church and state he remained typically medieval, showing no signs of the so-often-admired trend to a "modern" separation of the two seen in the majority of Anabaptists.[123]

Hut's first judgment was also conceived of in an eschatological context. And, contradictory as this may at first appear, it was the apocalyptical context that helped blur the lines between Hut's and the Swiss Anabaptists' goals. For, while an examination of Hut's practice would suggest that he did not necessarily baptise within the context of a pure congregation,[124] he did encourage separation from the corrupt and fallen religious establishment. Moreover, explicit passages advocating withdrawal from the world, and, therefore, at least implicitly also the establishment of separate brotherhoods, can be found in Hut's writings.[125]

> In this congregation all members are enemies to sin, who love and desire only righteousness. . . . There everything is held in common, nothing is private: Acts, 2, 3, 4. It has been this way since the beginning of the world, in part, but until now never in the whole . . . that can and will not happen in the whole until the tribulation of all fear and misery has humiliated the whole world. Matthew 24.[126]

Hut was here approximating the ideal of a covenantal brotherhood for whose members he advocated something close to sinless perfection and the communitarian ideal. The impulses for this separatist element of his thought and practice were, however, in the final analysis eschatological. For Hut's extraordinary zeal as a baptiser was directly related to his identification of baptism with the sealing of the 144,000.[127] Hut, encouraged by the uniqueness of his apocalyptical message, believed himself especially commissioned by God to seal the faithful remnant.[128] Some of his followers would later maintain that they had not rejected pedobaptism, but merely accepted a sign indicating their willingness to improve their lives in view of the impending doom.[129]

Hut's second judgment concerning Christ's body was part of the same mystical and eschatological framework. The Lord's Supper above all symbolized the fellowship and unity of Christ's body with their Head. Hut's view in this regard approximated that of Erasmus and

Carlstadt.[130] However, in the eschatological context the Lord's Supper signified the identification of the members with Christ the Head in literal suffering. The last 3½ years before the end of the world were to be a time of persecution for Christ's true disciples. For judgment was to begin at the house of the Lord. The Lord's Supper was, therefore, a love and memorial meal of the faithful remnant, who were united in suffering, symbolizing their literal identification with and participation in the passion of Christ.[131].

The remaining five judgments further outlined Hut's specific apocalyptic programme. All evidence suggests that he awaited the end of the world some time in 1528. His timetable would suggest that his eschatology was an extension of Müntzer's own teaching. In fact, it has been persuasively argued that Hut identified Müntzer and Pfeiffer with the two prophets of Revelation 11:3-10. Significantly, their ministry had lasted 3½ years and their bodies had not been buried, as Scripture predicted. Another 3½ years remained before divine judgment would fall upon Christendom.[132] Thus the crucial seven last years of the world, predicted in Daniel and the Apocalypse, began around December 1521. This was approximately the time when the Zwickau Prophets began their ministry. Whether or not Hut arrived at this dating with the Zwickau Prophets in mind must remain speculation. What was significant was the fact that he gave the Peasants' War apocalyptic significance by placing it at the center of the last seven years.[133]

Other details included the prediction that the judgment of the godless would set in five months before the Parousia. The Turk would invade, but the faithful remnant would survive. Hut left the impression with his followers that he and they would then participate in the judgment of the world.[134] His tendency to identify the godless with the Obrigkeit proved particularly attractive to veterans of the Peasants' War, many of whom had become fugitives.[135]

Menius, who, as we noted earlier, appears to have been informed about the Anabaptist group centering upon Hut, gave the following description of Anabaptist apocalyptical teachings: God had now sent out His angels or messengers to seal the elect with the sign of the covenant. When the punishment of the world set in, the elect would gather from the four corners of the earth. Christ would enter their midst as leader and give them the sword to punish the godless. The end of the world was to be distinguished from the last judgment. Between the two was to be the millennium during which the elect would rule with Christ. The millennium was pictured as being without the rule of law and Obrigkeit, without conventional matrimony, without private property, and without clergy or Scripture. All men were to be taught by God directly. If Menius' report was accurate, then Hut and his followers held that the millennium would fall into history. In fact, it was to be the great seventh stage of human history—the Sabbath of the world. After these thousand years the last judgment would come. According to Menius, it would terminate in universal salvation. This latter article was considered a special secret and not explained to everyone.[136]

It is difficult to accept that Menius invented these details, including the supporting scriptural references he cited. His description certainly complements the other fragmentary sources we possess concerning Hut's teaching on the subject. The totality of these would suggest that Hut's view of the end of the world, as expressed in his last five judgments, was substantially indebted to the medieval apocalyptical tradition. Menius objected particularly to the idea of the two judgments, one before the millennium, the other after. He, too, like many of his contemporaries, was expecting the Parousia in the near future. However, what distinguished him from the Anabaptists was their expectation of vengeance on the Obrigkeit and the establishment of an egalitarian *Reich*.[137] Under the impact of persecution and as a result of objections raised by other Anabaptists, including Hubmaier and Dachser, Hut was to become more reticent about this part of his programme, raising his seven judgments to what has been labelled the "arcane" level, where they were reserved for a core of the most trusted initiates.[138]

We can now turn to an examination of the peculiar concept of judgment *per se*, and to a series of related concepts with primary significance for Hut's scriptural exegesis. The recurrence in Hut's confession, concordance, catechism, and *Of the Mystery of Baptism* of a distinctive concept of judgment is probably the strongest evidence that they were all Hut's work.[139] Hut's catechism contained the questions, "What is God's covenant, what are God's commandments, what God's judgments, what God's moral precepts, what God's witness, what God's law?"[140] Interestingly, the catechetical fragment attributed to Landsperger and preserved in the *Kodex Braitmichel* addresses itself to the last five of these questions.[141] Since the piece was clearly written either by Hut or someone close to him, it merits discussion here. The commandments were contained in the Decalogue and summarized by Christ as "Thou shalt love the Lord thy God with all thy heart and thy neighbour as thyself." But the inner meaning of the commandments could be grasped only by a clear understanding of the scriptural judgments. For the particular commandments were found to be "often against each other."[142] The contradictions were illustrated by scriptural citations concerning the oath and the sword. The author concluded:

> In this fashion one must keep the judgments through the whole Scripture. Therefore, it is necessary to cry with David to God and beg Him that He might teach us His judgments, which are incomprehensible to the world, but are revealed through the Spirit to those who love and fear God . . . and where the judgment is not and is not kept, there is nothing but great error. Because the judgments . . . teach us to keep all of God's commandments rightly.[143]

It appears, therefore, that the judgments were key concepts which were supposed to provide insights into the inner meaning of the whole Scripture. They were attained only when all the conflicting commandments were brought together and illuminated by the Spirit.

> Therefore, to each judgment there belongs not a statement or sentence, but as found in Scripture they are presented in fragments, as Paul says: we know in part and we prophesy in part. But when that which is perfect is come, then that which is in part shall be done away. Therefore, just as no part is the whole, but many parts come together and must become perfect, so also many commandments put together in order make one complete judgment.[144]

The author then distinguished between general judgments and those relating to biblical prophecy.

> There are also some judgments which are called extended judgments, which will happen in the last days. Therefore, it is not our duty to keep them, but to learn them. Such are the judgments against the godless. . . .[145]

The general judgments were clarified by an allegorized interpretation of the Mosaic ceremonies. The visible ceremonies witnessed to the invisible reality. The sacrificial rites illustrated the principle of suffering in all creation.[146] Christ repeated the Mosaic message by means of parables.

> Therefore, Christ presented such moral precepts to the people through parables, also to His disciples, when He sent them and commanded them to preach the Gospel of all creatures, so that the creatures give us witness and teach us about their relation to human beings, so that human beings will assume the same relation towards God.[147]

The gospel witnessed to by Moses and the one preached by Christ and by Paul were the same, except for the outer mode of expression. The principles revealed through Moses were therefore still applicable in the Christian era.[148] Those who had neither the Mosaic nor the Pauline message still had the law placed in all creation.

Those who do not have the Law keep the Law according to [its] content in nature. Nature teaches every heathen that all creatures must be justified before he [the heathen] uses them, so also man, if he keeps still before God, observes all ceremonies and moral precepts.[149]

The author of this early South German Anabaptist treatise, therefore, explicitly denied that the differences between the Old and New Testaments were differences in kind. He also implied that the Scripture's special historical revelation granted through Moses, Christ, and Paul had as its content the same moral precepts as the revelation in all the creatures. The judgments provided not only an overall purpose to God's individual commandments, but also the inner meaning of the moral precepts hidden in the Scriptures. The "witness" encompassed the three categories of "commandments, judgments and moral precepts."[150] Scripture was a witness to divine revelation. In this framework it served a dual function of witnessing to the historical experience of true believers and of communicating moral precepts to believers now living. With regard to the conduct expected of the believer, all of Scripture could be considered as letter or law, a position explicitly defended by Hut.

The theme of law was, however, pursued further. Three laws were distinguished: (1) "of works and life," (2) "of sin and death," and (3) "of spirit and faith." The three laws appear to have corresponded roughly to the activity of the Trinity in the viator. The first law confronted man with specific divine precepts. But man found himself unable to fulfil these because of the law of sin. He needed first to submit to the cross— the second law. Through the inner cross the third law of the spirit and faith became active and enabled him to escape the law of sin and the flesh and to fulfil the first law.[151] This somewhat awkward exposition of the three laws fitted well with Hut's fondness for the trinitarian pattern. It also harmonized with his general soteriology and supported the pronouncedly moralistic thrust of his message.

That an understanding of Hut's hermeneutical principles is best sought against a background of medieval allegory may be supported by

reference to another source. We are referring to the anonymous fragment preserved in the Hutterite codices as an exposition of the four
beasts of Revelation 4.[152] It contained references to the gospel of all
creatures, as well as to the four stages of the believer's road to conformity with Christ. Both these concepts originating with Hut were to
be found among his Austrian followers, particularly Schiemer and
Schlaffer.[153] The document, therefore, even if not originating with Hut
directly, provides some insights into the ideas current among those who
were drawn into his movement. The fragment illustrates a peculiar
fondness for symbolic numbers. The number four is related to the sevenfold activity of the Spirit in the viator.

> For this number is found . . . in many places in Scripture, [and]
> when one pays close attention it always has the same meaning. Just
> as the seven spirits are a secret of the united Spirit, [so] the number
> four is also found in many places having a single sense and meaning
> about a proper, genuine and perfect life, and none [of these
> qualities] can exist without their being all together in a perfect
> person.[154]

Christ was this perfect man, and the four beasts of the Apocalypse were
a fourfold witness of His perfect life.

> These beasts enclose in them a man; He is Christ, the patient
> lamb of God, who receives the sin of the world. And everything was
> seen together undivided and is one. Similarly, it must also be found
> undivided in man. However, this no one can believe or find unless
> he has engendered and imparted the four secrets. . . .[155]

The four beasts were then allegorically interpreted as the witness of
the evangelists Matthew, Mark, Luke, and John, whose message was the
same as that of the four major prophets, Isaiah, Jeremiah, Ezekiel, and
Daniel. All revealed the same secret, namely that the four stages in
Christ's life (conception, birth, death, and resurrection) had to be
experienced by every true follower of Christ.[156] The fourfold secret was
then placed into an eschatological framework hardly understandable to
the unilluminated mind. Because it was also

> . . . the wagon and the four wheels on which the Lord with all His
> elect will come to the judgment of the world and distribute the four
> plagues—the sword, hunger, the horrible beasts and pestilence—
> until He has made an end of all those who have not these four
> secrets of the four animals.[157]

If this was in fact one of Hut's own expositions, then his boast that no one could interpret Scripture as he did becomes understandable. It would also lend credence to the rumours which suggested that he possessed the book with the seven seals, shown to Daniel, but kept to be revealed during the last days. Interestingly, Christian Entfelder, whom we will discuss later, and who proved to be a master of allegory, gave an almost verbatim exposition of this particular allegory in one of his works.

Nevertheless, as this discussion of Hut's ideas would suggest, Hut himself was no doubt capable of producing homilies like the one above. Certainly neither Hut nor his followers recovered pure primitivist visions from the pages of Holy Writ. In many of their assumptions and modes of thought they broke less radically with the generation preceding them than did Luther. Hut's transference of Müntzer's cross mysticism to the Anabaptist protest made it one of the distinguishing features of early South German Anabaptism. His understanding of the Word of God, the gospel of all creatures, faith, justification, baptism, and his fondness for symbolic number patterns all support the thesis that his theology of protest is best understood as a Reformation derivation of popular medieval mystical motifs.

4

HANS HUT AND THE EARLY
SOUTH GERMAN
ANABAPTIST MOVEMENT

A. Hut's Franconian Ministry

While we will forego a detailed narrative account of Hut's missionary itinerary, an analysis of his teachings would remain incomplete without an examination of his impact on his followers. Some of these were educated and their writings provide excellent primary sources. Others, in particular the immediate circle, were from the less literate classes and we must rely heavily on their court records. Although these reflect the opinions of the accusers and provide only limited background material regarding Hut's early converts they remain the only historical sources permitting some insights into the ideas current in Hut's early movement.

The first evidence of Hut's activity on behalf of the Anabaptist cause comes from Königsberg and Uetzing in Franconia. From the statements of his initiates we can reconstruct Hut's message eight months after his baptism[1] as having been one of undisguised vengeance. He predicted an invasion by the Turk, and admonished his followers not to help anyone, but to remain in ambush until the Turk had decimated the supporters of the Obrigkeit. Then, as Christ's representative on earth, he would give the signal for the slaying of the rest. Until then his followers needed to be patient and suffer for Christ's sake.[2] These statements suggest that Hut sustained his hope of a new order by counting on divine intervention which was to feature an invasion by the infidels as God's instrument of judgment.

In Hut's eschatological framework the peasants had been replaced by the Turks. Evidence also indicates that Hut was already preaching the gospel of all creatures. Thus the distinguishing features of his Anabaptist message had been formulated. Yet, some of his converts at first denied having been baptised as adults.[3] How is the historian to interpret this evidence? Were the denials of adult baptism solely the result of fear? Or did they mirror an ambivalence in Hut's message? One thing is clear: neither Hut nor his followers were as yet consciously labouring in an Anabaptist tradition. They were in the process of creating one that would bridge the gap from Müntzer and the peasants' revolt to the future sectarians.

Sometime in January 1527 Hut with his companions Eucharius Binder (Kellermann), Joachim Märtz, and Kilian Volkhaimer left the area around Königsberg and Uetzing, moving south to visit Nuremberg and Augsburg, intending to obtain literature for his followers. They planned to return within three weeks.[4] On his way Hut held what has been rather pretentiously described as his first "Anabaptist synod" (*Täuferkonzil*) at Alterlangen.[5] Actually Hut did little more than propagate his ideas about the immediate future. He then moved on to Nuremberg and Augsburg.[6]

While his followers awaited his return in Erlangen, rumours reached them of the first arrests in Königsberg.[7] Hereupon the brothers dispatched Thomas Spiegel and Jörg Volck to investigate the fate of their comrades. Both hoped to be back in Erlangen for another meeting with Hut around February 17.[8] However, Spiegel, who separated from Volck in Bamberg, was shortly thereafter apprehended in the Königsberg area. His interrogations provide further insights into Hut's Anabaptist operations. We learn why Hut had no difficulties financing his travels. Some of his supporters contributed liberally with an eye to the windfall profits to be obtained after the punishment of the wicked.[9] About the latter, Spiegel was able to provide the further details that, besides the expected invasion of the Turks, God intended to reduce the population by one third through divine plagues. A kind of Armageddon would take place near Nuremberg. For Hut and his followers God had provided certain places of refuge. From these they would emerge and strike the final blows, which included the slaying of the remnant of the Obrigkeit and the stoning of the clergy. Then that which Hut and his followers now held in secret would be made manifest to all and preached from the rooftops.[10]

These, then, were the ideas current in Hut's circle early in 1527. It is difficult to number him and his followers, a significant number of whom were veterans of the Peasants' War,[10a] among the "stillen im Lande." He and his followers were foiled revolutionaries, feeding their vengeful hopes on apocalyptic fantasies. The defeat of Müntzer in 1525, rather than the conversion experience at his baptism, had been responsible for moving the revolutionary goal into the future, and for convincing Hut to sheathe his sword temporarily.

During his interrogations Spiegel implicated Hans Nadler of Erlangen and Wolfgang Vogel of Eltersdorf near Nuremberg as baptised members of Hut's circle.[11] Vogel's contact with Hut probably preceded Hut's own so-called conversion to Anabaptism. At his trial Hut indicated that he had preached in Eltersdorf several years previously.[12] This would indicate that Vogel, like so many of Hut's closest friends, may have been implicated in the peasants' revolution.[13] Vogel also repeatedly visited Hut while the latter was employed in Nuremberg. Hut eventually won him for the Anabaptist cause.[14] Thereafter Vogel appears to have believed and taught doctrines very similar to Hut's. These were not yet the ideals of separated brotherhood, but more like a manifesto of a potentially revolutionary secret society. After embracing Hut's mode of baptism Vogel remained at his post as pastor of a state-sponsored church in Eltersdorf.

Vogel had come to the attention of the Nuremberg authorities early in January because of a pastoral letter written to his old congregation in Bopfingen. This letter, while taunting the princes who were trying to reinstate Catholicism, did not reveal any revolutionary intentions on Vogel's part. Vogel's connections to Hut remained concealed and he was released after questioning.[15] The harsh treatment meted out to him a few weeks later has often puzzled scholars conditioned to thinking of South German Anabaptists as harmless evangelicals. They expressed astonishment that an open letter which was later read with profit by Lutheran Pietists should have brought Vogel the death penalty.[16] The amazement would have been justified had the letter been the evidence leading to Vogel's execution. However, as noted above, this appears not to have been the case. The real significance of the letter lies in its theological content. It indicated that Vogel was familiar with the gospel of all creatures, combining the Great Commission with the immanence theme of Colossians 1:4-6. This clearly identified Vogel with Hut's camp, a fact not immediately appreciated by the authorities.[17] On February 17, only three days after Vogel had been questioned, the Nuremberg authorities received the first confessions of Hut's followers arrested in Königsberg.[18] Between the nineteenth and twenty-first of the same month Vogel was mentioned by name in Thomas Spiegel's confession.[19] On February 22 the Nuremberg council issued warrants for his arrest. However, Vogel had left the nest. He was not apprehended until March 7 or 8. Condemned on the twenty-second of the same month, he was executed four days later.[20]

It is quite possible that the nervous authorities in Nuremberg overreacted. Numerically, Vogel and his companions remained harmless. However, their teachings appear to have been less peaceful than sympathetic scholars would like to believe. Although he at first denied everything, Vogel was compromised through the confessions of Hut's followers in Königsberg.[21]

Unfortunately, the records of Vogel's trial are no longer extant. Nevertheless, by inference we can conclude that during the trial Hut's seven judgments surfaced for the first time.[22] In all probability they were materials among Vogel's possessions which were confiscated on March 16. In the letter sent to Regensburg on the eighteenth, the Nuremberg authorities summarized the teachings of Hut's followers as:

> They do not believe that Christ has redeemed us. Further, they hold and believe that the devil will be saved also, that Christ will shortly return to earth and begin a new kingdom. He will punish with death all those who are not Christians and in their brotherhood. . . . They have also been ordained to kill and exterminate all governmental authorities. Then there will be one shepherd and one sheepfold.[23]

The charges with regard to Christ's satisfaction and Hut's chiliasm later reappeared in the Nicolsburg Articles, suggesting that Hut's seven judgments were also discussed in Nicolsburg. It is also possible that news of Hut's teachings reached Nicolsburg via Nuremberg and predisposed Hubmaier against Hut. Or could the reverse have been true?[24]

Unfortunately our sources are singularly defective with regard to Hut's whereabouts during February and March. We do not know how the arrests affected his teachings and ministry. In all probability the veteran, who knew "when the shooting was becoming too thick," decided to move on and "visit the brethren in other places." According to our sources he appeared in the little village of Uttenreuth not far from Erlangen some time later in March.[25] It is hardly possible to describe his activity there as *Gemeindebildung*. He baptised at least nine persons. Many of these quick converts later reappeared in the "Dreamers' sect."[26] Hut was obviously in a hurry. He tarried only one night. His destination appears to have been Nicolsburg.

One of those who fled with Hut from the Franconian area was Hans Nadler, whose home in Erlangen had been the central meeting place for Hut and his followers. Nadler's wife testified later that her husband had left her and the children despite her pleading, in order to "explore the new and old faith."[27] Similar motives must have inspired Hut's other intimates, among them the Maiers. They too were veterans of the peasants' uprising and their contact with Hut probably dated back to 1526 or earlier.[28] Hut had lodged his nine-or-ten-year-old son with them. The boy had helped to build the movement by reading to the illiterates when his father was absent.[29] Marx Maier was one of the messengers sent ahead by Hut to Nicolsburg. Nadler, too, found his way to this Anabaptist Mecca, only to "scatter in horror" because he found "the proper Christian order" was lacking there, too.[30] As for Hut he stopped first in Augsburg.[31] The situation in the imperial city is well worth a closer examination before we go on to deal with Hut's difficulties in Nicolsburg.

B. Hut and the Augsburg Anabaptists

Augsburg played a significant role as melting pot of early South German Anabaptism, and for a short time in 1527 became a haven for dispossessed and persecuted religious dissenters. Some of this dissent preceded the Reformation and, no doubt, had local economic and social roots. In 1484 Augsburg citizens were treated to the spectacle of a weaver, Georg Breuning, preaching to large crowds from a tree. His devotional sermons remained popular long after, and later one of his descendants became an Anabaptist. Popular interest in religious topics continued high and was stimulated by the Reformation. By 1524 there was talk of "true brothers and sisters" separating themselves from the fallen church.[32] By the end of that year Hut from Nuremberg was providing copies of Müntzer's writings for interested parties. An anonymous tract addressing itself to the Augsburg situation and reflecting popular concerns warned the Obrigkeit of the consequences of permitting the preaching of the gospel but not following its precepts.[33]

During 1525 Ludwig Hätzer was active in the city. Whether or not he "assumed leadership of a gathering of apostolic brethren" who were the forerunners of the later Anabaptists is not clear.[34] However, it is very likely that he contributed to the controversy concerning the Lord's Supper which captured the imagination of the radicals during this period.

Among those embracing a Zwinglian position were the later Anabaptist leader Hans Leupold and the patrician Hans Langenmantel.[35] Shortly after Hätzer's expulsion Denck arrived, resuming contact with Hätzer's supporters.[36] Hätzer or Denck quite possibly brought the first Anabaptist tract to be published in Augsburg.[37] Other Anabaptists driven from Switzerland arrived in 1526. Among them was Jacob Gross who in Waldshut had dissented from Hubmaier's teaching that Christians might use the sword.[38] Gross together with Denck, Hut, Sigmund Salminger, and Jacob Dachser belonged to the group of early Augsburg Anabaptist leaders who baptised others. One of his better-known converts was the weaver Augustin Bader.

The arrival of Anabaptist refugees coincided with a local "mystical revivalist movement" which reached a peak in 1526-27.[39] The first official Anabaptist leader, Sigmund Salminger, actively participated in this revival by editing and printing mystical treatises. One of these, *Out of What Ground Love Originates, and What Great Powers It Has, and How Useful It Is, to Reform the Inner Man, so That the Outer May Die,* printed in 1526, developed a theme which, as we noted earlier, also preoccupied Denck who was still in Augsburg at the time.[40] In 1527 Salminger brought out *Two Epistles About the Love of God Written by Georgen Preining, Weaver at Augsburg in Years Past.*[41] Later he included three of Breuning's songs in a printed collection.[42] All these productions reflected popular mystical presuppositions shared by Denck and later Spiritualists.

When Hut made his entrance with a letter of introduction from Nuremberg in 1527, he found conditions among Augsburg radicals truly "ripe unto harvest." What attracted the leading dissenters to him was the mystical side of his message, in particular the first two of his seven judgments relating to baptism and the Lord's Supper. The five apocalyptical judgments were, for the time being, wisely kept secret by Hut. Within a short time he had baptised Hans Langenmantel, Sigmund Salminger, Jacob Dachser, and a host of lesser people. Johannes Landsperger had earlier written a favourable introduction to Hut's *A Christian Instruction.*[43] A new dimension, perhaps not entirely dependent on Hut's initiative, now appeared in his ministry. Augsburg represents the first visible effort at establishing something approaching a separated brotherhood in South German Anabaptism. Salminger was chosen the first minister and Gross and Dachser appointed his assistants. A common fund was set up to provide for the poor.

Through the writings of Salminger, Langenmantel, and Dachser[44] we gain an insight into the issues and ideas that occupied the early Augsburg Anabaptists. Of the three Dachser provided us with the most significant document in his *A Godly and Thorough Revelation About the True Anabaptists: Revealed in Godly Truth.*[45] Since the tract provoked a specific reply by Urbanus Rhegius, the leader of the Reformation party, it is particularly valuable for our understanding of what separated some of these educated Anabaptist leaders from the magisterial Reformers.[46] It is, therefore, surprising that Dachser's treatise has received little attention from Anabaptist scholars. Perhaps his abandonment of Anabaptism at a later date tarnished his reputation in the eyes of some. However, a brief sketch of the man's life should convince even the sceptics that early Anabaptism could not have been represented by a more sincere defender.

Like Hubmaier and Denck, Dachser had connections to the University of Ingolstadt. Here he became involved in radical protest and upon expulsion suffered imprisonment at the hands of the Bishop of Eichstädt.[47] It is not clear when he arrived in Augsburg, but it is possible that he knew both Hätzer and Denck before Hut arrived and baptised him. The acceptance of Hut's message by a man of Dachser's calibre is best explained by reference to similar theological and anthropological assumptions.

Although Salminger by lot became the official leader of the congregation in Augsburg, Dachser, nicknamed the *Pfäfflein* or *Jäcklein*, was probably its main pillar. It was to Dachser that Langenmantel brought his own tracts for proofreading.[48] It was Dachser who baptised Hans Leupold, the successor of Salminger.[49] Perhaps more significantly, Dachser appears to have been the backbone of resistance against Hut's chiliasm during the Martyrs' Synod in August 1527. Dachser's disciple, Leupold, declared that he and others had walked out when Hut revealed his future expectations to his Augsburg converts. Dachser later stated that he had only accepted those teachings which had been wholesome, "but since some from among them put themselves forth, prophesied and held strange opinions, he spoke against it, so that he fell into such disfavour that they wanted to excommunicate him."[50]

Dachser's claim cannot be easily disregarded. According to our knowledge of Hut's ideas and Dachser's own steadfastness in the face of persecution Dachser's account can be accepted as trustworthy. He, the first Augsburg leader to be imprisoned,[51] for three years resisted every attempt at persuasion to recant.[52] When he finally did recant it was in Latin and at a time when few were present.[53] While imprisoned he managed to publish his *Form and Order of Spiritual Songs and Psalms.* It included four songs by Müntzer and two attributed to Hut. How Dachser received the songs of Müntzer and how he achieved the feat of delivering this collection to Ulhart's press while imprisoned remains a puzzle.[54] One year after his release he was appointed vicar of the Protestant parish of St. Ulrich, a post which was to bring him more grief and persecution, although from different quarters.[55]

We can now turn to an analysis of Dachser's important Anabaptist tract, which originated during the spring or summer of 1527.[56] Dachser opened his tract with a lamentation about the confusion caused by the quarrels among the Reformers. God could not be the author of such confusion and disunity.[57] He then moved to a general ethical and moral critique of the achievements of the Reformation. Predestinarianism was singled out as the theological root of all evil. The gospel preached by the Reformers abnegated human responsibility; it stood condemned by its fruits.[58] Significantly, Rhegius in his reply was willing to recognize the problem.[59] However, he attributed antinomian tendencies to the work of "the evil spirit" and ignorance. He adamantly rejected the conclusion that the Reformation gospel was one of false and cheap grace. It contained both the preaching of the law for recognition of sinfulness and the good news of forgiveness based on Christ's role as mediator of God's grace.[60]

Rhegius then went to the attack and countered that the Anabaptist writer lacked the proper understanding of the condemning function of the law because of his semi-Pelagian view of man, which in turn rested on a shallow view of man's fall. Drawing on his knowledge of Hubmaier's writings, Rhegius accused Dachser of making too much of the *imago Dei* in man. True, man had been created in the image of God, but the fall had corrupted the total man, both body and soul. To leave one part of man untouched by sin as Hubmaier had done was to reopen the door to human merit. And one error followed the next. The incorrect anthropology contained the germs of sinless perfectionism, a heresy held by the Romish priest Novatus and the Cathars. It prevented the Anabaptist from understanding the meaning of grace and faith as gifts of God irrespective of the recipient's condition.[61] Above all, it detracted from the sufficiency of Christ.

> Very well, Anabaptist, say on, where do you leave the suffering of Christ? Where is grace? Where is Christian liberty?
> One error follows the next. The Anabaptist still considers the

natural man to be so healthy in his soul that he thinks the strength to do good resides in him, and that he needs only to use it and not to neglect it. It follows that Christ is only looked upon as a teacher like another prophet and apostle, who came and gave good regulations about how one is to live a Christian life and become pious.

You must go further and also believe that He cleanses you through His blood and reconciles you with the Father . . . so that you can say in true faith, Christ is my righteousness, His innocence covers my guilt, His payment redeems me from the devil. He is my only mediator, bishop, reconciler before God, . . . all has been purchased by Christ and is given without my merit to me, the un-worthy. Because He is the only one who maketh righteous. He is alone just and justifieth him who believeth in Jesus Christ.[62]

Rhegius in lecturing his Anabaptist opponent on the merits of Christ took a classical Reformation stance. He was not about to assume that his opponent's ideas were logical extensions of his own insights. The dif-ferences extended well beyond hermeneutics and different biblical emphases, although these were also noted by Rhegius. In his view he and Dachser moved from essentially different anthropological assump-tions. The question to be answered is whether Rhegius' charges had some foundation.

Caution is particularly appropriate since Rhegius, who did not know the real author of *A Godly and Thorough Revelation,* supple-mented his knowledge of Anabaptist teachings from other sources, in particular from his knowledge of Denck and Hubmaier.[63] Con-sequently, unaware of or purposely ignoring the real differences existing between individual leaders, Rhegius eclectically combined evidence as it served his polemical purpose. Nevertheless, Rhegius' charges of semi-Pelagianism were not without foundation from his perspective. Dachser's focus was not on the fall of man and human depravity but rather on the "living breath" or "heavenly ghost" granted to every human being and "gone out" from the Father. The Spirit of God active in the hearts of all men was giving continual witness of good and evil.[64] In this framework the fall was not the cataclysmic event which separated the Creator from the creatures. Man had lost the super-added grace of holiness, but retained an inner connection, an "inner guide" (*zuchtmaister in uns*).[65] Thus basic late medieval motifs remained part of Dachser's anthropology. He was both unable and unwilling to follow Rhegius' view of man.

Rhegius, preceding from the normal assumptions of the Reforma-tion, with its transcendent God and clear division between the natural and supernatural orders, could conceive of human resources as natural only. However, in Dachser's *Weltanschauung* the natural and supernatural had not yet suffered that Copernican rupture. He could insist that the internal connection to the Divine was "all through grace" and complemented by the providential order of nature. Both the fall and the incarnate Christ were part of the same design that unfolded with creation. The universe did not veil God's design but revealed God's mercy existing for man's well-being.[66] God had graciously provided man from within and without with the necessities for his physical and spiritual welfare. Logically, with such a view of man and nature the emphasis shifted from man the helpless sinner in need of grace and redemption to man the morally responsible being provided with the necessary means enabling him to obey God's law. The role of the historical Christ, as Rhegius recognized, was indeed consciously or unconsciously minimized to that of a teacher of Christian ethics.[67] A mixture of mystical and nominalist motifs provided the prerequisites for this Christology.[68]

From the analysis above it becomes explicable why Dachser was favourably predisposed to receive Hut's message. Hut too assumed a graciously foreordained order of nature which revealed God's will. He too subscribed to an anthropology which conceived of salvation as "becoming just" (*Gerechtmachung*) rather than "being justified" (*Rechtfertigung*). He viewed grace as a quality bestowed on man and active to progressively purify him, producing proper moral behaviour. Thus Dachser and Hut shared the same moralistic and soteriological presuppositions. The creatures demonstrated to man the utility of obedience and that cleansing by necessity involved suffering. Suffering itself became the ordained means of dealing with evil and sin. Dachser, who here showed his strong indebtedness to Hut, provided one of the clearest expositions of the gospel preached by the creatures. It is well worth quoting him directly:

> So that one may understand what the Gospel of all creatures is, all creatures will give witness in our hearts at the last judgment how they were obedient and submissive to us, how [they] had to be patient and suffer our chastisement, as we disciplined them according to our will. They were obedient to us unto death. But they have been obedient because God commanded them to be obedient unto us. And God has made us lords over them that we might enjoy them and eat them like the green herbs of the whole earth. . . .
> I must briefly speak further about the creatures. . . . When you

take into your hands a creature which has been given to you by God for food, you know that God has created it pure and good. But because God has set you to be lord over it, and the creature belongs in your house [that is, in your body as food], you will not let it go into your house unless it is first prepared, so that there is nothing unclean on it. . . . [If] it has skin above the flesh, the skin has to go. Therefore it has to die. [If] it has feathers on its body, you pluck the feathers, and you leave not a single one on its body. And when you have plucked out the feathers, and have cleansed it totally, you tear open the body and what does not please you of the innards you [pull] out and throw away. Because you say it is unclean, it does not belong in your house. Therefore the creature is obedient to you unto death, for the sake of Him who made it obedient to you.

O almighty eternal God, give grace and strength through Your Son Jesus Christ that we may understand what is the significance of such a creature. I speak from God, that it means nothing else but that we are all created for the house of God. . . . Hence you should know that nothing unclean may enter into the house of God. . . . [Therefore] let us be obedient to God as all creation is obedient to us through His godly word. . . .[69]

Dachser's last admonition suggests that for him the gospel of all creatures revealed primarily the relationship of obedience regulating man's standing before God. Unity with God could be achieved only through a relation of obedience. Thus Dachser's attenuated mysticism showed definite nominalistic traits. It would be best described as penitential mysticism. He compared the thick skin and feathers to outward sins. The intestines represented internal impurities. Man needed cleansing from both inner and outer sins. He had to submit to the cleansing work of God and die to all creatureliness. Only in this way could he escape eternal death.[70] Suffering itself, as illustrated in the creatures, therefore, became the redemptive principle for Dachser. There are no signs of a Lutheran understanding of law and gospel, and, as Rhegius noticed rightly, one will look in vain for the good news of forgiveness based on Christ's atonement. The one comforting thought offered by Dachser was that God treated man more patiently than man the creatures.

Dachser's tract clearly illustrates the impact of Hans Hut on the early Augsburg Anabaptists. Dachser had obviously been exposed to Hut's homily, *Of the Mystery of Baptism*. However, Dachser's defence of "true baptism" was by no means an endorsement of Hut's total programme. The absence of the apocalyptic context of Hut's teaching is striking. Similarly the mystical strains were less pronounced. Without equivocation Dachser insisted that faith should precede outer baptism.

He supported this view by an appeal to a literal interpretation of the Great Commission—preach, believe, baptise. This was the ordained order; whoever followed it was a "true baptist," while those engaging in pedobaptism were the "false baptists" who introduced an unchristian order and practice.[71] The message to be preached and believed before baptism was the gospel of all creatures—the need of man to suffer God's purifying work in and on him. Unlike Hut, Dachser did not turn the gospel of all creatures as a natural revelation against the Reformation principle of sola scriptura. His intentions appear to have been primarily devotional. His emphasis on the believer's need for suffering marked a milestone on the road to a later Anabaptist martyrology. His use of Hut's concepts and illustrations help to blur the lines between Hut's followers and what might be described tenuously as evangelical Anabaptism. Dachser in some respects showed greater similarities to Denck and the Swiss Brethren than to Hut. He certainly represented the more evangelical tendencies of early Augsburg Anabaptism. Hut's impact on the Augsburg Anabaptists ought, therefore, not to be exaggerated.

On the other hand, major theological assumptions separated Dachser from the Reformers. These were not a product of a more radical biblicism nor of a more primitivist ecclesiology recovered from the illuminated pages of Holy Writ, but leftovers of medieval motifs which the major Reformers attempted to overcome. It would, therefore, be theologically inaccurate to describe Dachser and the Anabaptists he represented as "radical children of the Reformation." We conclude that the Anabaptists in Augsburg, while not carbon copies of Hut's Franconian disciples, were united with and attracted to Hut because of their similar theological presuppositions. We can now turn to Hut's clash with Hubmaier in Nicolsburg.

C. Hut and the Anabaptists in Nicolsburg

Hut's visit to Nicolsburg and his clash with Hubmaier has long been a major problem in Anabaptist historiography. Part of the problem centered on the mysterious Nicolsburg Articles purporting to contain the teachings of Hut.

(1) The Gospel should not be preached in churches but only secretly and clandestinely in houses.
(2) Christ was conceived in original sin.
(3) The Virgin Mary is not the mother of God but only the mother of Christ.

(4) Christ was not God but a prophet to whom the speech of God or Word of God was commanded.
(5) Christ did not make satisfaction for the sins of the entire world.
(6) Among Christians there should be neither force nor authority.
(7) The day of judgment is to be expected within two years.
(8) The angels were conceived with Christ and accepted the flesh with Him.[72]

Sympathetic scholars found it difficult to believe that these articles represented Anabaptist teachings. Complicating the problem was the fact that the articles originated with Hubmaier. Hubmaier, seeking to hurt another Anabaptist, sounded "downright contradictory." Such articles were more likely the work of the prosecutors and persecutors, but not of Hubmaier, "who today is greatly revered by Baptists all over the world as a forerunner. . . ."[73] With these assumptions a discrepancy in the sources must have been welcomed with a sigh of relief. The Nicolsburg Articles, it was discovered, made their appearance in March 1527, hence before the debate between Hubmaier and Hut, which was alleged to have occurred in May.[74]

Even if the debate took place in May, however, the alleged appearance of the Nicolsburg Articles two months earlier can now be explained. The document found in the Strassburg *Täuferakten* which contained the Nicolsburg Articles was dated wrongly by its editors. The material in question, which had been dated as originating in Nuremburg during March 1527, was really part of the correspondence between Nuremberg and the city of Goslar during March 1528. The letters were detoured to the Strassburg archives, where they were filed under the wrong date.[75] The earliest appearance of the Nicolsburg Articles seems to have been after all in Oecolampadius' report to Zwingli on July 19, 1527.[76] (This report was based on information supplied to Oecolampadius by the Catholic vicar general Johann Fabri, whose connections with Hubmaier we shall discuss below.) Thus the fortuitous discrepancy which absolved Hubmaier in the eyes of some historians from being a defamer of a fellow Anabaptist never existed, but neither did the largely mythical evangelical Hans Hut.

Whatever the date of the debate, all evidence suggests that the clash between these two early Anabaptist leaders went well beyond "minor emotional antagonism."[77] In all probability Hut entered an atmosphere already charged with tension.[78] His message was received favourably by the common people. He later claimed that Hubmaier had been jealous of his popularity. Some of the other ministers, including

Oswald Glaidt, a certain Augustin from a nearby village, and one Bastian, the assistant of Bishop Martin Göschl, were favourably impressed by Hut.[79] Hubmaier proved less receptive to Hut and the heralds of his coming. He was particularly annoyed by the fact that Hut appeared to inspire many of the common people to irresponsibly leave their homes, their possessions, their work, their wives and children.

An examination of Hut's writings did not alleviate his misgivings.[80] He discovered that Hut predicted that the final judgment would come within two years.[81] According to Hubmaier Hut's dating rested on faulty, "unlearned" reasoning. Hut had misinterpreted the seven days of the week mentioned in Daniel as seven ordinary years. According to the more learned Hubmaier they were "sun and Daniel years." An ordinary year was one day in a sun year. Thus the 3½ years—half week—of persecution prophesied for the house of God in Daniel, according to Hubmaier, were not 3½ ordinary years but 1,277 ordinary years. This figure was produced by turning the days of the 3½ years into years, thus arriving at the 1,260 years already enshrined in Joachimist tradition. By adding a certain number of days for the leap years Hubmaier came to the total of 1,277 as the number of years during which the house of the Lord would be subjected to persecution. He did not elaborate upon when these years began, leaving the hour to God.[82]

A private meeting with Hut left the latter unconvinced of Hubmaier's mathematical accuracy. Neither could agreement be reached on other points drawn up by Hubmaier. Hubmaier, therefore, invited Hut to a public disputation in the church. Hut, fancying himself cast in the role of Paul resisting Peter before the church council, agreed.[83]

Hubmaier appears to have been determined to turn the situation into a general rout of the opposition. He summarized Hut's errors in fifty-two articles and packed the meeting with his own supporters. The disputation from Hut's point of view turned into a mock trial. Hut and the other three defendants were summarily accused of teaching all the erroneous articles drawn up by Hubmaier.[84] When they refused to plead guilty and attempted to debate the articles point by point Hubmaier cut them off. As Hubmaier himself later admitted he had not minced words, but had rebuked Hut severely.[85] As Hut recalled the event, Hubmaier's overbearing manner prompted even some of the nobility present to intercede on his behalf.[86]

Unfortunately, Hut at his trial could only remember eleven of the points discussed:

(1) that Christ was not God's Son
(2) that Christ was merely a prophet
(3) that Mary had more than one husband
(4) that the angels had become men with Christ
(5) that when a man is possessed by a good angel he can do only good, and when possessed by a bad angel only evil
(6) that Hut and his followers put stock in visions and dreams
(7) that Hut had set a definite date for the pending judgment
(8) that with Scripture one received the truth and also falsehood
(9) that Christians would judge the world
(10) that no prince or power in this world has accepted or recognized the truth
(11) that power should be taken from the government and given to the Christians.[87]

An analysis of these statements indicates that four of them reappear in the Nicolsburg Articles, substantiating the genuineness of the latter. We can, therefore, add to Hut's own list the other four Nicolsburg Articles not mentioned by him. From the statements of Hut's follower Hans Nadler, who was also in Nicolsburg, we know that the first two of Hut's seven judgments—the sacraments of the Lord's Supper and baptism—were also points of debate. Similarly, it is now well established that the other judgments dealing with Hut's eschatology were major topics of disputation.[88] We have, therefore, the topics of at least sixteen, or one third of the fifty-two articles debated between the two Anabaptist leaders.[89]

Hut at his trial claimed he had only defended two of the eleven articles he remembered. These related to Scripture and dreams. He believed that Scripture contained both truth and falsehood for those not imbued with a discerning spirit. Scripture could not be accepted as an external objective criterion of truth. Even the papacy used it to argue on behalf of its position.[90] Hut further defended dreams and visions as legitimate modes of revelation. His explanation echoed Müntzer.[91] Not all dreams and visions were accepted. Three types could be distinguished:

(1) dreams originating in the flesh, that is, arising out of everyday concerns
(2) evil dreams stimulated by the forces of darkness
(3) genuine divine revelations which came from on high and through the power of the Spirit, authenticated by means of trustworthy signs and oracles

In this manner God had spoken to His prophets. Whoever

understood it would receive it, and much was being revealed in this fashion, as it had been promised in the fourth book of Moses in the twelfth chapter.[92]

All this was further supported by Hut's eschatological framework. God had promised to pour out His Spirit in these last days and the very young would see visions and the old would have dreams and prophesy.

The other nine articles which Hut remembered he denied outright, or claimed that Hubmaier had misinterpreted his point of view. All this would suggest that real differences existed between Hubmaier and Hut.

When the public disputation broke down, Hut was escorted to the Liechtenstein castle. There, in the presence of Leonhart von Liechtenstein, Hubmaier repeated his charges and accused Hut of having disturbed the peace. Hut again protested his innocence. He was then warned by Bishop Martin Göschl that plans were afoot to turn him over to Ferdinand of Austria. That same night Hut made his escape out a window and down a net apparently provided by sympathizers.[93] Some of the other disputants who had taken his side were less fortunate. One brother had been separated from the others and was required to give a written reply to the charges drawn up by Hubmaier. When he refused he was lowered into the tower where Hubmaier, who had earlier suffered similar treatment at the hands of Zwingli, now cast himself in the role of inquisitor and unsuccessfully tried to obtain the proper confession. Hut later learned from this follower and from some of the other ministers present at the disputation that Hubmaier tried to procure their signatures as witnesses against him in a published report of the disputation. Hubmaier then attempted unsuccessfully to have his articles published in Nicolsburg and Vienna.[94]

Hut's claim to substantial sympathy among the citizens in Nicolsburg is supported by a report in the *Hutterite Chronicle*. After Hut's escape the people began to murmur against the lords of Liechtenstein because of the unfair treatment meted out to Hut. The uproar provoked a public explanation by Hubmaier and his assistants.[95] By inference we can assume that Hubmaier reiterated how Hut had taught doctrines which were religiously and socially detrimental to the well-being of the community. His flight underlined his guilt, for, had he been innocent, there would have been no need to flee from the disputation.[96]

Unfortunately, the report in the *Hutterite Chronicle* confused the Hubmaier-Hut conflict with a later controversy between Jacob Wiedemann, the proto-Hutterite, and Johann Spittelmaier.[97] It left the impression that Hubmaier took issue primarily with Hut's nonresistant stance on the sword.[98] This incorrect impression appeared to be substantiated by Hubmaier's own writings. His *On the Sword*, which was published closest to the debate supposedly held in May, was full of allusions to difficulties with some brethren.[99] Throughout the tract Hubmaier defended his own "real political" ethic reminiscent of Zwingli against a Swiss Brethren position.[100] We conclude that Hut's apocalyptic message, to the effect that the Turk's punishment of the Christian Obrigkeit should not be resisted, was in retrospect confused by the Hutterites with their own teaching of nonresistance to evil.[101] Hubmaier did not make that mistake. In several writings touching on the subject he very clearly distinguished between his opponents, using different arguments to counter their positions.[102] Close examination of Hubmaier's *On the Sword*, therefore, would suggest that it represented a continuation of his running battle with the Swiss Brethren rather than with Hut's followers.[103]

This line of reasoning is supported by Hubmaier's attitude towards Scripture in *On the Sword*. It is hardly credible that Hubmaier would, when writing against Hut, have been overly concerned to stress the paradoxical nature of Scripture. Hut, with his defence of extrascriptural revelation and view of the Bible as a passive tool, had already overlearned this lesson. Yet such was the tactical position assumed by Hubmaier against the "dear friends" who in a literalist spirit plucked half-truths from the Bible. Like Denck and Hut he now presented evidence that some scriptural passages were outwardly contradictory. What counted was the proper understanding of the whole.[104] These statements have misled some historians into believing that Hubmaier, possibly influenced by Denck and Hut, assumed a more mystical position near the end of his life.[105] However, the scholastic Hubmaier carefully avoided the spiritualizing tendency of Denck and Hut. He accused his Swiss Anabaptist opponents not of literalism but of a one-sided emphasis on specific portions of Scripture. His utilization of Denck's and Hut's methods without appropriating their principles gives credit to his astute perception. We conclude that *On the Sword* does not reflect the Nicolsburg Disputation, but Hubmaier's opposition to Anabaptists of Swiss Brethren derivation.

One problem still to be explored is how the Nicolsburg Articles fell into the hands of the authorities. The articles appear to reflect Catholic concerns, in particular with regard to Mariology. The conclusion is, therefore, not farfetched that they represented a "Catholic selection" from the fifty-two articles drawn up by Hubmaier.[106] Johann Fabri could have played the role of original distributor. As noted earlier, he remains the oldest discernible source of the articles, and probably the originator of the Catholic tradition that the Nicolsburg Articles represented Hubmaier's own, rather than Hut's, views.[107]

It is not easy to understand why Providence would permit the Nicolsburg Articles to fall into the hands of Johann Fabri, a former friend and colleague of Hubmaier, who mistakenly or maliciously accepted them as genuine beliefs of Hubmaier. It is easier to understand how Fabri, after Hubmaier's trial, triumphantly boasted of having moved Hubmaier to "recant some articles."[108] It appears that Fabri received Hubmaier's personal papers shortly after the latter's arrest in July 1527. Fabri claimed later that his published defence of Hubmaier's condemnation and burning was based on a personal examination of Hubmaier's manuscripts.[109] Unfortunately, Fabri did not consult with Hubmaier personally until several months after he had sent abroad the first report of Hubmaier's blasphemous errors.[110] The description which Fabri later gave of Anabaptist teaching fitted Hut admirably, but not Hubmaier. Shortly after the completion of his tract justifying Hubmaier's burning, Fabri concluded a series of special services for the benefit of the Moravian nobility. He attacked five specific heresies: (1) Hut's apocalyptic predictions, (2) the denial of Christ's divinity, (3) psychopannychism, (4) the ultimate salvation of all things, and (5) the rejection of Obrigkeit as unchristian.[111] If these five topics reflect Johann Fabri's knowledge of Anabaptist teaching gleaned from Hubmaier's papers, then universalism was another of the accusations which Hubmaier levelled against Hut. This charge had earlier been directed against Denck and reappeared in information that surfaced during Wolfgang Vogel's trial.

We conclude that according to all the evidence available the Nicolsburg Articles do reflect the debate between Hubmaier and Hut. The differences between these two leaders went well beyond mere emotional antagonism and circumscribed a whole body of doctrines. Hubmaier appears to have repeated charges against Hut which he had earlier raised against Denck, in particular with regard to Scripture and universalism, but perhaps also with regard to Christology.[112] Hut dismissed the accusations as not representing his views. This does not mean, however, that Hubmaier deliberately falsified Hut's teachings. Hubmaier merely attributed to Hut those erroneous views which he disliked in other Anabaptists, Denck included, with what mixture of in-

genuousness or disingenuousness it is now impossible to judge. The
Nicolsburg Articles, therefore, even though they cannot be accepted
uncritically, do provide a valuable source concerning Hut's difficulties
with Hubmaier in Nicolsburg

D. Hut's Impact on Austrian Anabaptists
1. Leonhart Schiemer

Hut's difficulties with Hubmaier are echoed in the writing of
Leonhart Schiemer and Hans Schlaffer, two of the most influential early
Austrian Anabaptists. Both contributed substantially to early Anabaptist
literature. Schiemer, who has been labelled "the first Anabaptist bishop
in Upper Austria,"[113] had been a Franciscan for six years, while his
ministry as an Anabaptist lasted only six months. During that brief period he managed to baptise others in Steyer, Salzburg, Bavaria, and the
Tyrol. His letters from prison were highly esteemed by later Hutterites
and Pilgramites alike. In fact, it was Schiemer's trial and death that
moved Pilgram Marpeck to resign his judicial post in the Tyrol and
move to Strassburg.[114]

After leaving the Franciscan order disillusioned and disappointed,
Schiemer had learned the seamster's trade in Nuremberg. Unfortu-
nately we can no longer determine whether he made contact with any of
the radicals in Nuremberg at the time. He later drifted to Nicolsburg.
There the controversy between Hubmaier and Hut aroused his interest.
He followed Hut to Vienna and by ruse gained entrance to one of his
meetings. Hut's reaction would suggest that Schiemer had been on
Hubmaier's side in Nicolsburg. Hut treated him as a spy.[115] However,
Schiemer was able to persuade Hut that he was only searching for the
truth. During the next two days Hut won Schiemer to his position.
Schiemer was then baptised by Oswald Glaidt, who had also left
Nicolsburg for Vienna. From Vienna Schiemer, either accompanying
Hut or following him, moved through Austria to Augsburg, where he
participated in some of the meetings of the Martyrs' Synod. Through
marriage he became part of Hut's inner circle.[116] On his honeymoon trip
back to Austria he baptised as he went. He was finally apprehended on
November 25, 1527, and imprisoned in Rattenburg on the Inn. He died
a true martyr on January 14, 1528.[117]

It would be implausible to argue that Schiemer with two days of
instruction from Hut began the formulation of his Anabaptist ideas as
on a *tabula rasa*. His background in pre-Reformation theology is clearly
evident in his writings.[118] We can surmise that he identified with the

practical mystical tradition. He registered strong criticism of the scholastic preoccupation with Latin definitions and of the fruitless speculations about the reality of universals. Nominalism had taken such an approach to the point of absurdity.[119] However, one will search in vain for a more fundamental critique of pre-Reformation presuppositions. If anything, Schiemer remained to a great measure a child of the medieval tradition of "pious ignorance." Like Müntzer and Hut, he extended his critique of scholasticism and higher learning to the Reformers, who were stealing their knowledge from one another and out of books, assuming that knowledge of God and faith could be mediated through externals.[120] Schiemer differentiated the true faith born in man from false belief mediated through externals.

> They [the scribes] think that faith relates only to an event outside of them, namely at Bethlehem, Nazareth, or Jerusalem . . . but they can give no account of the truthfulness of such faith—when or how one begins to believe and what it is that he means by faith. . . . They have only found faith beside them, and not in them, perchance in a dead letter, or in a song sung about it, or have heard only outer talk about it. They think faith comes only through physical hearing, and do not want to notice that the Lord says: Whoever hears it from the Father, and learns, the same comes to me. Yes, they do not know what the Father has spoken to them; therefore, they have never experienced faith.[121]

This true faith was born in suffering. Suffering experienced by the believer became itself the means of salvation, for only through it could man's grasp of the particular be loosened and could he be brought to the point of being united with the One (*ainigen*).[122] In good mystical fashion Schiemer internalized the life of Christ. Conception, birth, death, and resurrection were all to be relived in the believer.

> It is true, Christ's suffering purges sin. Yes, it does this if He also suffers in the believer. Because, just as the water does not quench my thirst unless I drink it . . . so also Christ's suffering does not prevent me from sinning as long as He does not suffer in me.
> They say that He has suffered for them. That is true. But notice, whoever permits Christ to die for him, and does not die with Him, will stay behind here below when Christ ascends to heaven, instead of rising with Him.[123]

Like Hut and Haug he displayed familiarity with numerical symbolism. Drawing a typically mystical analogy from Christ's descent to hell,[124] Schiemer spoke of seven degrees of purgatorial suffering. The seventh was the stage of total Godforsakenness. Here, stripped of all creatureliness, the love of God sprang forth in full purity. Of this the "crazy scribes" had, of course, no personal knowledge. Therefore, the "sevenfold sealed Scripture" remained locked to them.[125]

Schiemer coupled his anti-clericalism with a genuine feeling for the poor, accusing the magisterial Reformers of aggravating the division between laity and clergy, ignorant and educated, poor and rich.[126] Like Müntzer, Denck, and Hut he supported his opposition to the Reformers by an appeal to the inner cosmological Christ. The Reformers had never learned to distinguish the inner Word from the outer. They knew nothing of the universal witness active in all men by virtue of the creative logos.[127]

Some of the anthropological assumptions which remained implicit in Hut's writings were made explicit by Schiemer. Again, unlike the Reformers, he accepted a soteriologically significant divine spark in man which the fall had been unable to wipe out.

> The light [*imago Dei*] witnesses to all that is good, the flesh to all that is evil. The soul stands in the middle. Since we all, with the exception of Christ, have turned to the flesh with our soul, we all died in the soul.[128]

According to this genuinely medieval tripartite psychology of man not the total man was corrupted but a good two thirds. Therefore, original sin could not have the devastating results it had for the Reformers. Children remained innocent until they were old enough to understand the inner witness. They became guilty when they consciously chose to disobey the inner light.[129]

With these anthropological assumptions it was logical that justification remained literally a "becoming righteous." The pre-Reformation view of man was basic.[130] So was the complementary understanding of grace as an ontological enabling force subsistent in man.[131] Schiemer's by-now-familiar attacks on the "belly preachers" whose preaching had brought no moral improvement cannot be separated from this larger anthropological framework. Reformation theology, as he understood it, shifted every responsibility to God, undermining man's moral independence and obligations. On the contrary, he stressed man's free will and moral accountability precisely because he reckoned with God's immanence in man.[132] Schiemer's moral critique, like that of other South German Anabaptists, proved to be rooted in the mystical tradition. It grew as much out of its intellectual antecedents as out of the existential moment.

What remains amazing is the clarity with which Schiemer repeated key concepts of Hut. Hut must have been an eloquent and persuasive person. Schiemer expounded Hut's gospel of all creatures perhaps even more clearly than Dachser.

> Paul says, . . . God has created all visible things so that the invisible may be recognized therein. He says further that the Gospel which I preached to you is preached in all creatures. God created all creatures in five days, for the reason that they might be of use to man when he was created on the sixth day. Then the creature has its rest. Similarly, man was not created that he remain in the sixth day as a man, but that he come into the seventh day, yes, that he would become godly or deified and would come to God. Then comes the true human rest and true feast day . . . and precisely the same means whereby all creatures become useful to man [are God's way with man], that is, through suffering, by which man kills, cuts and prepares and the creature submits to man and suffers for faith's sake. And just as the animal [for instance a lamb] is of no nutritious value to man unless it dies, so no man can become blessed unless he dies for Christ's sake.[133]

In Schiemer's version the mystical context re-emerges more clearly than in Dachser's exposition. The message of the creatures was not merely illustrative of relations of obedience but revealed the purpose of these relations—that man ought to be deified and united with God. The statement also suggested that Schiemer understood the six phases of the Genesis process as God's foreordained order which regulated the relationships within the external world. The revelation in the creatures was based on the order of Genesis 1:26. That order showed not only characteristic medieval, hierarchical relations, but assumed a special inner connection of the created order to God by virtue of the cosmological Christ and His role in creation as the logos. It was the inner connection rather than the outer witness which for Schiemer proved to be more significant, for it alone guaranteed man's proper perception of the outer order.[134] Thus Schiemer appears to have reinterpreted Hut's gospel of all creatures within a more consistently mystical context, suggesting that a secondary revelation in the creatures could harmonize with the mystical focus on the unmediated revelation in the heart.

Nuances in Dachser's and Schiemer's interpretations of Hut's gospel of all creatures suggest divergent levels of comprehension of Hut's message among his followers. This is more easily illustrated with reference to Hut's apocalypticism.

Unlike Dachser, Schiemer appears to have been well acquainted with Hut's eschatology. Moreover, some of his statements suggest that he defended Hut's view against Hubmaier's criticisms.

> If, however, there is someone who would like to interpret year for day, as for example with the seventy weeks of Daniel, I answer, no, to it. Because the Scripture calls the days shortened, [therefore] little time will remain. For if someone would take days for years, then the persecution would not be short, but the longest ever, namely 1290 years. No persecution has ever lasted that long before.[135]

As we noticed earlier, Hubmaier arrived at 1,277 years. Schiemer's statement would, therefore, counter Hubmaier's arithmetic. How Schiemer arrived at the number 1,290 is no longer clear. As we will see, the number 1,260, which was prominent among the reckonings of Joachimists, was also used by Schiemer.[136]

Schiemer believed that he was living during the last week prophesied in Daniel. The middle of the seventh week which saw the predicted beginning of the persecution of God's true servants was identified with the persecution of brothers in Solothurn, Switzerland. This was an innovation by Schiemer, to whom Hut's identification of the two apocalyptic witnesses as Müntzer and Pfeiffer (killed in 1525) either remained hidden or did not make sense. Schiemer thereby grafted Hut's eschatology onto an Anabaptist movement which saw its genesis in Zürich. The significance of the date 1521, which marked the beginning of the last seven years, if it was clear to Hut was lost to Schiemer. So was the apocalyptical significance of the Peasants' War. Schiemer concentrated on the last half of the week predicted in Daniel, which covered the events to take place during the last 3½ years.[137]

> These days of the greatest tribulation are shortened, as Daniel says in chapter 2 and 9. . . . He says further, when the daily sacrifice, that is the Christians, will be killed, and the desolate abomination will be raised up, and will sit in the holy place of God, one thousand two hundred and ninety days will pass. Isaiah 14: the man in the linen cloth baptizes, one time and a half time. (A time is a year.) Revelation 12, II Corinthians 11: The holy place, that is, the Christian people, will be trampled and tempted by the heathen for forty-two months. The woman, which is the holy Church, dressed with the sun of Christ, will flee before the dragon for 1260 days. God will prepare her a place in the desert for three years, that is, He

will nourish her miraculously for forty-two months. The judgment
begins on the house of God— understand, on God's people. Thus is
the shortening of the days of our great tribulation described [ac-
cording to] time in years, months and days in many texts in the
Scriptures, as recorded above. [138]

The statement that the man in the linen cloth baptised 1½ years
could have been a reference to Hut. If true, it would tend to pinpoint
the beginning of Hut's activity as a baptiser in the fall of 1526, which is
confirmed by our sources. [139] At the time of his own imprisonment late in
1527 Schiemer believed that the crucial seventh year predicted in
Daniel was in full swing. The godly had to endure only a little longer.
The book of the seven seals of Apocalypse 5 would be opened, Christ
would return, and God's sevenfold judgment would begin on the godless. Their weeping would last five months. [140] This would be followed
by a general resurrection. Those who had suffered faithfully with Christ
their Head would judge and rule the world with Him. [141] Schiemer here
proved his familiarity with Hut's last seven judgments. These were supported by a view of history which drew heavily on St. Augustine, and in
all probability also on the Joachimist tradition, for it combined
Augustine's major text on creation with favoured texts of the Joachimists. Schiemer believed that the sixth age of the world, the sixth age
of the church in its sixth hour of tribulation, had been reached. There
remained the great seventh Sabbath age for man to enter. In this setting
the gospel of all creatures took on a new meaning as a revelation of creation's historical and eschatological purpose.

> God created all creatures in five days, but He did this so that
> they would come into the sixth day to be of use to man, who was
> created on the sixth day. . . . And the medium is . . . suffering. . . .
> E.g., in the Revelation of John we find that Antichrist's number is
> 666. Here read three times: six, six, six, because Antichrist with all
> his followers, Pharisees and scribes, wants to force [us] six times to
> remain in the six days in which man and all creatures have been
> created. He prohibits us the seventh day, so that we should not be
> obedient to God. He sets himself in God's place in this fashion. Read
> Daniel 2, 7, 11, 12; Isaiah 14; Matthew 24. [142]

Thus Schiemer rounds out our picture of Hut's gospel of all creatures as well as of Hut's eschatology. However, this by no means made
of him a wild-eyed chiliast. In fact, an impartial reader of Schiemer's
prison epistles finds himself immersed in the noblest thought of early

South German Anabaptism. Schiemer, like Denck, perceived the established religious authority (Antichrist with the Pharisees and scribes) to be coercive aggressors who sought to stem the course of history and delay the coming of the kingdom. Yet unlike some of Hut's lesser disciples, Schiemer's focus was not on the expected vengeance on the godless. His mission was to comfort and strengthen Christ's true followers in their tribulation. Better than Hut, Schiemer in his own person epitomized the transition from a purely internalized cross mysticism to an Anabaptist theology of martyrdom. The bridge from one to the other was provided by the eschatological expectations. Again and again Schiemer repeated the need for the members of Christ's body to suffer with and for their Head. Eschatology and cross mysticism were blended through the experience of persecution. The true followers and martyrs of Christ became a sacrificial offering to God.

> The believers are the meal offering, but meal offering and daily offering are the same thing. The Lord says with clear words, whoever wants to follow me must deny himself and take up his cross daily. . . . But when Ezra says, after seven days my Son Christ will be killed, one must not separate Christ from His members but [understand it] as it is written, 'The Lamb was slain from the beginning of the world.' Even though Christ as head has only been slain once. . . . in His members, the Lamb began to be slain with Abel and will [be slain] until the last half week, so that the number of fellow travellers *(Mitgesell)* and brothers who must be slain might be fulfilled. [143]

This increased emphasis on discipleship was complemented by an explicitly elitist ecclesiology. Schiemer advocated the establishment of separated brotherhoods.[144] This is particularly evident in some of his writings that have hitherto received little attention.[145] It is possible that Schiemer had made contact with Swiss Anabaptists. As noticed earlier, he dated the beginning of the persecution of Christ's true followers with the persecution of Swiss Brethren. He also advocated the use of strong congregational discipline.[146] Whoever was not in harmony with the true Christian Gemeinde on earth would be unacceptable in heaven. The practice of foot washing alluded to in one of his letters may also have been of Swiss origin. In all these matters Schiemer appears closer than Hut to the Denckian and Swiss New Testament hermeneutic with its greater appreciation of the *nova lex Christi*. He approximates the image of the evangelical Anabaptist subscribed to by sympathetic scholars. This proves how difficult it becomes to retain the artificial boundaries drawn between Spiritualists and Anabaptists. Schiemer's theological assumptions in general remained every bit as mystical as those of Denck and Hut.

2. Hans Schlaffer

Hans Schlaffer's spiritual kinship to Schiemer has long been recognized. His writings indicate full understanding of and agreement with Schiemer's view of history and the future.[147] Like Schiemer he had been strongly influenced by Hut. Besides Hut, Schlaffer had also made personal acquaintance with many of the other early South German Anabaptist leaders, including Denck, Hätzer, Kautz, and Oswald Glaidt.[148]

Like so many of the early South German Anabaptist leaders, Schlaffer had received much of his training in pre-Reformation thought. According to his own confession it had been the writings of Luther and others which forced him to rethink his own position. The study of Scripture convinced him that salvation could be attained through faith in Christ alone. He began to preach this new faith in his parish. When this was forbidden him, he ceased to perform his public duties as a priest and gave himself to private reading of Scripture.[149] This presumably took place prior to 1526, for by that date Schlaffer had left his parish and the Catholic Church and found temporary lodging with the lords von Zelking near the city of Freistadt.[150]

It is not clear when he first heard of the Anabaptists. He later claimed that he had first opposed them, even written against them.[151] This would suggest some time lapse before Schlaffer embraced Anabaptism. For Schlaffer the acceptance of adult baptism must have been a consciously significant step. Who were the Anabaptists he at first rejected? Unfortunately, we do not know. But we know that he was eventually drawn into the movement under the impact of Hut. Whether he was actually baptised by Hut or was personally in Nicolsburg during the latter's debate with Hubmaier remains conjectural. It is certain only that he joined the group of dissenters who supported Hut's case against Hubmaier. He disapproved particularly of the fact that Hubmaier conducted mass baptisms without requiring individual professions of faith.[152] A similar claim, as we noted earlier, had been made by Hans Nadler.[153] Like Schiemer's, Schlaffer's career as an Anabaptist was of short duration. He himself heard the news of Schiemer's martyrdom in prison and, refusing to give up his newfound faith, shortly thereafter suffered a similar fate.[154]

One of Schlaffer's prison epistles proves particularly enlightening for our purposes. It suggests that the debate between Hubmaier and Hut left some ripples among the South German and Austrian Anabaptists. Schlaffer's letter was a reply to some questions sent to him by a "dear brother" who showed concern over the content of some doctrines circulating among the brethren.[155] One of these concerned the person of Christ.

> I do not know very well what I should say to this, that Christ is not true God and man, but is supposedly only a prophet. I fear there is in some persons more meddlesomeness than love. But I do not want to judge anyone. It is difficult and dangerous to talk about it. . . . It is true that there is only one God, as Moses says: 'Hear, oh Israel, your God is one God, etc.' Here the Jews and Christians are annoyed with one another (*ergern sich*). The Jews would put up with almost anything rather than accept that Christ is God. This is their greatest stumbling block. Human reason cannot comprehend such a thing, that there is one thing and that it is three things.[156]

Schlaffer sought to explain the apparent paradox by analogy to man's own makeup.

> Namely man in himself is one, his word and speech are something else, his breath or wind . . . a third thing. . . . Now because the Father is God, and Word and Spirit are one with the Father, so one may well call the Word and the Spirit also God. Yet all three remain only one God from eternity to eternity.[157]

Schlaffer concluded that the Scriptures proclaimed Christ to be both a prophet and the Son of God.[158] The significance of this passage lies not so much in Schlaffer's own views, in which he strove to be orthodox, as in the fact that Christ's divinity was being questioned in Anabaptist circles, a subject reappearing from the Nicolsburg Articles.

Other questions concerned the Lord's Supper and the ban, touching congregational organization and discipline. These issues, too, had been a point of disagreement between Hut and Hubmaier. The Lord's Supper was interpreted in terms of cross mysticism, as commemorating and celebrating the members' oneness with their Head in suffering. With regard to church organization, Schlaffer, even more than Schiemer, advocated the strongest possible separation from the world. Those outside the true fold were to be regarded as "bucks, wolves, lions, dragons, dogs, and the like."[159]

More interesting for our purposes were the next questions which concerned Schlaffer's correspondent. These, judging from Schlaffer's answer, covered the eschatological articles of Hut's seven judgments, with which Schlaffer was obviously acquainted. As in his answers relating to the Trinity and Christ's divinity, Schlaffer feared that some brothers were showing an unbecoming curiosity for these secrets. He struck a note of caution. The dear brother needed to be patient and ought not to worry about things he did not yet understand. The apostles had also been with Christ for three years without understanding Him fully. Besides, "secrets were secrets."[160] One needed to be careful in outward discussions of them lest they should be defiled by dogs or false brethren. He, therefore, advised his reader to turn inward to the One with the key of David, who could unlock the secrets to him directly.

> The further secrets of the covenant and its main elements, the end of the earth, the time and the day of the Lord's judgment, how and in what form we will be resurrected, where we will have our dwelling place and where we will remain during this time before the judgment, about the kingdom of Christ, eternal judgment and similar matters, one should in humility commit to God the Father. To whom, however, through the key of David one or more of such secrets are opened (as, no doubt, out of God's grace happens often, especially during this time), and he is assured of this in his heart, he should praise God. But he should show circumspection that the noble gems and pearls are not thrown before swine and that the holy [not] be given to dogs, who would thereafter turn upon him and tear him apart. It is also necessary to beware of the false brethren, because it is possible to speak about these things outwardly—but to open the book and read it internally . . . belongs to no other than to the Lamb through the key of David.[161]

Schlaffer's letter illustrates well the ideas that preoccupied the early South German and Austrian Anabaptists under Hut's influence. Not all of these were of the evangelical variety.[162] Schlaffer demonstrates perfectly the considerable discussion provoked by Hut's well-developed eschatological timetable. Schlaffer himself, as his statements indicate, belonged to the more moderate spirits who showed reticence in speaking publicly about some of these apocalyptic expectations.

In other matters Schlaffer indicated greater willingness to endorse Hut's ideas openly. One of these was Hut's gospel of all creatures.[163] Perhaps more clearly than any of Hut's students Schlaffer retained the original orientation of this concept toward the illiterate poor. The revelation in all creatures could be read by all. Schlaffer repeated the illustration used by Dachser of the feathers that need to be plucked. He supplemented it further with reference to the cleaning of fish. In this context expressions first coined by Müntzer reappear. Christ is said to have quoted Scripture only because of the "stiff-necked scribes." But Scripture repeated the message of creation—the Lamb has been slain since the beginning of creation. The poor and suppressed of this world, therefore, have a natural affinity to the suffering Christ.[164]

Like Schiemer, and perhaps more so than Hut, Schlaffer accentuated the internalized Christ—the Word which has become flesh and dwells in us. The incarnation became a universal symbol of the birth of the Son in the believer's flesh. The sola fide doctrine of Christ's satisfaction as taught by the Reformers was criticized as too simplistic. The true disciple had to experience suffering in and on his own body for Christ's sake.[165] The concept of the four-dimensional Christ which we met earlier in Hut is further expounded by Schlaffer in terms of His length, height, depth, and width.[166] Thus all the evidence would suggest that in Schlaffer we meet an early Austrian Anabaptist leader influenced by Hut's, and therefore indirectly Müntzer's, ideas. In fact, some of the ideas which remain implicit in Hut's fragments, such as his pre-Reformation anthropology, are made explicit in Schlaffer. Like Schiemer, Schlaffer argued that children, until they became of age, had neither sin nor condemnation. Only the flesh, not the spirit, had been corrupted by the fall.[167]

Yet, in spite of the obvious and striking similarities between Hut and Schlaffer, it remains difficult to classify him as a mere disciple of Hut. Schlaffer's endorsement of Hut's message is perhaps again best explained by a theological predisposition (like the one we noted in Schiemer and Dachser) to the practical mystical tradition. Other circumstances, including a common antipathy for Hubmaier's behaviour and teachings, helped to bring these men together. However, unlike the foiled revolutionary, Hans Hut, and like Schiemer and Dachser, Schlaffer outlined a religious doctrine in which the focus was not on the expected vengeance on the godless. For him the cost of discipleship for true followers of Christ was central.[168] He also thought in more practical, empirical terms of congregational structure. Thus Schlaffer's ideas represented a step forward in sect formation. His theology and ecclesiology represent a new permutation of the mystical theology coming from Müntzer via Hut, as it combined with a nova lex Christi tradition coming from Denck and possibly from the Swiss Brethren as well. Influences are usually reciprocal, and it is not at all impossible that Hut himself was moving in the direction of Schlaffer, that is, away from a movement almost entirely feeding on social frustrations to a more quietistic religious sect. It is also likely that Schlaffer knew only the chastened, post-Nicolsburg Hut. In the constellation of South German and Austrian Anabaptism both Schlaffer and Schiemer personified the transition of a sizable part of Hut's movement in the direction of what has been in the past conceived as typically Anabaptist—a more confessional sectarian movement. The martyrdom of Schlaffer and Schiemer helped to demarcate, and accelerate the formation of, a new ethos in which the internalized cross mysticism of Müntzer and Hut underwent an externalization into a full-blown martyr theology, later institutionalized in the sectarian Hutterite movement.

5

THE DEVOLUTION OF
HUT'S MOVEMENT

A. The Disintegration of Early South German
Anabaptism

The decline of Hut's movement began with the doom of Hut himself. Persecution which set in after Hubmaier's arrest drove Hut and many of his disciples from Austria. The refugees converged in Augsburg, one of the few places still relatively unaffected by persecution. The not entirely accidental concentration of so many transient Anabaptist leaders in Augsburg during August 1527 has misled some historians into viewing events in Augsburg as the proceeding of a synod similar to the one that produced the Schleitheim Confession. Since many of those present shortly thereafter fell to the sword of the executioners, the synod became known as the "Martyrs' Synod." Depending on perspective, scholars have seen either Hut or Denck presiding over the meetings. However, to describe the goings-on in Augsburg in the fall of 1527 as a synod is misleading.

Hut's return and the divulgence of his apocalyptic expectations led to dissent among the local Anabaptists.[1] So did the requests by some to introduce polygamy.[2] Hut found it necessary to circulate a letter in which he promised to be even more reticent about his knowledge of the future. But he by no means surrendered his convictions. Denck's contribution appears to have been insignificant. His friend Hätzer, perhaps because of fear of arrest, did not participate at all. Denck attended only two meetings. Together with Hut he was present at the ordination and commissioning of new Anabaptist leaders, among them Jörg Nespitzer.[3] It was at this gathering that Denck and Hut harmonized their teachings about the expected revolution.[4] That Denck dissented at the Martyrs' Synod from Hut's apocalypticism, as has been generally assumed by historians, is not at all clear. Denck was also present when Dachser registered his protest against Hut's apocalypticism. About Denck's role in that controversy the sources are again silent. This gathering must have taken place before August 25, 1527, for on that date Dachser was apprehended.[5] Salminger and Gross were next, and on September 15 it was Hut's turn.[6] The trial of Hut marked the beginning of the end for the phase of the movement that had been stamped by his peculiar personality and unique eschatology.

During the early part of Hut's trial questions arising out of the Nicolsburg Articles and Hut's seven judgments loomed large.[7] The latter were provided by Nuremberg.[8] It is not entirely clear from whom the Augsburg authorities received the Nicolsburg Articles. Hut answered the questions by repudiating the Nicolsburg Articles and by seeking to give the impression that his seven judgments, in particular those concerned with the end of the world, were intended primarily to move sinners to repentance.[9] Unfortunately for Hut the authorities possessed specific information about his conflict with Hubmaier. They considered his answers unsatisfactory.[10] Similarly, the suspicious authorities were not about to accept the harmlessness of the seven judgments.

Information reaching them from Ambrosius Spittelmaier's trial in Ansbach suggested that Hut's eschatology included the vision that one of the righteous would slay a thousand of the wicked, and two, ten thousand. More significantly, the name of Thomas Müntzer appeared in one of the booklets taken from Spittelmaier. Spittelmaier could not remember why Müntzer's name was written into the margin.[11] His claim is by no means incredible. He considered himself a disciple of Hut, but his knowledge was limited to Hut's post-Nicolsburg teachings.[12] He knew nothing about Denck, Hätzer, and Hubmaier.[13] Less credible was Hut's response that he did not know Spittelmaier and that his contact with Müntzer had been casual.[14] An examination of one of Hut's booklets convinced the authorities that his apocalypticism was more incriminating than he cared to admit.[15]

Meanwhile, news of Hut's trial had reached his hometown. Hans von Bibra, the suzerain in Hut's area, had heard that Hut claimed to have been driven from his home for the sake of the "pure gospel."[16] He now tried to set the record straight. Hut, he informed the Augsburg government, had distributed Müntzer's writings in the area. Around Pentecost 1525 he had preached from the open pulpit that the time had arrived when the subjects should take the sword and rid themselves of the Obrigkeit. He disappeared when troops of the Swabian League arrived. Attention was also drawn to Hut's activity in Königsberg.[17] Understandably, Hut had not been anxious for an investigation into what he taught while in Königsberg. Now, under torture, he confessed that he had preached there on such edifying texts as these:

> Whoever has two coats should give up one and buy a sword. [Christ] had not come to bring peace, but a sword.
> The holy will be happy and have two-edged swords in their hands, so that they may do vengeance in the land among the people, to bind the kings with chains and the nobles with iron casks. So that they may bring to pass the judgment about which it is written: 'Cursed be the one who does God's work unfaithfully, and cursed be the one who withholds his sword from the punishment.'[18]

To bring out the paradoxical nature of scriptural political ethic a bit more clearly, he added the story of Peter severing the ear of Malchus. Christ commanded Peter to sheathe the sword. Hut saw in this an application to the peasants' cause. The peasants failed because they acted rashly and because they had sought their own honour rather than God's. The end-product was at best ambivalent. Some time in the near future—3½ years after the Peasants' War to be exact—"God would overturn the thrones of the mighty and the mighty would suffer terrible pain."[19]

Hut had earlier assured his interrogators that he knew of no other Parousia of Christ than that announced in the Holy Scripture. He was not awaiting a physical but a spiritual kingdom.[20] He had also attempted to brush off his contact with Müntzer and the accusations contained in the Nicolsburg Articles. But on all points his protested innocence proved entirely unconvincing. In fact, to the authorities it appeared that Hut was not only evasive but untruthful. The turning point was reached in Hut's confession of November 26. His contact with Müntzer, he now admitted, had been more than casual. No doubt the interrogators were hoping for greater revelations in the near future. Hut himself must have realized the hopelessness of his situation. A few days later he was found unconscious in his cell suffering from smoke inhalation. He was moved to better quarters, and while recovering admitted to having planned his escape. The plan, according to official reports, included the killing of the guard, who was to have been attracted by the fire.[21] When Hut suddenly died a few days later, rumours spread that he had committed suicide in order not to divulge any further secrets.[22] He became the object of a posthumous condemnation for his conspiratorial involvements and intentions, and his body was burned early in December 1527.[23]

Hut's trial and death by no means ended Anabaptism in Augsburg. If anything, the movement had not yet reached its peak. Even while the trial of Hut and the three Anabaptist leaders, Dachser, Gross, and Salminger, was in progress, proselytising and secret baptisms continued in Augsburg and environs. It was not a lack of leaders that brought on the disintegration. If anything, the reverse was true. Among those at least temporarily exercising the right to baptise late in 1527 and early in 1528 were Melchior from Salzburg,[24] Hans Greul (also appearing in the documents as Hans von Geltendoerf),[25] Georg Schachner (also known as Jörg von Munich, or Jörg Gschachner and Scheurer),[26] Thomas Waldhauser,[27] Burkhart Braun von Ofen,[28] Leonhard Dorfbrunner (the *"Deutschherr"*),[29] Bartholomäus Nussfelder, Gregorius from Chur in Switzerland,[30] Hans Leupold, Jörg Nespitzer, and Hans Bechthold.[31] Others joined in as they moved through the area.

With such a profusion of leaders it should be obvious that generalizations about the South German Anabaptist movement during the crucial period immediately following Hut's death are almost impossible. Even assuming the illuminating presence of the Holy Spirit and the Bible as the common and sole sources of their religious ideas, it strains credibility to believe that all those mentioned above were of the same mind, preaching the same message. The fragmentary sources permit only limited insights into their teachings. Nevertheless, they indicate that many of them preached primarily a "repent or perish" gospel. Their main aim appears to have been the moral improvement of their adherents. The mystical and apocalyptical elements of Hut's message, while they may have been in the background, do not appear dominant.

This moralistic and practical Anabaptism found a diligent advocate in Leonhard Dorfbrunner. Dorfbrunner had been a priest in Bamberg. He suffered imprisonment for reading the Mass in German. After his release he learned the trade of knifesmith and then moved to Steyer. Some time during June or July 1527 when Hut came into the area Dorfbrunner joined the Anabaptist cause. Together with Schiemer he was commissioned by Hut to baptise.[32] He later followed Hut to Augsburg, on the way baptising the first Anabaptists of Munich.[33] He arrived in Augsburg during the crucial period of arrests, and in spite or because of the climate of persecution a most fruitful ministry unfolded.[34] He baptised around one hundred persons during a five-week period.[35] Shortly after the burning of Hut's corpse in December Dorfbrunner decided to return to Austria.[36] En route through Munich he discovered that his converts there had meanwhile been arrested. The same fate overtook him a few weeks later in Passau. By that time, according to some sources, he had managed to baptise three thousand persons in all. He was executed before March 15, 1528.[37]

Dorfbrunner's crisp confessional statement made during his trial indicates a strong emphasis on submission to God's will. Baptism was understood as the dual covenant between the viator and God. The theologically complex opposition of the inner to the outer, so pronounced in Denck and Hut, had given way to a strong one-sided emphasis on outer baptism in the service of practical piety. The Lord's Supper signified the suffering and brokenness of Christ's genuine followers united as His true body. Echoes of Hut's gospel of all creatures reappeared. So did the four stages in the journey of the viator from conception to resurrection. Yet the original mystical thrust was muted. Even the doomsday predictions appear to have served clearly as trumpet calls to repentance. We conclude that in Dorfbrunner we face a change from the largely mystical orientation of Hut to a practical moralism. The original cross mysticism was taken one step further in the direction of discipleship and theology of martyrdom.[38] Dorfbrunner belonged to a current among Hut's following that flowed into the sectarian evangelical stream of Anabaptism.

Similar observations could be made about some of the other Anabaptist leaders. Melchior von Salzburg, although more cautious, appears to have also preached a practical moralistic message.[39] Burkhart Braun's activity, as well as the statements of his converts, convey the same impression.[40] This is also true for the local leader, Hans Leupold. Leupold, as we noticed earlier, continued the less apocalyptic tradition of Jacob Dachser.[41] A seamster by trade, he had joined the radical dissenters in Augsburg very early. Like so many others he had been arrested in the wake of Hut's trial. He refused to recant and was expelled from the city together with a tough core of the faithful. These elected him *Vorsteher* and dispatched him to Esslingen and Worms.[42] Leupold arrived in Esslingen late in November and remained there for five weeks. However, his ministry appears to have been a limited one. The sources record only two baptisms by him during this period.[43] From Esslingen he carried letters to Worms. Here his presence was more productive. He baptised fifteen or sixteen persons. Then he returned with correspondence to Esslingen and from there to Augsburg. He entered Augsburg secretly on March 26, 1528.[44]

When Leupold returned to Augsburg after three months of absence the Anabaptist cause there was experiencing a revival. Leupold found the meetings inflated by outside refugees and saw many new faces.[45] The real mover behind the new flurry of Anabaptist activity was the enigmatic Jörg Nespitzer (Jörg von Passau). Nespitzer, earlier Hut's host in Passau, was one of the numerous followers of Hut who had now taken to the road. After participating in the Martyrs' Synod in Augsburg he led a missionary expedition into Hut's old stamping ground in Franconia. Accompanying him was Hut's faithful follower, Hans Weischenfelder. Other contacts included Hut's oldest disciples, the Maier brothers and Jörg Volck. Nespitzer participated in the appointment of Marx Maier as Vorsteher.[46] His own teachings in Franconia were of a distilled apocalyptical nature.[47] According to his later confession he had believed that the judgment of the godless would set in 3½ years after the Peasants' War.[48] Thus, unlike Leupold, he must be regarded as a disciple of Hut in the true sense of the word.

When Nespitzer returned to Augsburg around February 9, Anabaptist fortunes were at a low ebb.[49] The actions of the authorities had intimidated many and it was difficult to find meeting places for prophetic Bible studies. Nespitzer's solution was a simple one. One of the victims later testified how Nespitzer walked in with ten others trailing behind him while she and her family were having dinner. The surprised hostess and her husband abandoned their house to the visitors. Nespitzer was obviously desperate. He had already been refused entry at another place.[50] A similar situation arose when Leupold upon his return contacted Nespitzer and the two decided to call a general meeting for April 4.[51] Nespitzer had chosen a familiar meeting place. The owner had been exiled from Augsburg for her Anabaptist beliefs. When her relatives refused the upper part of the house Nespitzer and his group moved into the basement.[52] The candlelight service lasted all night with between sixty and one hundred persons in attendance and Nespitzer, Leupold, and Augustin Bader presiding. Besides reading and preaching they celebrated the Lord's Supper together. Upon Nespitzer's request two new Vorsteher, Claus Schleifer and Peter Ringmacher, were elected.[53]

On the next day another meeting took place. The two new ministers were to be instructed and commissioned by the legitimate leaders. Leupold, who had been received warmly the night before, heard of this council only indirectly and surprised the other participants when he arrived in broad daylight. Present were the newly elected Vorsteher, Nespitzer, Augustin Bader, and another Anabaptist leader, Leonhard Freisleben. According to Leupold they compared their teaching with each other so that no one might introduce errors. Where one was mistaken the others taught him differently.[54]

It is not clear whether Hut's eschatology was discussed at the council. According to our sources Nespitzer exercised considerable restraint in preaching about the expected judgment. Augsburg was not Franconia. He even told some to pay no attention to Hut's predictions. Even if the day of judgment would not come as predicted, there would be no less need to repent of one's sins.[55] Perhaps this was partly due to the influence of Leupold; for Nespitzer, as his later confession shows, was still convinced that Hut's predictions would prove true.[56] Moreover, Hut's apocalyptical teachings were not entirely forgotten among Augsburg Anabaptists. This is evident from a letter that circulated among them during this period.

The letter in question was later published by Rhegius in seeking to expose and combat Anabaptist teaching.[57] The author has remained anonymous. One could suspect Hut of having been the writer were it not for evidence that the letter originated during January 1528.[58] It contains only a few clues about its author and place of origin. Indirect evidence suggests that the author had left Augsburg because of persecution. He found, however, that persecution was also in effect one hundred miles from Augsburg.[59] Other particulars included the information that he was married and had children. Other brothers were with him. His host was a certain brother "Oschwald."[60] The only Oswald who figured prominently among early South German Anabaptists and whose first name could have identified him to those in Augsburg was undoubtedly Oswald Glaidt. If so, the letter originated either in Moravia or Silesia, where Glaidt was active during January 1528.[61]

Although the identity of the writer is no longer discernible,[62] the document remains significant. It presents clear evidence of a tendency in Hut's immediate following to rely on special visions and dreams. It will be remembered that Oswald Glaidt had sided with Hut against Hubmaier in defending the legitimacy of special revelation. Rhegius in his reply to Dachser's tract had earlier warned against this belief.[63] Now in this letter there was evidence that the writer had been blessed by special visions of the impending judgment.

> Rejoice with your whole heart and with all your strength . . . because the Lord has revealed to us brethren during what time He will punish those who have persecuted and scattered you. . . . For the Lord has truly much declared in godly revelation that the time is short . . . but if the time is not written to you, it is for this reason. The Lord does not want the time to come before the godless, for He speaks in all Scripture that they will not know until the day when He will fall upon them with His punishment. For we prayed to God for eight days that He should reveal the time unto us once more, as He had done four times earlier, if it was His will that we should write about the time. . . . This the Lord did not want to do and we are not certain either whether the letter will get to you.[64]

Fortunately for the historian, even at the risk of the pearls falling to the swine the writer could not restrain himself from including some details about the expected judgment. In one vision granted to him he saw hailstones the size of human fists falling from the skies. A tremendous famine would sweep Europe from which the Anabaptists would be spared because God had appointed places of refuge for them. This would presumably take place after the scattering of the faithful. He admonished them further to be ready to move through the Red Sea lest they should fall into the hands of Pharaoh. Whether this was an illusion to baptism remains unclear. Coupled with the expectations of judgment was a barely disguised spirit of vengeance. The writer declared that the bodies of those who had separated faith from baptism would be literally separated into halves. All those who had wounded and killed with the sword would soon suffer the same fate. Some of the soft-hearted brothers needed to steel themselves against any pity they might feel for the godless once judgment set in.[65] That all this was related to Hut's eschatology becomes clear from the writer's distinction between the Lord's punishment and Christ's return in the clouds. This distinction followed Hut's seven judgments. About the timing of the final return of Christ the writer was unwilling to speculate.[66]

The rest of the letter sounded the trumpet call to repentance and discipleship. Christ was to be followed in humble obedience. The arguments for adult baptism could mislead the casual reader into believing that the letter originated among followers of Conrad Grebel. The Zwinglian equation of baptism and circumcision was explicitly rejected as an invented swindle of the false scribes. Christ's Great Commission was to be accepted literally. Anyone who taught differently—even if he carried the whole Bible under his arm and read from it three days continuously, assuring his listeners in all humility that these were not his own ideas but God's—spoke against God's express will. The writer was obviously drawing on concrete experience, for throughout the letter he alluded to false brethren who had been persuaded to give up their commitment to adult baptism. Through another vision God had warned him of one particular brother who had become a traitor, and was now aiding the enemy.[67]

The content of the letter, then, permits the conclusion that Hut's apocalyptic ideas were still occupying the minds of some. These persons were now practising what Hut had taught about dreams and visions. In fact, it can be argued that this strain in Hut's teachings was eventually responsible for the Dreamers' sect and for the aberrations of Augustin Bader. But during March and early April 1528 these ideas were still basic ingredients of Anabaptism reviving as a result of Nespitzer's activity in Augsburg.

After the council of April 5 only two further meetings materialized. On April 11 Elisabeth Vischer, the wife of Gall Vischer, opened her house to Nespitzer for a meeting. It had earlier been used by Hut. About sixty persons came to hear Nespitzer.[68] On the next day, Easter Sunday, April 12, 1528, almost one hundred persons gathered in the house of Susanna Adolphine, who took advantage of the absence of her husband. The spirit of this last meeting was one of foreboding. Not only was Hut's predicted judgment imminent, but the warning reached those assembled that the authorities were about to make new arrests.[69] Nespitzer and Leupold who presided at the meeting told those who were weak to return home because the cross was before the door. Only one frightened sister rose asking the others to pray for her weakness.[70] The others decided to persevere. Eighty-eight were arrested. The government acted swiftly. On the next day the non-citizens were expelled from the city, among them the fortunate Nespitzer with his wife and sister. The authorities were apparently unaware of his significance. The less fortunate Leupold was executed on April 25.[71]

Ironically, with this action the authorities succeeded in breaking the backbone of Hut's movement during the time which the dead leader had predicted would be critical for his followers. When the other part of the predictions, the punishment of the godless by means of supernatural plagues and the invasion of the Turk, failed to come true, interest in Anabaptism began to wane. By July Philip Plener, the new Vorsteher in the Augsburg area, complained that no one would support him and that he could not find employment.[72] Some time in August 1528 Plener together with Georg Schachner, the only other original minister remaining in the area, met with a faithful remnant on a meadow outside Augsburg. Only twenty persons attended. The decision was reached to suspend all further meetings, "since the time was past during which God sufficiently revealed and verified true baptism." Subsequently each one would do that which God would individually reveal to him.[73] This action constituted, in effect, the official dissolution of the early South German Anabaptist movement in the area. No doubt the action was to a considerable extent a bowing to reality, and was directly related to the disintegration and inner crisis which set in after the failure of Hut's predictions.[74] Henceforth only sporadic and isolated Anabaptist activity was reported in the Augsburg area.[75] It appears, therefore, historically questionable to see a direct evolution from early South German Anabaptism to Pilgram Marpeck, a later resident in the imperial city. The Anabaptist movement inspired by Hut was a transitional phenomenon of which the later more purely religious and sectarian Pilgramites were a new permutation.

The disintegration of the early South German Anabaptist movement is well illustrated in the subsequent careers of the last ministers in the Augsburg area. Philip Plener had earlier been active in the Palatinate, where he forbade his followers to drink, play, blaspheme, take the oath, or enter churches, those "houses of idolatry." His message was, therefore, explicitly separatist. While in the Augsburg area he exhibited a particularly harsh attitude towards those outside the fold.[76] He reappeared briefly in Strassburg and then led an Anabaptist community in Rossitz and Auspitz, Moravia. The writings that have survived from this group suggest that either Plener or other leading members of his following absorbed much of the mystical world-view of Müntzer, Hut, and Denck.[77] Eventually Philip and his followers found it difficult to cope with the strict communitarianism of Jacob Hutter. Plener left Moravia and disappeared into the Rhineland. Many of the Philippites followed his example.[78]

Even more illuminating was the case of Georg Schachner. By November 1530 he had settled in Nuremberg.[79] Thirty years later he reappeared as a follower of Schwenckfeld. Answering questions of his in-laws as to why he had become unfaithful to the Anabaptist vision and not joined them in Moravia, he replied that original Anabaptist teaching had by no means been as pure as those in Moravia believed. He had per-

sonally known and heard "horrible doctrines" from Müntzer, Hut,
Hätzer, Balthsar Hubner (Hubmaier?), and Leupold who , "my dear
brother-in-law, were the first Anabaptists." Among other things they
had taught that God would entrust the sword to them for the punishment of the wicked. While Schachner's statement given thirty years
later is obviously of limited value, it retains autobiographical significance.[80] No doubt the mystical content of Hut's, and particularly
Denck's, message predisposed him favourably towards Schwenckfeld's
rather than Marpeck's teachings. Similarly, the failure of Hut's predictions must have contributed to his disillusionment with the Anabaptist
cause.

The disintegration which set in after Hut's prophecies failed to
come true is also illustrated in the subsequent fate of Jörg Nespitzer.
Two of his letters, originating during the crucial period after his expulsion from Augsburg, and his recantation of one year later have survived.
In the document addressed to Hut's followers in Franconia he conveyed
greetings from the brothers in Augsburg and Esslingen and expressed
the conviction that "the time had come to be silent before the world."
Everyone was to remain in the order until the Lord would come. The
brothers were not to arouse unnecessary attention by frequent meetings; once every eight or fourteen days was to be enough. Nespitzer also
announced his intention to visit Basel and there consult with "the elders
of the Gemein." Whom he considered the elders in Basel is no longer
clear. Neither is the purpose of the mission. The letter suggested that
differences of opinion existed which he hoped to overcome.[81] Perhaps
these related to Denck's recantation. Denck had travelled to Basel after
leaving Augsburg. His *Widderruf* must have been common knowledge
by this time.

Nespitzer's letter also contained evidence that the disillusioned
followers of Hut were now sustaining their hopes with an appeal to the
miraculous. One dear brother who had been condemned to death and
imprisoned in Bohemia for one year and seven weeks, like St. Peter of
old, had been miraculously delivered "through seven locked doors."
Prior to that he had heard a voice commanding him to visit all the
brethren and to admonish them that henceforth they ought no longer
"to seal and enclose but to reach for the perfect."[82]

The other fragment contained even stronger evidence that
Nespitzer was seeking to readjust Hut's apocalyptic schemata to the
changed circumstances. He requested prayers on his behalf that God
might reveal to him "who the four angels" were. According to Matthew

24:31 and Isaiah 11:12 they were sent out to gather the elect from the four corners of the earth. As we will see, Augustin Bader eventually identified them with his four most trusted disciples.[83] Whether Nespitzer ever received the illumination he prayed for is unclear. The sources are also silent about his success in Basel. In all probability he got no further than Strassburg. Here he was temporarily imprisoned early in 1529 and then released after recanting.[84] One further imprisonment in Alterlangen cured him of his Anabaptist beliefs. By June 1529 he was working as a linen weaver in Leutershausen. Here he was arrested once more during June 1530. At that point he claimed to have had no further contact with Anabaptists since the spring of 1529. He also maintained that he had given up Hut's chiliasm shortly after the latter's predictions failed to come true.[85] He had re-entered society hoping to forget his Anabaptist past.

For some of the early Anabaptists the road from disillusionment to normality was more difficult. A remnant of Hut's followers in the area of Uttenreuth, including the veterans Marx and Hans Maier, eventually ended among the wife-swapping Dreamers. Both Marx and Hans were imprisoned and disavowed their Anabaptist beliefs in 1530.[86] One year later they were compromised by the Dreamers.[87] Even the authorities recognized the Dreamers as a new permutation not to be equated with the Anabaptism which itself had undergone a greater Swiss Brethren orientation.[88]

Yet the teachings of the Dreamers cannot be simply written off as the product of "psychopathic minds," and, therefore, left unrelated to early South German Anabaptism.[89] Under the pressure of persecution they dissociated themselves from the practice of rebaptism, but they amplified Hut's views on dreams and direct revelations.[90] Even the unconventional marriage relationships which surfaced during their trial had antecedents in Hut's early movement. Jörg Volck, one of Hut's earliest and most active converts, had taken a second wife when his first lady refused to embrace Anabaptism and follow him on his missionary journeys. Together with others he had seriously proposed polygamy at the Martyrs' Synod. It appears, therefore, not farfetched to conclude that the Dreamers represented an understandable variation of Hut's movement caught in the process of disintegration. Driven by circumstances—persecution and the failure of Hut's predictions—they clung to those strains of Hut's legacy which permitted their escape into fantasy. We can now turn to Augustin Bader whose bizarre career illustrates a similar phenomenon.

B. Augustin Bader, from Anabaptist *Vorsteher* to
Viceroy of the Messiah

Augustin Bader's development, when examined in the context of general disintegration following the failure of Hut's predictions, appears much less of a deviation from early South German Anabaptism than has generally been accepted. The salutary neglect with which Bader has been treated by Anabaptist scholars is, therefore, not altogether justified. Particularly during his early stage Bader was by no means a marginal figure. Baptised by Jacob Gross, and arrested in the wake of Hut's trial, he belonged to those who on October 19, 1527, recanted their Anabaptism and were permitted to remain in the city.[91] One week earlier the city council with much fanfare published a decree forbidding private meetings.

No sooner was Bader released than he sat down with twenty likeminded brethren to celebrate the Lord's Supper.[92] His zeal brought about his election as Vorsteher.[93] From then on he exercised the right to baptise, and his name reappears repeatedly in the confessions of Augsburg Anabaptists. Among his more notable converts was Franz Preuning (Breuning), the son of the poet-weaver who had preached three decades earlier from a tree. Another of his converts, Blasie Daniel, was to be elected Vorsteher under Bader's own watchful eyes. In fact, Bader figured prominently at most of the meetings held in the aftermath of the massive arrests in the fall of 1527.[94]

Some time during December or early January Franz Breuning was arrested and Bader's activity must have come to the attention of the authorities. Breuning was exiled on January 20, 1528.[95] On February 25 the city guards smashed their way into Bader's house, but were unable to discover his secret compartment.[96] Why such a belated attempt to arrest him? Had Bader been absent during January? Around Christmas he was still active in Augsburg, but the sources are silent about his activity during January. Three of those present during the last documented meeting in 1527 left Augsburg shortly thereafter.[97] During late December and January Schachner was baptising in the circles formerly frequented by Bader.[98] Could Bader have been the visionary letter writer from Moravia against whom Rhegius polemicized? We will never know with certainty. He later boasted of having been in Nuremberg, Strassburg, Switzerland, and Moravia. His presence in those areas with the exception of Moravia can be verified.[99] In any case, it is certain that Bader very early showed signs of following Hut's example in claiming special revelations and a prophetic status for himself.[100]

Bader was one of the Anabaptists who showed keen interest in Hut's apocalyptic expectations. On February 2 he met with other leaders in Göggingen near Augsburg and discussed Hut's seven judgments. Their host, who was serving them wine, was not allowed to participate in the discussion since these secrets were "not for the weak."[101] Bader then returned to Augsburg, where the authorities failed to apprehend him on February 25.[102] Shortly thereafter he visited the exiled Hans Langenmantel in Leittersheim and requested a copy of either Hut's *Little Book of Mission (Missionsbüchlein)* or his concordance of the seven judgments.[103] Hermann Anwalt, Langenmantel's servant who made copies for several interested persons, later testified that they did not give out Hut's secrets indiscriminately. In fact, both Anwalt and Langenmantel assured their interrogators that they themselves had seen and heard Hut's eschatological teaching only after they had been baptised. Both obviously felt uncomfortable about some of its contents. They tried to convince the interrogators that they always understood the predicted judgment to be the work of angels. Five of the more incriminating points in question read:

(1) Do not damage the earth until we have sealed the co-servants of our God on their foreheads Rev. 7.
(2) Sign my people with a sign on their foreheads. Ezk. 14.
(3) Those who do not have the sign will be killed by the angel. Ex. 14.
(4) Those who do not have the sign will be punished and will suffer. Rev. 9.
(5) Those who do not have the sign, you shall strangle without sparing any, including all women and children. Ezk. 9.[104]

Besides Bader, Anwalt implicated several others as having obtained knowledge of Hut's apocalyptic teachings, among them Gall Vischer, who was singled out as particularly knowledgeable about Hut's "little book."[105] This is not surprising. Vischer, who had been appointed treasurer, was to be Bader's faithful companion to the bitter end.[106] His home had been one of the earliest meeting places of Hut's followers and Hut performed some of his earliest baptisms there. It was in Vischer's house that Hut upon his return from Austria clashed with those rejecting his prophetic insights. Bader's and Vischer's fondness for Hut's eschatology would suggest that they were not among the dissenters.[107]

Some time in March 1528 Bader and Vischer visited Kaufbeuren. The Anabaptists there had requested a Vorsteher from Augsburg to teach them. Unfortunately the sources permit no insights into Bader's teachings at this point. He later claimed that they had taught, among other matters, the community of all things.[108] He also supervised the appointment of two Vorsteher and the election of two treasurers, thus giving the group a congregational organization. One of the newly appointed Vorsteher in turn baptised forty others. Soon the city council of Kaufbeuren received notice of dangerous Anabaptist strength in the city. Bader and Vischer departed just before mass arrests were made. Five of the leaders—the two Vorsteher, the two treasurers, and Bader's host—were beheaded on May 13, 1528.[109]

Meanwhile Bader and Vischer secretly returned to Augsburg. Here Bader participated in the election of the two Vorsteher and their instruction at the council of April 5. Three days later he and Vischer were on their way once more "to comfort and proclaim the Word to the Gemeinden abroad."[110] When Bader returned to Augsburg some time in June, conditions had changed. The execution of Leupold and the expulsion of Nespitzer and a host of lesser Anabaptists had broken the Anabaptist movement in Augsburg. But the expected punishment of the godless Obrigkeit tarried. However, Bader, who probably from the beginning stood for a popularized apocalypticism among Hut's followers, continued to speak of the imminent judgment.[111]

His first recorded visions come from this period. In one of them he saw Christ with His five wounds as a "mighty strong man" dressed in an overcoat. Bader revealed the extraordinary vision of the dressed Christ to two others, one of whom began to dance with joy. In another vision Bader saw two Christs, one ascending into heaven, the other descending to earth and then disappearing. In a third vision Moses appeared to him at night, took him by the hand and led him and his followers singing and dancing into the Red Sea. When the water reached his knees, Bader grabbed two stones, lifted them above himself, but then awoke back in Augsburg.[112] While the significance of these visions is no longer clear, if it ever was, it is obvious that they later enhanced Bader's standing in the eyes of other disillusioned Anabaptists. It appears Bader was accentuating one element of the Müntzer-Hut tradition, and moving in the same general direction as the Dreamers mentioned above. He soon found followers willing to acclaim him a new prophet in whom the spirit of Elijah was active.[113]

Bader did not suddenly fall from grace. He represented a legitimate strain in Hut's tradition, and was one of the few among Hut's disciples who with much prayer and searching of heart attempted an updating of the fallen leader's eschatological teachings.[114] One month after Plener and Schachner shut down operations near Augsburg, Bader called for a conference of Anabaptists to meet with him in a hayloft at Schönberg between Esslingen and Strassburg.[115] Only sixteen or seventeen persons attended. Among them were Bader's stalwart friend, Gall Vischer, and a certain Oswald Leber, who was to exercise a considerable influence on Bader's further development.

In all probability Leber was introduced to Bader by another participant, Ulrich Trechsel. Trechsel had been one of the messengers sent by Hut to Worms. He settled in Strassburg from whence he attended the conference in Schönberg.[116] On the agenda was a re-evaluation of the teaching concerning baptism, the ban and the Lord's Supper. Bader announced to those present that the time to baptise and teach was over.[117] His explanation was a reversal of Hut's mystical doctrine of baptism. He equated suffering itself with baptism. Water baptism had been an outer witness to baptism in suffering and to true spiritual baptism. Bader now built the tripartite theory of baptism into an externalized chronological sequence. Water baptism had been the signal symbolising the general tribulation to fall upon Christ's true disciples. All those who suffered during this period of tribulation were experiencing true spiritual baptism of which the water had been an outer symbol. Thus Bader achieved the negation of outer baptism by replacing the sign of water with suffering.[118]

The Lord's Supper was given a similar tripartite division. Its substance remained natural elements, its reality signified the washing away of sins, and its purpose lay in the remembrance of Christ's suffering.[119] In all probability Bader now argued for discontinuing the Lord's Supper, since a higher historical stage had been reached. How Bader explained the ban is no longer clear. He claimed later that during the perfect stage all evildoers would be banned and readmitted only after they had undergone suffering. Those who refused to submit to the new order would be banned with the sword.[120] Besides discussing baptism, the ban and the Lord's Supper, Bader also hinted at new revelations concerning the future. But God did not yet want them disclosed to others. In all probability God's future plan was not entirely clear to him either. Revelations were coming bit by bit as Bader prayed often for divine illumination.[121] Still, some of those present were unwilling to accept Bader's new insights and boasts of special revelation. Joachim Fleiner, who later suffered a martyr's death and was only fifteen or sixteen years of age at the time, brought upon himself Bader's disfavour by challenging some of his proposals. Fleiner left the conference one day later, detecting "a spirit of arrogance" in Bader.[122]

This must have been the spirit in which Bader arrived a few months later to discuss the problems of Anabaptism in Switzerland. As noted earlier, Nespitzer had announced similar intentions to counsel with leaders in Basel. Two of Bader's followers temporarily settled there[123] and may have been the source of Bullinger's description of the *Augustiner Tauffbrüder*. According to Bullinger, their teaching reflected that of Hut with regard to dreams and visions, but they held some other strange opinions. "God had closed heaven once more and . . . would keep everyone safe in his particular place."[124] Whether these were teachings of Bader's disciples or not, Bader's inflated sense of mission was given a strong rebuff by the less futuristic Swiss Brethren whom he met around Christmas 1528 in Teufen in Appenzell. When his appeal to special visions and revelations did not have the desired effect, Bader rose and declared that those present could not discern the Spirit of God.[125] The final result was mutual excommunication,[126] leading to Bader's departure and his break with the Anabaptists.[127]

From Switzerland the rejected prophet returned to his home area. Here he and four of his closest followers set up a commune near Westerstetten. With him was the aging but irrepressible Gall Vischer, the most generous contributor to the common fund. Bader was soon to spend the money as if expecting windfall profits. Vischer's wife, who had suffered two arrests for her Anabaptist beliefs, was found wanting for the new experiment and sent back to Augsburg. In all, the commune consisted of five men, three women, and eight children.[128]

The most significant member of Bader's entourage was doubtless Oswald Leber. Leber, formerly trained as a priest, was another veteran of the Peasants' War.[129] After the collapse of the uprising he had moved to Worms. Here he must have come into contact with Anabaptists around Denck, Kautz, and Hätzer. Unlike some of Bader's other followers he retained his faith in adult baptism until his death.[130] The persecution that set in after the expulsion of Kautz affected him also. Before joining Bader's commune he had settled in Schönberg, the place of Bader's last conference. Leber appeared to have taken an extra draught from Denck's and Hätzer's mysticism. His jailor later reported that Leber, the most learned of the prisoners, was able to speak so eloquently about the inner and the outer and the *Ordnung gottes* that he as a poor uneducated layman was unable to follow.[131] At the same time Leber proved an ardent student of biblical prophecy. Benefiting greatly from the insights of Jewish scholars in Worms, he was able to provide some new answers for the searching Bader. As Bader related:

> Oswald, the minister, had given him much instruction and strengthened him in his beliefs regarding the revolution (*Veränderung*), because the Jew at Worms instructed him about it in Hebrew. One of the Jews had travelled to Jerusalem. . . . The same informed Oswald in detail about the revolution, and told him that the revolution would take place within the year. He had gone to Jerusalem for this purpose and requested that Oswald join him, indicating to him in what house and in which street he might find him there.[132]

It is understandable that some of the homeless veterans of the peasants' uprising felt an affinity to the Jews. The Jewish community was experiencing new anti-Semitic pressures. The Spanish expulsion of 1492 heightened apocalyptical expectations which mingled with a strong mystical tendency. In South Germany Jews were accused of collusion with the Turk.[133] Hubmaier during his early ministry had led a movement that expelled them from Regensburg. In 1524 Phillip of Hesse ordered the expulsion of the Jews from his territories.[134] Under these circumstances it was not surprising that messianic hopes were revived, and that some expected the Messiah in 1530.[135]

Under Leber's tutoring Bader began an intensive reexamination of biblical prophecy. The Old Testament apocryphal books and the Book of Ezra were his favourites. Bader's landlady in Westerstetten testified that he studied day and night and thought more of Jewish practise than of the Christian faith. Her husband made similar observations. Bader and his colleagues no longer worshiped Christ but only God.[136] Bader and his friends were obviously holding opinions which the Nicolsburg Articles had earlier attributed to Hut and his followers. Christ had been a prophet or one of the many incarnations of God's Word. Jewish predictions, in which astrological calculations may have played a part,[137] now led Bader to await the end-time Messiah before 1530.[138] He arrived just in the nick of time.

Sabina Bader gave birth to a son late in 1529. It was not a virgin birth but a star was seen standing above the shack which Bader had made his headquarters. Rumours spread that wonderful things would be heard of this child, things not heard since the days of Christ. He would correct all wrongdoings (*misbrauch*) within three years.[139] Leber provided the theological rationalization for the new incarnation. The child was not God's Son but a symbol of the Son of God, who once before "through His child Christ had accomplished much on earth."[140] The physical messiah was really only the external manifestation of the inner Christ.[141]

After the successful arrival of the messiah, Bader made contact with the Jewish community announcing to them parts of the great changes about to begin.[142] Some of the ideas of Hut surfaced again in these expectations. The Turk would invade sometime early in 1530, destroy both the secular and religious authorities, and rule outwardly while sin ruled the hearts of men inwardly.[143] A chosen few who accepted the message of the prophet (Bader) would escape.[144]

After 2½ years the Turk would realize that another people existed who had refused to bow their knee before him. At that point, so Leber related in epic biblical language, God, as of old, would arise and intervene on behalf of His people. Hail, thunder, and lightning would break the Turkish power. Bader would then in the name of his son declare the new order, ushering in a thousand years of peace and prosperity. The new order would be one of social equality and justice. Payment of interest, the tithe, all rents—even the monetary system itself—would be abolished. All means of production would be held in common, and all men would engage in productive labour. All social distinctions would cease. Capital punishment would be abolished, and even the natural aging process and death would be less painful.[145]

The new political structure was to embody the representative principle. In all districts the congregations would elect their representatives, who in turn were to elect the king God would reveal to them. The king would appoint twelve assistants with whom he would set up an itinerant court. It would be the duty of each district to provide for the king's court when in its territory.[146] Bader obviously believed himself and his descendants to be cut out for the royal dignity, but he assured his interrogators at his trial that he would have submitted to the general will and the election process.[147] Religiously the new order was to do away with the distinction between laity and clergy. The veneration of saints would be discontinued and no sacred places recognized. All outer ceremonies, including the sacraments, would become unnecessary, for Christ would rule directly in the hearts of all. Eventually a truly spiritual kingdom would result.[148] After the thousand years the godless would once more gain the upper hand. Shortly thereafter the glorified Christ would return in final judgment. The exact date had not yet been revealed.[149]

Bader's utopian ideas of the future were, no doubt, part of the great millennialist tradition, and may have absorbed some elements of Joachimism. This is evident from Bader's insistence that the millenniun would be a spiritual kingdom during which Christ revealed divine truths spiritually as He formerly had revealed them physically.[150]

As noted earlier, Bader expected the spiritualizing process to be a gradual one that would involve some reeducating. To help him in this task he designed some visual aids in the shape of three uniforms illustrating the three stages in the believer's life. The first of these, a simple gray-brown garment without a lining, represented the creaturely life. It was to be worn by Oswald Leber, the most eloquent and learned in worldly matters. It was assumed that he would prove most effective in convincing those still totally absorbed with the creaturely. A second uniform of brown and red, representing the middle stage between the creaturely life and the perfect, was to be worn by Gastel Miller. His task was to instruct those in the transitional stage. The last and most impressive, as well as most expensive, of the uniforms represented the perfect spiritual stage.[151] It was to be worn by Bader himself. In a piece of allegorical exegesis he compared the three stages to the patriarchs of old— in reversed chronological order—Jacob typical of the creaturely life, Isaac of the transitional stage, and Abraham of the perfect stage.[152]

Meanwhile, Bader's visions had become contagious. The aging Vischer was now blessed by visions of his own. He saw the roof opening and a golden crown and sceptre descending and remaining suspended above Bader. The vision disappeared when he called the others. However, Bader recognized its significance almost immediately, declaring it to be a "great thing."[153] God wanted him to fill in as regent for the newborn messiah. He ordered the symbols made after the heavenly pattern revealed to Vischer. To the sceptre and the crown were added a gilded sword, a knife, a chain, a canopy embroidered with stars, and a ring with the inscription, "I have made an eternal covenant with you." The royal equipment was to be passed on to Bader's posterity. It must have been fortuitous that the vision occurred to Vischer, the most generous contributor to the messianic budget, for the gear reduced the common fund by over half. With the collection of symbols complete, Bader staged a full dress rehearsal. His five-year-old son substituted for the six-month-old messiah, who was still incapable of supporting the crown. Bader sat next to him, accepting the homage of his followers who now addressed him as lord.[154]

At this stage the preparations for the millennium were crudely interrupted. On January 16, 1530, Bader and his comrades were arrested.[155] His plans had been to send out the four disciples around Easter of that year and then make his entrance wherever the response would be most favourable to their message.[156] Between Easter and Pentecost he expected another Peasants' War. Once imprisoned, he challenged his jailors to keep him until Pentecost. If his predictions would fail he would be willing to suffer any punishment.[157] Unfortunately (or fortunately, one might say, for his state of mind), the authorities did not heed his request. He was executed on March 30, 1530, convinced that his predictions would come true.[158] The young messiah and his mother proved to be more fortunate, outliving the predicted disaster. The attractive Sabina escaped at the time of the arrest through questionable application of her feminine charms. Within a week she was requesting to be reunited with her five children, and a few weeks later she asked permission to return to Augsburg. When the request was turned down, she moved to Strassburg.[159] Here she left such a favourable impression on Wolfgang Capito that, had Martin Bucer not restrained him, he would have become the stepfather of the messiah. With the recommendations of both Capito and Bucer, Sabina was able to return to Augsburg on October 24, 1531.[160]

Sabina Bader's return closed the chapter of early Augsburg Anabaptism which began with the arrest of Hut in the fall of 1527. Sabina, we recall, had been expelled from Augsburg a few days after Hut's arrest.[161] When she returned four years later, the original Anabaptist movement largely inspired by Hut's mystical and apocalyptical message had disintegrated or evolved into a more sectarian form. The majority of early leaders in the area who had not suffered martyrdom had recanted, among them the influential Nespitzer, Dachser, Salminger, Gross, Schachner, and, as we will see later, the Freisleben brothers, Entfelder, Bünderlin, and Kautz. The spiritual odyssey of Bader himself was not an isolated phenomenon. The members of the Dreamers' sect escaped similarly into fantasy. Both Bader and the Dreamers were manifestations of the process of disintegration of early South German Anabaptism. Next to persecution the major single factor contributing to that disintegration was the failure of Hut's apocalyptic schedule. The latter, as the millennial hopes of Bader once more illustrate, had been largely inspired by social revolutionary impulses. Behind the facade of Hut's moderate "interim political ethic" stood primarily social revolutionary expectations. Bader's spiritualistic utopia implied a social and political revolution every bit as radical as the revolution hoped for earlier by Müntzer or the one initiated four years later by Jan of Leyden.

6

THE EVOLUTION OF
EVANGELICAL SECTARIAN ANABAPTISM

Through persecution, defections, and escape into fantasy Hut's movement in Swabia and Franconia had practically disappeared by 1530. However, it would be historically inaccurate to limit Hut's legacy to the disillusioned, the Dreamers, and the messianic prophet Augustin Bader.

As we noticed earlier, Hut's impact extended into Moravia and Austria, where he left a strong influence on the two early martyrs, Schiemer and Schlaffer, whose deaths became part of the martyr tradition with which both the later Hutterites and Pilgramites identified. The question that remains to be examined is to what extent this later tradition which ran from Schiemer to Pilgram Marpeck and from Brandhuber to Jacob Hutter and Peter Riedemann marked a continuation of Hut's form of Anabaptism. Or was there another tradition which preceded Hut in Austria that was to be more consequential for the Hutterites and the Marpeck circle?

Again and again scholars expressed the opinion that Anabaptists— even whole congregations—existed before Hut entered the Austrian territories.[1] The idea of actual congregations existing prior to Hut's arrival has now been largely abandoned. Hut has been given credit by many for having introduced Anabaptism to Austria, particularly to the Tyrol.[2] Unfortunately, the latest edition of Austrian *Täuferakten* has provided no further clues with regard to the genesis of Austrian Anabaptism.[3]

However, evidence does exist that individual radicals were proselytising prior to Hut's activity in those areas. By January 2, 1527,

Archduke Ferdinand had been notified of itinerant "corner preachers" (*Winkelprediger*) in his territories. A certain Wölfl, interrogated on January 19, 1527, died later as a Hutterite martyr. Ferdinand's reaction suggests that the new ideas were introduced by strangers from other territories.[4] It is possible that Swiss Anabaptists were among them. Müntzer's adherents also infiltrated the area.[5]

In Austria as in other areas the appearance of Anabaptism shortly after the brutal defeat of the peasants' rebellion would suggest that a social and historical relationship existed between the two movements. Several participants in the rebellion led by Michael Gaismaier later resurfaced as Anabaptists. Among them were Hans Bünderlin (Vischer), (Hans) Gasser, and Friedrich Brandburger, one of Jacob Hutter's travelling companions.[6] At least for some Anabaptists pacifism became a binding religious conviction only when open rebellion was no longer feasible. The existence of contacts between those who had been sympathetic to the rebels could help to explain the quick growth of Anabaptism in the area.

Luther's teachings, too, penetrated into Austria and helped to prepare the exodus from the Roman Catholic fold. Luther's followers were at first difficult to distinguish from the other radicals. One of those active for Luther's gospel was Dr. Jacob Strauss, who contributed eighteen different pieces of literature to the Reformation cause.[7] The Austrian territories profiting from his ministry later proved extremely receptive to Schiemer's and Schlaffer's message.[8]

Another representative of Lutheranism in Austria was Michael Stiefel, a renegade monk from Esslingen. Stiefel, although he remained a Lutheran, shared Hut's preoccupation with the Apocalypse. He identified Luther as the angel of Revelation 14. Later in 1533, as a Lutheran pastor, he caused a sensation when he sold his books and household goods and encouraged his parishioners to do likewise because the end was in sight. When the expected return of the Lord tarried, his impoverished followers tore him out of the pulpit and led him bound to Wittenberg. However, the failure of his predictions, which would have been sufficient to ruin a disreputable Anabaptist, did not irreparably damage Stiefel in the eyes of Luther. He soon overcame his "*kleine Anfechtlein*" and with Luther's favour remained in the ministry, eventually moving to the more suitable calling of professor of mathematics at the University of Jena.[9]

While in Austria Stiefel had met two exiles from Wels who appeared to be Catholics but were really sacramentarians. It has been argued that these were Christoph Eleutherobios and Leonhard Freisleben, who at the time served as schoolteachers in Wels and nearby Linz respectively.[10] Both were drawn into the Anabaptist movement and their subsequent careers illustrate the transitional character of early South German and Austrian Anabaptism.

In 1523 Leonhard Freisleben helped to draw up a church order for the city of Elbogen.[11] It appears that Leonhard became involved in the local issues aroused by the Reformation. Among those clamouring for more radical reforms was Wolfgang Rappolt, who in 1525 published an open letter to his followers in Elbogen.[12] Rappolt represented a radical Lutheranism similar to that of Stiefel. He had fled because of Catholic reaction to his message. The major issue between him and his Catholic opponents, according to Rappolt, hinged on the question of authority. The "Romanists" attempted to extend the inspiration of Scripture to church traditions. To this he could not agree.[13]

It is possible that Leonhard Freisleben sided with the Lutherans during this debate, for his second literary effort was a translation of one of Johannes Bugenhagen's sermons. This translation of Bugenhagen's sermon has been hailed as the first Austrian publication defending Luther's position.[14] In the sharply polemical introduction Leonhard attacked the scholastic tradition, which utilized Aristotle rather than Scripture in support of its doctrines, as guilty of the sin against the Holy Ghost. He also manifested strong anticlerical tendencies.[15] Whether or not this made him a full-fledged Lutheran is difficult to judge. His brother Christoph's relation to the Reformation remains still more obscure, as does the first contact of the two brothers with Anabaptism. Several leaders were to emerge from Linz, among them Wolfgang Brandhuber and Hans Bünderlin. The latter, a native of Linz, may have been the first Anabaptist in the area.[16] The Freislebens, Ambrosius Spittelmaier, and others were baptised by Hut in Linz some time during the summer of 1527.[17]

No sooner had the two brothers embraced Anabaptism than official persecution began in earnest. By July 29, 1527, Ferdinand was in the possession of Hubmaier's preliminary confession. Through it he must have learned of Hut's activity in his territories, for a few days later Balthasar Thanrädl, his majesty's representative near Freistadt, was instructed to search out Hut and his followers. Thanrädl discovered that Hut had been in Freistadt and had made converts there. However, the city government proved uncooperative until Ferdinand threatened it with severe punishment. Not until August 22 were six of Hut's followers arrested.[18] In the meantime Hut had moved on to Augsburg. The subsequent trial in Freistadt is of historical interest because the six accused claimed to understand the "sign" they had received from Hut not as baptism but as a pledge to moral improvement of their lives. They had heard nothing unbecoming from Hut, only the gospel of all creatures. To underline the harmlessness of their teachings they submitted a copy of Hut's original *Of the Mystery of Baptism*.[19] All six eventually recanted and returned to the mother church. However, their arrests provoked panic among Hut's other followers in the area.

Sometime during September the Freislebens left Linz and moved up the Danube. By September 29, Christoph was baptizing in Passau.[20] From Passau they moved to Regensburg. A host of Anabaptist visitors were active in Regensburg during the fall and early winter of 1527. Among the more significant ones were Hätzer, Glaidt, Schlaffer, Brandhuber, and Burkhart Braun. A very interesting pattern now began to unfold. Anabaptist leaders travelling in opposite directions exchanged information on possible contacts and sent instructions to their converts. Hans Stiglitz, Jr., baptised by Christoph in Passau, now received news from Regensburg that he had been appointed Vorsteher and authorized to baptise. Stiglitz promptly turned missionary and baptised around fifty new converts in the Freislebens' home area of Wels and Linz.[21]

Early in November Leonhard and several other Austrian refugees living with him were arrested in Regensburg. His brother Christoph had moved on earlier. The confessions dated November 15, 1527, are the only source permitting a glimpse into Leonhard's teachings at this time. He and his friends, as we suggested earlier and as his confession substantiates, had left Linz because of persecution. His fellow traveller, Hans Schuster, testified that as long as he had gambled and sworn he had remained unmolested in Linz. As soon as he had committed himself to God and taken up the cross of discipleship he had become undesirable. Of particular interest is the fact that Leonhard Freisleben understood the seal not like those in Freistadt but as adult baptism by affusion.[22] There is not the slightest evidence that Leonhard and his companions were driven by Hut's chiliasm. On the contrary, indications suggest that in these converts of Hut we find the beginning of a more sober, realistic Anabaptism concerned less with eschatology than with ethics.[23] Yet, as the Freisleben brothers' subsequent movements indicate, it is almost impossible to separate these followers of Hut from those fired by apocalyptical enthusiasm.

Leonhard's imprisonment in Regensburg left little visible effect on his convictions. He resumed his proselytising efforts one day after expulsion from the city.[24] Among his new converts was Augustin Würzlburger. Würzlburger's career as an Anabaptist leader once again illustrates the pattern we noted above. No sooner had Leonhard moved than Burkhart Braun, travelling in the opposite direction, stopped to visit Würzlburger.[25] Three months later a messenger from Augsburg announced that either Würzlburger or a certain Hans, formerly schoolmaster in Weiden, should assume the office of apostle. The message had, no doubt, come through Peter Ringmacher. Leonhard participated with Bader, Leupold, and Nespitzer at the council in Augsburg where Ringmacher received his instructions and was sent to Regensburg. Since neither Hans nor Würzlburger had hitherto felt a special calling to the full-time ministry, they drew lots to determine who was to assume the new responsibility. The lot fell on the unfortunate Würzlburger.[26] Reluctant but obedient he began to evangelize among his friends. Besides defending believer's baptism he denied the real presence of Christ in the elements, forbade his converts attendance at Mass, and the removal of their hats in honour of the saints. He also encouraged them to collect a common fund for the needy among them and to exercise the ban against those not living in conformity with Christ. Würzlburger's message therefore was explicitly separatist. Anabaptism, as represented by him, was indeed becoming overtly sectarian. Würzlburger, although he had been exposed to elements of Hut's gospel of all creatures, was not a revolutionary. He aimed his teaching primarily at practical piety, hardly deserving the capital punishment to which he fell victim.[27]

After April 1528 Leonhard Freisleben disappeared from the Anabaptist sources. His brother Christoph had appeared several months earlier in Esslingen.[28] Esslingen, at the crossroads between Augsburg, Strassburg, and Worms, had its quota of Reformation radicalism. It had been the home of Stiefel, the Lutheran apocalypticist. Late in 1527 and early in 1528 rumours spread in Esslingen that the Anabaptists were secretly plotting the overthrow of the established authorities. An army, seven hundred strong, would meet in or near Reutlingen. These rumours originated with Hans Zuber who, his Anabaptist brother-in-law commented, had always been given to overeating and overdrinking.[29] Social grievances mixed in Esslingen with religious aspirations. One of the predictions making its rounds told that the rich would dump their silver on the streets some time in 1528. It was said to be the one biblical prophecy yet unfulfilled.[30]

Only slowly as the Anabaptists in the area matured did the overtly social and revolutionary aspirations give way to a more confessional phase of Anabaptism. Even then, traces of Hut's influence survived. When Leonhart Lutz, the main pillar of the Anabaptist congregation in Esslingen, was forced to flee early in January 1528, he comforted those who remained behind with a revelation granted to "a dear sister" that the persecution of God's faithful would last only ten weeks and thirteen days. Two weeks after Easter the tables would be turned on the godless. The Son of Man would then appear and punish those who had not heeded His Word and law. Like so many other early South German Anabaptist leaders, Lutz later defected when the predicted moment passed uneventfully.[31]

Yet charismatic elements survived as late as 1529. At one of the meetings two strangers preaching in the area behaved in such a peculiar manner that one of the less heavenly – minded brethren asked himself, "God, where will this end?"[32] One of the local youth tried to convince other members of the community that Christ had been a human being just like them. All those who did the will of God were true sons of God. Christ had been merely a prophet. The Jews, he told them, were still God's chosen people and their faith was better than that of institutionalized Christianity.[33] Similar ideas had been repeatedly expressed within early South German Anabaptism and were formulated at the time by Augustin Bader.

However, such unorthodox manifestations as these do not adequately summarize the type of Anabaptism practised in Esslingen. It would be historically inaccurate to describe all Anabaptists in the area as full disciples of Hans Hut. This remains true for Christoph Freisleben also, even though he "proclaimed the Day of the Lord" in Esslingen.[34] Christoph arrived, as we noted earlier, in the company of Hans Leupold from Augsburg. Leupold belonged to a faction critical of Hut's apocalypticism.[35]

In Esslingen Christoph joined the efforts of the veteran Anabaptist Wilhelm Reublin.[36] The effect of these two on the Esslingen congregation has been preserved for us by an account given in 1529.

> In the beginning came one of the learned of this faith to us. He supported his teachings mightily with the Scriptures: how until now the right faith no longer existed; how it had been totally obscured through the papacy and how now the Word of God shines forth again brightly; how they should believe this Gospel of Christ; and how they ought to be baptized upon the confession of their

faith. . . . Thereupon we stood still for more than half a year and searched the Scriptures which he showed to us. Meanwhile another, a learned man from Linz, arrived. He proclaimed this teaching even more adamantly and more seriously than the first. And he [taught us] that this was the right faith and baptism which a true Christian should and must confess, because without this faith and baptism no man can be saved, etc. For the pope's pedobaptism had no basis in Scripture. . . . Therefore, we should repent and be baptized, for the Day of the Lord was at hand.[37]

Fortunately, we can compare this description of Christoph's teachings with one of his treatises originating in his controversy with the representatives of Lutheranism. When forced to leave Esslingen in late 1527 or early 1528[38] Christoph took the manuscript north and published it under the title *On the Genuine Baptism of John, Christ and the Apostles.*[39] The printer was a former assistant of Peter Schofferl, the publisher of Denck's and Hätzer's works in Worms.[40] In a letter addressed to the Esslingen Anabaptist leader, Leonhart Lutz, Freisleben credited Reublin with having strongly influenced the tract. He included one exemplar and begged Lutz to send news to those in Augsburg that more copies could be obtained in Frankfurt.[41]

Reublin's influence at this stage was in the direction of the Swiss Brethren. He himself had been strongly impressed by Michael Sattler's martyrdom a few months earlier. Christoph Freisleben's tract gives evidence to this effect. The composition of *On the Genuine Baptism* demonstrated familiarity with *On Distinguishing Scripture*, a publication attributed to Sattler.[42] In that booklet "Sattler" had reopened the question of pedobaptism. Scripture was to serve as the plumb line. If pedobaptism could be substantiated from Scripture it was to be retained; if not, it should be discarded. A *tour de force* through Scripture demonstrated the divinely ordained order: (1) teach, (2) hear, (3) believe, (4) baptise, (5) receive the Spirit, and (6) produce good works. In the supporting arguments appeared practically all the passages utilized by Christoph Freisleben in 1528. Of particular interest was the contention of "Sattler" that Noah's flood rather than circumcision foreshadowed baptism. Circumcision had been suspended during the forty years of wandering in the wilderness and again during the Babylonian captivity. It was finally abolished by the prophets as unnecessary.[43] It could, therefore, not serve as a symbol of baptism. "Sattler" closed with a call to repentance because Christ was about to separate the wheat from the chaff.

Freisleben's production, which has received scant attention in Anabaptist literature,[44] went well beyond the earlier work attributed to Sattler. It proved to be one of the more significant public statements coming out of early South German and Austrian Anabaptism. Christoph was particularly thorough in refuting pedobaptism as the practice of Antichrist. He drew both on his knowledge of church history and the Scriptures to castigate the unholy practice. The custom had evolved because Tertullian, Cyprian, and Augustine had placed too much emphasis on the importance of outer baptism. Because of the exaggerated significance attributed to the outer act, children with poor health were baptised before adulthood lest they lose this blessing by premature death. Eventually it became customary to baptise all children as soon as they could recite the Lord's Prayer and give their names. By the year 862 under Pope Nicolas pedobaptism had become the officially sanctioned norm. Things had now gone so far that baptism was performed before the newborn had fully emerged from the mother's womb.[45]

One evil led to another. Unchristian and superstitious rites and practices became associated with pedobaptism.

> The Antichrist has to salt the child, give it the sign of the cross, spit on it, soil it with saliva, open its ears, anoint it with oil, dress it in a particular gown, tie it with money, pawn or pledge it, drink to it and many more fantasies.[46]

Next the idea of godparents had to be invented. Someone else had to assume responsibility for the child's faith. Thus faith became an impersonal thing. Finally God's order of "hear, understand, and believe" had been totally perverted. Pedobaptism, therefore, marked not the entrance into Christ's sheepfold but into the kingdom of Antichrist. The church's loss of moral purity was a logical consequence of this unscriptural practice. It had become difficult to retain the proper discipline in an institution which accepted members as babes and *en masse*. Moreover, fallacious doctrines followed. For instance, the lagging zeal for discipline and moral purity in the adult member was rationalized and partially defended by an appeal to original sin. Human depravity was stressed to a point where innocent children were declared guilty and in need of baptism at the time of birth.[47]

Christoph then turned to the arguments utilized by Catholics and Reformers to support pedobaptism. These included the argument that children were blessed with a sleeping faith, that Christ "suffered the children to come unto Him," and that the apostles baptised whole households. All of these were proven unconvincing. With regard to the latter Christoph remarked that it would also logically follow that the cats and dogs of Christian households were to be baptised. He rejected the appeal to 1 Corinthians 10, which compared baptism to Israel's escape through the Red Sea and in the eyes of traditional churchmen implicitly included children under the symbol of baptism. Freisleben argued that it was incorrect to make inferences about the parts from symbolic statements about the whole, and vice versa. Just because the Bible reported that all of Samaria had received the gospel and had been baptised did not warrant the assumption that children were baptised. The Bible also recorded that the whole church "remained in the apostles' teachings and in the breaking of the bread." However, it was ridiculous to argue that this meant babes were breaking and eating bread.[48]

Christoph also dealt explicitly with the favourite Zwinglian argument which equated baptism with circumcision. The Bible stated that only true believers were the descendants of Abraham. True circumcision was a matter of the heart, not external mechanics. Nevertheless, except on this spiritual plane, equation of baptism and circumcision was ridiculous. Circumcision was limited to males. The apostles never advocated the substitution of baptism for circumcision. Otherwise they would have left specific instructions to baptise children on the eighth day.[49] Thus no scriptural text advocating the baptism of children existed.

On the positive side, adult baptism was explicitly commanded by God, initiated by John the Baptist, taught by Christ, and practised by the apostles. In contrast to circumcision, baptism was the sign of the new spiritual covenant revealed by Christ. Freisleben, therefore, possibly under Reublin's tutoring and Sattler's influence, accepted the Swiss Brethren distinction between the Old and New Testaments. Christ's own baptism illustrated the differences between the old covenant symbolized by circumcision and the new covenant symbolized by adult baptism. Christ, although circumcised eight days after birth, received baptism at the age of thirty. As the descending dove indicated, baptism signified the reception of the Spirit as the seal of the new covenant. The New Testament was, therefore, initiated at Christ's baptism. This raised an exegetical problem with regard to John the Baptist. How could John introduce the sign of the new covenant while being himself still part of the old? Christoph found the solution in the exception granted to the ordained. John the Baptist was an exception. Just as Balaam's ass had through God's omnipotence been granted the power to communicate in human language, so John the Baptist had been miraculously blessed with the seal of the new order before it had become chronologically effective. Thus all Scripture indicated that baptism belonged to the new dispensation. It was intended for adults who "asked questions, repented of their sins, believed and received the Holy Spirit—some before, others after water baptism." Baptism itself "signified a washing from sin, the drowning of the old Adam." It was an outer witness to the inner occurrence of Christ's death, burial, and resurrection, that is, new conduct in the viator.[50]

Apart from the refutation of pedobaptism and the defence of adult baptism Christoph's treatise contained little of theological substance. Much of the rambling argument consisted of polemical outbursts against Antichrist, the "great harlot," and the "evangelical scribes." In particular the latter drew Freisleben's ire. The "evangelical hypocrites" attacked the Catholics only because it brought tangible profits. The average income of Catholic priests was twenty-four *Gulden*. The evangelicals, sitting idly on soft upholstery all week, complained when they received two hundred *Gulden*.[51]

The tract also contained some veiled threats against the host of Antichrist. Those who refused to accept proper baptism—suffering with Christ—would suffer baptism by fire, divine punishment.[52] But these general allusions to pending doom are not sufficient to permit the classification of Christoph as a disciple of Hut in regard to apocalypticism. Similarly, it remains difficult to categorize Freisleben's theology as either mystical or biblicist. The tract contains evidence of both plus traces of humanism. The most that can be concluded is that Freisleben represented an early Austrian Anabaptism akin to that of Dachser, Schlaffer, and Dorfbrunner. This tradition contained elements both of Hut and of Swiss Brethren teachings.[53] Freisleben's polemic against the magisterial Reformers reflects similar theological assumptions with regard to original sin, freedom of the will, etc., to those one finds in the majority of early South German and Austrian Anabaptists. These assumptions were in the final analysis motifs retained from a pre-Reformation heritage. Stiefel's description of the two men from Wels whose sacramentarianism retained a Catholic appearance certainly fitted Christoph, whether or not he had been its original object.

Unfortunately, little is known about Christoph Freisleben's experience during the crucial three years after the completion of his influential tract. In all probability he remained in South Germany and there at firsthand experienced the disintegration and metamorphosis of early South German Anabaptism. It appears that he himself was soon affected by the general disillusionment. His mystical inclinations and humanistic tendencies may have contributed to the process. By April 1531 he was in Augsburg and corresponding with Erasmus.[54] The letter would suggest that his interest had shifted from true baptism to classical literature. Scholars who tend to see Erasmus as a progenitor of Anabaptism[55] should take note that Erasmus' influence appeared to have the opposite effect on Christoph. A similar tendency can be noticed in Bünderlin and Entfelder, who together with Denck came closest to the ideals of Erasmus. Christoph soon returned to the mother church, accepting a position with the Catholic Collegiate of St. Moritz in Augsburg.[56] Correspondence with Schwenckfeld would suggest that an interest in the more mystical elements of early Anabaptism helped to prepare his way back into "the world."[57]

By 1539 Christoph was providing theatrical entertainment in Ingolstadt, which was under the watchful eye of John Eck and therefore a stronghold of "Antichrist."[58] One decade later Christoph's zeal for Anabaptism was even more obviously a thing of the past. In 1547 he rose to the rank of *Syndikus* of the University of Vienna. He now unfolded his literary gifts in the cause of the Catholic Reformation.[59] Reublin, who had exercised such a profound influence on Freisleben's Anabaptist treatise, now followed the example of his former student. Having dedicated the productive years of his life to the establishment of true Christian brotherhoods, he returned to the Catholic church and spent the evening of his earthly existence petitioning Ferdinand of Austria for the restoration of his confiscated worldly possessions.[60]

The fate of Christoph's brother Leonhard remains less certain. It was generally assumed that he followed in his brother's footsteps.[61] However, his marriage and his children would have made it more difficult for him to re-enter a clerical career. In fact, his return to Catholicism is not at all certain. It has been suggested that he assumed a position similar to that of Bünderlin.[62] One of Leonhard's publications of 1532 suggested that he had withdrawn into hiding and, like his brother, was dedicating himself to a study of Erasmus and the Church Fathers. He was now writing about the Word of God in terms similar to Denck and Müntzer. All externals, including the outer Word, were exposed to corruption. Only the internal Word, the "immediate, invisible" connection between man and God, remained beyond all corrupting influences.[63] This immanence theme now identified Leonhard generally with the predominant tendencies of early South German Anabaptism.

Apart from this publication of 1532 we have only one other document which we can attribute with certainty to Leonhard's pen. This was his *An Amusing and Gay Play About Wisdom and Folly in Which Are Included No Unchastity, But Many Good Lessons and Ridiculous Tales*[64] Published in 1550 the pamphlet suggests that Leonhard by that date had followed his brother's example and escaped into the entertainment world. Of his theological views at the time, or of his theological development since 1530, and 1550 writing contains no clues. However, it is possible that we possess one or even two other anonymous documents of Leonhard's authorship.

A tract of 1531 or 1532 had earlier been attributed to the Freisleben brothers. *The Dialogue,* a conversation between a nobleman and his servant, assailed the *Pfaffen* who were ignorant of the true inner Word in terms not heard since Müntzer.[65] They knew nothing of Christ come into the flesh; yes, they had lost Him altogether. They feared the experience of the bitter Christ, yet wanted the sweet benefits of ascending with Him. But he who would not suffer could not reign with Christ.[66] If this treatise was in fact the work of one of the Freisleben brothers, then Leonhard was its author. This would support the thesis that his development was in the direction of Bünderlin.

The problems of authorship of *The Dialogue* are intertwined with those of one further Anabaptist source. This second book, entitled *The Uncovering of the Babylonian Whore,*[67] was written in a spirit reminiscent of Christoph's tract of 1528. The ornamentation of the title page was identical to that of *The Dialogue* discussed above. It contained a double-headed Austrian eagle and a coat of arms with a horizontal bar. The latter was the coat of arms of several Austrian cities and would suggest some connection to Austria. Unfortunately, neither date nor place of publication are given. But it has been tentatively dated as having originated during the same period as *The Dialogue*—some time in the early 1530s.[68]

The few autobiographical hints could describe the experiences of several Anabaptist leaders including Leonhard and Christoph Freisleben. The author had been committed to the man-made ordinances of the church of Rome until his eyes were opened by the new evangelical preachers. He had soon become disillusioned with them also. The polemical vocabulary was reminiscent of Christoph's tract of 1528. So was the methodology. The author had utilized all sorts of writings, including works of church history, to combat the errors of Antichrist. What has so far escaped Anabaptist scholarship is the fact that *The Uncovering of the Babylonian Whore* was printed not only on the same press as *The Dialogue,* but also on the same press as *On Distinguishing Scripture,* attributed to Sattler and mentioned above.[69] Could Reublin have been its author?

The Uncovering of the Babylonian Whore contained echoes of mystical themes which would identify it with early South German Anabaptism. The Christ "in you," the inner Word, was directed against the evangelicals who refused to follow Christ in suffering. Suffering alone—the cross which every viator must bear himself—could liberate man from the flesh and make him a new creature. The evangelicals had preached only half-truths. They had personally refused to shoulder the cross of persecution, seeking protection from the rulers of this world.[70] However, in spite of these polemics, the unknown writer, unlike Hut, explicitly distanced himself from the spirit of vengeance. The spirits of Elijah and of Christ were different.[71] The author also clearly differentiated between Old and New Testament political ethic. The discussion of political ethic contained a unique, proto-Hutterite connection between rejection of the sword of the magistracy and rejection of property.[72]

An overall evaluation would lead to the conclusion that in this document we have a transitional chapter in an evolution from the Anabaptism of Hut to something akin to the later Hutterites. Many of the strains of cross mysticism were now directed towards a more ethically oriented form of Anabaptism. We are probably on safe ground if we detect the influence of Swiss Anabaptism at work in this permutation. Evidence of a similar tendency in some of the Anabaptists loosely associated with Hut has been noticed earlier. These more ethically oriented leaders represent a link between Hut's early movement and later South German and Austrian Anabaptism. Among them we include Dachser, Leupold, Dorfbrunner, Schlaffer, and possibly Schiemer. The influence of the Freisleben brothers, in spite of their later development, contributed in a similar direction. This is illustrated by their impact on their fellow citizen from Linz, Wolfgang Brandhuber.

Although an uneducated seamster,[73] Brandhuber became a leading reorganizer and propagator of Anabaptism in Passau, Linz, Wels, and the Tyrol during 1528-29. Like the Freisleben brothers Brandhuber left Linz because of persecution. In the fall of 1527 he was in Regensburg. From Regensburg he returned to Passau after Dorfbrunner's martyrdom there. He won back the faltering and tried to rebuild the movement. He also kept lines of communication open to brethren in other places. One of the letters he sent from Passau to those in Freistadt has been preserved, thanks to the memory of the one who wrote the letter for him.

Brandhuber sought to comfort those imprisoned with reports that the true gospel was continuing to make progress. His own brother was now secretly baptising in Linz. God would soon take pity on their fetters.[74] God's compassion took a different shape than Brandhuber expected. First, news of the recantations and the release of those in Freistadt reached him, and he decided to visit the brethren in person. As a consequence he escaped the arrests that followed shortly after his disappearance from Passau.[75] His fortunes in Freistadt have not been documented. Later during the same year (1528), he ventured on a successful missionary journey into the Tyrol. Then he rebuilt the Anabaptist congregations in Wels and Linz.[76] Late in 1529 he and seventy others were arrested in Linz. After a lengthy trial during which he refused to recant he suffered the fate of Dorfbrunner, Schlaffer, and Schiemer.[77]

According to Hutterite tradition Brandhuber taught the community of goods, nonresistance, and strong church discipline.[78] Fortunately, we are able to verify this account by an analysis of one of Brandhuber's surviving pastoral epistles. The letter, which originated in Linz some time in 1529, was directed to the Gemeinde in Rottenburg.[79] It is significant because it links Brandhuber to the Freisleben brothers. In the last paragraph mention is made of a "little book about baptism" which the brothers in the Tyrol requested. We can now conclude that this was a reference to Christoph Freisleben's publication of 1528 and not to Hut's pamphlet.[80] There exist several indications that this was so. Brandhuber's own description of pedobaptism as the "sign of the beast" echoed Christoph's earlier polemics. More specifically, Brandhuber closed his own letter with a salutation identical to that found in Christoph's booklet: "All you of the household of Lot, remove yourselves from Sodom and Gomorrah."[81]

The letter itself reveals strong moralistic and puritanical strains coupled with an authoritarian tendency in church discipline. It is the first piece of Anabaptist literature that explicitly advocates a proto-Hutterite position of communalism in very empirical terms. The communal stage itself appears to have evolved out of the dual practice of (1) keeping a common fund for the poor and (2) individual sectarian households sharing all their possessions with their servants. Apparently not all Anabaptists in Austria were ready to accept the communal ideal. Brandhuber warned against them as "false brethren" who had gone "out from among [us] but were not of [us]."[82]

Brandhuber's understanding of discipleship extended well beyond an internal conformity to Christ. Even proper attire was now involved in separation from the world. With the expertise of a master seamster he listed all the superfluous items of clothing which served no utilitarian purpose, appealing only to the lust of the eyes. Brandhuber here ran directly counter to statements made by Hut earlier that such emphasis on externals was undesirable.[83] He also assumed an unequivocal position on the sword. In this regard his own position was different from that of both Hut and Hubmaier. He warned explicitly against false brethren who published a book in which they sought to demonstrate that the political ethic normative for the Old Testament remained effective for the New Testament. Not so, according to Brandhuber. This meant an unwarranted equation of the revelation granted to the servant Moses with that of the Son Christ. The New Testament did not permit participation in war or the use of the sword, not even for self-defence.[84] The book referred to was obviously Hubmaier's *On the Sword*.

As we know, Johann Spittelmaier and others in Nicolsburg continued to hold to Hubmaier's political ethic. In this sphere Hubmaier had more in common with the Spiritualists Entfelder and Bünderlin than with the type of Anabaptism forged by Brandhuber. Both the clear separation between Old and New Testaments and the regulations about proper dress and total segregation from the world would suggest that a strong Swiss Brethren influence had penetrated Austrian Anabaptism, or that Austrian Anabaptism had arrived at a similar phase of sect formation as Swiss Anabaptism had earlier.

Theologically, the letter gave evidence of a lingering mystical influence. There were references to the *imago Dei*, the inner Word, and the internal law in man. Brandhuber absorbed without critical re-examination the basic anthropological assumptions shared by Müntzer, Denck, Hut, Hubmaier, and other theologically formative thinkers of early South German Anabaptism. However, the mystical immanence theme was no longer explicitly directed against the Reformation's doctrines of justification and biblical authority.[85] The focus had clearly shifted to a dry moralism. The cross mysticism of Müntzer and Hut had undergone an externalizing transformation. Even the gospel of all creatures reappeared in a different context as primarily a lesson in humility, an illustration of obedient discipleship.[86] The theological end-product was an incongruous lingering of mystical vocabulary, now subsumed within the overarching concern for a pure Gemeinde circumscribed in visible, temporal dimensions.

Thus we can conclude that in the Anabaptism represented by Brandhuber and his followers in Linz there is a new permutation of the Anabaptism brought to Austria by Hut. Brandhuber's emphases, which reflected a development in the direction of sectarianism, would continue and become dominant in Austria through the contribution of leaders like Peter Riedemann and Jacob Hutter. Later development, therefore, justified the claims of Hutterite chroniclers to see in Brandhuber a representative of their tradition. Hut himself was partly responsible for this tradition. He had been one of the earliest and most effective propagators of the Anabaptist cause in Austria, leaving behind a host of converts and strings of martyrs who were to become the soil and seed for the new religious sect. This new creation differed from Hut's early movement, becoming more sectarian, more evangelical, less mystical and apocalyptical. Among the factors producing this change were (1) continuous persecution, (2) the infiltration and mingling of Swiss Anabaptist ideas, and (3) the influence of indigenous leaders like Schlaffer, Dorfbrunner, and Brandhuber, who had never been passive mouthpieces of Hut's ideas. Among the latter, although less obviously so, were also the Freisleben brothers who at first, at least, contributed to the evolution of South German Anabaptism in an evangelical direction. We can now turn to a third outcome of early South German Anabaptism besides devolution and evangelical sectarianism. It was to a large extent the antithesis of the evangelical development we sought to document in this chapter.

7

THE EMERGENCE OF THE "HOMELESS MINDS": HANS BÜNDERLIN AND CHRISTIAN ENTFELDER

A. Hans Bünderlin

So far we have traced two streams emerging from the disintegration of the Anabaptist movement built up by Hans Hut. The first, discussed in Chapter 5, devolved into fantasy. It was exemplified in the Dreamers' sect and Augustin Bader. The second, dealt with in the previous chapter, evolved into a morally realistic, sectarian evangelical Anabaptism. In spite of direct connections to Hut and his disciples this latter development also showed traces of many typically Swiss Brethren attitudes with regard to hermeneutics, political ethic, and ecclesiology. It found its earliest representatives in leaders like Dachser, Dorfbrunner, Schlaffer, Schiemer, the Freisleben brothers, and, above all, in Brandhuber. This tributary by no means constituted the main stream of South German-Austrian Anabaptism prior to 1530. Many of the early leaders, including some of the evangelicals, left Anabaptism altogether and evolved in no particular direction, simply rejoining one of the established religious groups. This was not true of a third stream, the mystical Spiritualists, best represented by Hans Bünderlin and Christian Entfelder.

Hans Bünderlin, as some of his contemporaries observed, continued the mystical humanist tradition of Denck.[1] This assertion has been repeated by every scholar who seriously compared the writings of the two men.[2] In fact, it has been argued that Bünderlin's ideas represented "the development of Denck's thought to its logical spiritualist conclusion."[3] If accepted, this thesis would see in Denck a forerunner of Sebastian Franck[4] and a kindred spirit of Schwenckfeld.[5] However, such an interpretation runs counter to a second line of argument which considers Denck a founding father of South German Anabaptism. This second thesis incorporated the distinction between sectarian Anabaptists and Spiritualists in terms derived from Troeltsch. Accordingly, Bünderlin and similar-minded dissenters represented an unbalanced spiritualism, a by-product rather than the logical extension of ideas coming from Denck.

The influence of Denck was salvaged for a continuous, tangible, religious sect, South German Anabaptism, soon to be crystallized by Marpeck and his Pilgramites. A combination of insights from Denck and Marpeck, in the conception of this school, was constituted into an amiable Anabaptist vision—not one-sidedly literalist, not subjectively spiritualist, not narrow-mindedly separatist—with which any twentieth-century evangelical Baptist could identify.[6]

Unfortunately, neither the separation of Spiritualists from Anabaptists nor the combination of elements from Denck and Marpeck into a continuous and consistent whole can do justice to the complexity of the early South German Anabaptist movement. The latter bore more resemblance to a religious and social protest movement than the models borrowed from Troeltsch would suggest. Spiritualistic, mystical, apocalyptical, and evangelical biblical ideas were inextricably interwoven in the expressions of protest. During the crisis years, 1528-30, the protagonists of the movement became conscious of the latent differences existing in their own camp. A polarization between the more biblicist and spiritualistic elements contributed to the process of disintegration which, as we noted earlier, set in around 1528.

The ideas of Denck, we maintain, favoured the evolution towards the more spiritualistic pole personified in Bünderlin and Entfelder.[7] These two leaders represented the most intellectual and sophisticated mystical tendencies within early South German-Austrian Anabaptist thought. The cardinal tenets of the mystical legacy, as the experience of disintegration was to prove, were better suited to sustain individual dissent than disciplined brotherhoods.

Hans Bünderlin, also appearing in the documents as Hans Vischer, like the Freisleben brothers and Brandhuber came from the Anabaptist congregation in Linz. Prior to his involvement with Anabaptism he received clerical training at the University of Vienna and had been employed as a secretary to one of the local nobles.[8] He was probably the same Hans Vischer who supported the peasant rebellion in the Tyrol led by Michael Gaismaier. In May 1526 he participated at a disputation between Zwinglians and Catholics. Although probably not a true Zwinglian, he attacked extreme unction and the Mass as superstitious magic.[9] It is not clear when he joined the Anabaptists. In the past some scholars expressed doubts about his Anabaptist credentials.[10] However, his brief confession made in Strassburg during 1529 stated explicitly that he had received baptism in Augsburg.[11] Presumably this took place before the fall of 1527, for Bünderlin appears as Vorsteher together with the Freisleben brothers in the documents relating to Passau.

He must have left with the Freislebens when persecution broke out in Linz.[12] The similarity of his ideas to those of Denck, plus the fact that his baptism took place in Augsburg, would suggest that he was baptised by Denck as early as 1526.[13] If so, he was one of the pioneers of the Anabaptist cause in the area around Linz. When driven from his home by persecution he stopped temporarily in Nicolsburg.[14] Early in 1529 he surfaced in Strassburg.[15]

Bünderlin's arrival in Strassburg from Nicolsburg as a mystical-spiritualistic Anabaptist permits certain interesting conclusions about the evolution of Anabaptism in the latter area. In Nicolsburg Bünderlin must have witnessed the exodus of Jacob Wiedemann and his *Stäbler* from the Liechtenstein domain.[16] The main issue concerned political ethic. Wiedemann and his followers assumed a nonresistant position like that defended by Brandhuber and the later Hutterites. Johann Spittelmaier and his helpers defended a position similar to that of Hubmaier.[17] However, from Spittelmaier's later association with Bünderlin we can infer that he represented Hubmaier only with regard to political ethic. On other issues he reflected a more mystical Anabaptism,[18] which evolved in the purely spiritualistic, individualistic direction exemplified by Entfelder and Bünderlin.

The group with which Bünderlin became associated in Strassburg retained connections with Denck's and Hätzer's ministry in that city two years earlier. One of the historical links was the notary, Fridolin Meyer.[19] Meyer himself had been baptised by Kautz after the latter's expulsion from Worms.[20] He was in contact with Reublin, Ulrich Trechsel, and Pilgram Marpeck. Trechsel, as we noted earlier, had been sent by Hut to Worms and settled in Strassburg, from whence he participated in Augustin Bader's conference in Schönberg.[21] During October 1528 Meyer was arrested together with Kautz and Reublin. Marpeck was also implicated. According to Meyer he had met with them seeking to establish an Anabaptist order.[22] Marpeck explained that the meeting had been held to organize relief for the refugees pouring into the city.[23] Both Meyer and Marpeck remained unmolested.[24] Kautz and Reublin were less fortunate, suffering lengthy imprisonment and expulsion.[25]

Meanwhile Bünderlin arrived on the scene. His reception would suggest that he was accepted as an Anabaptist leader. His meetings were well attended. The more spiritualistic message he conveyed left a particularly favourable impression on Fridolin Meyer. Perhaps this was not accidental, since an outside informer claimed that those associating with Fridolin considered themselves especially blessed by the Spirit and looked down on those not part of the group as in bondage to the "stinking flesh."[26] Fridolin himself gave readings from one of Bünderlin's booklets for the edification of assembled Anabaptists.[27]

The new flurry of activity soon reached the attention of the authorities. Among the more familiar figures appearing upon the list of Anabaptists arrested was Jörg Nespitzer, formerly from Passau, now giving his home as Lauingen.[28] Bünderlin himself was interrogated and expressed the desire to return to Nicolsburg. After his release he made a brief appearance in Constance. A few years later he participated at the Synod of Rastenburg called by Albrecht von Hohenzollern, Duke of Prussia. Apparently he had earlier returned to Nicolsburg, for with him were two veterans of the Nicolsburg debate—Johann Spittelmaier and Oswald Glaidt. When Albrecht opted for Lutheranism Bünderlin and his companions were obliged to leave Prussia. The sources are silent about Bünderlin's subsequent fate.[29]

All four of Bünderlin's surviving works originated during the crucial years of 1528-30. All were published in Strassburg.[30] The first three contained no explicit attacks on the Anabaptists. Only in his last treatise, *The Explanation*, did he turn against his former colleagues.[31] He now argued that the time had come to abolish outer baptism and the Lord's Supper as unnecessary externals.[32] This suggestion, coming as it did in 1529 or early 1530, was by no means an isolated insight. At least three factors contributed to this conclusion: (1) the disintegration and disillusionment of Hut's early movement, (2) the continued oppression of those embracing adult baptism, and (3) the infiltration of the more militantly literalist Swiss type of Anabaptism, which was slowly emerging as a dominating tendency in the Anabaptist movement itself (e.g., Wiedemann and Brandhuber).

Bünderlin, who had earlier assailed the magisterial Reformers for associating the true Word of God too closely with the external, historically given Word,[33] now battled against a similar tendency among the Anabaptists. The Anabaptist movement, as he understood it, was it-self undergoing changes in a sectarian direction which he could not ap-prove. The effect was to push Bünderlin in an opposite direction. From his perspective, this did not imply a defection or forsaking of earlier principles. In fact, he believed himself true to the early spirit of the movement.

Interestingly, Bünderlin rationalized his opposition to the new sectarianism by his understanding of history. Since the beginning of the physical universe God had repeatedly revealed the true spiritual nature of His kingdom. Man had again and again become preoccupied with the historical means of communication, losing sight of the truths they were intended to communicate. Hence each mode of revelation could serve only for a limited time. Typical was Israel's involvement with the letter of the law but its neglect of the spirit of the law.[34]

A new and higher revelation was given in Christ, who once more testified to the purely spiritual nature of God's kingdom.[35] Christ taught that divine truth was directly communicated to man without externals.[36] Thus outer baptism, as carried out by John the Baptist, Christ, and His disciples, witnessed primarily to a true, inner spiritual occurrence. The external witness was necessary only because that generation was still preoccupied with externals. One could, therefore, not argue for a con-tinuation of baptism from their practice. Some persons in Christ's day were baptised as many as three times. Those who were now insisting on external baptism were regressing into Judaistic concern with the letter. Water baptism should have ceased with the apostles had that generation understood the inner significance of the outer rite. But Antichrist had assured the survival of the external rite and constructed a second visible kingdom to succeed that of external Israel. Those who now insisted on the proper external mode to separate true believers from the world were playing once more into the hands of Antichrist, whose aim it was to keep them entangled in externals.[37] What mattered was the Spirit, the internal significance of the external rites. Thus Bünderlin's philosophy of history was now directed not only against sacramentalism but also against Anabaptist sectarianism.

Bünderlin's spiritualism and dispensationalism suggest an exposure to elements of the Joachimist tradition.[38] He believed that the true spiritual church, foreseen by Daniel, was beginning to unfold in these last days.[39] There is also evidence of a strong indebtedness to the mystical tradition which had been formative for Müntzer, Denck, and Hut. Inferences left implicit in Denck and Hut became explicit in

Bünderlin, among them the denial of eternal punishment and the rejection of a personal devil.[40] Both Denck and Hut had been charged with those views. Bünderlin also held to the apokatastasis as a logical consequence of his Neoplatonic presuppositions.[41] Eventually all creation would be spiritualized and flow back into its origin.[42]

Neoplatonic assumptions, which provided the backdrop to Bünderlin's Weltanschauung, are illustrated on the title pages of two of his publications. They picture a triangle and a circle. The triangle represented the spiritual reality of the omnipotent Father, the righteous Son, and the merciful Spirit.[43] The circle symbolized physical and temporal reality—stars, birds, mountains, water, and deer. Man was pictured as partaking of both these worlds. He was represented by the parts of the triangle—Holy Spirit and the Son—which intersected the circle. Men's spiritual counterparts, not part of the creaturely, were the angels.

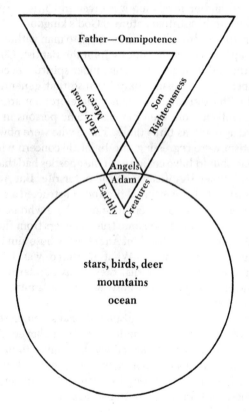

The text further expounded a typically mystical anthropology. Central to the understanding of man was the immanence of God. The seed of God, the *imago Dei* in man, provided the divine connection.[44] In fact, Bünderlin's stress on the divine in man was so pronounced that he could accept all other witnesses about God only as secondary, pointing to the true, inner universal presence of God in men.[45] These anthropological teachings were implicitly antipredestinarian, as in practically all early South German Anabaptists. It seems, therefore, logical to see a relation between Bünderlin's voluntaristic thrust and his pre-Reformation anthropology.[46]

A logos theology provided the scaffolding for the anthropology with its emphasis upon immanence.[47] The focus on the transhistorical Christ as the creative principle carried the same Christological tendencies first noted in Denck. The historical Jesus differed from the average man quantitatively rather than qualitatively. In Him divinity had become more fully incarnate. His role had been primarily pedagogical like that of all prophets.[48]

All the other mystical themes first expounded by Müntzer and Denck reappeared. But they assumed an accentuated spiritualistic dress. Bünderlin's attitude toward Scripture perhaps best illustrates this point. He argued that a biblicist mentality was responsible for the proliferation of divisions and strife among the followers of Christ. His polemics against the "scribes" were the harshest heard since Müntzer.[49] An appeal to Scripture as an objective authority was impossible. Scripture was capable of being bent to all sides. "Antichrist, too, has his seat there for he, too, comes in the name of the Lord."[50]

The question arose why Christ and St. Paul in their day had utilized Scripture to such an extent. Bünderlin's reply was consistent with his view of history. It had been necessary because that generation had not yet totally emerged from the dispensation when God communicated through the letter of the law. But Christ initiated the change from the age of external law to the stage when God would be worshipped in spirit and truth. This was particularly difficult for the Jews to grasp. Therefore, Christ and Paul appealed to Scripture to communicate the change to them.[51]

Like Müntzer, Denck, and Hut before him, Bünderlin reiterated that Scripture gave witness of the truth but was in itself not the Word of God. "God's Word is Spirit and life, John 6, image, simile, seed, son and kingdom of God in and not outside us, Luke 17."[52] It was impossible to bring the Word of God to where it was not. It could not be communicated through externals. Bünderlin, therefore, explicitly rejected the Lutheran correlation between a supposedly objectively communicated Word of God and faith. True faith was not imparted by the reading of the written, or the hearing of the preached, word. It was generated in the soul when the viator experienced true spiritual rebirth.[53] Faith, in the final analysis, was the recognition of the divine presence in man. Like Müntzer and Denck, Bünderlin assailed the Reformers for not explaining the arrival of faith, for not providing their listeners with the key of David that could unlock the inner meaning of Scripture. Scripture itself was, after all, full of paradoxes, if not contradictions, which could only be harmonized by a deeper penetration into their spiritual message.[54] In practice this meant an allegorical rather than a literalistic hermeneutic.

The rest of Bünderlin's rambling arguments—he himself admitted that he was writing "without particular order and with digressions"[55]— communicated the same pre-Reformation assumptions which we encountered earlier in Müntzer, Denck, Hut, Dachser, Schiemer, and Schlaffer. His Christology and anthropology were supported by a supplementary view of nature which testified of the Creator through His opposite. The gospel found in the creatures was that of obedience to the Creator.[56]

Bünderlin's soteriology similarly reflected strong pre-Reformation and mystical motifs. Like Müntzer, Denck, and Hut he conceived of salvation primarily in terms of reunion—*Wiederbringung*. In almost Eckhardian terminology he could write of "hastening" into the abyss of divinity through "the medium of the Son."[57] Here cross mysticism, first utilized by Müntzer against the "soft-living flesh in Wittenberg," made its reappearance. Bünderlin insisted that the bitter Christ must precede the Comforter.[58] The viator must experience a repetition of Calvary within him, as exemplified by Jonah's metaphorical descent into hell. After all, salvation was not effected by trusting in the spilling of substitutionary "strange" blood. It was a reunion of man with God which could be achieved only in personal death to all the creaturely.[59]

We conclude that in all essentials Bünderlin continued the mystical tradition of the early South German Anabaptist leaders. His thinking revolved around the cardinal doctrine of God's immanence. Christ's true disciples were those experienced in rebirth and committed to the guidance of the inner Word. Bünderlin's opposition to Reformation principles was ultimately derived from the inner logic of his mystical presuppositions. So was his early association with Anabaptism. Among the early Anabaptists he had found kindred spirits building on a similar mystical foundation and aiming at personal piety. The establishment of a new disciplined sect had never been part of his original intent.[60] In fact, when Bünderlin encountered this tendency in Anabaptism, those same mystical assumptions which earlier generated and sustained his opposition against the Reformers were turned against Anabaptism.

Bünderlin's attack on his former brethren was consequential for the subsequent development of South German Anabaptism. His accentuated spiritualism had an opposite effect on those unwilling to forsake all commitment to external discipline. His *Explanation* provoked Pilgram Marpeck's defence of a more sectarian Anabaptism.[61] The result was a new consciousness of the subversive implications of extreme mystical and spiritualistic tenets, which set the stage for Marpeck's later controversy with Schwenckfeld. It is possible that the rethinking forced on the heirs of early South German Anabaptism resulted in the retroactive expurgation of Denck's writings from the *Kunstbuch*, allegedly a Pilgramite collection.[62] However, this leaves inexplicable why Christian Entfelder, whose ideas, as we will see, closely resembled those of Denck and Bünderlin, received the honour of contributing to that same *Kunstbuch*.

B. Christian Entfelder

Christian Entfelder was probably the most speculative mind associated with the early Anabaptist movement. His early life remains veiled in obscurity. Scion of a wealthy family from the Enns Valley, he had studied law prior to his involvement with the Anabaptists.[63] Some time in 1526 he made contact with Hubmaier in Nicolsburg.[64] Thereafter he took the leadership of a radical conventicle in Eibenschitz, Moravia. According to later reports he had here exercised the prerogatives of an Anabaptist Vorsteher.[65] Some time in 1529 he appeared in Strassburg.[66] Whether or not he associated with Bünderlin is not clear but an analysis of his writings would suggest that the two agreed on most issues.[67] Unfortunately the sources provide no further clues about Entfelder's whereabouts during the next five years.[68]

In 1536 he surfaced as councillor to Albrecht von Hohenzollern. In this capacity he negotiated the first substantial settlement of Anabaptists from the Netherlands in East Prussia.[69] He evidently remained sympathetic to the Anabaptists and other radical Reformers without identifying himself with any group. In a letter dating from this period Schwenckfeld lamented that "our beloved brother Christianus" was still not able to see things as he did.[70] A few years later the new militancy of Lutheran orthodoxy made Entfelder's position at the court untenable. After 1547 he disappears from our sources. Schwenckfeld mentioned him once more in a letter written in 1560. Here he grouped him with Denck as one of the "fine, God-blessed men" who had recognized how much damage the well-intentioned but over-zealous Anabaptists had done to the cause of the true gospel.[71]

Schwenckfeld's assessment was not without merit. An analysis of Entfelder's writings suggest strong similarities between him and Denck.[72] In fact, as with Bünderlin, Entfelder's ideas appear to be extensions of Denck's thought world into the changed circumstances of the 1530s. Three published treatises have survived, all of them subsequent to Entfelder's involvement in Anabaptism and written between 1529 and 1533.[73] In particular his first treatise, originating in late 1529 or early January 1530, provides valuable insights into the reasons for Entfelder's exodus from the Anabaptist movement.

In his *Widerruf* Denck had dissociated himself from the practice of adult baptism and argued that a special divine commission was necessary to exercise the right to baptise. This line of argument provided the excuse for others to cease baptising. Entfelder argued strenuously that both the practice of baptism and the Lord's Supper should be suspended because those who had God's express command to initiate the external rite had passed away.[74] He supported this reasoning by reference to the three types of baptism carried out by John the Baptist, Christ's disciples before Christ's death, and the apostles who baptised after Pentecost. Each baptiser had acted on special command. The commission was null and void when the commissioned died. Strife and divisions set in when those who had no specific command began to baptise and bind their disciples to external custom. The result could only be idolatry. Thus Entfelder did not question Anabaptist baptism in principle; he merely insisted that the specially sent ones alone had the right to baptise.[75] For to alter traditionally accepted ceremonies which had fallen under the corrupting influence of Antichrist necessitated a special portion of the spirit of Elijah.[76] He implied, however, that the special messengers of his own day had come and gone. As support he cited the opinion of other brethren that the time to baptise was over because the time of wrath had begun.[77]

No doubt this explicit refusal to baptise without special divine command was not solely the result of Denck's *Widerruf*. It was to some extent an escapist rationalization to avoid martyrdom. It also reflected the evaporating enthusiasm of the early South German and Austrian Anabaptist leaders. Indeed, the baptisers, of whom there had been no dearth in late 1527 and early 1528, were becoming a rare breed. Even those who remained committed to adult baptism now insisted on proper authorization before baptising others.[78]

Entfelder's disaffection with Anabaptism appears to have had other causes. In tones again reminiscent of Denck he reminded his brothers in Eibenschitz of the divisive, narrow-minded, and cantankerous spirit in their midst. He himself had been guilty by condoning the practice of separation from others who refused to believe as he did. Loyalty to his flock had muzzled the inner witness which had faithfully reminded him that the spirit of separation was due to creaturely zeal rather than Christ's spirit. He had acquiesced in a pharisaical and critical attitude towards outsiders. His eyes were opened when he was forced to disengage from his involvement with the brethren in Eibenschitz. He now admonished them to judge no one but themselves and to leave the separation of godly and ungodly to God alone.[79]

An analysis of Entfelder's three writings reveals that he remained entirely consistent with the basic principles which had guided him even as an Anabaptist. These, in spite of an anti-intellectualism on the surface,[80] were largely inherited from the medieval mystical and metaphysical tradition. At the heart of Entfelder's concern was the knowledge of God—how God revealed Himself and how that revelation related to man. His views were expressed in trinitarian patterns. In fact, Entfelder is best described as a trinitarian thinker. *Of God's Perception* (*Erkandnuss*), his most substantial theoretical statement, was divided into three major sections:

(1) The first discourse: how the one God through the sole cause of His goodness revealed Himself with grace in threefold power, which is spoken of as three persons.

(2) The second discourse: how multiple, diversified man is through a variety of causes reminded of God's revealed message.

(3) The third discourse: about the perception of the true mediator together with an introduction into some of the matters previously mentioned.[81]

Entfelder began his discussion with the premise that God in His goodness wanted to be known. To be known, He externalized and objectified Himself. The result was creation.[82] Divine disclosure in creation involved an enclosure, a limitation of God, a division of the unchanging, united One into changing physical parts. Yet in His wisdom God created a perfect whole which reflected His own unity.[83] Man fell out of harmony with this unity when, out of his own will, he became preoccupied with parts of the design, losing touch with and sight of the whole.[84] In order to redirect man to unity, God revealed Himself through the parts.[85]

It was in the revelation in and through the parts (the creature) that the division of the Godhead into three made its appearance. Entfelder here deliberately put aside the anthropomorphic description according to which divine revelation occurs in three persons.[86] The result was a complex panentheistic process theology in which the metaphysical and visible realms fused into one reality.

Divine revelation through the parts of creation was designated by Entfelder in traditional scholastic language as revealing divine Being (*essentia, Wesen*). Divine Being was the indivisible, unmovable, and unchanging source from which all other being received its existence. Each creature partook in some measure of the fulness of divine Being.[87]

The Being, equivalent to the Father, was made known through its *operatio (Wirklichkeit)*. the German word combines two conceptions in its meaning—reality and activity. Physical reality was in the Neoplatonic vision the manifestation of divine activity. The *operatio* was, therefore, the medium that related Being, the unmoving, unchanging, with the transient, ever-changing external phenomena of creation. It was the universal of universals, proceeding from the Being in essence without being separated from it.[88] The close relation of the *operatio* with the temporal and finite raised the question of whether this second aspect of divinity could be considered eternal. The answer was in the positive.

> Just as a house is always in the architect's mind, so also is the earth, eternally, without time, in its creator. One species rises, the other declines, and yet all this is prepared from eternity in the divine Being's reality and activity, although revealed in time like the master's skill in building.[89]

The *operatio* was, therefore, more than blind activity. It was, in fact, the master plan itself. Here the Neoplatonically inspired logos theology made its reappearance.

> Because there can be no activity without speech or word . . .

this *operatio [Wirklichkeit]* is called God's speech. It is also in name the Word, through which all things which are something before God have become.[90]

The Word was the intelligence of God, the archetype of creation itself, literally incarnate in all creation, the medium through which the Being objectified and externalized itself: "The *operatio [wirklichkeit]* . . . is itself the Word, a real and working image and mediating power through which all creaturely images are mediated."[91]

Entfelder here proved himself part of the medieval mystical world in which the Creator did not stand in a mechanical, causal relation to creation. Through the logos God retained an immanent organic and ontological potency through which He sustained the dynamic process of creation.[92]

To the Being and *operatio* revealed in the creation process Entfelder added the Spirit, literally, the wind or breath of God. As he explained:

> Now no word or speech can be spoken without wind, breath or spirit. Hence there appeared so soon in this work of God [His creation and regeneration] the wind, . . . whose office it is to seal with its power the created, justified being.[93]

This latter statement serves as a convenient link between Entfelder's description of the threefold revelation of divinity through creation and his understanding of redemption. Salvation was through the *unio mystica*, the bringing again of "divided man into the whole."[94] It was the reversal of creation—since it moved in the reverse direction, from diversity to oneness. The redemptive activity of God was experienced by man as "wise omnipotence, just mercy and holy goodness."[95] This was regeneration itself, perceived by man as proceeding through three stages of ascent firmly enshrined in the medieval mystical tradition: (1) purification, (2) illumination, and (3) unification.[96] Outer baptism was understood as symbolic of this regenerative experience in which the viator recognized the severity of the Father, the mercy of the Son, and the goodness of the Spirit.[97] Sanctification and justification were subsumed under the one movement of mystical reunion.

This becomes clear from Entfelder's description of the seven phases of the believer's experience. Significantly, these stages are typified by the miracle of incarnation. The experience is illustrated in Mary. The Word becoming flesh went through the following phases: (1) God

saluted her with favour and good will, (2) God announced His desires
and will, (3) Mary was gripped by fear and sadness, (4) she waited on
God in patience and He aided her in tenderness *(Sanftmut)*, (5) she
resigned herself totally to God, (6) God's love and power embraced her,
and (7) union was achieved between divine and human desires. The
results of the mystical experience were allegorized in almost nontrans-
latable terms:

> Whoever, therefore, has gone into God's Sabbath day of rest, as
> through six tiresome working days, so that God in him and he in
> God, through Christ in the Holy Spirit, have become one united
> One [*ain ainigs ain*], that same person can also achieve all his outer
> desires through the power of the One who is in him. [He will] not
> only feel a power . . . but also a desire . . . to do and fulfill what God
> commands. Yes, it would be hard for him if he had to transgress one
> iota of the law of his God knowingly.[98]

Mary's example was of universal application. The stages represented the
internal order loosening the believer's preoccupation with the creaturely, reuniting him with his origin.[99] The seven stages also reflected
the activity of the sevenfold Spirit, a concept earlier found in Haug and
Hut.

Entfelder understood the union between the human and the
Divine not merely as a union of wills but metaphysically, if not ontologi-
cally. This becomes plain from an analysis of his anthropology, which
supported and complemented his trinitarian view of God's revelation.
Here the medieval assumption that only equals could know each other
reappeared. True knowledge of God, therefore, presupposed the bringing together of God and man in union. For God this involved incarnation, for man, deification—two sides of the same movement.[100]

With regard to man Entfelder distinguished between *mentem*
(Gemüt) and *ratio (Vernunft)*. *Mentem* related man to the inner
presence of the Divine. *Ratio* related man to the created world. Through
its sensory powers, sight, hearing, smell, *ratio* drew man to the creaturely. *Ratio* was, therefore, constantly tempted to focus on the
particular and to indulge in creaturely contradictions.[101] An example of
this was found in Mary. When the secret of divine conception was announced to her, she was astonished because her *ratio* turned outward
but could find no explanation through her knowledge of the creaturely.
God in His mercy permitted her a creaturely lesson in Elisabeth.
Thereafter Mary "withdrew her senses, committed *ratio* to the divine

works and permitted the inner man, who was created unto the image of God, to speak."[102] Another example cited to illustrate the believer's need to withdraw the *ratio* from the creaturely was Peter's historic walk on the water. Because he had withdrawn his senses incompletely from the creaturely he remained suspended in the water, sinking halfway.[103]

The point was that man could be addressed through the divine presence in him or through the creatures from without. In his *On the Division* Entfelder drew the following illustration:[104]

Voice	Father		heard		Spirit	
of	Son	is	felt	in	Soul	of
God	Holy Spirit		at work		Body	Man

Voice	Letter		heard		
of	Man	is	felt	in	Man
Creature	Evil Spirit	not	at work		

The illustration demonstrated that Entfelder conceived of man as patterned after God.

> Man, too, has an *essentia [Wesen]*, but unclean in himself. He also has an *operatio [Wirklichkeit]*—but not light because he loves darkness. He has also a goodness *[gute]* to the extent that he loves the good, but not separate from evil.[105]

Like the medieval mystics Entfelder related the inner man to the concept of *scintilla*, the divine spark or seed in man, still alive even after the fall. This inner potency was present in all men and remained within man even in hell.[106] However, the mere presence of the divine potency was not sufficient to restrain man's desires for the creaturely. Only when man experienced the reorientation (regeneration) from the creaturely to the Divine was the purpose of the *scintilla* fulfilled in union between the human and the Divine. But this reorientation and regeneration implied a literal purification from the creaturely.

> Therefore, to the extent that man is purged, he is illuminated [and] is accordingly united with the true light. To the extent that he is united with the true light he perceives (knows) the united One who illuminates him and cleanses him with truth.[107]

Here typically mystical assumptions with regard to man as the *homo spiritualis* came to the fore again. Justification could only be conceived of as literal cleansing from the creaturely. The law of "the less of a sinner, the more of a saint" was operative in this framework which was supported by a strong spirit-matter dualism. The cathartic process of purification was expressed in terms typical of cross mysticism. In fact, it was given back its original purely internalized thrust by Entfelder. To pick up one's cross with Christ meant not an external martyrdom, but rather to commit oneself

> . . . with Christ to a simple, poor, sincere life, dead [to the creaturely]. . . . To permit oneself in true resignation [*Gelassenheit*] to be threshed, swung, winnowed, separated, ground, bagged and baked. Then he [the viator] becomes true nourishment to God, the heavenly Father. In this process his creaturely and animal nature [is] thoroughly digested. [108]

Through the experience of the bitter inner cross, the viator lost all taste for the creaturely and turned totally to the "united oneness." There that which tasted bitter turned sweet.

> Then the heavenly nourishment begins . . . cooked by the fire of tribulation to spread its power through him [the viator]; and he begins to taste the true sweetness in which also our flesh tastes similar to and becomes conformed to the flesh of Christ. [109]

Thus the central mystical motifs already found in Müntzer reappear in Entfelder. The mystical experience of the cross was not seen as something to which man passively submitted, but something in which he cooperated. [110] When man cooperated with the divine activity in him his three virtues, faith, hope, and love, experienced proper reorientation and participated in the *unio mystica.* That Entfelder's understanding of faith was not that of Luther and the other Reformers becomes clear from the context. Faith, together with the other two virtues, was born in the twilight zone in which divine and human nature overlapped. Faith was the "power of being which unites being with being." [111]

The three virtues corresponded to the trinitarian movement of purification, illumination, and unification and were generated in the experience of mystical rebirth. Faith implied submission to the work of the Father, who prepared the viator for illumination by weeding out the creaturely. [112] Hope, designated as a "real operative power" (*wirkliche Kraft*), was set free by the cleansing activity of faith. Love, as "a power of goodness" (*gütige Kraft*), sealed the union of the human and Divine. "Thus God comes to man through faith. . . . Man, through hope, moves toward God. . . . And in these two true love runs [its course]."[113] The net result was that the *viator*, having experienced reorientation and regeneration, was now in control of his lower creaturely desires, literally living in harmony with God and, therefore, in holiness, fulfilling God's desires—God's law.[114]

True knowledge of God, then, came through the experience of mystical union. Mystical union was a reversal of the trinitarian creation process, and it was experienced by the *viator* as a literal spiritual regeneration. It was in the final analysis made possible through the immanence of God in creation, in man. All the other concepts of Entfelder's theology can be shown to be logical extensions of this cardinal presupposition. Nothing illustrates this better than his view of Scripture.

If the quantity of biblical citations found in Entfelder could serve as the criterion for determining his biblicism, then, in fact, Entfelder was the biblicist of biblicists. He thoroughly peppered his publications with biblical references. However, like Müntzer, Denck, Hut, and most South German Anabaptists, he maintained that Scripture was a mere witness (Zeugnis) to the inner living Word, although not in contradiction to it.[115] The mystical assumptions of his thought made it impossible for Entfelder to accept the Reformation's normal understanding of the Word of God. His focus on the inner Word designated all outer witness as inferior. Above all, he deplored creaturely zealousness, in which category he included literal interpretation of the Bible.[116]

The Reformation's appeal to sola scriptura he regarded as the cause of sectarian bickering and division.[117] Like Müntzer, Denck, and Hut, Entfelder advocated a clearer distinction between the living Word and the historically given dead letter. The latter belonged to the creaturely and was incapable of communicating true living faith.[118] Satan cast himself in the role of a literalist, tempting Christ in the wilderness with citations from Scripture. But Christ remained unmoved by Scripture and showed "that Scripture is at all times against Scripture."[119] Here the concept of scriptural paradoxes, already present in Müntzer, Denck, and Hut, reappeared in its mystical context. It was directed again against the "fleshly scribes" who had never experienced the cathartic inner cross. Against them Entfelder pointed to the inner experience of regeneration which provided the key of David. "The personal experience of a withdrawn life (taken from the world and submitted to God) does more than all the Scripture and books on earth."[120] What was new in Entfelder was that this anti-intellectualism, which had earlier been the cutting edge of the polemic against the Reformers, was now directed against the Anabaptists as well.

> I . . . must with surprise experience through all sects what let-
> ter without spirit [and] zealousness without understanding are ca-
> pable of. One error is born after another. . . . All those who believe
> they will find Christ in the Scripture are seeking the living among
> the dead. The Scripture witnesses about Christ. That is true. But the
> letter does not learn to know Him. That is demonstrated by all
> scribes . . . through their manner of life on earth.[121]

This was also applicable to the "new scribes," who believed they were
taught by God because they had no formal education. They used Scripture
without proper understanding more often even than the learned whom
they despised.[122]

In practice Entfelder's view of Scripture reflected a medieval hermeneutic. He indicated the same fondness for allegorical interpretation that
we noticed in our discussion of the mystics, Hut, and Bünderlin. In
particular the symbolic number patterns of three, seven, and four figured
prominently in his works. As noticed above the revelation of God came to
man through a threefold creative and redemptive activity.

The believer's own experience of the activity of the inner Word went
through either seven stages or four stages. The believer's three virtues
were reoriented and rekindled in purification, illumination, and union.
A good sample of the application of the allegorical hermeneutic was
found in Entfelder's exposition of Isaiah's vision of the cherubim. The
three pairs of wings on the cherubim signified the three virtues of faith,
hope, and love. To be specific, the two wings covering the face
represented faith and purification, those covering the feet, love and
union, and those in the middle with which they propelled themselves,
hope and illumination. The latter symbolically raised the believer from
the parts to the whole.[123]

Entfelder gave a similar explanation of the four wheels which Ezekiel
saw in that same vision. They signified the witness found in the four evangelists: (1) Matthew, symbolized by the lion, testified to faith and purification, (2) Mark, symbolized by the ox, testified to hope and illumination,
(3) Luke, symbolized by man, testified to union and love, and (4) John,
symbolized by an eagle, testified to perception *(Erkenntnis)* and divinity.[124]

With the interpretation of John as representing perception and divinity we return to Entfelder's major concern—knowledge of God. True
perception necessitated equality of subject and object, hence divinity on
man's part and humanity on God's part. True knowledge could, therefore,

come only in mystical union. It followed that the testimony of the evangelists was conceived by Entfelder in an internalized, existential fashion. Not surprisingly, therefore, he gave the historical record of Christ's life the same internalized application which we have found already in Hut, Schiemer, and other South German Anabaptists. In fact, his ideas so closely resembled Hut's on this subject that it is tempting to conclude that he had firsthand knowledge of Hut's teachings or at least drew on identical sources. Like Hut, but perhaps in a less literal fashion, he insisted that those who wanted to participate in the first resurrection and reign with Christ needed to suffer other, preliminary stages—conception, birth, passion, and death—with Him beforehand. [125]

This internalized view of Christ's life was supported by a Christology which stressed the imitatio Christi. The historical Christ was ultimately only a pedagogue and exemplar of the universally applicable mystery of incarnation—union between God and man. [126] His cross and death represented not a vicarious sacrifice for the propitiation of God's implacable justice, but an illustration that union involved death to the creaturely, hence suffering—the cross. In the human Jesus the principle of suffering as the divinely ordained means to cleanse from sin had been fully manifested. [127]

The principle of the cross was also revealed through nature to those who had experienced cathartic inner suffering. The design of the whole was revealed through the parts to those purified, illuminated, and united with God. Here Hut's gospel of all creatures reappeared.

> Yes, every man can recognize his God and Lord in the works of His hands. So wonderful is the Lord in His creatures when they are considered with the internal eyes. [Then] the goodness of God is recognized—why, for what, from whom and for whose benefit they are created. . . . However, as no creature can find final rest on earth unless it becomes one with man to whom it has been subordinated, and none may become one with man unless it suffers his will, so also man finds no rest eternally until he becomes one with God. [128]

Entfelder in fact described the revelation in nature as *Evangelium Creaturarum*. Not only all animals on earth, in the air, and in the water, but also leaves and grass, useful for man's nutrition, preached salvation as the *unio mystica* They offered themselves freely to be united with man, testifying that God, too, waited to be reunited with him and was willing to bring him again into "the paradise of divine Being." [129] Here the principles of cross mysticism became normative on a cosmic scale. Entfelder expounded the gospel of the creatures within a consistent mystical context. The creatures illustrated not only the required relationship of obedience, but also the proper ontological relationship between man and God expressed in union. The regenerate viator could also perceive the trinitarian revelation in human history. Here Joachimist motifs made their reappearance. Entfelder discovered three periods in history, which corresponded roughly to the trinitarian activity present in creation and regeneration. The first stage began with creation and lasted until the giving of the law. In it the divine Being manifested itself as a Father and originator *(Ursprung)*. The second stage began with the giving of the law and lasted until Christ's ascension. It was literally the age of the "go-between," of the righteous *operatio*. Toward the close of this age the *operatio* took on flesh so as to reveal clearly the beginning, purpose, and end of history. The last stage, implicitly beginning with Pentecost, was the age of grace and of the "good Spirit." [130]

This tripartite division corresponded roughly to the witness of the creatures, the witness of the law and ceremonies, and the inner witness of the Spirit. [131] However, the threefold division of history did not mean the limitation of any particular element of the Trinity to one of the three stages of history. All three elements were active together, even though one of them dominated each period. As an example of trinitarian interaction, Entfelder cited Abraham, Isaac, and Jacob from the first stage. Abraham, as father of many nations, symbolized the *essentia (Wesen)*. Isaac, the "blessed seed" and "holy sacrifice," symbolized the righteous *operatio*, and Jacob, the overcomer, the "good spirit." [132]

Above all, Entfelder was concerned with preserving the unity of God. Here the monistic thrust of his system, foreshadowed in Denck and Hätzer, became explicit. Abraham, he reminded his readers, had encountered three manifestations of divinity but he worshipped only one. It was an error when Christians began to worship the divided three. [133]

This brief analysis would suggest that in Entfelder we meet another representative of the same mystical tradition which flowed through Müntzer, Denck, and Hut into early South German Anabaptism. In fact, it becomes obvious that in Entfelder more of the mystical substrata underlying early South German Anabaptism emerge to the surface than in any of our other protagonists. Entfelder must have had firsthand knowledge of the writings of some of the mystics including Tauler and the author of the *Theologia Deutsch.*

Entfelder illustrates how the latent individualism of mysticism, excellently suited to inspire dissent, could also militate against the development of sectarianism. Entfelder, although full of pastoral concern for the brethren "who had been written into his heart," could not surrender the conviction that there were still many in the dark world who belonged to the kingdom of light. There were also not a few who considered themselves children of light but walked in darkness.[134] All of this would suggest that in Entfelder we meet a first-generation Anabaptist who was becoming uncomfortable as the conventicle of which he was a leading member began to absorb more and more sectarian traits. The tension within the early movement, partially the result of personality clashes, but in a more basic sense the result of an ever clearer polarization between individualist and sectarian impulses, drove Entfelder to reevaluate his own commitment.

The mystical presuppositions which had inspired Entfelder's earlier dissent from both Catholicism and Lutheranism eventually clashed with the sectarian tendency to institutionalize and dogmatize baptism and the Lord's Supper within a new church of the saints. Entfelder's internalized view of the sacraments was incapable of supporting the continuance of external rites under the strains of continued oppression. It is, therefore, a fair assumption that Entfelder's views on baptism and the Lord's Supper did not originate in an ecclesiology based on confrontation between the kindom of Christ and the kingdom of this world.[135] In fact, it was his exposure to practices derived from such a sectarian view of the world which destined him to join the "homeless minds of the Reformation." Together with Bünderlin he best personified the evolution of those early Anabaptist protestants who lost all confidence in approximating the ecclesiological idea of collective purity. The concept of the kingdom of God was again filled with its original mystical content as the "kingdom in you." Both Bünderlin and Entfelder withdrew to a purely internalized individualistic but tolerant religion.

8

CONCLUSION

As this study progressed we touched upon several historical and historiographical problems. For none of these do we claim to provide an ultimate answer or the only possible interpretation. Nevertheless, we believe that the evidence presented in these chapters does permit certain generalizations which we hope will contribute to a better understanding of the complex nature of early South German and Austrian Anabaptism.

Our first and strongest conclusion concerns the nature of the theology of early South German-Austrian Anabaptism. Only a Protestant historical imagination which was well intentioned but strained could characterize the major theological assumptions found in the writings of our protagonists as Reformation insights carried to a radical conclusion. The mere fact that practically the whole first generation of leaders—Denck, Hut, Dachser, Salminger, Schiemer, Schlaffer, the Freislebens, Bünderlin, and Entfelder, not to mention Hubmaier—received their early education in as yet unreformed, unprotestantized halls of higher learning should have warned against such a simplistic thesis.

We maintain that, contrary to the conventional wisdom which tended to see all Anabaptists as concerned with following Christ and His teachings in a simple and a more consistent biblical fashion, the thought world of our protagonists reflected historically-created presuppositions of considerable sophistication and consistency. Early South German Anabaptism inherited much of its theological inspiration from an earlier medieval, more specifically popularized mystical tradition. To put it most bluntly, the protagonists in our narrative represented a medieval mystical legacy within the Reformation context. It was, therefore, not merely a more consistent return to pre-Constantinian Christianity or a more thoroughgoing biblicism—although these may in fact have been intentions of our protagonists—which led to their dissent from the magisterial Reformers. On many of the crucial doctrinal issues they stood in opposition not only to the hierarchical Church of Rome, but also to the teachings of the Reformation.

This is not a denial of the fact that Anabaptist thought also mirrored the immediate circumstances of the sixteenth century. Particularly with regard to political ethic and ecclesiology did the immediate historical situation exert a strong influence. Understandably, therefore, in these realms Anabaptist ideas remained at first flexible and dynamic. External pressures, and the creation of its own ethos and tradition, eventually provided a unifying force and a stabilizing influence for the Anabaptist movement as a whole. However, as with most objects of historical inquiry, it is possible and legitimate to examine both immediate and long-range influences upon Anabaptist ideas. In the realm of specifically theological ideas the search for historical continuity proved in fact more fruitful than a stress upon innovation. We therefore deliberately chose a "medieval point of departure" for our investigation.

Early Anabaptist theology, we suggest, possessed a history that can be traced back through Müntzer, Denck, and Hut, or more directly, through the *Theologia Deutsch* to Tauler and even Eckhardt. We singled out the concept of the immanence of God in man as the structuring and interpretative theme for our theological analysis. It was the medieval and mystical *Leitmotif* present in the theological protest of early South German Anabaptism. It provided the background assumption with which the early Anabaptist leaders approached the problems of the Reformation and helps to explain the implicit synergism that pervaded much of their thought both in its mystical beginnings and in the moralism that emerged later on.

This focus on the mystical common denominator led us to narrow rather than to widen the distinctions between the revolutionary Thomas Müntzer and the early Anabaptist leaders Hans Denck and Hans Hut. As a transmitter of the mystical tradition Müntzer bequeathed a mysticism of suffering and the cross, mixed with apocalyptical expectations. Denck conveyed the values of the tradition of imitation of Christ, the Head, by His members, and stressed the *nova lex Christi* of the Sermon on the Mount. The apocalyptic element was minimized (without being totally absent). Denck had serious scholarly and humanistic commitments absent from Müntzer. And yet, on balance, Denck's spirit came closer to Müntzer than to the Reformers and a significant direct influence by Müntzer on Denck is not at all improbable.

For Hut we accepted most of the results of the historiographical tradition which Seebass culminated and enriched. We deny Hut's conversion to an evangelical model of Anabaptism originating in Zürich, and we maintain that his acceptance of adult baptism did not mark a decisive break with his Müntzerian past. Hut constituted a major direct link between Müntzer and the early South German and Austrian Anabaptists. And we are defending the thesis that in the realm of theology proper Müntzer undeniably left more than a passing impression on this part of the early Anabaptist movement.

The stress upon divine immanence carried implications which supported first Müntzer's, then the Anabaptists' dissent from Reformation teachings. Soteriologically most significant was the retention of a dualistic, at times tripartite, view of man, while Luther and those following him preached the total man as sinner. The Reformation emphasis on total human depravity and the denial of any human merit (including merit derived from human volition) were logical consequences of Luther's rejection of any division of man's nature. Predestinarianism provided a theocentric corollary to this wholistic anthropology in the realm of theology proper. In contrast, the tradition focusing upon the *unio mystica* assumed the cooperation of man with the divine presence in him as part of the salvation process. The maintenance of the dualistic matter-spirit dichotomy in man was a necessary prerequisite for such a view.

By maintaining that grace was in man while man found himself in a providential natural order, the mystics and the early South German-Austrian Anabaptists influenced by them could insist that salvation came *sola gratia Dei* without denying human freedom. By embracing suffering as the cosmologically normative principle of purgation and redemption from all creatureliness and sin, they appeared to argue with the Reformers that justification was a *iustitia passiva*. True justifying faith was born in the bitter catharsis of inner cleansing. However, in the final analysis, this did not imply an endorsement of Luther's justification by faith alone or his crucial *simul iustus et peccator*. In true mystical fashion the early Anabaptists conceived of justification as a literal becoming righteous through the mystical process of rebirth, the birth of the Son in the soul—literally God becoming flesh—man being deified as symbolized in the miracle of incarnation. Justification and sanctification were thus inseparably one and the same movement. For them, like the theologians of the old faith, the principle of gradualness was operative—the less of a sinner the more of a saint. The transhistorical logos played a crucial anthropological role, providing the connection between man and the Divine. In this capacity the inner Word was not only a source of divine revelation but also a resource providing the enabling power for man's volition to act and choose freely and properly. Ironically, therefore, while the Anabaptists did not share the deeper appreciation of original sin and the depravity of human nature as outlined by the Reformers, they did emphasize the moral accountability of man. In the realm of practical piety, therefore, it appeared as if they were treating the problem of sin more seriously than the Reformers. In fact, from the Anabaptist perspective the Reformers succumbed to antinomianism.

If Anabaptist Christology is examined within this anthropological and larger mystical context it becomes apparent that the Christological differences between our protagonists and the Reformers went beyond semantics. Luther's Christocentricism focused on the redemptive work of the unique Son of God, the historical Christ. His emphasis on the unity of the two natures of Christ led to an almost unorthodox differentiation between the three persons in the Trinity. Just the opposite was the case for many of the Anabaptists dealt with in our study. The mystical focus on the transhistorical logos on the one hand, and the imitatio focus on the human Christ as the great exemplar and pedagogue on the other, were fundamentally incompatible with an acceptance of the vicarious nature of Christ's work. In the mystical experience of the cross, the Lamb slain since the foundation of the world was again experienced in every viator. It was not enough to believe Christ had suffered for one's sins. The members were expected to suffer with their head. The Anabaptist theology of martyrdom and discipleship was directly related to this emphasis, although a more externalized version of it. Luther's dialectical understanding of law and gospel was a negation of this tradition.

Many of our protagonists, as a corollary of their mystical stress on the divine logos, held to a more traditional emphasis on the unity of the Godhead, as opposed to Luther's stress on the unity of Christ. (For them Christ had a dual nature, just as the ordinary human being did.) However, the ideas of some of the more extreme pointed beyond orthodoxy to a radical monotheism, which led not only to a denial of the Trinity but one step further to a denial of the divinity of the historical Christ. In Christ the presence of the divine logos shone with greater clarity but was not qualitatively distinct from that in other prophets. The reappearing charges against the Anabaptists, as well as traces of an evolution towards such conclusions in Denck, Hätzer, and later Entfelder, are best explained by the presence of this radically monotheistic tendency. However, the majority of Anabaptists remained within the borders of orthodoxy. For them the appeal to the inner Word was of a more utilitarian nature. As representatives of an anticlerical, lay movement it provided them with a rallying point of opposition against the Reformers' close association of the Word of God with the Scriptures. An exaggerated view of the importance of the letter supported an unwholesome division between laity and clergy. A new class of scribes, claiming a monopoly on God's revelation, was the consequence. In contrast the inner Word was accessible to all men, even the illiterate.

However, opposition to the Reformers extended well beyond this popular anticlericalism and anti-intellectualism. Some of the intellectual leaders of early South German Anabaptism, like Denck and Hut, consciously rejected both the Catholic authority of Scripture plus tradition and the Reformation authority of sola scriptura. Final authority rested with the inner Word, there where the Father addressed the Son. The tendency to interpret Scripture allegorically, plus the insistence that Scripture was very difficult to understand and filled with paradoxes, if not contradictions, was part of this larger mystical framework. Later, when a more biblicist and literalist spirit asserted itself in South German Anabaptism, some of the more consistent mystical thinkers deserted the movement, blaming a literalist hermeneutic for producing a divisive sectarian spirit.

This later development introduces the second major conclusion of our study. When turning from a theological content analysis of early Anabaptist thought to an evaluation of its functional role, we were confronted with the more basic question of the nature of the early South German-Austrian Anabaptist movement. Taking seriously the uniqueness of that movement, we were faced with the problem of how South German Anabaptism produced such unlikely progeny as the Marpeck circle and the Hutterites. We suggested a partial explanation of this issue in terms of a triad of mutations evolving from the Hut-Denck Anabaptism. At the same time we sought to show the dynamic nature of early South German Anabaptism in its development from a foiled revolutionary movement to an institutionalized sect. The early movement represented a transitional phenomenon between these two poles. Theologically it marked a transition from medieval mysticism to Protestantized sectarianism or Spiritualism. Sociologically it was a metastasis from a revolutionary movement largely inspired by social grievances left unresolved by the defeat of the peasants to a movement with a more consciously religious content. The functional role of Anabaptist ideology itself shifted under the changing circumstances from social protest to sectarian apologetics and confessional proselytising. The prominence of Hut and his apocalyptical ideas until mid-1528 permit the generalization that until that time the social impulses were more significant than later. However, the social inspiration varied in intensity from Hut's most immediate circle to those Anabaptists less influenced by him, and was focused geographically in Hut's original stamping ground in Franconia, existing in different degrees in Swabia, Moravia, and Austria. The historical Hut himself remains a chameleon who adjusted his message to changing circumstances. In his own mind the religious and social motifs remained inextricably interwoven. The defeat of the peasants and Müntzer shifted his expectations from active rebellion to divine intervention and invasion by the Turks. The punishment of the world, primarily the Obrigkeit, was to take place 3½ years after the abortive revolution of the peasants. He and the faithful remnant who had received adult baptism as the sign of the covenant would then inherit Christ's kingdom.

The resistance of leaders like Dachser and the controversy with Hubmaier in Nicolsburg indicate that not everyone in early South German Anabaptism accepted Hut's message of vengeance and of the imminent Parousia. Yet it is also clear that Hut's ideas had a powerful effect among an inner circle of followers. Many of these had been compromised by their involvement with the peasants. In fact, it is not an exaggeration to see Hut's apocalypticism as reflecting revolutionary impulses which had been thwarted by the impact of successful oppression. When Hut's predictions failed disintegration of the early revolutionary movement set in. The devolution of the Dreamers and Augustin Bader into illusions even less realistic than Hut's marked the final separation of the fantastic elements in the movement from those tendencies which were socially feasible and realistic. Bader crystallized Hut's apocalypticism into its "pure" form, postponing the date once more in a parody of the operation Hut had performed upon Müntzer.

Hut's movement also evolved in a moralistic and sectarian direction, no doubt influenced by the similar preoccupations of the Swiss Brethren. One group of Anabaptists externalized the Müntzerite mystical stress on internal suffering into moralism and a theology of martyrdom. Not all of them had accepted Hut's radical apocalypticism. We noticed different shades of what might be labelled evangelical Anabaptism present in leaders like Dachser, Schiemer, Schlaffer, Dorfbrunner, and the Freis-lebens. The chastened Hut, after his experience in Nicolsburg, may have himself moved in a similar direction. In any case, for many of his followers the social motives were gradually pushed into the background by the concern for the establishment of a pure Gemeinde. Under the proto-Hut-terite, Wolfgang Brandhuber of Linz, one can observe a new stress on the ban and nonresistance, probably resulting from the mingling of Hut's Anabaptism with the direct or indirect influence of Swiss Brethren refugees. Beyond that, in Linz we are met with the spectacle of Hut's former hopes for millennial equality crystallizing into sectarian communi-tarianism. It is, therefore, legitimate to see continutiy between the early revolutionary movement and the later South German and Austrian Anabaptist sects including the Hutterites and Pilgramites.

The emergence of the more quietistic, but also better disciplined, Anabaptist sectarians out of the devolution of Hut's original movement in 1528-29, brought with it its own inner tensions. Here a different dialectic was operative. In Austria, where the harshest persecution was experienced, the movement was welded together both by external pressures and by the enforcement of internal discipline, resulting in an un-flinching and inflexible attitude toward the persecutors and toward all those outside the fold. This development was encouraged by the emergence of a strong leader in the person of Jacob Hutter, who succeeded in imposing communitarian uniformity in Austria and Moravia. In this evolution theological purity was subordinated to the concern to keep the new community undefiled and separated from the world. Systematic or apologetic theology became merely instrumental for the Hutterites, be-ing directed outward and absorbed in a strong missionary thrust.

Consequently there survived in the writings of the Hutterite com-munity a rather colourful mingling of what to theologically trained eyes must appear to be contradictory motifs. These internal contradictions were negated by the overarching concern for the survival of the com-munity of brothers in a hostile environment. This partially explains why the ideas of Müntzer, Haug, Denck, and other even more mystical thinkers were not felt to be subversive, but loyally preserved as *Glaubens-zeugnisse*.

Yet the defection of the more consistent mystical thinkers such as Bünderlin and Entfelder would suggest that the mystical legacy carried within it internalizing tendencies which were incompatible with the institutionalization which set in after 1528-29 in Austria and Moravia. These "homeless minds" were not only disturbed by internal rifts originating in the struggle for leadership within the brotherhood, but also by the militantly separatist spirit of the emerging sect. From the mystical point of view this implied a return to an unbecoming concern with the creaturely and external. Moreover, the latent individualism of mysticism had to clash with the attempt to impose conformity through externals. The communitarian spirit, although a necessity in the struggle for survival, was felt as something stifling the creative and personal impulses of the mystical individualists.

The exodus from Anabaptism of the more consistently nonconformist but also more generously ecumenical spirits was, therefore, almost inevitable. These spiritual cousins of Denck (Hans Bünderlin, Christian Entfelder, and the Freisleben brothers) had not fled the externalism and quarrels of the religious establishments only to see them reproduced on a lilliputian scale. They retired into a purely individualistic, inward religiosity, cultivating the kingdom of God within. We are, therefore, suggesting a synthesis of the antithetical interpretations of Karl Holl and Ernst Troeltsch. On the one hand, Holl's approach, which stressed the continuity of mysticism and Anabaptism, was the more useful in grasping the content of early South German Anabaptist theology. The eventual parting of ways between the Anabaptist sectarians and the Spiritualists, on the other hand, supports Troeltsch's thesis of the incompatibility of mystical individualism and sectarian discipline. Yet, both Holl and Troeltsch erred because each had approached his problem ahistorically, one from the eternal verities of dogma, the other from the hypothetical stasis of the "ideal type."

An evolution towards a quietistic religious sect without the vigorous external communitarian controls of the Hutterites took place in South Germany under the leadership of Pilgram Marpeck. The Marpeck circle grew from persons at first in a loose communion with the communitarian *Stäbler* of Moravia. Unable to rest in the relative theological confusion of the Hutterites Marpeck was also reluctant to accept the parochial outlook of the Swiss Brethren. He aimed at establishing uniformity within the Anabaptist movement and to prevent its disintegration, not by imposing communitarian conformity—for this his followers were at any rate too scattered—but by clarifying, purifying, redefining, and systematizing the theological doctrines of the movement. Not surprisingly, the more mystical ideas of the spiritualizers who had been part of the intellectual leadership of the early movement proved subversive to Marpeck's endeavour. During the ensuing controversy, first with Bünderlin and later with Schwenckfeld, Marpeck himself was driven to assume a more or less

Protestantized position on many theological issues, including the Word of God and justification. Thus the more sectarian and quietistically religious nature of the later movements which grew from Hut's beginnings was achieved by two different routes—in Austria and Moravia through external pressures and internal discipline, in South Germany by theological and doctrinal redefinition. Neither the Pilgramites nor the Hutterites represented a simple continuation of the early movement which has been the subject of our inquiry.

Thus we have reiterated our contention that later developments ought not to be read back into the early movement. Swiss Anabaptist influence was present from the beginning but neither it nor the influence of Hubmaier was decisive in early South German and Austrian-Moravian Anabaptism. In contrast Müntzer exercised considerably greater influence than the demythologizers of the Schwärmer have hitherto been willing to admit. This fact helped to prejudice the traditional Protestant historiography which was in its formative stage during the period covered in our study. The devolution of Hut's movement provided further anecdotes for the Reformers' stereotyping of all Anabaptists.

The revisionists rendered excellent service in dismantling the polemical picture painted by historians within anti-Anabaptist confessional traditions. However, they too went beyond what was warranted by historical fact when they sought to make evangelical currents into a main stream of Anabaptism while arbitrarily making other parts of the movement into peripheral eddies. We suggest that, at least for the Anabaptists in South Germany and Austria from 1526 through 1531, a dynamic model which takes account of the diverse and transitional nature of much of the early movement is historically more fruitful than either of the two static interpretations noted above. And we are hopeful that this study may help to bridge the gap between the more traditional, dominantly European, and the revisionist, dominantly North American, interpretations of Anabaptism.

NOTES

Chapter I. A Medieval Point of Departure

1. Cf. a summary of the problem as relating to Luther in Heiko Oberman, "Simul Gemitus et Raptus," *The Church, Mysticism, Sanctification and the Natural in Luther's Thought*, ed. by Ivar Asheim (Philadelphia, 1967), p. 21. Karl-Heinz zur Mühlen, *Nos Extra Nos. Luthers Theologie zwischen Mystik und Scholastik* (Tübingen, 1972).

2. Karl Holl, "Luther und die Schwärmer," *Gesammelte Aufsätze zur Kirchengeschichte*, I (Tübingen, 1932), p. 420. A typical example of an historian in the Holl tradition is Heinrich Bornkamm, who credited Holl with rediscovering Müntzer as a theologian of some standing and then concluded as regards Müntzer's mysticism: "Ich brauche kaum darauf hinzuweisen, wie Luthers Gotteserlebnis und sein Bewusstsein der Freiheit durch den Geist der schöpferische Anstoss zu dieser Mystik gewesen sind." *Mystik, Spiritualismus und die Anfänge des Pietismus* (Giessen, 1926), p. 6.

3. Ernst Troeltsch, *Die Soziallehren der Christlichen Kirchen und Gruppen* (Tübingen, 1912) (hereafter referred to as *Soziallehren der Kirchen*), pp. 811, 967.

4. Alfred Hegler had been one of the first to differentiate between the more spiritualistic followers of Müntzer and Carlstadt and the Anabaptists, although he conceded: "... der Zusammenhang der Prinzipien und zum Teil auch die geschichtliche Verbindung ist eng." *Geist und Schrift bei Sebastian Franck. Eine Studie zur Geschichte des Spiritualismus in der Reformationszeit* (Freiburg, 1892), p. 4.

5. The most sophisticated results are found in George Williams and Heinold Fast. Fast, who distinguished between *Täufer, Spiritualisten, Schwärmer*, and *Antitrinitarier*, included influential Anabaptists among *Schwärmer* and *Spiritualisten*. Fast, ed., *Der linke Flügel der Reformation: Glaubenszeugnisse der Täufer, Spiritualisten, Schwärmer und Antitrinitarien* (Bremen, 1962); Williams, *The Radical Reformation* (Philadelphia, 1962).

6. Typical are the works of Fritz Blanke, specifically *Aus der Welt der Reformation* (Zürich/Stuttgart, 1960), pp. 73, 81, 83, and those of John Horsch and Harold Bender. The most sophisticated approach appears in the writings of John Howard Yoder.

7. This was recognized by Walter Klaassen with regard to the problem of Word and Spirit. "Troeltsch's approach ... prejudiced any real contribution immediately, because the real question here is doctrinal and not sociological...." "Word, Spirit, and Scripture in Early Anabaptist Thought" (unpublished PhD dissertation, Oxford, 1960) (hereafter referred to as "Word, Spirit and Scripture"), p. XVI.

8. Troeltsch, *Soziallehren der Kirchen*, p. 939.

9. Albert Ritschl, Adolf von Harnack, and Ludwig Keller were major advocates of medieval continuance into Anabaptism. Keller's thesis of Waldensian connections became the whipping boy for Reformation historians. Recently Claus-Peter Clasen again raised the question of possible Anabaptist links to medieval heresies. "Medieval Heresies in the Reformation," *CH*, XXXII (1963), p. 392. Bernd Moeller, claiming that the medieval heretical movements "came to an end in the late fifteenth century," rejected Clasen's contention. "Even if the covert survival and influence of medieval sects cannot simply be denied, the conclusion as a whole is not compelling. It does not take into consideration the fact that the breadth of variation in sectarian themes within the realm of Christianity is relatively limited." "Piety in Germany around 1500," trans. by Joyce Irwin. *The Reformation in Medieval Perspective*, ed. by Steven Ozment (Chicago, 1971), p. 66.

10. George Williams, "Popularized German Mysticism as a Factor in the Rise of Anabaptist Communism," *Glaube, Geist, Geschichte: Festschrift für Ernst Benz*, ed. by Gerhard Müller and Winfried Zeller (Marburg, 1967) hereafter referred to as "Popularized German Mysticism"), p. 290.

11. See the article by Klaus Deppermann, Werner Packull, and James Stayer, "From

Monogenesis to Polygenesis: The Historical Discussion of Anabaptist Origins," *MQR*, XLIX (1975) (hereafter referred to as "From Monogenesis to Polygenesis"), pp. 83-121.

12. This has led John Howard Yoder to date the formation of Anabaptism proper from the Schleitheim Confession. "Der Kristallisationspunkt des Täufertums," *MGB*, XXIX (1972), pp. 35-47. On the question of whether or not Michael Sattler's relation to the Strassburg Reformers also implied a sectarian stance see Klaus Deppermann, "Die Strassburger Reformatoren und die Krise des oberdeutschen Täufertums im Jahr 1527," *MGB*, XXX (1973), pp. 24-41.

13. See the recent articles by James M. Stayer, Martin Haas, and Heinold Fast in Hans-Jürgen Goertz, ed., *Umstrittenes Täufertum 1525-1975; Neue Forschungen* (Göttingen, 1975); also Stayer's paper read at Colloque sur les débuts et les caractéristiques de l' anabaptisme au XVIe siécle entitled "Reublin and Brötli: The Revolutionary Beginnings of Swiss Anabaptism."

14. Kenneth Davis, *Anabaptism and Asceticism: A Study in Intellectual Origins* (Scottdale, Pennsylvania, 1974).

15. David Steinmetz, "Scholasticism and Radical Reform; Nominalist Motifs in the Theology of Balthasar Hubmaier," *MQR*, XL (1971), p. 137. Christof Windhorst, *Taüferisches Taufverständnis Balthasar Hubmaiers, Lehre zwischen traditioneller und reformatorischen Theologie* (Leiden, 1976). (PhD dissertation, Heidelberg, 1974); "Wort und Geist; Zur Frage des Spiritualismus bei Balthasar Hubmaier im Vergleich zu Zwingli und Luther," *MGB*, XXXI (1974), pp. 7-24. "Initial Stages and Aspects in the Theology of Balthasar Hubmaier" (paper read on February 22, 1975, at Colloque sur les débuts et les caractéristiques de l' anabaptisme au XVIe sie'cle.

16. Hans-Jürgen Goertz, *Innere und Äussere Ordnung in der Theologie Thomas Müntzers* (Leiden, 1967) (hereafter referred to as *Innere und Äussere Ordnung); "Der Mystiker mit dem Hammer," *Kerygma und Dogma*, XX (1974), pp. 23-53; Gordon Rupp, *Patterns of Reformation* (London, 1967); Steven Ozment, *Mysticism and Dissent: Religious Ideology and Social Protest in the Sixteenth Century* (New Haven and London, 1973) (hereafter referred to as *Mysticism and Dissent).

17. For a discussion of the two traditions and their relationship to late medieval nominalism see Heiko Oberman, *The Harvest of Medieval Theology* (Grand Rapids, Michigan, 1967), pp. 323-361. Steven Ozment, "Mysticism, Nominalism and Dissent," *Pursuit of Holiness*, ed. by Haiko Oberman and C. E. Trinkaus (Leiden, 1973), pp. 67-92.

18. Kurt Ruh, *Bonaventura Deutsch* (Bern, 1956), pp. 56 ff.

19. This information was brought to my attention by Dennis Martin, graduate student of the History Department, University of Waterloo, Canada.

20. Ozment, "Mysticism, Nominalism and Dissent," pp. 73, 77, 78.

21. Ozment, *Mysticism and Dissent*, p. 13.

22. Konrad Weiss speaks of the *Grundgedanke*, "dass die Seele der Ort unbedingter Verbundenheit zwischen Gott und Mensch sei, und zwar wesenhaft, ihrer Natur nach...." "Die Seelenmetaphysik des Meister Eckhart," *ZKG*, LII (1933) (hereafter referred to as "Seelenmetaphysik"), pp. 491, 504.

23. St. Augustine has generally been accepted as the source of trinitarian speculation. Kurt Ruh, "Die trinitarische Spekulation in deutscher Mystik und Scholastik," *Zeitschrift für deutsche Philologie*, LXXII (1953) (hereafter referred to as "Spekulation"), p. 25. Ruh contrasts the mystical Neoplatonic dynamic concept of God,". . . dessen neidlose Güte es zur Selbstmitteilung drängt" with the Aristotelian scholastic tradition which emphasises God as the unmoved mover (p. 41). Within this frame of reference Ruh sees the scholastic tradition as concerned with pure doctrine and clear formulations, mysticism with "Umformung, Umkehr, Wandlung, Neugeburt des menschlichen Herzens" (p. 51).

24. Josef Quint, ed. and trans., *Meister Eckharts Predigten*, Vol. 1 (Stuttgart, 1958), p. 180.

25. Franz Pfeiffer, ed., *Meister Eckhart*, Vol. II: *Deutsche Mystiker des Vierzehnten*

Jahrhunderts (Aalen, 1962), pp. 527-533, 578-580.

26. Quint, *Meister Eckharts Predigten*, V. pp. 46-47.

27. Weiss, "Seelenmetaphysik," p. 468. As to the controversy over whether Eckhardt taught the uncreatedness of the rational powers of the soul see also pp. 494-500.

28. Quint, *Meister Eckharts Predigten*, I, p. 152; Pfeiffer, *Meister Eckhart*, II, p. 188. Frederick, Copelston, *A History of Philosophy*, III, *Late Medieval and Renaissance Philosophy*, Part 1: *Ockham to the Speculative Mystics* (New York, 1963) (hereafter *History of Philosophy*, III, Part 1), pp. 196-197.

29. Quint, *Meister Eckharts Predigten*, I, pp. 49-50, 55.

30. *Ibid.*, p. 177. Weiss, "Seelenmetaphysik," pp. 521, 523, 524.

31. Quint, *Meister Eckharts Predigten*, I, p. 476.

32. Leopold Naumann rightly observed, "In der Entwicklung der Mystik spielt der Logos, das Wort, die bestimmende Rolle. Der Logos bildet das Bindeglied zwischen der wesenlosen Gottheit,... und der Welt mit ihren Erscheinungen." *Deutsche Mystik* (Leipzig, 1925), p. 6.

33. Quint, *Meister Eckharts Predigten*, V. p. 509; Pfeiffer, *Meister Eckhart*, II, pp. 239-240. Ozment, *Mysticism and Dissent*, pp. 1-2; Heinrich Ebeling, *Meister Eckharts Mystik* (Stuttgart, 1941; reprint Aalen: Scientia, 1966), pp. 173 ff.; Bardo Weiss, *Die Heilsgeschichte bei Meister Eckhart* (Mainz, 1965), pp. 147-159.

34. A good example is Eckhardt's interpretation of Christ's conversation with the woman at the well who is asked to bring her husband. Her husband is interpreted as meaning her will. Her former five husbands are interpreted as the five senses through which she sinned. Thus the historical encounter is given a universal, spiritual application.

35. Zur Mühlen has pointed out that in mystical thought salvation was inconceivable without attributing to human nature some soteriological quality. *Nos Extra Nos*, p. 97.

36. Christine Pleuser has claimed that Tauler had first-hand knowledge of Eckhardt and that Eckhardt's influence was pronounced. *Die Benennung und Begriff des Leidens bei J. Tauler* (Berlin, 1967) (hereafter referred to as *Benennung und der Begriff des Leidens*), pp. 42, 52. For Tauler's and Eckhardt's relation to the *Theologia* see Joseph Bernhart in the Introduction to *Theologia Germanica*, trans. by Susanna Winkworth (New York, 1949) (hereafter referred to as *Theologia*), pp. 101, 103.

37. The many editions of the *Theologia* and of Tauler's works on the eve of the Reformation attest to their popularity. See Joachim Seypel, ed., *Texte deutscher Mystik des 16. Jahrhunderts Unruhe und Stillstand* (Göttingen, 1963) (hereafter referred to as *Texte deutscher Mystik*).

38. Copleston, *History of Philosophy*, III, Part I, p. 208.

39. Recent literature has argued that Tauler's *unio mystica* did not imply ontological or substantive union between man and God. Steven Ozment, *Homo Spiritualis: A Comparative Study of the Anthropology of Johannes Tauler, Jean Gerson and Martin Luther (1509-16) in the Context of their Theological Thought* (Leiden, 1969) (hereafter referred to as *Homo Spiritualis*), p. 36.

40. Bengt Hägglund has claimed that Tauler and the *Theologia Deutsch* embraced a strictly Augustinian position on human sinfulness. *The Background of Luther's Doctrine of Justification in Late Medieval Theology* (Philadelphia, 1971) (hereafter referred to as *Background of Luther's Theology*), p. 10.

41. Ferdinand Vetter, *Die Predigten Taulers* (Dublin/Zürich, 1968), p. 19; Susanna Winkworth, *The History and Life of the Reverend Doctor John Tauler of Strasbourg with Twenty-five of His Sermons* (London, 1857) (hereafter referred to as *History of Tauler*), pp. 190-191; Pleuser, *Benennung und Begriff des Leidens*, p. 181.

42. Winkworth, *History of Tauler*, pp. 264-265. Vetter, *Die Predigten Taulers*, pp. 229, 233.

43. Pleuser, *Benennung und Begriff des Leidens*, pp. 206-207.

44. *Theologia*, p. 162.

45. *Ibid.*, pp. 99, 117-118, 154.

46. *Ibid.*, pp. 216, 223-225.

47. This was basically the thesis of Hägglund seeking to reject Horst Quiring's contention that the mystical *resignatio* unlike Luther's *resignatio ad infernum* never cut loose from an anthropocentric religiosity which in its essence remained disguised selfishness. Hägglund, *Background of Luther's Theology,* pp. 7, 13; Horst Quiring, "Luther und die Mystik," *ZST,* XIII (1936), pp. 159, 217.

48. This is part of Joseph Lortz' thesis, *The Reformation in Germany,* trans. by Ronald Walls, vols. I and II (London, 1968).

49. This ambivalence is shared by all the mystics. Ozment, *Homo Spiritualis,* p. 33.

50. *Theologia,* p. 210.

51. For Tauler see Winkworth, *History of Tauler,* pp. 380-381 and the discussion by Hägglund, *Background of Luther's Theology,* p. 13; Pleuser, *Benennung und Begriff des Leidens,* p. 182.

52. *Theologia,* p. 127.

53. Ozment, "Mysticism, Nominalism and Dissent," p. 81.

54. *Ibid.*, pp. 77-81

55. *Ibid.*, p. 82.

56. I am indebted to Ozment for the discussion of the dual covenant above; see *Homo Spiritualis,* pp. 25, 43, 199; Ozment in turn adapts his terminology about the *potentia ordinata Dei* from Oberman, *The Harvest of Medieval Theology.*

57. *Theologia,* p. 114, and pp. 222 and 142, respectively: "If the creator shall enter in, all creature must depart." "The more the Mine, the I, the Me, that is I-hood and self-hood abate in a man, the more does God's 'I,' that is, God Himself, increase in Him."

58. The *Theologia* speaks of purification, illumination, and union. *Ibid.*, p. 137.

59. It has long been recognized that later many of the Anabaptists "tended to interpret justification in the sense of sanctification." George Williams, "Sanctification in the Testimony of Several So-called *Schwärmer,*" *The Church, Mysticism, Sanctification and the Natural in Luther's Thought,* ed. by Ivar Asheim (Philadelphia, 1967) (hereafter referred to as "Sanctification"), p. 206.

60. This is so regardless of the question as to whether grace was in man or infused. Otto Scheel, "Taulers Mystik und Luthers reformatorische Entdeckung," *Festgabe für Julius Kafton* (Tübingen, 1920). p. 311; see also Ozment, *Homo Spiritualis,* p. 4.

61. This was basically Tauler's understanding of justification. Ozment, *Homo Spiritualis,* pp. 28, 46.

62. *Ibid,* pp. 2-4, 23, 24, 152, 197, 215, 216.

63. Oberman, "Simul Gemitus et Raptus," pp. 32, 33-35; Quiring had believed that Luther's break with this central mystical assumption of the divine in man was not complete until 1519. Such a view opposes the popular misconception that Luther turned against mysticism only when he recognized its dangers in debate with the "left wing" of the Reformation. Quiring, "Luther und die Mystik," p. 182-183, 203, 204, 206.

64. Zur Mühlen, *Nos Extra Nos,* pp. 105-106, 111, 113, 174, 175, 198-199. It goes without saying that a citation of Zur Mühlen or any of the other Lutheran scholars in this context does not imply agreement with their general assumption that Luther rediscovered St. Paul pure and simple.

65. This is Hägglund's conclusion, who, it will be remembered, sought to counter Quiring's attempt to separate Luther altogether from the mystical tradition. Hägglund, *Background of Luther's Theology,* pp. 15-16, 34; see also Quiring, "Luther und die Mystik," p. 183; U. Saarnivaara, *Luther Discovers the Gospel* (St. Louis, 1951), pp. 75, 76, 81, 117.

66. Erwin Iserloh contrasts *Logosmystik* with *Christusmystik,* but sees mystical overtones in Luther's concept of faith. However, Iserloh's existentialized interpretation of Luther is suspect. Iserloh, "Luther und die Mystik", *The Church, Mysticism, Sanctification and the Natural in Luther's Thought,* ed. by Ivar Asheim (Philadelphia, 1967), pp. 61, 66, 68.

67. Regin Prenter, *Luther's Theology of the Cross* (Philadelphia, 1971), p. 3, Zur Mühlen, *Nos Extra Nos*, pp. 34, 91, 92, 162, 252.

68. This appears to be the tendency of Gordon Rupp. In one of his articles, "Protestant Spirituality in the First Age of the Reformation," *Popular Belief and Practice*, ed. by G. J. Cuming and D. Baker (Cambridge, 1972)(hereafter "Protestant Spirituality"), p. 156, Rupp was indebted to Werner Hälsbusch, a Catholic scholar who demonstrated similarities between Luther and "Elements of a Theology of the Cross in Saint Bonaventura."

69. Goertz, *Innere und Äussere Ordnung*, pp. 47, 58. Goertz here differs with Günther Goldbach who distinguishes between Denck, the mystic, and Müntzer, the spiritualist. "Hans Denck und Thomas Müntzer—ein Vergleich ihrer wesentlichen theologischen Auffassung. Eine Untersuchung zur Morphologie der Randströmung der Reformation" (unpublished DTh dissertation, University of Hamburg, 1969) (hereafter referred to as "Morphologie"), pp. 61-64, 68-69.

70. *Thomas Müntzer, Schriften und Briefe*, ed. by Günther Franz (Gütersloh, 1968) (hereafter *Müntzers Schriften*), p. 224.

71. Goertz, *Innere und Äussere Ordnung*, p. 49, and "Der Mystiker mit dem Hammer," pp. 28-36.

72. This observation was made by Goertz, *Innere und Äussere Ordnung*, p. 66; Ozment, *Mysticism and Dissent*, p. 89.

73. *Müntzers Schriften*, p. 251.

74. *Ibid.*, pp. 237, 489.

75. Goertz, *Innere und Äussere Ordnung*, pp. 86-87.

76. The conventional definition is given by G. Born: "Geht die Mystik von der im Grunde immer schon gegebenen Einheit des Menschen mit Gott aus, so ist dieses dem Spiritualismus versagt. Für diesen ist zwischen Gott und Mensch eine Kluft, die nur von Gott durch den . . . Geist überbrückt werden kann." "Geist, Wissen und Bildung bei Thomas Müntzer und Valentin Icklsamer" (unpublished dissertation, Erlangen, 1952), pp. 13-14.

77. Rudolf von Stadelmann made the point that mysticism provided the roots of both spiritualism and humanism. *Vom Geist des Ausgehenden Mittelalters: Studien zur Geschichte der Weltanschauung von Nicolaus Cusanus bis Sebastian Franck* (Halle/Salle, 1929), pp. 37-39.

78. *Müntzers Schriften*, pp. 279-280.

79. Goertz, *Innere und Äussere Ordnung*, pp. 69, 119; see also Ozment, *Mysticism and Dissent*, pp. 83-84.

80. Müntzer's alleged biblicism grows out of the functional role of Scripture in his system as well as the fashion of the day. Besides the confirming function (*Zeugnis*) above, he also permits Scripture a role as law or letter. With regard to the latter, both Old Testament and New Testament fall into the same category and as law can aid a preliminary purification process which loosens man from the creaturely and directs his attention to the inner Word. Goertz *Innere und Äussere Ordnung*, pp. 73-79.

81. *Müntzers Schriften*, p. 327.

82. This appears to be the misunderstanding of Müntzer which perpetuates itself in scholarship which views him one-sidedly as a wayward disciple of Luther. Goldbach, "Morphologie," pp. 47, 64-66, 107.

83. Goertz, *Innere und Äussere Ordnung*, pp. 59, 66, 115.

84. *Müntzers Schriften*, p. 339, n 35.

85. *Ibid.*, p. 224: "Do einander vor ir leidet, do bewbt er ein stargken glauben."

86. For similarities between Tauler and Müntzer on this point see Gordon Rupp, *Patterns of Reformation*, p. 290. I disagree with Goldbach, who maintained that Müntzer's understanding of suffering was not derived from mysticism. "Morphologie," p. 53.

87. This is a fitting description given to Müntzer by James Stayer, *Anabaptists and the Sword* (Lawrence, Kansas, 1972), ch. 4.

88. Müntzer's references to *auserwählte*—chosen ones—must be understood within

this context as meaning self-selected instruments of God rather than in the Reformation framework of predestinarianism.

89. For a further discussion of Müntzer's revolutionary theology see Carl Hinrichs, *Luther und Müntzer; ihre Auseinandersetzung über Obrigkeit und Widerstandsrecht* (Berlin, 1952, p. 174; Stayer, *Anabaptists and the Sword*, pp. 73-90; Carl Braaten, "Theologie der Revolution," *Luther. Monatshefte*, V (1968); Thomas Nipperdey, "Theologie und Revolution bei Thomas Müntzer," *ARG*, LIV (1963), pp. 145-181; Gottfried Maron "Thomas Müntzer als Theologe des Gerichts. Das 'Urteil'—ein Schlüsselbegriff seines Denkens," *ZKG*, LXXXIII (1972), pp. 195-225.

90. John Oyer, *Lutheran Reformers Against Anabaptists: Luther, Melanchthon and Menius and the Anabaptists in Central Germany* (The Hague, 1964) (hereafter referred to as *Reformers Against Anabaptists*), p. 238; see also Gerhard Neumann, "Eschatologische und chiliastische Gedanken in der Reformationszeit, besonders bei den Täufern," *Die Welt als Geschichte*, XIX (1959), p. 59.

91. Wolfgan Schäufele, *Das missionarische Bewusstsein und Wirken der Täufer* (Neukirchen, 1966), p. 84.

92. See my comments on Michael Stiefel below. P. 140.

93. See the references by Melanchthon and Myconius to medieval prophecies fulfilled in Luther cited by Marjorie Reeves in *The Influence of Prophecy in the Later Middle Ages* (Oxford, 1969) (hereafter referred to as *Influence of Prophecy*), pp. 233-234.

94. Reeves, *Influence of Prophecy*, pp. 96, 258-259; Steven Ozment, ed., *The Reformation in Medieval Perspective* (Chicago, 1971, pp. 4-5.

95. Reeves, *Influence of Prophecy*, p. 262.

96. *Müntzers Schriften*, p. 398.

97. Abraham Friesen, "Thomas Müntzer and the Old Testament," *MQR*, XLVII (1973), pp. 5-19; Günther List, *Chiliastische Utopie und Radikale Reformation. Die Erneuerung der Idee vom Tausendjährigen Reich im 16. Jahrhundert* (Munich, 1973) (hereafter *Utopie und Reformation*), p. 139. However, List in speaking of Müntzer's "Gerichtsapokalyptik" and his concern to collect a church of the elect is overly dependent on Nipperdey's interpretation of Müntzer.

98. Norman Cohn, *The Pursuit of the Millennium* (New York, 1961), pp. 3-31; Reeves, *Influence of Prophecy*, p. 175: "A Joachimite view of history produced a mood somewhat akin to that of an early Marxist, a mood of certainty and urgency."; also pp. 138, 245-248.

99. One of the puzzles that awaits further examination is how Peter Olivi's *Postil on the Apocalypse*, translated into German, became part of the Hutterite heritage. Robert Friedmann, "A Hutterite Book of Medieval Origin," *MQR* XXX (1965), pp. 65-71; *Die Schriften der Huterischen Täufergemeinschaften. Gesamtkatalog Ihrer Manuskriptbücher, Ihrer Schreiber und Ihrer Literatur 1529-1667* (Vienna, 1965), pp. 57, 76-77; and "Olivi, Petrus," *ME*, IV (1959), p. 1113. Reeves found traces of Joachimism in Müntzer, Melchior Hoffmann, and David Joris. *Influence of Prophecy*, pp. 473, 482-483, 492.

100. Saint Augustine, *The City of God*, ed. by Vernon Rourke (abridged ed., New York, 1958), pp. 544-545.

101. "Für den dazwischen liegenden sechsten Zeitraum ist 'Millennium' nicht unbedingt eine exakte Zahlenangabe, sondern vor allem ein mystischer Begriff der Vollkommenheit." List, *Utopie und Reformation*, pp. 68-69.

102. Franz Förschner, "Concordia, Urgestalt und Sinnbild in der Geschichtsdeutung des Joachim von Fiore. Eine Studie zum Symbolismus des Mittelalters" (unpublished PhD dissertation, Albert-Ludwig University, Freiburg, 1970) (hereafter referred to as "Joachim von Fiore"), p. 19; Cohn, *The Pursuit of the Millennium*, pp. 13-14; Herbert Grundmann, *Studien über Joachim von Fiore* (reprint of 1927 edition, Darmstadt, 1966), p. 77.

103. Förschner, "Joachim von Fiore," p. 2.

104. Grundmann, *Studien über Joachim von Fiore*; List, *Utopie und Reformation*, pp. 81-85.

105. Grundmann, *Studien über Joachim von Fiore*, pp. 58-60; Marjorie Reeves and Beatrice Hirsch-Reich, *The Figurae of Joachim of Fiore* (Oxford, 1972), p. 7; Reeves, *Influence of Prophecy*, pp. 198-199.

106. Marx Maier spoke of a fleshly Christ, a spiritual Christ incarnate in the true disciples, and a clarified Christ. *TA: Bayern*, I, pp. 193, 213-214.

107. See in particular Schiemer in A. Zieglschmid, "Unpublished Sixteenth-Century Letters of the Hutterian Brethren," *MQR*, XV (1941), pp. 10, 14.

108. Reeves and Hirsch-Reich, *The Figurae of Joachim of Fiore*, pp. 5-6; Reeves, *Influence of Prophecy*, pp. 5, 191, 196.

Chapter II. Hans Denck: the Ecumenical Anabaptist

1. This label was given to Denck by G. Haake, *Hans Denck, ein Vorläufer der neueren Theologie: 1495-1527* (Norden, 1897) (hereafter referred to as *Denck, ein Vorläufer*), p. 45.

2. Adolf Schwindt, *Hans Denck, ein Vorkämpfer undogmatischen Christentums, 1495-1527* (Habershof, 1924) (hereafter referred to as *Denck, ein Vorkämpfer*).

3. S. Cramer, "Die geschichtliche und religiöse Bedeutung Hans Dencks und der Täufer," *Protestantische Kirchenzeitung für das evangelische Deutschland*, XXX (1883); see also Richard Heath, "Hans Denck, the Anabaptist," *Contemporary Review*, LXII (1892).

4. Arthur Kreiner, "Die Bedeutung Hans Dencks und Sebastian Francks," *Mitteilung des Vereins für die Geschichte Nürnbergs*, XXXIX (1944).

5. Traces of this attitude can be found in the writings of John Horsch, Harold Bender, William Klassen, and even Heinold Fast.

6. *ZHVSN: Hut*, p. 224.

7. Werner Packull, "Denck's Alleged Baptistm by Hubmaier. Its Significance for the Origin of South German-Austrian Anabaptism," *MQR*, XLVII (1973) (hereafter referred to as "Denck's Alleged Baptism").

8. Jan Kiwiet, "Hans Denck and His Teaching (ca. 1500-1527)" (unpublished BD thesis, Baptist Theological Seminary, Rüschlikon-Zürich, 1954); "The Life of Hans Denck," *MQR*, XXXI (1957); "The Theology of Hans Denck," *MQR*, XXXII (1958) and *Pilgram Marbeck*, 2nd edition (Kassel, 1958).

9. "Introduction," *LCC: SAW*, pp. 32-33.

10. See my discussion of recent interpretations of Denck in Stayer, Packull, Deppermann, "From Monogenesis to Polygenesis," pp. 100-111.

11. For a brief biography of Denck see *TA: Denck*, Part II, pp. 8-19.

12. An edition of Tauler's writings appeared during Denck's stay as proofreader in Basel. Goldbach, "Morphologie," p. 51, n. 3. That Denck was a student of Tauler and mysticism is evident from Hätzer's edition of the *Theologia Deutsch*, which appeared with Denck's *Schlussreden*. Denck's indebtedness to mysticism is, therefore, one of the few axioms on which a general agreement exists among all scholars.

13. "Von der Nachfolgung des willigen Sterbens Jesu Christi," *Johannes Staupitzens sämtlichen Werken*, ed. by J. K. Knaake, I (Potsdam, 1867), pp. 52 ff. Ludwig Keller, *Johann von Staupitz und die Anfänge der Reformation* (Nieuwkoop, 1967), pp. 29-35.

14. Gottfried Seebass, "Die Reformation in Nürnberg," *Mitteilung des Vereins für Geschichte der Stadt Nürnberg*, LV (1967-1968), p. 254; Friedrich Roth, *Die Einführung der Reformation in Nürnberg 1517-1528* (Würzburg, 1885) (hereafter referred to as *Einführung Nürnberg*), pp. 16-20.

15. On Osiander see Gottfried Seebass, *Das reformatorische Werk des Andreas Osiander* (Nuremberg, 1967) (hereafter referred to as *Osiander*).

16. Claus-Peter Clasen, "Nuernberg in the History of Anabaptism," *MQR*, XXXIX (1965), p. 25; Günther Bauer, *Anfänge täuferischer Gemeindebildungen in Franken* (Nuremberg, 1966), pp. 115-127.

17. Gerhard Pfeiffer, ed., *Quellen zur Nürnberger Reformationsgeschichte* (Nuremberg, 1968), p. 6.

18. Seebass, *Osiander*, p. 115.

19. Theodor Kolde, "Zum Prozess des Johann Denck und der drei gottlosen Maler" von Nürnberg," *Kirchengeschichtliche Studien* (Leipzig, 1888) (hereafter "Prozess"), p. 229.

20. *TA: Denck*, Part II, p. 10. Carlstadt, during this period, was influenced by the mystical tradition. Ronald Sider, *Andreas Bodenstein von Karlstadt. The Development of His Thought 1517-1525* (Leiden, 1974).

21. A list of seven of Greiffenberger's tracts in Theodor Kolde, "Hans Denck und die gottlosen Maler in Nürnberg," *Beiträge zur bayerischen Kirchengeschichte*, VIII (1901) (hereafter referred to as "Denck und die Maler"). pp. 12-13.

22. Philoon Thurmann, "Hans Greiffenberger and the Reformation in Nuernberg," *MQR*, XXXVI (1962) (hereafter "Greiffenberger"), p. 66.

23. Reinhardt, expelled from Jena, had dedicated *Anzaygung wie die gefallene Christenheit widerbracht mäg werdn in jren ersten standt. . . .* to Pirkheimer and the Nuremberg city council. He was expelled as a *Schwärmer* on December 17, 1524. Pfeiffer, *Quellen zur Nürnberger Reformationsgeschichte*, p. 32.

24. *Ein Sermo/von Fest der heiligen drey Konig/gepredigt/durch Simonen/Haferitz zu Allsted/MD 1524.* Haferitz is only mentioned once in Müntzer's correspondence. *Müntzers Schriften*, p. 401. According to Kolde, he matriculated from Wittenberg in 1522 and later, in 1530, once more enjoyed Luther's confidence. Kolde, "Denck und die Maler," pp. 24, 27.

25. Kolde, "Denck und die Maler," p. 27.

26. *Ibid.*, pp. 24-26.

27. *Ibid.*, p. 27.

28. *ZHVSN: Hut*, pp. 207, 224, 229. Hut may have been Denck's guest several times in 1524. Hans-Dieter Schmid, *Täufertum und Obrigkeit in Nürnberg* (Erlangen, 1972), p. 11.

29. Müntzer had entrusted the manuscript to Hut in Bibra after he and Pfeiffer had been driven from Mühlhausen. Kolde had mistakenly believed that Müntzer was in Nuremberg in October and did not identify the *Buchführer* from "Mellerstadt with Hut, Kolde, "Denck und die Maler," p. 9. This has been done since then. Gottfried Seebass, "Müntzers Erbe: Werk, Leben und Theologie des Hans Hut (gestorben 1527)," (Habilitationsschrift der Theologischen Fakultät der Friedrich-Alexander Universität zu Erlangen-Nürnberg, 1972) (hereafter "Müntzers Erbe"), pp. 102-104; Schmid, *Täufertum und Obrigkeit in Nürnberg*, p. 12; *Müntzers Schriften*, p. 265; Georg Baring, "Hans Denck und Thomas Müntzer in Nürnberg 1524," *ARG*, L (1959), p. 152.

30. The fact that one hundred copies were sent to Augsburg indicates that connections existed between Nuremberg radicals and circles in that city. Hans Langenmantel's servant later testified that Hut had been recommended in a letter by one "Martin from Nuremberg." *ZHVSN: Langenmantel*, p. 22.

31. Pfeiffer, *Quellen zur Nürnberger Reformationsgeschichte*, pp. 25-26; Ozment, *Mysticism and Dissent*, p. 116.

32. Pfeiffer, *Quellen zur Nürnberger Reformationsgeschichte*, pp. 292-293; Kolde, "Denck und die Maler," pp. 28-29.

33. Pfeiffer, *Quellen zur Nürnberger Reformationsgeschichte*, pp. 25-27.

34. The *Hochverursachte Schutzrede* was printed by Hötzel, who also produced a larger edition of Carlstadt's writings. *TA: Denck*, Part II, p. 10; *Müntzers Schriften*, p. 321.

35. *Müntzers Schriften*, pp. 449-450.

36. Baring claimed that Müntzer lived for four weeks with Denck. "Hans Denck und Thomas Müntzer in Nürnberg," p. 154. Fellmann noticed that the sources do not reveal whether personal contact was made between Müntzer and Denck. *TA: Denck*, Part II, p. 10. Goldbach, whose thesis was diametrically opposed to Baring, seconded Fellmann, finding it incredible that Müntzer could have been in Nuremberg for four weeks without being discovered. Goldbach, "Morphologie," p. 30.

37. *Müntzers Schriften*, p. 544. Ernst Stähelin, *Briefe und Akten zum Leben Oekolam-*

pads, 2 vols. (Leipzig, 1927/34), I, pp. 330, 390, 419.

38. Pfeiffer, *Quellen zur Nürnberger Reformationsgeschichte*, p. 27.

39. Rupp, "Protestant Spirituality," p. 164.

40. Pfeiffer, *Quellen zur Nürnberger Reformationsgeschichte*, p. 343. Capito on February 6, 1525, informed Zwingli that Denck was denying the orthodox formula on the Trinity. Ulrich Zwingli, *Huldreich Zwinglis sämtliche Werke*, ed. by Emil Egli, et al (Leipzig, 1905-) (hereafter referred to as *Zwinglis Werke*), VII, p. 362, also p. 302.

41. Pfeiffer, *Quellen zur Nürnberger Reformationsgeschichte*, p. 40: "Die 3 gefangen maler ruen lassen, biss die sach mit dem schulmaister geortert wird...."

42. *TA: Denck*, Part II, p. 26.

43. Pfeiffer, *Quellen zur Nürnberger Reformationsgeschichte*, p. 42. See also a letter by one of Denck's former students in June 1525. He connected Denck's expulsion with that of the "godless painters" (p. 424).

44. Kiwiet's approach can hardly be considered historical on this issue. "Hans Denck and His Teaching," p. 18:" It is however very misleading to call Denck a mystical thinker.... Denck's teaching ... starts off from the Bible...." *Pilgram Marbeck*, p. 41: "Am Luthertum enttäuscht, fing er an, selbständig die Probleme seiner Zeit zu durchdenken."

45. A notable exception, seeking to separate Denck from Müntzer even at this stage, was Goldbach. Goldbach reacted against Baring who saw in Müntzer a determining influence on all of Denck's thought. Seebass believed that Denck was under Müntzer's influence in Nuremberg, but thereafter developed independent views. Seebass, "Müntzers Erbe" Appendix, p. 189, n. 81.

46. See letter of April 1525 by Oecolampadius to Pirkheimer, in Ernst Stähelin, ed., *Briefe und Akten zum Leben Oekolampads*, I, p. 365. The objections which Christian Neff raised against a stay of Denck in Mühlhausen are not convincing. "Hans Denck," *ML*, I, pp. 401-404; William Stoez, "At the Foundation of Anabaptism: A Study of Thomas Müntzer, Hans Denck and Hans Hut" (unpublished PhD dissertation, New York, Union Theological Seminary and Columbia University, 1964) (hereafter "Foundation of Anabaptism"), p. 159.

47. Baring, "Hans Denck und Thomas Müntzer in Nürnberg," p. 178.

48. *TA: Ostschweiz*, p. 274.

49. Traditionally it was believed that Denck arrived in the area sometime in June 1525. *TA: Denck*, Part II, p. 11. However, Heinold Fast dated Denck's appearance in St. Gall as September 1525. "Hans Krüsis Büchlein über Glauben und Taufe; ein Täuferdruck von 1525" *Zwingliana*, XI (1962) (hereafter referred to as "Krüsis Büchlein"), p. 474, n 78.

50. Fast, "Krüsis Büchlein," p. 464.

51. On a popularized level, this was said to mean that Denck taught the salvation of the devil. *Johannes Kesslers Sabbata, St. Galler Reformationschronik 1523-1539*, ed. by Traugott Schiess, *Schriften des Vereins für Reformationsgeschichte*, XXVIII (1911), p. 50; Stähelin, *Briefe und Akten zum Leben Oekolampads*, I, p. 364 and II, pp. 52-53.

52. Among these were Kiwiet, "Hans Denck and His Teachings," p. 31; Alvin Beachy, "The Concept of Grace in the Radical Reformation" (unpublished ThD thesis, Harvard University, 1960) (hereafter referred to as, "Concept of Grace"), p. 89, and specifically William Klassen, "Was Hans Denck a Universalist?" *MQR*, XXXIX (1965).

53. Kiwiet, "Hans Denck and His Teachings," pp. 31, 36.

54. W. Klassen, "Was Hans Denck a Universalist?" pp. 153-154. Cf. a similar cautious approach in David Steinmetz, who limited Denck's universalism to a "universalism of opportunity and responsibility." *Reformers in the Wings*, (Philadelphia, 1971), p. 216.

55. *TA: Bayern*, II, p. 8; *TA: Bayern*, I pp, 19-20; Paul Wappler, *Die Täuferbewegung in Thüringen von 1526-1584* (Jena, 1913), pp. 245-246. See below pp. 83, 91, 105.

56. List, *Utopia und Reformation*, pp. 160-166.

57. Denck arrived from St. Gall some time in late September 1525. *TA: Denck*, Part II, p. 12.

58. Packull, "Denck's Alleged Baptism by Hubmaier," p. 327-338.

59. Urbanus Rhegius, *Ein Sendbrieff Hans huthen etwa ains furnemen Vorsteers im*

widertaufferordem verantwort (Augsburg: A. Weyssenhorn, 1528) (hereafter referred to as *Ein Sendbrieff huthen*), sig. D iv v, E i v.

60. *TA: Denck,*, Part II, pp. 13-14.

61. Justus Menius, *Der Widdertauffer lere un geheimnis/aus heiliger schrifft widderlegt/Mit einer schönen Vorrede Martini Luther* (Wittemberg: Nickel Schirlentz, 1530) (hereafter referred to as *Der Widdertauffer lere*) sig. X iii v; also sig. V r See below p. 83.

62. Martin Bucer, *Martin Bucer: Deutsche Schriften*, ed. by Robert Stupperich, II (Gütersloh, 1962) (hereafter referred to as *Bucer Deutsche Schriften*), pp. 256-257; Johann Bader, *Brüderliche warnung für dem newen Abgöttischen orden der Widdertäuffer* (n. p., 1527 hereafter referred to as *Brüderliche warnung*), sig. K iii v.-K iv r.

63. The letter is printed in Stähelin, *Briefe und Akten zum Leben Oekolampads*, II, cited in *TA: Elsass,*, I, p. 80. I used a German translation found in J. P. Gelbert, *Magister Johann Baders Leben und Schriften; Nikolaus Thomae und seine Briefe* (Neustadt a. H., 1968) (hereafter referred to as *Baders Leben und Schriften*).

64. Gelbert, *Baders Leben und Schriften*, p. 190.

65. They were: Ezekiel 18:23, 33:11; Psalm 77:8-10; Romans 11:33; 12:18; 1 Corinthians 15:22-25; Ephesians 1:7-10; Colossians 1:12-20; 1 Timothy 2:4; 1 Peter 3:19-20, 4:6; John 4. *Ibid.*, pp. 161-162.

66. *Ibid.*, pp. 162-163.

67. *TA: Denck*, Part II, pp. 139-140.

68. This was recognized by Haake, *Denck, ein Vorläufer*, p. 51; also by Albrecht Hege, "Hans Denck 1495-1527" (unpublished DTh dissertation, Tübingen, 1942), p. 108.

69. *TA: Denck*, Part II, p. 29. Hans Denck, "Whether God Is the Cause of Evil" (hereafter referred to as "Cause of Evil"), trans. by George Williams, *LCC: SAW*, p. 90.

70. This is basic to a proper understanding of Denck's "Was geredt sey, das die Schrift sagt, Gott thuoe und mache guots und boeses." *TA: Denck*, Part II, pp. 27-47.

71. *Ibid.*, p. 29.

72. *Ibid.*, p. 30.

73. Denck was unconsciously labouring in what may be described as the Irenean tradition, which if the outline provided by John Hick's treatment is not deceptive, was not rediscovered until Schleiermacher. Hick, *Evil and the God of Love* (London, 1968).

74. *TA: Denck*, Part II, pp. 28-29.

75. *Ibid.*, p. 92.

76. Ludwig Keller, ed., "Sebastian Francks Aufzeichnung über Joh. Denck (1527) aus dem Jahre 1531," *Monatshefte der Comenius-Gesellschaft*, I (1901), p. 178. Franck also recorded Denck's universalism in another passage (p. 174).

77. This is a point made by Albrecht Hege, "Hans Denck 1495-1527," pp. 70, 107, and by Diakonus Heberle, "Johann Denck und sein Büchlein vom Gesetz," *TSK*, XXIV (1951), p. 162.

78. *TA: Denck*, Part II, p. 51.

79. Nikolaus Thomae (Sigelspach) in a letter to Oecolampadius. Stähelin, *Briefe und Akten zum Leben Oekolampads*, II, p. 51, cited in *TA: Denck*, Part II, p. 15.

80. Throughout the Middle Ages the Trinity and therefore Christ's divinity—virgin birth, etc.—were bones of contention between Jews and Christians. Wolfgang Seifert, *Synagogue and Church in the Middle Ages: Two Symbols in Art and Literature* (New York, 1970) (hereafter referred to as *Synagogue and Church*), pp. 37, 93.

81. The statements in the introduction have often been interpreted as referring to Denck's and Hätzer's Anabaptist connection. This is not the whole truth. "Nun haben wir beyd also unsern hoechsten vleiss unnd verstand, . . . nitt gespart, Unns zu fragen, da wir antwurt verhofften, nit geschaempt, Keyn lesen underlassen, nichts veracht. . . . auch der weilen von wegen der kurtz abgebrochnen art Hebraischer spruch, welche denen bekannt so damit umb gehen." Cited in Georg Baring, "Die 'Wormser Propheten.' Eine vor-Lutherische evangelische Prophetenübersetzung aus dem Jahre 1527," *Deutsches Bibel-Ar-*

chiv Hamburg, 3. Bericht (1933) (hereafter referred to as "Wormser Propheten"), pp. 40-41.

82. Baring, "Wormser Propheten," p. 3: "Aber es sind Juden dabey gewest, die Christo nicht grosse hulde erzeigt haben, sonst were kunst und vleis gnug da."

83. Heinrich Bullinger, *Der Widertoufferen Vrsprung, fürgang, Secten, wäsen, fürnemme vnd gemeine jrer leer Artikel ouch jre gründ, vnnd warummb sy sich absünderind vnnd ein etc.* (Zürich: Christoph Froschauer, 1561) (hereafter referred to as *Widertoufferen Vrsprung*), sig. di v.

84. See below, pp. 135-136.

85. This could be a valuable exercise not only with regard to the Wormser Propheten, but also in relation to Tyndale's work, which was carried out at Worms in 1526.

86. Gershom G. Scholem, *Major Trends in Jewish Mysticism* (New York, 1967), p. 86. See specifically the teachings of Elezar Jehudah of Worms. Scholem speaks of a "logos mysticism" (pp. 111-114).

87. *Ibid.*, pp. 108-110.

88. Seifert, *Synagogue and Church*, pp. 153-154.

89. *TA: Elsass*, I, p 96. A report of the public debate between Bucer and Denck has been preserved in the diary of Nik. Gerbel. According to Gerbel, Denck left his audience bewildered as to where he stood on the points at issue. *TA: Elsass*, I, pp. 60-61.

90. *Bucers Deutsche Schriften*, II, p. 239.

91. Presumably this was Hubmaier's *Von dem Christlichen Tauff der gläubigen*.

92. Rinck singled him out as the one to whom he made confession of his sin. Oyer, *Reformers Against Anabaptists*, pp. 54, 55.

93. Bader, *Brüderliche warnung*, sig. Biiiv.

94. *Ibid.*, sig. Avii v.

95. *Ibid.*, sig. Aviii r.

96. The person in question was the weaver Hans Wolff, expelled from Strassburg on July 30, 1526. Wolff, among other things, was also accused of teaching that the demons would be saved. *TA: Elsass*, I, pp. 52-57, 91, 109.

97. Bader, *Brüderliche warnung*, sig. Avii v.-Br.

98. John Howard Yoder, "The Hermeneutics of the Anabaptists," *MQR*, XLI (1967), pp. 298-299.

99. The letter was dated May 31, 1527, in *TA: Elsass*,, I, pp. 87-91. On the same day Capito and several preachers had drawn up and sent a "Fürbitte für die zu Horb gefangengesetzten und verurteilten Wiedertäufer," vouching for their innocence (pp. 80-87).

100. On December 10, 1526, Capito reported to Zwingli that Denck was attacking the keystone of the Christian faith by minimizing the sufficiency of Christ's redemptive work. *Ibid.*, pp. 59, 62; Gelbert, *Baders Leben und Schriften*, pp. 157-158.

101. *TA: Elsass*, I, pp. 110, 114. For a discussion of Sattler's relation to the Strassburg Reformers, see Klaus Deppermann, "Die Strassburger Reformatoren und die Krise des oberdeutschen Täufertums im Jahre 1527," *MGB* XXX (1973) pp. 24-41 and Klaus Deppermann and John Yoder, "Ein Briefwechsel über die Bedeutung des Schleitheimer Bekenntnisses," *MGB*, XXX (1973), pp. 42-52.

102. *TA: Elsass*, I, p. 114.

103. This was the conclusion of Walter Fellmann, the editor of Denck's writings, in "Theological Views of Hans Denck," trans. by Walter Klaassen, *Mennonite Life*, XVIII (1963), p. 44. A similar interpretation was given by Walter Klaassen in "Word, Spirit and Scripture," p. 145.

104. *TA: Denck*, Part II, p. 20.

105. *Ibid.*, pp. 59-60.

106. Ozment has seen Denck's immanence theme as "the cornerstone of his soteriology." *Mysticism and Dissent*, p. 30.

107. This observation was made by Goldbach, "Morphologie," pp. 40-41; Albrecht

Hege, "Hans Denck 1495-1527," pp. 71-72, 75; Haake, *Denck, ein Vorläufer*, p. 50; Schwindt, *Denck, ein Vorkämpfer*, p. 17.

108. Observed by Alvin Beachy, "The Grace of God in Christ as Understood by Five Major Anabaptist Writers," *MQR*, XXXVII(1963)(hereafter referred to as "Grace of God") p. 18 Otto Vittali, *Die Theologie des Wiedertäufers Hans Denck* (Offenburg, 1932), p. 29.

109. *TA: Denck*, Part II, p. 94.

110. An observation made by Coba Boerlage, *De Geestverwantshap van Hans Denck en de Middeleeuwsche Mystieken* (Proefschrift, Amsterdam, 1921), pp. 20-22; Cramer, "Die geschichtliche und religiöse Bedeutung Hans Dencks und der Täufer," pp. 1149-1150; Ozment, *Mysticism and Dissent*, p. 126.

111. "Cause of Evil," *LCC: SAW*, pp. 100-101.

112. This was accurately assessed by Goldbach, "Morphologie," p. 98; Williams, "Sanctification," p. 205.

113. "Cause of Evil," *LCC: SAW*, p. 101.

114. *Ibid.*; *TA: Denck*, Part II, p. 39.

115. *TA: Denck*, Part II, p. 53.

116. "Cause of Evil," *LCC: SAW*, pp. 98-99; *TA: Denck*, Part II, pp. 52, 58.

117. Similar conclusions by Haake, *Denck, ein Vorläufer*,, p. 17; Vittali, *Die Theologie des Wiedertäufers Hans Denck*, pp. 34-35.

118. Among them Hätzer, Bünderlin, and Entfelder, Augustin Bader and his colleague, Oswald Leber.

119. See Gerhard Goeters' discussion on Hätzer's "Booklet concerning Christ," in *Ludwig Hätzer (ca. 1500 bis 1529): Spiritualist und Antitrinitarier. Eine Randfigur der frühen Täuferbewegung* (Gütersloh, 1957) (hereafter referred to as *Hätzer: Randfigur*), pp. 139-147.

120. Ernst Güss, *Die Kurpfälzische Regierung und das Täufertum bis zum Dreissigjährigen Krieg* (Stuttgart, 1960)(hereafter referred to as *Kurpfälzische Regierung und Täufertum*), p. 4. Goldbach noticed that Tauler had already left the question of the Trinity "to the learned" and Denck "hat dieser dogmatischen Frage doch innerlich fremd gegenübergestanden." "Morphologie," p. 38, n. 1.

121. See below, pp. 101-102.

122. *TA: HS*, p. 472.

123. *TA: Denck*, Part II, pp. 77-78.

124. *Ibid.*, p. 76.

125. *Ibid.*, p. 97; cf. *Müntzers Schriften*, p. 339; see also above, p. 31.

126. *TA: Denck*, Part II, p. 90.

127. Walter Klaassen and Alvin Beachy tried to establish that for Denck the inner Word or resource was not part of human nature as such. This supposedly distinguished him from Müntzer. Klaassen, "Word, Spirit and Scripture," pp. 161-162; Beachy, "Concept of Grace," pp. 251-252. More accurate was Albrecht Hege when he described the divine resource in man as a "Zwitterding . . . etwas, das von Gott kommt, aber im Menschen ist, das als menschlicher Besitz etwas Göttliches und Uebernatürliches ist." "Hans Denck," p. 84.

128. Denck's opposition to the Reformation on this score was first commented on by the Catholic historian J. Döllinger in *Die Reformation, ihre innere Entwicklung und ihre Wirkung* (Regensburg, 1846), I, p. 196. He was followed by Heberle, "Johann Denck und sein Büchlein vom Gesetz," p. 168. and Albrecht Hege, "Hans Denck," p. 119.

129. *TA: Denck*, Part II, p. 39.

130. *Ibid.*, pp. 55-57.

131. Albrecht Hege, "Hans Denck," p. 117-118; Beachy, "Concept of Grace," p. 134 and "Grace of God," pp. 17-18.

132. Denck raised similar questions regarding the arrival of faith as Müntzer. *TA: Denck*. Part II, pp. 21-22.

133. "Cause of Evil," *LCC: SAW*, p. 104.

134. *TA: Denck*, Part II, p. 23.

135. *Ibid.*, pp. 52-53.

136. Denck, therefore, argued that the "gospel of love," rather than moral precepts, should be preached to the non-Christians. *Ibid.*, p. 81; also p. 64.

137. *Ibid.*, p. 58; also pp. 54-55.

138. *Ibid.*, p. 58.

139. *Ibid.*, p. 54.

140. *Ibid.*, pp. 54, 57, 60, 64.

141. *Ibid.*, p. 80.

142. *Ibid.*, p. 53. Ozment was correct when he wrote: "In a historical sense the fulfillment of the law demanded by Denck is as objectless as faith in the eternal Christ of the heart."

143. This observation was made by Walter Klaassen, "Word, Spirit, and Scripture," pp. 176-177.

144. Goldbach, "Morphologie," pp. 66, 60-61, 68-69, 63-65, maintained that for Müntzer, unlike Denck, God's revelation in man was not natural but supernatural. While Denck would, therefore, appear as a more consistent mystic, Müntzer was really a Spiritualist. For my critique of Goldbach see Stayer, Packull, Deppermann, "From Monogenesis to Polygenesis," pp. 106-107.

145. *TA: Denck*, Part III, p. 44.

146. Denck's allusions to the opposites can be traced to Eckhardt. Goldbach, "Morphologie," p. 52. It reappears in Bünderlin.

147. *TA: Denck*, Part II, p. 111. Was Denck here alluding to themes found in Bonaventura and Nicolas of Cusa?

148. *Ibid.*, pp. 21-22.

149. *Ibid.*, p. 22.

150. *Ibid*

151. Kolde, "Prozess," p. 239; *TA: Denck*, Part III, p. 138.

152. *TA: Denck*, Part II, p. 59.

153. *Ibid.*, p. 61.

154. *Ibid.*, p. 63. Erasmus also used that phrase. Albrecht Hege has argued that Erasmus, Müntzer, and Denck borrowed it from the mystics. "Hans Denck," p. 95.

155. *TA: Denck*, Part II, pp. 67-74. The concept of *Widerschriften* is found in Tauler, Müntzer, Carlstadt, and Erasmus, and reappears in Hut. *TA: Glaubenszeugnisse*, pp. 29-31; Albrecht Hege, "Hans Denck," pp. 94, 89. Goldbach's contention that Denck was here influenced by Erasmus rather than by Müntzer, while it fits his thesis, is meaningless in the larger context. Goldbach, "Morphologie," p. 74. The point is that Denck was here on common ground with all those drawing from medieval mystical sources.

156. *TA: Denck*, Part II, p. 68.

157. Ozment commented: "By making the Spirit the key to true understanding in this as in all matters of religious truth, alternative conclusions from the most eminent historical authorities need not be seriously entertained." *Mysticism and Dissent*, p. 32.

158. I disagree with Goldbach who saw differences between Müntzer and Denck on this point, arguing that for Müntzer Scripture was in no way considered as the "Quelle der Erkenntnis," and because Müntzer understood the concept of "Zeugnis" in a more "äusserlichem Sinne" as authenticating the direct revelation of visions and dreams. Goldbach, who here followed the old Lutheran interpretation of Müntzer, overestimates the importance of dreams and visions for him. He also overlooked the fact that Denck believed God revealed His Word existentially in "dreierlei weissen . . . im schlaff, im gesicht und mündtlich." *TA: Denck*, Part III, p. 87; Goldbach, "Morphologie," pp. 71-73.

159. Goeters sees "a clearly recognizable second epoch in Hätzer's theological thinking" which he attributes to his contact and friendship with Denck. Hätzer was clearly a "Lernender." *Hätzer Randfigur*, p. 92.

160. Goeters, *Hätzer: Randfigur*, pp. 127, 131: "Denkt man an den massiven Biblizismus

198   *Mysticism and the Early South German-Austrian Anabaptists*

der ersten Schriften zurück, so ist ein Wandel kaum grösser vorstellbar. In der Auffassung von Schrift und Geist hat eine Verkehrung ins genaue Gegenteil stattgefunden...."
  161. *Ibid.*, pp. 130-131: "... es kann mit dem Bilde des 'Spazierens im Kreuzgang' gekennzeichnet werden."
  162. *Ibid.*, p. 131.
  163. Friedrich Roth, *Augsburgs Reformationsgeschichte, 1517-1527*, I (Munich, 1881), p. 213.
  164. Timothy Röhrich, "Zur Geschichte der strassburgischen Wiedertäufer in den Jahren 1527 bis 1531," *ZHT*, XXX (1860), pp. 44-46, 64. By 1536 Kautz had settled somewhere in Moravia as a schoolmaster. After his death his children returned to Worms. Heinrich Boos, *Geschichte der rheinischen Städtekultur von ihren Anfängen bis zur Gegenwart mit besonderer Berücksichtigung der Stadt Worms*, IV (2nd ed., Berlin, 1901), pp. 267, 271.
  165. This has been recognized by the Mennonite scholar Gerhard Hein, who wrote: "In Worms trat das Täufertum im Jahre 1527 ganz in der Form des reinen Spiritualismus auf. Das zeigen vor allem die 'Sieben Artikel' von Jacob Kautz, ... Typisch sind hier die ... mystischen Unterscheidungen und negativen Wendungen...." Hein contrasted this early Anabaptism with the biblicist Anabaptism which spread in the area after 1529. "Die Täuferbewegung im Mittel-Rheinischen Raum von der Reformation bis zum Dreissigjährigen Krieg," *Ebernburg-Hefte* (1972/73), pp. 98, 104.
  166. Christian Hege, *Die Täufer in der Kurpfalz. Ein Beitrag zur badisch-pfälzischen Reformationsgeschichte* (Frankfort, 1908), pp. 38-42. Not surprisingly Hege found it puzzling that Sattler received a different treatment from Denck in Strassburg; neither could he understand why Hätzer distanced himself from Sattler, yet was close to Denck (pp. 12, 45). A similar attitude appears in William Klassen, "Was Hans Denck a Universalist?" p. 152. Klassen in seeking to clear Denck of the charge of universalism, attributed the same to Kautz, suggesting that he might have fathered the "Nicolsburg Articles."
  167. A conclusion reached by Goeters, *Hätzer: Randfigur*, p. 106.
  168. This beginning is lacking in the copies that have been preserved. *Bucers Deutsche Schriften*, II, p. 227. Queries at the Stadt Archiv Worms indicated that all the earlier documents relating to Anabaptists have been lost or destroyed. It is, therefore, not clear why Güss, covering this area in a specialized study, could write: "Für Stadt und Bistum Worms liegt leider noch keine Täuferakten Publikation vor." *Kurpfalzische Regierung und Täufertum*, p. 4, n. 19.
  169. Letter by W. von Affenstein to Ludwig V of the Palatinate, written on June 13, 1527. *TA: Baden und Pfalz*, p. 115.
  170. *Ibid.*, p. 113.
  171. See articles nos. 2, 3, and 4 in *Ibid.*, pp. 113-114.
  172. *Ibid.*, p. 114.
  173. For a similar conclusion see Goeters, *Hätzer: Randfigur*,, p. 106.
  174. *TA: Baden und Pfalz*, p. 115.
  175. Johannes Cochlaeus, "Articuli aliquot, a Jacobo Kautio Oecolamadiano, ad populum nuper Wormaciae aediti, partim a Lutheranis, partim a Johanne Cochlaeo doctore praestantissimo, reprobati (MDXXVII)" (hereafter referred to as Cochlaeus, "Articuli (MDXXVII)"). A German copy of the tract was obtained on microfilm from the Stadtbibliothek Frankfurt. Unfortunately the title page was missing.
  176. Cochlaeus, "Articuli (MDXXVII)," sig. A iv v. - C r.
  177. *Ibid.*, sig. C iii r. Among other things, Cochlaeus renewed the charge of universalism (sig. C ii r.- C ii v.).
  178. *Getrewe Warnung der Prediger des Evangelii zu Strassburg über die Artikel, so Jacob Kautz Prediger zu Worms kürtzlich hat lassen aussgohn....* July 2, 1527. *TA: Elsass*, I, pp. 91-115; *Bucers Deutsche Schriften*, II, pp. 225-258. The two Lutheran Reformers of Worms, Ulrich Preu und Johann Freiherr, replied earlier.

179. The judgment of Heinrich Bornkamm cited in Walter Fellmann, "Martin Bucer and Hans Denck," *MGB*, XXIII (1966), p. 31.

180. Kautz, he claimed, had been sound until influenced by Denck. *TA: Elsass*, I, p. 95.

181. This emerges also from a letter which Bucer wrote to Zwingli six days after his reply to Kautz' articles was published. *Ibid.*, p. 115; Fellmann, "Martin Bucer und Hans Denck." p. 30.

182. Denck is described as "ein schwerer feynddt der erlösung Christi, des liechts der schrifft und gotlicher ordnung der Oberkait." *Bucers Deutsche Schriften*, II, pp. 234, 248-250, 254-255; *TA: Elsass*, I, pp. 93, 105-109.

183. *TA: Elsass*, I, pp. 107-108.

184. *Bucers Deutsche Schriften*, II, p. 238.

185. Goeters, *Hätzer: Randfigur*, p. 93: "In der Tat hatte Butzer damit die entscheidenden Gegensätze Dencks zur reformatorischen Theologie bezeichnet."

186. *TA: Denck*, Part II, pp. 82-86.

187. For a discussion of the problem see *TA: Denck*, Part I, pp. 35-36, 55-56; Part II, p. 75; Fellmann, "Theological Views of Hans Denck," p. 45; Robert Friedmann, "Eine dogmatische Hauptschrift der hutterischen Täufergemeinschaften in Mähren," *ARG*, XXIX (1932), pp. 9-17, specifically pp. 12-13.

188. James Stayer, *Anabaptists and the Sword*, p. 147.

189. We shall not discuss Denck's views of the sacraments here. This has been done in relation to baptism by Rollin Armour, *Anabaptist Baptism* (Scottdale, Pennsylvania, 1966). It should be of interest, however, that Denck used Müntzer's text on baptism and John 6 to support his views on the Lord's Supper. The same reference appears in Tauler, Erasmus, and Carlstadt in that connection. Armour, *Anabaptist Baptism*, p. 63; Goldbach, "Morphologie," p. 85; Albrecht Hege, "Hans Denck," p. 134.

190. *TA: Denck*, Part II, p. 84.

191. Many of these accusations, (1) that he baptised without a special commission, (2) that the Anabaptists were running to and fro in such a way as to disturb public order, and (3) that he rejected Paul's pronouncements about human depravity, are reflected in Denck's last statement.

192. German translation of the letter in Wilhelm Wiswedel, *Bilder und Führergestalten aus dem Täufertum*, I (Kassel, 1928), p. 146.

193. *Ibid.*

194. Cf. a similar conclusion in Ernst Stähelin, *Das Theologische Lebenswerk Johannes Oekolampads* (Leipzig, 1939), p. 393; Steinmetz, *Reformers in the Wings*, pp. 213, 217; Ozment, *Mysticism and Dissent*, pp. 132-133; Albrecht Hege, "Hans Denck," pp. 58-59.

195. *TA: Denck*, Part II, pp. 106-108.

196. Fellmann believed that Denck did not give up his Anabaptist views, but merely recognized the failure of his personal mission. *Ibid.*, pp. 18-19.

197. *Ibid.*, p. 108.

198. *Ibid.*, p. 109.

Chapter III. Hans Hut: the Foiled Revolutionary

1. A point made by Hans-Dieter Schmid, "Das Hutsche Täufertum. Ein Beitrag zur Charakterisierung einer täuferischen Richtung aus der Frühzeit der Täuferbewegung," *Historisches Jahrbuch* XVI (1971) (hereafter referred to as "Das Hutsche Täufertum"), pp. 327-344, Hut's movement according to Schmid was "zahlmässig zweifellos die bedeutendste Richtung des frühen Täufertums in Süddeutschland" (p. 328).

2. Werner Packull, "Gottfried Seebass on Hans Hut: A Discussion," *MQR*, XLIX (1975) (hereafter referred to as "Seebass on Hut").

3. *ZHVSN: Hut*, p. 243.

4. See above, p. 38.

5. *ZHVSN: Hut*, pp. 239, 241.

6. Jörg Haug, *Ain Christliche Ordenung, aines warhafftigen Christen, zu verantwurt-ten, die ankunfft seines Glaubens* (Nicolsburg: Simprecht Sorg, genannt Froschauer, 1526) (hereafter referred to as *Ain Christliche Ordenung*), obtained from the Stadtbib-liothek Augsburg. It was unsatisfactorily republished in *TA: Glaubenszeugnisse*, I, from Hutterite sources.

7. Harold Bender, "The Zwickau Prophets, Thomas Müntzer and the Anabaptists," *MQR*, XXVII (1953) (hereafter referred to as "Zwickau Prophets"), p. 6.

8. Bender is referring both to Rinck and Hut in his article. "Zwickau Prophets," p. 16.

9. Herbert Klassen, "Some Aspects of the Teaching of Hans Hut. A Study of their Origins in South Germany and their Influence on the Anabaptist Movement" (unpublished MA thesis, University of British Columbia, 1958) (hereafter referred to as "Aspects of Teaching of Hut"). Parts of the thesis were published in *MQR*, XXXIII (1959), "The Life and Teaching of Hans Hut," Parts I and II, pp. 171-205, 267-304; see "Aspects of Teaching of Hut," pp. 59-60, 65, 155-156 and "The Life and Teaching of Hans Hut," Part I, pp. 189-190.

10. *ZHVSN: Hut*, p. 218.

11. Here Schmid's criticism of Mennonite historiography is basically correct. "Das Hutsche Täufertum," pp. 328-329.

12. *ZHVSN: Hut*, p. 251.

13. *Ibid.*, pp. 241-242.

14. *Ibid.*, pp. 223-224. Gottfried Seebass has argued that the three artisans were of Swiss origin. If this was so, one wonders why Hut made inquiries in Wittenberg and not in Switzerland. "Das Zeichen der Erwählten. Zum Verständnis der Taufe bei Hans Hut," *Umstrittenes Täufertum 1525-1975. Neue Forschungen*, ed. by Hans-Jürgen Goertz (Göttingen, 1975) (hereafter referred to as "Das Zeichen der Erwählten"), pp. 138-164.

15. *ZHVSN: Hut*, pp. 224, 245.

16. *Ibid.*, pp. 227-228.

17. For the significance see Packull, "Seebass on Hut."

18. This was the contention of Lydia Müller, *Der Kommunismus der mährischen Wiedertäufer* (Leipzig, 1927), p. 74; Grete Mecenseffy, "Die Herkunft des oberöster-reichischen Täufertums," *ARG*, XLVII (1956), p. 257; Walter Klaassen, "Hans Hut and Thomas Müntzer," *Baptist Quarterly*, XIX (1962), pp. 209-228; Gerhard Zschäbitz, *Zur mitteldeutschen Wiedertäuferbewegung nach dem grossen Bauernkrieg* (Berlin, 1958), pp. 32-35; Armour, *Anabaptist Baptism*, pp. 58-96; more recently Schmid, "Das Hutsche Täufertum"; Claus-Peter Clasen, *Anabaptism; a Social History, 1525-1618: Switzerland, Austria, Moravia, South and Central Germany* (Ithaca, New York, 1972) (hereafter refer-red to as *Anabaptism; a Social History*), p. 444, n. 6; Ozment, *Mysticism and Dissent*, pp. 98, 101, 115; Seebass, "Müntzers Erbe"; Gordon Rupp, "Thomas Müntzer, Hans Hut and the 'Gospel of all Creatures,'" *Bulletin of the John Rylands Library*, XLIII (1961) (hereafter referred to as "Müntzer, Hut and 'Gospel of all Creatures'"), p. 43; Stayer, *Anabaptists and the Sword*, pp. 150-166.

19. Among these scholars are Bender, Friedmann, Herbert Klassen and, in a different variation, Kiwiet.

20. Among these authors are Baring, Stoesz, Armour, and Walter Klaassen, albeit with differing emphases.

21. Among the scholars representing this standpoint are Seebass, Schmid, and Stayer.

22. *TA: Hubmaier*, pp. 486-487.

23. This axiom was left unchallenged not only by Seebass but also by Schmid, "Das Hutsche Täufertum," p. 329; Friedwart Uhland, "Täufertum und Obrigkeit in Augsburg im 16. Jahrhundert" (unpublished PhD dissertation, Eberhard-Karls-Universität zu Tübingen, 1972), p. 76; Werthan Gerhard, "Zur Geschichte der Augsburger Täufer im 16. Jahrhundert" (Wissenschaftliche Prüfung für das Lehramt an Gymnasien, University of

Munich, 1972), p. 59.

24. Seebass, "Müntzers Erbe," pp. 196, 199, 471.

25. *Ibid.*, Appendix, p. 348, n. 215.

26. This was the thrust of Goldbach's thesis which was diametrically opposed to that of Baring with regard to an influence of Müntzer on Denck.

27. Seebass, "Müntzers Erbe," p. 198.

28. Packull, "Denck's Alleged Baptism by Hubmaier," pp. 328-329.

29. Hans Wiedemann, "Die Wiedertäufergemeinde in Passau 1527-1535," *Ostbayrische Grenzmarken: Passauer Jahrbuch für Geschichte, Kunst und Volkskunde*, VI (1962/63), p. 266.

30. See above p. 46.

31. *TA: Denck*, Part III, p. 49.

32. Seebass, "Das Zeichen der Erwählten," p. 160, n. 127.

33. This remains true regardless of the objections raised by Seebass, "Das Zeichen der Erwählten," pp. 160-161.

34. Armour argued that Hut's baptismal theology was a synthesis of Müntzer's, Hubmaier's, and Denck's views. *Anabaptist Baptism*, p. 95. Seebass, in his most recent pronouncement, has taken issue with Armour arguing that Hut incorporated incompatible elements into his view of baptism. Seebass, "Das Zeichen der Erwählten," pp. 138-139, 144.

35. A similar observation in Seebass, "Müntzers Erbe," p. 514.

36. Unfortunately the critical edition of Hut's writings now being prepared by Gottfried Seebass is not yet available. The author is especially indebted to Dr. Seebass for making his pioneering work on Hut available in manuscript form. The critical discussion of primary source materials on Hut is embodied in the first major section of Seebass, "Müntzers Erbe."

37. Hut actually speaks of becoming a partaker of the threefold activity through Christ, "in welchem wir eingeleybt müssen werden, und der aynnigen tryfältigkait tailhaftig werden." (Hans Hut), *Ain Christliche Unterrichtung, wie die Götlich geschrifft vergleycht und geurtaylt soll werden,*, etc., *Mittheilungen aus dem Antiquariate Calvary*, III and IV (Berlin, 1869) (hereafter referred to as *Christliche Unterrichtung, Mittheilung aus dem Antiquariate*), p. 163; *TA: Glaubenszeugnisse*, I, p. 34.

38. (Hut), *Christliche Unterrichtung, Mittheilung aus dem Antiquariate*, p. 161; *TA: Glaubenszeugnisse*, I, pp. 28, 32. A similar statement in *TA: Denck*, Part II, p. 112.

39. (Hut), *Christliche Unterrichtung, Mittheilung aus dem Antiquariate*, p. 158.

40. During his trial Hut stated that the original draft of his *Ein christlicher Unterricht* had been an exposition of the "three articles of faith." *ZHVSN: Hut*, pp. 235-236.

41. The trinitarian message in Scripture is (1) Scripture testifies to the witness of God the Father in all creatures; (2) Scripture witnesses to the Son—the necessity of suffering in order to be loosened from all creatureliness; (3) Scripture tells of the Spirit—a life in harmony with the will of God. (Hut), *Christliche Unterrichtung, Mittheilung aus dem Antiquariate*, pp. 158-159; *TA: Glaubenszeugnisse*, I, pp. 28-29, 36.

42. *TA: Glaubenszeugnisse*, I, p. 36; see also p. 13.

43. *Ibid.*, pp. 32, 33, 35.

44. For Hut's claim to private revelation see *ZHVSN: Hut*, pp. 225, 232, 240, 242.

45. The "bitter-sweet" Christ is mentioned several times by Hut in *Vom Geheimnis der Tauf, TA: Glaubenszeugnisse*, I, pp. 25, 26.

46. (Hut), *Christliche Unterrichtung, Mittheilung aus dem Antiquariate*, p. 163. *TA: Glaubenszeugnisse*, I, p. 34. The appeal that Christ must be born, even as in Mary, reappears in most of Hut's followers.

47. (Hut), *Christliche Unterrichtung, Mittheilung aus dem Antiquariate*, pp. 163-164.

48. *TA: Glaubenszeugnisse*, I, p. 35.

49. Staatsarchiv Nürnberg, *Ansbacher Religions Akten* (hereafter referred to as *Ansb. Rel. Akten*), XXXIX, f. 218. r. -v.: "Last euch nit bekummern, lieben bruedern, das misstrauen, das etliche hie gegen mir hetten dess doctor Balthauser halben zu N. Wiewohl es mich schon betruebet hat, so hab ichs doch mit gedult tragen. . . . Ich nim Gott zu zeugen, das ich des dings entschuldig bin." See also Seebass, "Müntzers Erbe Appendix," pp. 9-10.

50. *Ansb. Rel. Akten*, XXXIX, f. 218. r.-v.

51. Packull, "Seebass on Hut," p. 62.

52. The issues arising from Hut's gospel of all creatures have occupied Gordon Rupp, Walter Klaassen, Rollin Armour, Steven Ozment, and continue to be debated by Hans-Jürgen Goertz and Gottfried Seebass. In our discussion we are aiming less at a solution of the complex problem raised by these scholars, than at a proper assessment of this concept within the constellation of our general problem—the relation between mysticism and early Anabaptist thought.

53. *TA: Glaubenszeugnisse*, I, p. 17.

54. *Ibid.*, pp. 18-19.

55. Cf. Müntzer's statement: "Die gantze heylige schrifft saget nit anderst (wie auch alle creaturen aussweysen) dan vom gecreützigten sone Gottes, der halben er auch selber anfing vom Mose durch alle propheten zu eroffnen seyn ampt, das er muste also leiden und eingeen in den preyss seines vaters." *Müntzers Schriften*, p. 324.

56. Ozment, *Mysticism and Dissent*, p. 105, n. 28.

57. *TA: Glaubenszeugnisse*, I, pp. 12-14; (Hut), *Christliche Unterrichtung, Mittheilung aus dem Antiquariate*, p. 160.

58. Walter Klaassen was probably the first to recognize this thrust of Hut's gospel of all creatures. His view has received support from Ozment, *Mysticism and Dissent*, p. 106; Klaassen, "Word, Spirit and Scripture," pp. 199, 202, 213.

59. A stubborn exception has been Hans-Jürgen Goertz, who in a recent review of Rollin Armour's *Anabaptist Baptism* claimed: "Dass der Grundgedanke von dem 'Evangelium aller Kreatur' ein genuin Müntzerscher Gedanke sei, hat Armour ebenso wenig wie Rupp erwiesen." Goertz, "Die Taufe im Täufertum," *MGB*, XVII (1970), p. 47, n. 4.

60. Rupp, "Müntzer, Hut and the 'Gospel of all Creatures,' " p. 519. A similar interpretation in Williams, *The Radical Reformation*, p. 305.

61. Seebass, "Das Zeichen der Erwählten," p. 140.

62. I am here in agreement with Goertz, "Der Mystiker mit dem Hammer," p. 37.

63. Goertz has argued against Rupp and Seebass that the "Ordnung Gottes in den Kreaturen" referred not to a natural order but to an inner order governing the mystical salvation process. Ozment has seconded Goertz. Goertz, "Der Mystiker mit dem Hammer," p. 38, and *Innere und Äussere Ordnung*, p. 41; Ozment, *Mysticism and Dissent*, p. 109. Goertz has contended that Hut's gospel of all creatures was not consistently mystical and that Hut here went beyond Müntzer. Seebass in turn has drawn attention to passages in Müntzer which become explicable when read in the light of Hut's gospel of all creatures. *Müntzers Schriften*, pp. 38, 324.

64. Hut preached the gospel of all creatures as early as 1526 in Königsberg. Georg Berbig, "Die Wiedertäufer im Amt Königsberg i. Fr. 1527/28," *Deutsche Zeitschrift für Kirchenrecht*, XXXV (1903) (hereafter referred to as "Wiedertäufer im Amt Königsberg") p. 313.

65. *TA: Denck*, Part II, p. 34.

66. *Müntzers Schriften*, p. 503. What sort of speculations about the deeper meaning of this text overshadowed the discussion of literal salvation in the minds of some may be seen from Clemens Ziegler's comments on Mark 16:15. Ziegler, as early as 1524, used this text not to argue for baptism on confession of faith but, following Origen, to speculate about universal salvation of all creatures. *TA: Elsass*, I, p. 13.

67. *TA: Denck*, Part II, pp. 24, 83; Part III, p. 102.

68. Seebass has shown very convincingly that Hut's views on baptism reflected somewhat eclectically and not entirely consistently elements of Luther, Müntzer, Carlstadt, Swiss Anabaptists, Hubmaier, and Denck. Seebass, "Das Zeichen der Erwählten," pp. 143-146.

69. *TA: Glaubenszeugnisse*, I, p. 13. See also (Hut), *Christliche Unterrichtung, Mittheilung aus dem Antiquariate*, p. 167.

70. *TA: Glaubenszeugnisse*, I, p. 213.

71. *Ibid.*, p. 23.

72. *Ibid.*, p. 213.

73. *Ibid.*

74. *Ibid.*, pp. 213-214.

75. *Ibid.*, p. 23.

76. *Ibid.*, p. 213.

77. *Ibid.*, pp. 213-214.

78. *Ibid.*, pp. 28-29.

79. *Ibid.*, p. 29

80. Seebass has drawn attention to the fact that in the original tract published by Landsperger only three paradoxes appear, while in the manuscript preserved by the Hutterites and edited by Lydia Müller there are forty paradoxes. Thirty-nine of these were the same as those appearing in Denck's *Wer die warhait warlich lieb hat*. Traditionally this has been interpreted as strong evidence for Denck's influence on Hut. Seebass, who was interested in distinguishing between Denck and Hut, believed that the additional scriptural references were added by Hutterite copyists from Denck's tract. One could, therefore, not argue for a dependence of Hut on Denck. Seebass, "Müntzers Erbe," pp 18-19, Appendix, pp. 82-83, n. 56.

81. A good example of this literalism is Hut's insistence on adult baptism, based on an exposition of the Great Commission (which was, incidentally, also threefold).

82. The tendency to make Hut a biblicist in the sense of the Reformers was most pronounced in Herbert Klassen, "The Life and Teaching of Hans Hut," Part II, p. 267. Seebass has probably adopted the most convenient interpretation, that Hut was a biblical Spiritualist or spiritualistic biblicist. Packull, "Seebass on Hut," p. 63.

83. *TA: Glaubenszeugnisse*, I, p. 212.

84. *Ibid.*, pp. 212-213.

85. *Ibid.*, pp. 14, 214.

86. *Ibid.*, p. 214.

87. Ozment saw correctly that the mystical presupposition which "dehistoricized" and "existentialized" the traditional Christology provided the thrust against the *solus Christus* as understood by Luther. Ozment, *Mysticism and Dissent*, p. 105.

88. Letter in *Ansb. Rel. Akten*, XXXIX, f. 220 r.-v. Cf. (Hut), *Christliche Unterrichtung, Mittheilung aus dem Antiquariate*. p. 161.

89. *ZHVSN: Hut*, p. 229.

90. *TA: Glaubenszeugnisse*, I, p. 16.

91. *Ibid.*, p. 22. Schiemer later repeated Hut almost verbatim on the subject.

92. The emphases on Christ's passion and the *nova lex Christi* are not mutually exclusive. This helps to explain why some scholars could easily misread Hut's views as a Swiss Brethren emphasis on discipleship. We are here confronted by two different emphases originating in the same tradition.

93. This was also Seebass' conclusion in a qualified sense. Packull, "Seebass on Hut," p. 64.

94. This was Seebass' contention. *Ibid.*, p. 65.

95. *TA: Glaubenszeugnisse*, I, p. 20. Cf. Hut's baptismal theology in Armour, *Anabaptist Baptism*, Ch. III.

96. For a more detailed discussion of Hut's baptismal theology see Armour,

Anabaptist Baptism, Ch. III, and Seebass, "Das Zeichen der Erwählten," pp. 138-164.
    97. *TA: Glaubenszeugnisse*, I, pp. 20, 24. Baptism was, therefore, not a testimonial service witnessing to conversion or regeneration as present-day evangelicals would have it, but something preceding it.
    98. *Ibid.*, p. 13.
    99. Haug, *Ain Christliche Ordenung*, sig. A v.
    100. *ZHVSN: Hut*, p. 248. The information came from Ursula Nespitzer, the wife of Eucharius Binder and sister of Jörg Nespitzer, two of Hut's closest associates.
    101. *Ibid.*, p. 240.
    102. Lydia Müller wrongly believed the "book of the seven seals" to have been identical with Hut's larger work, *Vom Geheimnis der Tauf. TA: Glaubenszeugnisse,*, I, p. 11.
    103. *TA: Glaubenszeugnisse*, I, pp. 211-212. Commented on by Erich Meissner, "Die Rechtsprechung über die Wiedertäufer und die antitäuferische Publizistik" (unpublished PhD dissertation, Georg-August University, Göttingen, 1921), p. 50. Goeters, *Hätzer: Randfigur*, p. 115, n. 3; Williams, *The Radical Reformation*, p. 169.
    104. See for example the confessions of Ambrosius Spittelmaier, Hans Nadler, and Marx Maier, *TA: Bayern*, I, pp. 49-50, 134, 153 and 194 respectively.
    105. *ZHVSN: Hut*, p. 240.
    106. *Ansb. Rel. Akten*, XXXIX, f. 219 r.-v.: "Mitt den siben urteln wirt die gantz gschrifft des alten und neuen testament recht tractirt, so man darrauff achtung hat." Cited in Schmid, "Das Hutsche Täufertum," p. 331, n. 17; and Seebass, "Müntzers Erbe," Appendix, p. 11.
    107. I have followed Schmid, indicating in parenthesis deviations found in Hut's confession. The "Sieben Urteil" are in agreement with the concordance of the "Sieben Urteil" in the *Ansb. Rel. Akten*, which was reproduced by Seebass. The scriptural references are missing for the last two "urteil," but these can be supplied from Hut's larger concordance, the first seven points of which are the "Sieben Urteil." Of interest is the additional information given concerning the fifth "judgment." Hut distinguished two resurrections, one in the here and now for those ridding themselves of the creaturely, and a second at the time of judgment for those refusing that experience. Seebass, "Müntzers Erbe" Appendix, pp. 3-4, 11-12; Schmid, "Das Hutsche Täufertum," p. 230.
    108. From Hut's Sendbrief which he sent out after the Martyrs' Synod we know that the last five "judgments" had been responsible for the dissent. In his *Sendbrief* Hut listed all five and promised to keep their meaning secret, explaining them only to those who specifically asked about them. Rhegius, *Ein Sendbrieff huthen*, sig. C iv v.; *TA: Glaubenszeugnisse*, I, p. 12.
    109. *ZHVSN: Hut*, pp. 237, 240.
    110. *Ansb. Rel. Akten*, XXXIX, f. 219 r.
    111. *TA: Bayern*, I, pp. 211-212.
    112. See Hut's introduction to *Vom Geheimnis der Tauf, TA: Glaubenszeugnisse*, I, p. 12 and the undated letter by Hut in *Ansb. Rel. Akten*, XXXIX, f. 220 r.-v.
    113. Haug, *Ain Christliche Ordenung*, sig. A 3: "Das aber Gottes forcht ain anfang sey zu gottes weysshait bezeugen alle lebendigen Creatur/dan sy alle volfürn jr leben in der forcht. . . . "
    114. *Ibid.*, sig. A 2.
    115. Cited in Wappler, *Die Täuferbewegung in Thüringen*, p. 64.
    116. Seebass, "Müntzers Erbe," pp. 478-479.
    117. Other places where Hut's preference for the number seven appears are in his division of the last days of the world into two periods of 3½ years, and in his collection of seven city names in reference to the apocalyptic church, which he explicitly contrasted with seven names given to the Spirit.
    118. This was already recognized by Schmid, "Das Hutsche Täufertum," p. 331.

119. *TA: Glaubenszeugnisse*, I, pp. 14-15.
120. *Ibid.*, pp. 24-26.
121. This point was first made by Walter Klaassen, "Word, Spirit and Scripture," pp. 247-249. A similar argument is found in Ozment, *Mysticism and Dissent*, pp. 133-136.
122. Seebass has argued against Armour that Hut was primarily dependent on Müntzer and not on Denck. "Müntzers Erbe," p. 471.
123. Packull, "Seebass on Hut," p. 65.
124. This is a point readily conceded by Bauer, *Anfänge täuferischer Gemeindebildungen in Franken*, p. 62.
125. *TA: Glaubenszeugnisse*, I, p. 20.
126. (Hut), *Christliche Unterrichtung, Mittheilung aus dem Antiquariate*, pp. 165-166.
127. See above pp. 82-83.
128. He told Rhegius that he had received his commission at night from Christ Himself and signed his letters, "Hans Hut from the den of Elijah." According to Luke 4:25 Elijah had been miraculously nourished for 3½ years of drought. In his confession Hut admitted that "he had never heard of anyone who knew how to speak of these [apocalyptical] things as he. . . ." Rhegius, *Ein Sendbrieff huthen*, sig. A ii; *ZHVSN: Hut*, p. 240.
129. Packull, "Denck's Alleged Baptism by Hubmaier," pp. 327-338; see above p. 142.
130. Seebass, "Müntzers Erbe," p. 538.
131. This aspect of Hut's teaching has been excellently dealt with by Seebass, "Müntzers Erbe," pp. 17, 536-538.
132. Schmid has suggested that if January 1, 1525, was taken as the starting date for the last 1,335 days mentioned in Daniel 12:12, the end would fall exactly on Pentecost 1528. Schmid, "Das Hutsche Täufertum," p. 336, n. 50.
133. Packull, "Seebass on Hut," p. 66.
134. See the statements of Hut's followers around Königsberg in Franconia, below, pp. 88-89.
135. Schmid, "Das Hutsche Täufertum," p. 333. Seebass, "Müntzers Erbe," pp. 186, 202, 206, 216-218, 224, 235.
136. Menius, *Der Widdertauffer lere*, sig. B iii r.-v., D i r.-D ii v., E r.
137. This point was made by Seebass, "Müntzers Erbe," p. 410.
138. Hut's difficulties at the Martyrs' Synod reinforced this practice. Rhegius, *Ein Sendbrieff huthen*; also in *TA: Glaubenszeugnisse*, I, pp. 11-12.
139. The term "urteil" also recurs in Hut's larger concordance. Seebass, "Müntzers Erbe" Appendix, p. 4.
140. *Ibid.*, p. 3: "Was Gottes bund, was Gottes gepot, was Gottes urtl, was Gottes sitten, was Gottes zeukhnus, was Gottes gesetz?"
141. The tract is found in the *Kodex Braitmichel*, ff. 480 r.-482 r. A microfilm is at the University of Waterloo Library.
142. *Ibid.*, f. 482.
143. *Ibid.*
144. *Ibid.* This juxtaposition of parts to the whole is again strikingly Müntzerite. The idea that a judgment ought not to be explained literally, but presented simply as a collection of scriptural passages, is reminiscent of Hut. It was the practice he followed in his concordance.
145. *Ibid.*, f. 481 v.
146. *Ibid.*, ff. 481 r.-v. A very interesting allegory, the meaning of which is no longer clear but which reappears in the writings of Hubmaier and Bünderlin, admonished the reader to distinguish the judgments, as Moses distinguished the animals with the divided hoofs.

147. *Ibid.*, ff. 483 r.-484 v.
148. *Kodex Braitmichel*, f. 481 v.: "Darumb ist kain underschaid dan der buechstab. Darumb sein sie nit aufgehoben."
149. *Ibid.*, f. 482 r.
150. *Ibid.*, ff. 482 r.-v.
151. *Ibid.*, f. 482 v.
152. *Ein kurzer begriff und auslegung was da sein die vier thier Apoca. 4, Ibid.*, ff. 482 r.-483 v.
153. Seebass, "Müntzers Erbe," pp. 84-86.
154. *Kodex Braitmichel*, f. 482 r.
155. *Ibid.*, f. 483 r.
156. *Ibid.*, ff. 482 r.-483 v.
157. *Ibid.*, ff. 483 r.-v.

Chapter IV. Hans Hut and the Early South German Anabaptist Movement
1. Hut must have begun to proselytise in the area during the fall of 1526. He was still in the territory on Christmas Eve of that year. Wappler, *Die Täuferbewegung in Thüringen*, pp. 279, 314-315.
2. This emerges from the confessions of Hut's most loyal supporters in Uetzing—the brothers Veit, Mertheim, and Hans Weischenfelder. The first two were arrested in March 1527, and Hans, who travelled with Hut to Nicolsburg, not until January 1528. There was even talk about capturing the emperor and strangling him. *Ibid.*, pp. 239-240, 281.
3. *Ibid.*, p. 237.
4. This is supported by statements given to the authorities by Wolfgang Schreiner from Königsberg, the brother-in-law of Eucharius Binder, and by Hans Hübner, Veit and Mertheim Weischenfelder. *Ibid.*, pp. 239-240, 244; Berbig, "Die Wiedertäufer im Amt Königsberg," p. 316.
5. Bauer, *Anfänge täuferischer Gemeindebildungen in Franken*, pp. 37, 57.
6. This emerges from the confession of Thomas Spiegel, for whom Hut had left some books obtained in Nuremberg at Nadler's house in Erlangen. Wappler, *Die Täuferbewegung in Thüringen*, pp. 232, 234-235.
7. See letter of February 6 by Kunz Gotsmann, Berbig, "Wiedertäufer im Amt Königsberg," p. 302.
8. Wappler, *Die Täuferbewegung in Thüringen*, p. 235.
9. *Ibid.*, p. 234.
10. *Ibid.*, pp. 229-231, 235, 244, 247-248. Similar views were expressed by Hut's closest companions Eucharius Binder and Joachim März. Klaus Rischar, "Der Missionar Eucharius Binder und sein Mitarbeiter Joachim März," *MGB*, XXV (1968) (hereafter referred to as "Binder und März"), p. 20.
10a. Gottfried Seebass, "Bauernkrieg und Täufertum in Franken," *ZKG*, 85 (1974), pp. 140-156.
11. Wappler, *Die Täuferbewegung in Thüringen*, p. 232.
12. *ZHVSN: Hut*, pp. 229-230. The dating is not clear in this regard. The records literally state ten years previously (zehen) but in all probability this should read two years previously (zween).
13. A claim made by Adolf Engelhardt, *Die Reformation in Nürnberg*, II (Nuremberg, 1937), p. 59
14. *ZHVSN: Hut*, pp. 229-230, 243.
15. Wiswedel claimed that Hut and four others were also arrested with Vogel and released. I could find no evidence for this. *Bilder und Führergestalten aus dem Täufertum*, I, p. 157.
16. This was the line taken by Wiswedel; he was followed by Robert Friedmann. Since no records have survived from Vogel's trial, Wiswedel went so far as to suggest that

they had been deliberately destroyed to hide a case of injustice. *Ibid.*, p. 158; Friedmann, "The Nicolsburg Articles, a Problem of Early Anabaptist History," *CH*, XXXVI (1967) (hereafter referred to as "Nicolsburg Articles"), p. 401, n. 38. Wiswedel's allegations drew an angry response from Seebass, "Müntzers Erbe," p. 27, Appendix, p. 89, n. 127.

17. Wolfgang Vogel, *Ayn trostlicher sendbrieff unnd Christliche ermanung zum Euangelio an ain Erbarm Radt und gantze gemayn zu Bopfingen, und an alle die, so vom Euangelio unnd wort Gottes abgefallen seynd* (Nuremberg, 1526) (hereafter referred to as *Ayn trostlicher sendbrieff*), sig. C ii v.; an original copy of Vogel's open letter is in the Stadtbibliothek Nürnberg. Wiswedel, who lacked all historical context for the significance of this concept among early South German Anabaptists, read right past it. *Bilder und Führergestalten aus dem Täufertum*, I, p. 167.

18. Berbig, "Wiedertäufer im Amt Königsberg," pp. 309-316; also Schmid, *Täufertum und Obrigkeit in Nürnberg*, pp. 137, 139.

19. Wappler, *Die Täuferbewegung in Thüringen*, p. 232.

20. *TA: Bayern*, I, p. 11. Bauer, *Anfänge täuferischer Gemeindebildungen in Franken, pp. 129-133.*

21. *TA: Bayern*, I, p. 19.

22. Seebass, "Müntzers Erbe," pp. 231-232: "Die Schilderungen, die der Nürnberger Rat von den Lehren der Täufer gab, folgte im grossen und ganzen den 'sieben Urteilen', in den Hut seine Verkündigung zusammengefasst hatte. Da sie in keiner der Urgichten aus dem nördlichen Franken auftauchen, haben wir es einwandfrei mit einer auf Vogels Aussagen zurückgehenden Nachricht zu tun." A similar conclusion was reached earlier by Schmid, *Täufertum und Obrigkeit*, pp. 23-24.

23. *TA: Bayern*, II, p. 8.

24. In my dissertation I sought to show that the generally accepted date for the Nicolsburg debate in May remains problematic. I argued for the possibility that the debate may have taken place earlier. "Mysticism and the Early South German-Austrian Anabaptist Movement" (Ph D thesis, Queen's University, Kingston, 1974). *ZHVSN: Hut*, pp. 235-237.

25. It is possible that Hut had made contact with his wife, who was still in the area around Staffelstein. Wappler, *Die Täuferbewegung in Thüringen*, pp. 235, 242.

26. *TA: Bayern*, I, pp. 80-93, 311, 327.

27. *Ibid.*, pp. 13-15, 23.

28. Bauer, *Anfänge täuferischer Gemeindebildungen in Franken*, p. 43.

29. *TA: Bayern*, I, pp. 17-18.

30. *Ibid.*, pp. 132, 173-174; *TA: Bayern*, II, pp.177-178.

31. *ZHVSN: Hut*, p. 224. With him were Eucharius Binder, Joachim März, Hans Weischenfelder, and Endres Riess.

32. Uhland, "Täufertum und Obrigkeit in Augsburg im 16. Jahrhundert," pp. 68-70; Gerhard, "Zur Geschichte der Augsburger Täufer im 16. Jahrhundert," p. 52; see also Friedrich Roth, "Johann Schilling, der Barfüssermönch und der Aufstand im Jahre 1524," *ZHVSN*, VI (1879), pp. 1-32.

33. *Getrewe Christliche und nutzliche warnung etlicher oebrigkait die dass Euangelion zu Predigen zulassen und befehlen und straffen doch desselben volziehung* (n.p., 1525). A copy is found in the Stadtbibliothek Augsburg.

34. Williams, *The Radical Reformation*, p. 155.

35. Hans Leupold was arrested for the first time in June 1526 for open *Sakramentslästerung.* Similarly, Langenmantel underwent temporary imprisonment before his Anabaptist position was known. Ten others of the early sacramental radicals later emerged as Anabaptists. Gerhard, "Zur Geschichte der Augsburger Täufer im 16. Jahrhundert," pp. 53-57.

36. Mutual contacts reaching also to Hut were provided by the Regels. Friedrich Roth, *Augsburgs Reformationsgeschichte 1527-1530*, I (2nd edition, Munich, 1901)

(hereafter referred to as *Augsburgs Reformationsgeschichte*, I [2nd ed.]), p. 259, n. 20; Uhland, "Täufertum und Obrigkeit im 16. Jahrhundert," p. 73.

37. The tract appeared under the pseudonym Hans Nagel von Klingnau and was printed by Heinrich Steiner. It was probably a reproduction of one of Conrad Grebel's works by the St. Gall Anabaptist, Krüsi. Fast, "Krüsis Büchlein," pp. 473-474.

38. *TA: Elsass*, I, pp. 62-66. Another Anabaptist arriving at about the same time was the shoemaker Wilhelm Excel from Wallis. As we noted earlier Hubmaier and Hut both visited Denck in 1526. Roth, *Augsburgs Reformationsgeschichte*, I (2nd ed.), p. 222.

39. Schottenloher, *Ulhart*, p. 59.

40. A copy of Sigmund Salminger, *Ausz was grund die lieb entspringt, und was grosser krafft sy hab, und wie nutz sy sey, den innerlichen menschen zu Reformieren, dass der eüsserlich sterb* is in the Mennonite Historical Library, Goshen. The original text edited by Salminger was an excerpt from the anonymous *Das Buch von geistlicher Armut* or *Von der Nachfolgung des armen Lebens Christi*. It was printed with Salminger's preface by Ulhart. Max Radlkofer, "Jacob Dachser und Sigmund Salminger," *Beiträge für bayerische Kirchengeschichte*, VI (Erlangen, 1900), pp. 5-6.

41. A copy of *Zwen Sendbrieff von der Liebe gottes durch Georgen Preinig vor jaren weber zu Augspurg geschriben* was obtained from Stadtbibliothek Augsburg. See Friedrich Roth, "Der Meistersinger Georg Breuning und die religiöse Bewegung der Waldenser und Täufer im 15. und 16. Jahrhundert," *Monatshefte der Comensius-Gesellschaft*, XIII (1904), pp. 84, 92. This was the Breuning mentioned earlier.

42. Karl Schottenloher, *Phillip Ulhart: ein Augsburger Winkeldrucker und Helfershelfer der "Schwärmer" und "Wiedertäufer" (1523-1529)* (Nieuwkoop, 1967) (hereafter referred to as *Ulhart*), pp. 82-83. For Salminger's own songs see Philip Wackernagel, *Das Deutsche Kirchenlied*, II (Leipzig, 1864-1877), pp. 807-811. After his recantation in December 1530 Salminger's interest shifted to poetry and music, which brought him the admiration of Erasmus. His last years were spent in the pay of the Fuggers. Radlkofer, "Jacob Dachser und Sigmund Salminger," pp. 29-30. His last printed treatise was the *Guldin Schatz. Hauptschrift und Handzeugger, den Inhalt der gantzen Bibel, in sich schliessende. Auch all unsers glaubens und thuns, grüntliche zeügnuss, in 547. Titel und puncten gestelt und absolviert* (Strassburg: Sigmund Bosch, 1540). A copy is in the Stadtbibliothek Augsburg.

43. Schottenloher, *Ulhart*, pp. 62, 64, 134.

44. Hans Langenmantel, a scion from a local patrician family, was, no doubt, the most prolific publisher of the trio. At least seven of his tracts have been preserved. The most significant of these was probably *Ain kurtzer anzayg, wie Do. Martin Luther ain zeyt her, hatt etliche schriften lassen aussgeen, vom Sacrament, die doch stracks wider ainander, wie wirt dan sein, und seiner anhenger Reych bestehen* (Augsburg, 1527). This publication earned Langenmantel temporary confinement. Since he has received adequate attention in the past—he died as an Anabaptist martyr—we have foregone an analysis of his writings here.

45. Jacob Dachser, *Ein Göttlich und gründtlich offenbarung: von den warhafftigen widertauffern: mit Götliche warhait angezaigt* (n.p., 1527) (hereafter referred to as *Ein Göttlich offenbarung*); a copy is at the Mennonite Historical Library, Goshen. The tract, printed by Ulhart, had been attributed to Langenmantel. Schottenloher argued convincingly for Dachser's authorship. *Ulhart*, pp. 75-76.

46. Urbanus Rhegius, *Wider den newen Taufforden. Notwendige Warnungen an alle Christgleubig Durch die diener des Euangelii zu Augspurg* (Augsburg, 1527) (hereafter referred to as *Wider den newen Taufforden*). A copy is at the Mennonite Historical Library, Goshen.

47. Hans Saalfeld, "Jacob Dachser. Priester, Wiedertäufer, evangelischer Pfarrer," *ZBKG*, XXXI (1962) (hereafter referred to as "Dachser"), pp. 2-4.

48. *ZHVSN: Langenmantel*, p. 19. It is possible that in an anonymous Anabaptist

sermon on Jeremiah 7:3, 4 and 9:8 we have another work of Dachser. The tract, which contains echoes of the mystical immanence theme, is said to have originated in 1527 and appeared in Hutterite sources together with Langenmantel's exposition of the Lord's Prayer. It was translated into English by John Wenger, "Two Early Anabaptist Tracts," *MQR*, XXII (1948), pp. 34-42.

49. *ZHVSN: Augsburg*, p. 60.

50.*Ibid.*, p. 144.

51. Dachser voluntarily turned himself in between August 25 and 28 after he had gone into hiding earlier. Uhland, "Täufertum und Obrigkeit in Augsburg im 16. Jahrhundert," p. 92.

52. Particularly active in persuading Dachser was Pfarrer Wolfart who is said to have been a Schwenckfeldian. Saalfeld, "Dachser," p. 19.

53. Dachser was released in May 1531 after his wife had persuaded Georg von Brandenburg to intercede for him. She argued that Salminger, who had been released earlier, had been more deeply involved in Anabaptist errors than her husband. *ZHVSN: Augsburg*, p. 140.

54. August Kamp, *Die Psalmendichtung des Jacob Dachser* (Griefswald, 1931), pp. 26, 29. Schottenloher, *Ulhart*, p. 77; see also Saalfeld, "Dachser," pp. 14-19.

55. The rest of Dachser's life does not concern us here. It has been dealt with by Saalfeld, "Dachser," pp. 20-29.

56. We assume that it was completed before Dachser's imprisonment, and before his clash with Hut at the Martyrs' Synod—therefore, after his baptism in March and before August 1527.

57. Dachser, *Ein Göttlich offenbarung*, sig. A v.

58. *Ibid.*, sig. A iir.

59. Rhegius, *Wider den newen Taufforden*, sig. C i r.

60. *Ibid.*, sig. C i r.

61. *Ibid.*, sig. E iii r.; see also sig. D r.-F iv r.

62. *Ibid.*, sig. B iv r.; F iv r.; G r.

63. Rhegius saw Denck and Hubmaier as the real movers behind the scene. *Ibid.*, sig. A iv.

64. Dachser, *Ein Göttlich offenbarung*, sig. A iv r.

65. *Ibid.*, sig. B ii r.

66. *Ibid.*, sig. A iii v.

67. *Ibid.*, sig. B ii r.-v.; also D iii v., E iii v.

68. For the immanence motif see also Dachser's early hymns. Wackernagel, *Das Deutsche Kirchenlied*, II, pp. 701, 702.

69. Dachser, *Ein Göttlich offenbarung*, sig. D r., D ii r.-v.

70.*Ibid.*, sig. D iii v.

71. *Ibid.*, sig. C iv v.-D r.

72. *TA: Bayern*, I, pp. 65-66; *TA: Baden und Pfalz*, p. 392.

73. Friedmann, "Nicolsburg Articles," p. 399.

74. *Ibid.*, p. 406; Williams, *The Radical Reformation*, p. 177, n. 18.

75. Gottfried Seebass, "Apologia Reformationis. Eine bisher unbekannte Verteidigungsschrift Nürnbergs aus dem Jahre 1528," *ZBKG*, XXXIX (1970), pp. 21-22; "Müntzers Erbe," p. 264.

76. Stähelin, *Briefe und Akten zum Leben Oekolampads*, II, p. 87.

77. This was how Friedmann wanted to explain the differences. "Nicolsburg Articles," p. 407.

78. Jarold Zeman, *The Anabaptists and the Czech Brethren in Moravia, 1526-1628. A Study of Origins and Contacts* (The Hague, 1969) (hereafter referred to as *Anabaptists and Czech Brethren)* p. 185.

79. *ZHVSN: Hut*, pp. 231-232, 236.

80. Among the items examined by Hubmaier were (1) "a little book on the 'seven judgments,' " (2) a concordance with over one hundred references, (3) a tract about "three articles of faith" —Hut's "Ein christlich Unterricht," and (4) a manuscript containing "miscellaneous notations." *Ibid.*, p. 236.

81. If the debate took place in May 1527, the judgment as predicted by Hut was only one year away. This has led Seebass to the conclusion that Hubmaier got the dating from the "miscellaneous notations" which were Hut's *Missionsbüchlein*, completed before his ministry in Königsberg, that is, in the summer of 1526. Seebass, "Müntzers Erbe," p. 272.

82. *TA: Hubmaier*, pp. 475-476.

83. *ZHVSN:Hut*, pp. 231, 233.

84. *Ibid.*, p. 233.

85. *TA: Hubmaier*, pp. 475, 487, 489-490.

86. *ZHVSN: Hut*, p. 235.

87. *Ibid.*, pp. 231-233. a slightly different English translation is in Ozment, *Mysticism and Dissent*, pp. 101-102.

88. *TA: Bayern*, I, pp. 131-132, 153. Hubmaier also mentioned four topics discussed, namely baptism, the Lord's Supper, the end of the world, and the *Obrigkeit*. *TA: Hubmaier*, pp. 476, 486, 489; Torsten Bergsten, *Balthasar Hubmaier: Seine Stellung zur Reformation und Täufertum 1521-28* (Kassel, 1961) (hereafter referred to as *Hubmaier: Stellung*), p. 457.

89. This point was made by Seebass, "Müntzers Erbe," p. 271.

90. *ZHVSN: Hut*, p. 233.

91. Cf. *Müntzers Schriften*, p. 252.

92. *ZHVSN: Hut*, p. 232.

93. *Ibid.*, p. 233. Martin Göschl's role is dubious. It has been generally assumed that he was on Hubmaier's side. However, we noted that one of his assistants, a certain Bastian, was on Hut's side. Could it have been Göschl who engineered Hut's escape? Göschl's whole character is said to have been somewhat shady. Later a rumor spread that Hubmaier had sent a letter from prison to Göschl in which he admitted having treated Hut unfairly.

94. *Ibid.*, p. 235.

95. A. J. Zieglschmid, *Die älteste Chronik der Hutterischen Brüder* (Ithaca, New York, 1946), p. 50.

96. This was the attitude assumed by the Augsburg authorities during Hut's trial. They had specific knowledge of the Nicolsburg debate, including the fact that Hubmaier had summarized his accusations in fifty-two articles. *ZHVSN: Hut*, pp. 234-235.

97. Zeman, *Anabaptists and Czech Brethren*, pp. 191-192.

98. This myth was definitely destroyed by James Stayer in "Hans Hut's Doctrine on the Sword: An Attempted Solution," *MQR*, XXXIX (1965). *Anabaptists and the Sword*, pp. 162-165.

99. *TA: Hubmaier*, pp. 434-435, 439, 442, 444-445, 446; see also pp. 24-25; Bergsten, *Hubmaier: Stellung*, p. 465.

100. Stayer drew attention to the fact that practically all the arguments appearing in the Schleitheim Confession came up for refutation. Stayer, *Anabaptists and the Sword*, p. 142.

101. A similar conclusion in Seebass, "Müntzers Erbe," pp. 258-259.

102. A point made by Stayer, *Anabaptists and the Sword*, p. 163.

103. In his *Kurze Entschuldigung* written in 1526 Hubmaier recorded how some had interrupted his sermons and called him a "blood-sucker" who "vindicated the use of the sword by the 'Obrigkeit.' " Hubmaier promised to put his views on the sword into print later. Bergsten believed the incident occurred in Waldshut when Jacob Gross and Ulrich Treck refused to bear the sword for the city. *TA: Hubmaier*, pp. 271, 277.

104. Hubmaier may here have offered a metaphor repeated later by Bünderlin. *TA:*

Hubmaier, p. 450: "Darumb soll man die klawen der Schrifften spalten und sy wol widerklawen, ee man sy isset, das ist glaubt, oder man wirdt sonst den tod daran essen und durch halb warhaitten und halbe urtail weyt, weyt von der gantzen warhait abweychen und schwerlich irrgeen."

105. This appears to be Bergsten's conclusion. Bergsten, *Hubmaier: Stellung*, pp. 473, 475. Bergsten had difficulties in understanding why Hubmaier, therefore, remained so adamant in differentiating between his own and Hut's position. *Ibid.*, p. 473.

106. A conclusion arrived at by Seebass, "Müntzers Erbe," p. 270.

107. We are referring to Oecolampadius' letter of July 19, 1527. All eight articles were listed by Bonicius Amerbach in Basel on August 1, 1527. Needless to say, Oecolampadius found it incredible that they should reflect Hubmaier's beliefs. *TA: Elsass*, I p. 143; Bergsten, *Hubmaier: Stellung,* pp. 461-462.

108. Bergsten, *Hubmaier: Stellung,* pp. 461-463. Seebass has suggested that Fabri did so in order to partially retrieve his earlier "Falschmeldung." Seebass, "Müntzers Erbe," Appendix, p. 267, n. 130.

109. Johann Fabri, *Ursach warumb der wiederteuffer patron unnd erster Anfenger Doctor Balthasar Hubmeyer zu Wienn auff den zehnten tag Martij Anno 1528 verbrennet sey* (Vienna, 1528) (hereafter referred to as *Ursach warumb Hubmeyer*), sig. A iir. I found a copy of the tract in the Stadtbibliothek Augsburg.

110. He met with Hubmaier in December 1527. Fabri, *Ursach warumb Hubmeyer,* sig. B iv v.

111. Zeman, *Anabaptists and Czech Brethren*, p. 194, n. 76, p. 326; Bergsten, *Hubmaier: Stellung,* pp. 463-464. All five points reappear in sixteen articles which surfaced later. The articles were based on a document taken from an Anabaptist and brought to Archduke Ferdinand's attention by a "reputable" person. The salutation at the end of the articles supposedly identifies them as a genuine Anabaptist product. The content, in particular the argument for polygamy based on a puritan ethic, suggests that the articles may have originated in Hut's camp. Jörg Volk, one of Hut's early disciples and an active baptiser in his own right, made statements which indicate that he shared not only Hut's apocalypticism, but also denied the divinity of the historical Christ, taught universalism, and favoured polygamy. The latter idea was supported by others and seriously proposed during the Martyrs' Synod. It was rejected by the majority present. *TA: Glaubenszeugnisse*, I, pp. 201-202; *TA: Bayern*, I, pp. 61, 83-85; Wappler, *Die Täuferbewegung in Thüringen*, p. 323.

112. Packull, "Denck's Alleged Baptism by Hubmaier."

113. Johann Loserth, "Der Anabaptismus im Tirol. Von Seinen Anfängen Bis Zum Tode Jakob Huters (1526-1536)," *Archiv für österreichische Geschichte*, LXXVIII (1892), pp. 452-453.

114. This point was made by Heinold Fast, "Pilgram Marbeck und das oberdeutsche Täufertum. Ein neuer Handschriftenfund," *ARG*, XLVII (1956) (hereafter referred to as "Marbeck und Täufertum"), pp. 220-221. It is now confirmed in the newly published documents. *TA: Oesterreich*, II, pp. 32-33, 48, 52, 66.

115. *TA: Glaubenszeugnisse*, I, p. 80; *TA: Oesterreich*, II, p. 54. It is also plausible that Schiemer belonged to a third group, possibly influenced by Swiss Anabaptists, who accepted neither Hubmaier nor Hut as representative of their beliefs.

116. He married the sister of Thomas Paur. Paur, who was baptised by Hut, had married the sister of Eucharius Binder, Hut's most faithful companion from Franconia. Binder married a sister of Jörg Nespitzer. *ZHVSN: Augsburg*, pp. 47-48.

117. *TA: Oesterreich*, II, pp. 43-44, 53-58, 76.

118. A critical edition of the writings attributed to Schiemer is long overdue. The selection published by Müller in *TA: Glaubenszeugnisse*, I, is incomplete. A letter not included in the *Glaubenszeugnisse* was published by A. J. Zieglschmid, "Unpublished Sixteenth Century Letters of the Hutterian Brethren," *MQR*, XV (1941), pp. 5-15, 118-

140. There are other items attributed to him in Hutterite codices. Among them are two works in the question-answer format of a catechism, found in the *Kodex Braitmichel*. For a listing of these materials see Friedmann, *Die Schriften der Huterischen Täufergemeinschaften*, pp. 135-137.

119. *TA: Glaubenszeugnisse*, I, pp. 58-59: "Und hindennach, so man zusicht, so seind sy als hoch, das sy nimer realia sein, den res oder realia haist etwas, oder ein Ding. Es ist kain Ding, ist auch nit etwas, sonder werdt nur so lang, dieweil man daran gedenkt. So wirt zuletst gar nicht daraus und ist auch nicht; und welche am maisten von disem 'nicht' künen klaffen, die haist man mayster und doctores." Perhaps this antinominalist bent influenced Schiemer into opposition against Hubmaier and into the more mystical camp of Hut.

120. *Ibid.*, pp. 58-60, 74. How else could Luther, whose polemics against the whore of reason are well documented, receive the honour of being numbered with the scholastics?

121. *Ibid.*, p. 48; see also pp. 59-60, 73.

122. *Ibid.*, pp. 66.

123. *Ibid.*, pp. 52, 53.

124. A point which Erich Vogelsang made about the mystics' *Höllenfahrtmythos* is equally applicable to Schiemer. ". . . die Höllenfahrt ist zu einem Stück des Strafleidens Christi und damit der Rechtfertigungslehre geworden." Vogelsang, "Weltbild und Kreuzestheologie in den Höllenfahrtsstreitigkeiten der Reformationszeit," *ARG*, XXXVII (1970), p. 96.

125. Schiemer here speaks of the "key of David," which he clearly identifies as "the cross." The key is, therefore, the Lamb whose death must be experienced in the *viator*. *TA: Glaubenszeugnisse*, I, pp. 60, 74, 79.

126. Schiemer, "Ein wahrhaftig kurz Evangelium heut der Welt zu predigen," *Das Kunstbuch*, ed. by Georg "Maler" (Röthenfelder), sixteenth-century manuscript collection of Anabaptist tracts and letters at the Bürgerbibliothek in Bern, Switzerland (typescript copy at the Mennonite Historical Library, Goshen), pp. 141-143.

127. *TA: Glaubenszeugnisse*, I, pp. 60-61. Luther was explicitly attacked for denying the witness in man and deliberately falsifying Scripture. He had translated statements about the incarnation as God become flesh and dwelling "among men." According to Schiemer it should have been "in men."

128. *Ibid.*, p. 63.

129. *Ibid.*, p. 62.

130. *Ibid.*, p. 67; "Und ihe mer uns creatur entzogen wirt umb Christus willen, ihe mer erscheint das liecht und Gottes wort herfür."

131. Schiemer delineated three stages of grace. *Ibid.*, pp. 58-71.

132. *Ibid.*, pp. 46, 59, 63.

133. *Ibid.*, p. 49.

134. *Ibid.*, pp. 60-61.

135. *Ibid.*, p. 55.

136. Joachimists used both the figures 1260 and 1290 to fix the date when the great transformation would take place. However, they used these numbers as years dating either from Christ's birth, or, when that date passed, from Christ's passion, arriving at AD 1260 and AD 1290 respectively as crucial years. Reeves, *Influence of Prophecy, p. 59*.

137. Hut, Schiemer, and the other South German Anabaptists who predicted the end for 1528 may have been influenced by the prophecies of "ein alter Mann genannt Albrecht Gleicheisen" from Erfurt, whose prophecy has been preserved in *Das Kunstbuch*, p. 28. Gleicheisen in 1372 predicted that great changes would take place in 1528.

138. *Ibid.*, p. 133. This statement comes from the document preserved in *Das Kunstbuch*, which appears to be more accurate and complete than the one published by Müller, which was based on Hutterite sources. One of the differences is that Müller has

1200 days for the dragon's pursuit of the woman. *TA: Glaubenszeugnisse,* I, p. 55.

139. Assuming that the reference was to Hut: if Hut applied this prophecy to himself and believed his mission to baptise would carry on right until Pentecost of 1528, then he began to baptise in September or October 1526. If Schiemer included Hut's death in December 1527 in the 1½ years, then he would be saying that Hut began baptising in the spring of 1526.

140. *Das Kunstbuch,* p. 133.

141. *Ibid.,* pp. 63-64.

142. *TA: Glaubenszeugnisse,* I, pp. 49-50.

143. *Das Kunstbuch,* p. 134.

144. *TA: Glaubenszeugnisse,* I, pp. 71, 73, 79.

145. In *Prob des Geistes (ein Katechismus), Kodex Braitmichel,* f. 268 r.-v. Schiemer makes the characteristically separatist statement that he became a Christian, Sunday after St. Catherines, 1527. The works attributed to Schiemer in this codex await a thorough separate analysis.

146. Schiemer here followed the argument of Hubmaier, who transferred the keys from the supranational organization to the local community. He went beyond Hubmaier by attributing the power of the keys to the true believers separated from the world, including that of a local community. For the Swiss context of Hubmaier's church polity which Stayer has compared to the "non-separating congregationalism" of English Puritanism, cf. Stayer, "Die Anfänge des schweizerischen Täufertums im reformierten Kongregationalismus." *TA: Glaubenszeugnisse,* I, pp. 45, 57, 67-68, 73, 76.

147. He prayed, "In sechs Trübsalen wollest ihnen beistehen und in der siebenten (das ist in der letzten) nicht verlassen." Earlier he commented that "dear brother Schiemer's" predictions, particularly with regard to the suffering of God's people, had been correct. *Das Kunstbuch,* pp. 158-159.

148. He also listed Sigmund Hoffer, Jacob Wiedemann, and Wolfgang Brandhuber among the leaders. *TA: Glaubenszeugnisse, I, p. 118.*

149. Unfortunately we can no longer pinpoint the place of these occurrences. According to Schlaffer it was "im land," "ob der Enns." *Das Kunstbuch,* pp. 149-151; *TA: Glaubenszeugnisse,* I, pp. 119-120.

150. Karl Eder, *Das Land ob der Enns vor der Glaubensspaltung, Studien zur Reformationsgeschichte Oberösterreichs,* I (1933), p. 410, and *Glaubensspaltung und Landestände in Oesterreich ob der Enns 1525-1602, Studien zur Reformationsgeschichte Oberösterreichs,* II (1936) (hereafter referred to as *Glaubensspaltung in Oesterreich*), p. 35, n. 72.

151. *TA: Glaubenszeugnisse,* I, pp. 122-123.

152. *Ibid.,* p. 123. Schlaffer admitted that his judgment about Hubmaier might be prejudiced.

153. *TA: Bayern,* I, p. 132.

154. Schlaffer's trial and death received public sympathy which worried the authorities. *TA: Oesterreich,* II, pp. 64-65.

155. *TA: Glaubenszeugnisse,* I, p. 105. Unfortunately the questions are no longer extant, but we can reconstruct their content from Schlaffer's answers.

156. *Ibid.,* p. 108.

157. *Ibid.,* pp. 107-108.

158. *Ibid.,* p. 109.

159. *Ibid.,* pp. 109-110; cf. to *TA: Oesterreich,* II, p. 250.

160. *TA: Glaubenszeugnisse,* I, pp. 105, 110.

161. *Ibid.,* pp. 106-107.

162. In one place Schlaffer conceded that "vil seltzsam geschrei, das nit menschlich ist, geschweigen christlich, in der gemain ist." *TA: Glaubenszeugnisse,* I, p. 118.

163. Mecenseffy drew attention to this fact in "Die Herkunft des oberöster-

reichischen Täufertums," pp. 256-257.

164. *TA: Glaubenszeugnisse*, I, pp. 86, 88, 94, 95; see also *Das Kunstbuch*, p. 153.

165. *TA: Glaubenszeugnisse*, I, pp. 95-96.

166. The length denotes His presence as the slain Lamb from the beginning of creation to its end. His breadth signifies His universal presence in all peoples, transcending racial or national boundaries. His depth designates His presence even in hell and utter Godforsakenness. His height, although not specifically explained, suggests His ascension into heaven. *Ibid.*, p. 96.

167. *Ibid.*, p. 103.

168. *Das Kunstbuch*, p. 153; see also *TA: Glaubenszeugnisse*, I, p. 89.

Chapter V. The Devolution of Hut's Movement

1. See above, p. 94.

2. *TA: Bayern*, I, p. 199.

3. *Ibid.*, p. 187.

4. *Ibid.*, p. 199: "Und aber der Hut und Denck bei inen erschine. Und sich aldo verglichen, das solche verenderung in der benanten zeit komen wurde."

5. *Ibid.*, p. 28.

6. *ZHVSN: Hut*, p. 213.

7. The Nicolsburg Articles already appear in the "interrogatorium" for September 16. Seebass, "Müntzers Erbe" Appendix, p. 28. *Wiedertäuferakten*, Stadtarchiv Augsburg, f. 10 r. -13 r.

8. The Nuremberg authorities, as we noted earlier, had been in touch with Augsburg after Vogel's trial. They sent twenty-three questions including those concerning the "seven judgments" to Augsburg on September 23. These were the basis for Hut's interrogations on October 5. *ZHVSN: Hut*, pp. 229-231.

9. *TA: Bayern*, I, p. 44.

10. *ZHVSN: Hut*, p. 234.

11. Four books had been in Spittelmaier's possession when he was arrested. He was confronted with the same questions from Nuremberg as Hut. *TA: Bayern*, I, pp. 31-32, 39, 42, 44-47, 55.

12. The significance of Spittelmaier's confession has at times been overrated. Herbert Klassen, "Ambrosius Spittelmayr: His Life and Teachings," *MQR*, XXXII (1958), pp. 251-271.

13. This fact is derived from a comparison of Hut's and Spittelmaier's answers to questions #3, #4, and #5. *TA: Bayern*, I, pp. 41, 47.

14. *Ibid.*, pp. 40-41, 44.

15. *ZHVSN: Hut*, p. 243: "Sein Huten articul, die er in seinem buechlin zusamen gezogen, vergleichen sich mit den obgemelten articulen."

16. This information appears to have originated in Erlangen and travelled via Würzburg to Bibra. The letter of Hans von Bibra to Augsburg had originated in Würzburg on November 14. Cf. *ZHVSN: Hut*, pp. 238, 240-242, 249, 250-252; *TA: Bayern*, I, p. 60.

17. *ZHVSN: Hut*, p. 249.

18. *Ibid.*, pp. 241-242.

19. This has led Stayer to speak of Hut's political ethic as the "sheathed sword." *Anabaptists and the Sword*, p. 156; *ZHVSN: Hut*, p. 239; see also Berbig, "Wiedertäufer im Amt Königsberg," p. 313.

20. Stayer, *Anabaptists and the Sword*, p. 156, quoted from *Urgicht* of October 5. *ZHVSN: Hut*, p. 231.

21. *ZHVSN: Hut*, pp. 252-253. I find the explanation of the Augsburg council more plausible than the story mediated through Hut's son and found in the *Hutterite Chronicle*.

22. This was apparently the rumor circulating in Nuremberg and Würzburg. Lucas Osiander, *Grundtliche untterrichtung eins erbern Rats der Statt Nürmberg welcher*

gestalt ire Pfarrher und prediger in den Stetten und auff dem Land das volck wider etliche verfürische lere der Widertauffer in jren predigen auss heyliger Göttlicher schrifft zum getreülichsten ermanen unnd unterrichten sollen (Nuremberg: Jobst Gutknecht, [1528]) (hereafter referred to as *Grundtliche untterrichtung*), sig. E ii r. - E ii v; see also *TA: Bayern*, I, p. 60. The tract by Osiander has been traditionally attributed to Wenzel Link. Seebass has shown that it was the work of Osiander.

23. *ZHVSN: Hut*, p. 253.

24. *ZHVSN: Augsburg*, pp. 36, 48, 52, 80, 99.

25. *Ibid.*, pp. 14, 22, 33, 50, 69, 91, 97, 107, 110, 111.

26. *Ibid.*, pp. 25, 27, 29, 43, 49, 53, 55, 76, 79, 86, 98, 99, 110, 126, 127, 128, 130, 131, 136.

27. *Ibid.*, pp. 32, 47, 48, 51; about him see also Joseph Beck, ed., *Die Geschichtsbücher der Wiedertäufer in Oesterreich-Ungarn, 1526-1785* (Vienna, 1883), pp. 57, 65.

28. *ZHVSN: Augsburg*, pp. 35, 79, 94, 95, 97.

29. *Ibid.*, pp. 24-25, 32, 34-35, 43, 51, 53-54, 76, 84, 89-90, 99, 101, 103-104, 109, 110, 115, 132.

30. *Ibid.*, pp. 51, 67; *ZHVSN: Langenmantel*, pp. 21-23.

31. *ZHVSN: Augsburg*, pp. 11, 84.

32. *ZHVSN: Hut*, p. 248.

33. According to his confession he had stopped in Gmunden, Salzburg, and Wasserburg. Alexander Nicoladoni, *Johannes Bünderlin von Linz und die oberösterreichischen Täufergemeinden in den Jahren 1525-1531* (Berlin, 1893) (hereafter referred to as *Bünderlin*) pp. 205-207. Hans Rössler has Dorfbrunner in Munich by June/July 1527. "Wiedertäufer in und aus München 1527-1528," *Oberbayerisches Archiv*, LXXXV (1962), p. 43.

34. He was baptising by September 29. *ZHVSN: Augsburg*, p. 24.

35. Nicoladoni, *Bünderlin*, p. 206.

36. *ZHVSN: Augsburg*, pp. 53, 76, 99. I could find no evidence that Dorfbrunner had been sent to Linz from Augsburg in August and returned to Augsburg for a second time by November 10. This was a claim made by Paul Schwab, "Augsburg and the Early Anabaptists." *Reformation Studies: Essays in Honour of Roland H. Bainton*, ed. by Franklin H. Littell (Richmond, Va., 1962), p. 225.

37. Three hundred converts would sound more reasonable Nicoladoni, *Bünderlin*, p. 206; Wiedemann, "Die Wiedertäufergemeinde in Passau," p. 267; Schwab, "Augsburg and the Early Anabaptists," p. 225.

38. The above summary is based on an analysis of Dorfbrunner's own confession and statements made by his converts. Nicoladoni, *Bünderlin*, pp. 205-206, 210-211; *TA: Oesterreich*, 1, p. 63; *ZHVSN: Augsburg*, p. 55; *TA: Bayern, II*, pp. 10-12.

39. This is indicated by Elisabeth Leitlin's confession. *ZHVSN: Augsburg*, p. 36.

40. He was expelled from Augsburg on October 3, 1527, and reorganized the Anabaptists in Passau before Dorfbrunner arrived. He returned to the area of Augsburg during February 1528. *Ibid.*, pp. 13, 25-26; Nicoladoni, *Bünderlin*, pp. 190, 192, 195-196, 199, 203-204, 210.

41. *ZHVSN: Augsburg*, p. 65. See above, pp. 94, 98-99.

42. *ZHVSN: Augsburg*, p. 64. The Bossert collection of the *Esslinger Täuferakten* includes a letter by Jacob Wiedemann, Martin Veser, and Konrad Binder to the Anabaptists in Esslingen. It contained a response to queries from Esslingen concerning baptism and the *Obrigkeit*. It is possible that Leupold carried the letter. Its content corresponds to his own views. The Bossert collection, *Esslinger Täuferakten*, Generallandesarchiv, Karlsruhe (hereafter referred to as *Esslinger Täuferakten*).

43. *ZHVSN: Augsburg*, p. 60; Chr. Schnaufer and H. Haffner, *Beiträge zur Geschichte der Esslinger Reformation* (Esslingen am Neckar, 1932), p. 84.

44. He had baptised more converts in Göggingen near Augsburg. *ZHVSN: Augsburg*, pp. 58-60.

45. *Ibid.*, p. 60.

46. One of his missionary letters, written for him by Wolfgang von Iphof, was carried about by a brother Michel, probably Michael Maier. *TA: Bayern*, I, pp. 117, 171, 187; Bauer, *Anfänge täuferischer Gemeindebildungen in Franken*, pp. 96-97.

47. *TA: Bayern*, I, p. 112; Wappler, *Die Täuferbewegung in Thüringen*, p. 282.

48. *TA: Bayern*, I, p. 188.

49. *ZHVSN: Augsburg*, pp. 68-69.

50. *Ibid.*, pp. 34-35, 89.

51. *Ibid.*, pp. 58, 69.

52. The house belonged to a widow known as Schleiferin. Her two sons, Gall and Jörg, together with their sister Ursula, lived in the house. Ursula and Gall later blamed their brother Jörg for having permitted the use of the basement. Jörg was absent fighting the Turks when these allegations were made. *Ibid.*, pp. 80-81.

53. *Ibid.*, pp. 42-43; Claus Schleifer was related to Thomas Paur through marriage. Thus he was also related to Nespitzer, Eucharius Binder, and Schiemer (p. 47). Ringmacher was dispatched to Regensburg by Nespitzer (p. 46); see below p. 143.

54. *ZHVSN: Augsburg*, pp. 61, 63. Mrs. Sigmund Salminger was a silent observer.

55. Cf. the confessions of Els Knollin and Lux Miller. *Ibid.*, pp. 85, 122.

56. See the statements of Simprecht Widemann and Matheis Hieber. *Ibid.*, pp. 96, 102.

57. Urbanus Rhegius, *Zwen wunderseltzsam sendbrieff zweyer Widertauffer an ire Rotten gen Augsburg gesandt. Verantwurtung aller irrthum diser obgenannten brieff durch Urbanum Rhegium* (Augsburg: A. Weyssenhorn, 1528) (hereafter referred to as *Zwen wunderseltzsam sendbrieff*). I used the pagination found on the copy in the Mennonite Historical Library, Goshen. The second letter has been attributed to Hut. Seebass, "Müntzers Erbe," pp. 64, 67.

58. The letter was begun on January 4 and completed January 14. Rhegius, *Zwen wunderseltzsam sendbrieff*, p. 63.

59. *Ibid.*, p. 71: ". . . es ist überhundert meylwegs von euch grösser verspotung Christi, dan bey euch."

60. *Ibid.*, pp. 58-59.

61. Seebass arrived at a similar conclusion "Müntzers Erbe," p. 65.

62. The conclusion of the letter contains the initials V.S., but it is not clear whether they hide the identity of the writer or whether they are an abbreviated salutation. The Augsburg sources contain several hints as to letters circulating among Anabaptists. One of these was a letter by one Balthasar Berchtold intended for his wife. He had been exiled in September. *ZHVSN: Augsburg*, pp. 33, n. 1, 41-42,, 54, 90, 98. A more likely author or carrier of the letter was Burkhart Braun. Braun made a trip to Passau in December 1527 and from there he may have travelled to Moravia with some of his new converts. He returned to Augsburg some time in February 1528 bringing messages for a Chuonradt Miller from Radow. Nicoladoni, *Bünderlin*, pp. 190-192, 196, 199, 204, 207, 210; *ZHVSN: Augsburg*, p. 79.

63. Rhegius, *Wider den newen Taufforden*, sig. B r., A ii v., C v., F v.

64. Rhegius, *Zwen wunderseltzsam sendbrieff*, pp. 35, 38, 52.

65. *Ibid.*, pp. 36, 52-53, 58-62, 68. Rhegius' pointed comment was that the Anabaptists were concerned with removing the sword from the side but not from the heart (p. 37).

66. *Ibid.*, pp. 71-72. There is implicit evidence that the writer held to the apocatastasis. Satan could not "widerkeren biss das der herr kompt" (p. 32).

67. *Ibid.*, pp. 6, 9, 15, 20, 27, 31, 41, 51-52.

68. Gall Vischer had left Augsburg a few days earlier with Augustin Bader. *ZHVSN:*

Augsburg, pp. 32, 50-51, 75-76, 111.

69. Jörg Nespitzer and the new *Vorsteher* Claus Schleifer had predicted that by Pentecost such distress would fall on Augsburg that people should not be surprised if the city would disappear. *Ibid.*, p. 29.

70. *Ibid.*, p. 55.

71. Other old notables arrested on April 12 were Veronika Gross, Anna Salminger, and Marx Maier. *Ibid.*, pp. 12-17.

72. Plener was in the area for at least two months. His hostess for part of the time was the widow of Hans Leupold. Plener appears in the sources also under the name Weber and Jäger. *Ibid.*, pp. 127-128, 136.

73. See the statement by the participant Jacob Walch on September 9, 1528: *ZHVSN: Augsburg*, pp. 126, 131.

74. A similar conclusion was reached by Rössler, "Wiedertäufer in und aus München 1527-1528," p. 52.

75. Cases in point were Hans Kentner and Jos Riemer, who were active on behalf of the Anabaptist cause north of Augsburg. During March 1531 they came to Augsburg and interrupted one of the Reformed services. They were arrested, recanted, and were sent out of the city. Five years later Kentner was active in Dinkelsbühl. He recanted once more and then disappeared from the sources. Josef Seubert, *Untersuchung zur Geschichte der Reformation in der ehemaligen freien Reichsstadt Dinkelsbühl* (Hamburg, 1971), pp. 45-46.

76. *ZHVSN: Augsburg*, p. 130; Güss, *Kurpfälzische Regierung und Täufertum*, pp. 28-29.

77. Robert Friedmann, "Concerning the True Soldier of Christ. A Hitherto Unknown Tract of the Philippite Brethren in Moravia," *MQR*, V (1931) (hereafter referred to as "True Soldier of Christ"), pp. 91-92.

78. Christian Hege, *Die Täufer in der Kurpfalz*, pp. 62-63; Friedmann, "True Soldier of Christ," pp. 87-88.

79. Rössler, "Wiedertäufer in und aus München 1527-1528," p. 52.

80. This is a point already made by Rössler, *Ibid.*, p. 57, n. 100. The letter is in *Corpus Schwenckfeldianorum*, XVII, pp. 233-243. It was probably written for Schachner by Schwenckfeld (p. 234).

81. *TA: Bayern*, I, p. 170.

82. *Ibid.*, p. 169.

83. Gustav Bossert, "Augustin Bader von Augsburg, der Prophet und König, und seine Genossen, "nach den Prozessakten von 1530," *ARG*, X, XI (1912/1913, 1914) (hereafter referred to as "Bader," *ARG*), X, pp. 234-235. This is still the most comprehensive work on Bader.

84. See below p. 158.

85. This emerges from the document in *TA: Bayern*, I, pp. 174, 188-89, 196; *TA: Elsass*, I, pp. 265-267.

86. *TA: Bayern*, I, pp. 209-211.

87. *Ibid.*, pp. 269, 274.

88. *Ibid.*, p. 269.

89. This has been recognized by Bauer, who unsuccessfully tried to shift a larger influence from Hut to Georg Volck. *Anfänge täuferischer Gemeindebildungen in Franken*, pp. 54-55, 60-61, 162, 177; also Clasen, *Anabaptism; a Social History*, pp. 134, 456.

90. *TA: Bayern*, I, pp. 222, 228, 272, 287, 311, 327.

91. Forty-four others had preceded him and pleaded that they had been "verführt." Sabina Bader, Augustin's wife, proved to be more steadfast, refused to swear, and was led out of the city together with Salminger's wife. Others who were given severe penalties were Gall Vischer, Eitelhans Langenmantel, Endres Wildholz, Hans Kissling, and Peter Scheppach. Roth, *Augsburgs Reformationsgeschichte*, I (2nd ed.), pp. 236-238.

92. *ZHVSN: Augsburg*, p. 134. Roth's claim, that the meeting took place almost on

the same day that the new decree forbidding private meetings was published, is exaggerated. It must have been after October 19. Roth, *Augsburgs Reformationsgeschichte*, I (2nd ed.), pp. 236-237, 242.

93. Among those participating in his elevation were Nespitzer, Dorfbrunner, and Leonhart Freisleben. Bader at his trial wrongly believed that Freisleben had been burned with Dorfbrunner in Passau. *TA: Württemberg*, p. 936; Bossert, "Bader," *ARG*, XI, p. 108.

94. Bossert, "Bader," *ARG*, XI, pp. 107-108; *ZHVSN: Augsburg*, pp. 23, 26-27, 42, 52, 67, 74, 79, 96, 132-135.

95. *ZHVSN: Augsburg*, p. 137, n. 1.

96. Bossert, "Bader," *ARG*, X, pp. 125-126, XI, p. 106.

97. *ZHVSN: Augsburg*, p. 24.

98. Jacob Heiss testified that he was baptised by Jörg von München (Schachner) in the Ziegler woman's house. Hans Schlund, who arrived from Munich around Christmas and participated at meetings held during January, also fails to mention Bader. *Ibid.*, pp. 26-27, 29, 49.

99. *TA: Württemberg*, p. 938; Bossert, "Bader," *ARG*, X, pp. 134-135; XI, p. 44. List claims that Bader was in Nicolsburg early in 1528. *Utopie und Reformation* (p. 173).

100. *TA: Württemberg*, p. 926, n. 1.

101. Present also were Leonhard Freisleben, a certain Mang Schleiffer from Vienna, and Melchior from Salzburg. *ZHVSN: Langenmantel*, p. 26.

102. Bader's convenient escapes prompted rumors that he had always been warned about plans for his arrest. Bader was related to the *Vogt* of Augsburg. Bossert, "Bader," *ARG*, XI, pp. 56, 113.

103. With Bader was Matheis Harder. That Langenmantel probably possessed two writings by Hut emerges from contradictions between his statement and Hermann Anwalt's. Hermann claimed that he had received a document from Hut's son and also that Hut had given him permission to copy one of his documents. Langenmantel said that Hermann had received one of Hut's booklets from Laux Haffner, one of Hut's earliest and most influential followers in Augsburg. *ZHVSN: Langenmantel*, pp. 20, 23, 29-30; another copy of Hut's concordance was in the possession of Simprecht Widemann. *ZHVSN: Augsburg*, p. 96.

104. *ZHVSN: Langenmantel*, p. 20, 23, 29.

105. *Ibid.*, pp. 30-31. Others were Schachner, a certain Wildholz, and the Ziegler woman.

106. *ZHVSN: Augsburg*, p. 88.

107. Felicitas Huberin claimed to have been baptised in Vischer's house as early as Christmas 1526. Conrad Hubner was baptised there during March 1527. Throughout the summer of 1527 it remained a regular meeting place. *ZHVSN: Augsburg*, pp. 38, 40, 110, 113.

108. Bossert, "Bader," *ARG*, XI, pp. 119-120.

109. *Ibid.*, pp. 113-115, 119-120, *ZHVSN: Augsburg*, pp. 93, 133-134.

110. *ZHVSN: Augsburg*, p. 49.

111. He lived and worked secretly with Kürschner Obermayr for ten weeks, and although the latter was not an Anabaptist Bader revealed to him some of the things to come. Bossert, "Bader," *ARG*, XI, p. 106.

112. *Ibid.*, pp. 58, 60, 109.

113. *Ibid.*, pp. 29, 33, 61.

114. This emerges from statements made by Hans Köller and Gall Vischer. *Ibid.*, pp. 59-61. List has come independently to a similar conclusion. "Es gelang Bader nämlich, die von Hut angeregte revolutionäre Hoffnung am Leben zu erhalten und die Hauptmomente seiner Argumentation zu bewahren." *Utopie und Reformation*, p. 173.

115. The meeting, originally to be held in Esslingen, had been moved to Schönberg

for security reasons. It took place on September 29, 1528. Bossert, "Bader," *ARG*, XI, pp. 32, 34, 60, 108-109, 117.

116. Bossert, "Bader," *ARG, X*, pp. 145-146. *TA: Elsass*, I, pp. 180-181.

117. As noted earlier Nespitzer, Plener, and Schachner had reached similar conclusions by this time. Bossert, "Bader," *ARG*, XI, pp. 33-34, 108-109, 133.

118. This emerges from Bader's later confession. *Ibid.*, p. 46.

119. See Joachim Fleiner's confession of April 1, 1529, in the *Esslinger Täuferakten*; see also Bossert, "Bader," *ARG*, XI, p. 118.

120. Bossert, "Bader," *ARG*, XI, pp. 45, 47, 131.

121. *Ibid.*, pp. 58, 61.

122. *Ibid.*, p. 118; also p. 32.

123. They were Gall Vischer and Hans Köller. *Ibid.*, pp. 32, 35.

124. Bullinger, *Widertoufferen Vrsprung*, f. 44 r.-v.

125. Bossert, "Bader," *ARG*, XI, pp. 107, 132-133.

126. Clasen has drawn attention to the fact that a Swiss leader, Martin Linki, banned someone named Augustin. He has convincingly suggested that this may have been Bader. *Anabaptism; a Social History*, p. 455.

127. One of Bader's later followers, the miller Gastel, vehemently dissociated himself from the Anabaptists. Bossert, "Bader," *ARG*, XI, p. 28.

128. The adults were, besides Bader and his wife Sabina, Vischer, Leber and his wife, the seamster Köller, and the miller Gastel and his wife. *Ibid.*, pp. 36, 39, 47, 55, 75, 86, 108, 112, 113, 122.

129. He had been a priest in Nydenhain (Neudenau) near Hermbeltzen (Herbolzheim) in the Odenwald. *Ibid.*, pp. 110-111.

130. *Ibid.*, p. 31: "... den touf, den er ... in seinem alter empfangen, den halt und glob er und von dem kinder tauf nichts."

131. *Ibid.*, p. 28.

132. *Ibid.*, p. 46.

133. Seifert, *Synagogue and Church in the Middle Ages*, p. 148.

134. The expulsion was not rigorously enforced. Some were permitted to stay by purchasing a *Schutzbrief* that could be renewed for further payments. H. Kohls, "Die Judenfrage in Hessen während der Reformationszeit," *Jahrbuch der hessischen kirchengeschichtlichen Vereinigung*, XXI (1970), pp. 88-89.

135. Bossert, "Bader," *ARG*, X, pp. 142-144.

136. Bossert, "Bader," *ARG*, XI, p. 41; *TA: Württemberg*, pp. 939-940.

137. At his trial Bader was asked about a little booklet full of circles. He claimed that Oswald was most knowledgeable in it. Bossert, "Bader," *ARG*, XI, p. 49.

138. *Ibid.*, pp. 59, 128. Bader moved the date for the tribulation predicted by Hut to March 1530. See also List, *Utopie und Reformation*, pp. 175-180.

139. Bossert, "Bader," *ARG*, XI, p. 41.

140. *Ibid.*, p. 29: "In solcher sendung im, dem propheten, ain kind geborn, durch welches kind alle ding sollen geoffenbart werden, nit das diss kind also hailig, sonder sy das allain ain betutung dass sons gottes, der durch ain kind, sinen son Christum, vil uf erdrich gewirkt, also werd das auch sin. ..."

141. *Ibid.* Oswald Leber here gave the example utilized by Hubmaier and Bünderlin of the sign before an inn which was symbolic of the wine but was not the wine.

142. Contacts reached to Leyphaym, Gyntzburg, Bühel, and Würzburg. Ferdinand ordered the arrest of the Jews implicated. Their fate is not discussed in our sources. *Ibid.*, pp. 33, 42, 45, 59, 104, 132.

143. *Ibid.*, pp. 24, 29, 33, 129.

144. The authorities misinterpreted Bader as stating that he would join the Turks with his followers. Actually he intended to hide. Bossert, "Bader," *ARG*, XI, pp. 30, 62-63, 132.

145. *Ibid.*, pp. 30-31, 47-48, 57.
146. *Ibid.*, p. 48. Bader's ideas show striking similarities to those of Johann Hergott, *Von der newen wandlung eynes Christlichen Lebens.* Hütt dich Teuffel, Die Hell wirdt zurbrechen (Leipzig: Michael Blum, 1526 or 1527), pp. 56-57. This was the same Hergott to whose press Hut had brought Müntzer's manuscript.
147. Bossert, "Bader," *ARG*, XI, pp. 48, 61, 130-131.
148. Baptism was now allegorized into representing 2½ years of persecution under the Turks. All those having gone through the persecution, together with their descendants, were considered as baptised. The Lord's Supper was an inner understanding of the divine secret of the new order. *Ibid.*, pp. 47, 103, 129-130.
149. *Ibid.*, pp. 31, 47, 131.
150. *Ibid.*, p. 24. That the Joachimite tradition was alive at the time can be seen in Hergott, *Von der newen wandlung eynes Christlichen Lebens*, p. 53: "Es seynd gesehen worden drey wandlung, die erst hat Gott der vater gehalten mitt dem alten Testament. Die andere wandlung hat Gott der Sohn gehabt mitt der welt ym newen Testament. Die dritt wandlung wird haben der heylig geyst. . . ."
151. It consisted of a "märderin rock . . . daffatin lyprock, das schwarz samatin wammes und hosen." Bossert, "Bader," *ARG*, XI, pp. 127-129.
152. Bader further subdivided each of the three stages into three more stages, but the meaning is no longer discernible. *Ibid.*
153. *Ibid.*, pp. 33, 35.
154. *Ibid.*, pp. 20-22, 24-26, 33, 35, 38-40, 46, 51-52.
155. *TA: Elsass*, I, p. 181.
156. Bossert, "Bader," *ARG*, XI, pp. 24-25.
157. See unpublished letter of March 5, 1530, by Ulrich Neyhart to the privy council of Ulm. Bossert collection, *Ulmer Akten*, Generallandesarchiv, Karlsruhe.
158. *TA: Elsass*, I, p. 284.
159. Bossert, "Bade
160. *TA: Elsass*, I, pp. 344, 347-348, 523; *ZHVSN: Augsburg*, pp. 146, 154.
161. September 19, 1527. *ZHVSN: Augsburg*, p. 146.

Chapter VI. The Evolution of Evangelical Sectarian Anabaptism

1. Nicoladoni, *Bünderlin*, pp. 24-25. Joseph Jäkel, "Zur Geschichte der Wiedertäufer in Oberösterreich und speciell in Freistadt. Mit einer Einleitung über Entstehung und Wesen des Täufertums überhaupt," *Beiträge zur Landeskunde von Oesterreich ob der Enns* (Linz, 1889) (hereafter "Geschichte der Wiedertäufer"), pp. 9, 14-15, 22, 60-61; Rischar, "Binder und März," p. 21; Eder, *Glaubenspaltung in Oberösterreich*, p. 38, n. 82.
2. Eduard Widmoser, "Das Tiroler Täufertum," I, *Tiroler Heimat, Jahrbuch für Geschichte und Volkskunde*, XV (1951), pp. 49-50. Widmoser believed Hut may have been in Austria in 1526. Mecenseffy, "Die Herkunft des oberösterreichischen Täufertum," p. 253; Robert Friedmann, "Anabaptism in the Inn Valley," *Mennonite Life*, XV (1960), p. 109.
3. I addressed myself partially to this question in my article, "Denck's Alleged Baptism by Hubmaier," pp. 327-338.
4. Beck, *Die Geschichtsbücher der Wiedertäufer in Oesterreich-Ungarn*, pp. 108-109. *TA: Oesterreich*, II, pp. 1-4.
5. Christian Hitz from Salzburg republished one of Müntzer's tracts in 1526. Johannes Bergdolt, *Die freie Reichsstadt Windsheim im Zeitalter der Reformation, V: Quellen und Forschungen zur bayerischen Kirchengeschichte*, (Leipzig & Erlangen, 1921), p. 108; see also the case of Hans Sturm, Packull, "Denck's Alleged Baptism by Hubmaier," p. 336, n. 56.
6. I am indebted to Walter Klaassen for making his unpublished manuscript available to me. "Michael Gaismaier, Rebel and Reformer" (Conrad Grebel College, University of Waterloo), pp. 135-143. More research is necesssary to clarify the relationship between the

peasants' rebellion and Anabaptism in Austria. See below, p. 156-157.

7. For an analysis of Strauss' teachings see H. Barge, *Jacob Strauss. Ein Kämpfer für das Evangelium in Tirol, Thüringen und Süddeutschland* (Leipzig, 1937); also by Barge, "Die gedruckten Schriften des evangelischen Predigers Jacob Strauss," *ARG*, XXXII (1935) (hereafter "Schriften des Strauss"), pp. 100-121, 248-252.

8. Strauss was driven from Hall in the Tyrol during 1522. He later published one of his sermons preached there and addressed it to the brethren in Hall. Barge, "Schriften des Strauss," pp. 101-102.

9. Eder, *Das Land ob der Enns vor der Glaubenspaltung*, p. 416.

10. A point made by Bernard Raupach, *Presbyterologia Austriaca*, II (Hamburg, 1741), pp. 40, 51.

11. Eder, *Das Land ob der Enns vor der Glaubenspaltung*, p. 407; Otto Clemen, "Die Elbogener Kirchenordnung von 1522," *ZKG*, XXVI (1905), pp. 82-94.

12. Wolfgang Rappolt, *Eyn kurtze Epistel An die vom Elpogen* (Zwickau: Jörg Gästel, 1525,) sig. A iv r. A copy in the Universitätsbibliothek Heidelberg.

13. *Ibid.*, sig. A iv v.

14. Eder, *Das Land ob der Enns vor der Glaubenspaltung*, pp. 400-401, 408; Ulrich Gäbler, "Eine unbeachtete Uebersetzung des Leonhard Freisleben genannt Eleutherobius," *ARG*, LXI (1970) (hereafter "Uebersetzung des Freisleben"), p. 71.

15. Raupach, *Presbyterologia Austriaca*, II, pp. 42-44.

16. See below, p. 157, on Bünderlin, where it is suggested that he may have been baptised in 1526 in Augsburg.

17. *TA: Bayern*, I, pp. 47-48; *TA: Bayern*, II, pp. 11-12; Hermann Nestler, *Die Wiedertäuferbewegung in Regensburg. Ein Ausschnitt aus der Regensburger Reformationsgeschichte* (Regensburg, 1929), pp. 47-48.

18. This sequence of events emerges from Ferdinand's correspondence with the city council of Freistadt. *TA: Oesterreich*, II, pp. 6-7.

19. See the tract attributed to Jörg Schöferl in *TA: Oesterreich*, I, pp. 21-22; Seebass, "Müntzers Erbe," pp. 294-295.

20. Nicoladoni, *Bünderlin*, pp. 189, 201, 209.

21. *TA: Oesterreich*, I, pp. 66-67; Nicoladoni, *Bünderlin*, p. 191.

22. *TA: Bayern*, II, pp. 11-13; Nicoladoni, *Bünderlin*, pp. 195, 199, 202. Nestler, *Die Wiedertäuferbewegung in Regensburg*, p. 48.

23. This is also clear from Pfefferlein's confession. He was baptised by Freisleben in Göggingen. *ZHVSN: Langenmantel*, pp. 27-28, also pp. 14-15.

24. He was expelled on November 16, 1527. *TA: Bayern*, II, p. 27.

25. *Ibid.*, pp. 29, 32.

26. *ZHVSN: Augsburg*, pp. 62-63; *TA: Bayern*, II, p. 27.

27. This was recognized by Dr. Johann Rehlinger from Augsburg. Unfortunately the prosecution did not heed his advice. *TA: Bayern*, II, pp. 40-41, 49; also pp. 21-27, 33.

28. In all probability Christoph arrived in Esslingen in the company of Leupold and possibly Reublin, or another Anabaptist of Swiss origin, late in November or early in December 1527. "Aber darnach sein irer 3 ainer von Augspurg, der ander von Linz, der dritt us Schweiz. . . . komen. . . ." Hans Beyer's statement, June 13, 1528. *Esslinger Täuferakten*, Gustav Bossert, Jr.'s manuscript collection of the Täuferakten for the cities of Esslingen and Ulm, Generallandesarchiv Karlsruhe.

29. See the confessions of Hans Craft, Hans Graci, Wolfen Hans, and Hans Bayerlin, *Esslinger Täuferakten*; see also James Stayer's careful analysis of the Esslingen situation. "Eine fanatische Täuferbewegung in Esslingen und Reutlingen?" *Blätter für Württembergische Kirchengeschichte*, LXVIII/LXIX (1968-69), pp. 53-59.

30. See Mathias Dritschler's confession of January 15, 1528, *Esslinger Täuferakten*; also Clasen, *Anabaptism; a Social History*, p. 168.

31. Several of his letters, in which he explained at length the reasons for his break with

the Anabaptists, have survived. *Esslinger Täuferakten;* Claus-Peter Clasen, *Die Wiedertäufer im Herzogtum Württemberg und benachbarten Herrschaften* (Stuttgart: W. Kohlhammer, 1965) (hereafter *Wiedertäufer im Herzogtum Württemberg*), pp. 71-72.

32. Clasen, *Wiedertäufer im Herzogtum Württemberg,* pp. 76-77, and *Anabaptism; a Social History,* p. 130.

33. See the confession of Zunftmeister Anshelm and son sometime during 1528. *Esslinger Täuferakten.*

34. Clasen, *Anabaptism; a Social History,* pp. 167, 462-463, n. 30.

35. There is considerable evidence of Christoph's presence in Esslingen during December 1527. See the confessions of Hans Ultz, *Esslinger Täuferakten; TA: Elsass,* I, p. 182, n. 1; *TA: Württemberg,* pp. 5, 8.

36. For Reublin's role in early Swiss Anabaptism see Stayer, "Reublin and Brötli: The Revolutionary Beginnings of Swiss Anabaptism.

37. *Esslinger Täuferakten.*

38. *TA: Württemberg,* pp. 5, 8.

39. The tract carried the signature of Stoffel Eleutherobios and the date 1528. The full title reads: *Vom warhafftigen Tauf Joannis Christi und der Aposteln, Wenn und wie der kindertauff angefangen und eingerissen hat. Item Wie alle widerreden der Widerchristen wider den Tauff sollen verantwortet werden* (hereafter referred to as *Vom warhafftigen Tauf*). I was able to use a copy preserved in the Stadtbibliothek Frankfurt. It is found bound together with a handwritten treatise of Melchior Rinck.

40. *TA: Elsass,* I, p. 151.

41. It is possible that this was one of the letters brought back by Leupold, who was in Worms and environs at this time. Freisleben appears not yet to have had knowledge of the fact that Lutz himself fled Esslingen on January 21. Christoph's letter, *Esslinger Täuferakten.*

42. A copy of this "Sattler" tract is in the Stadtbibliothek Augsburg. *Wie die Gschrifft verstendigklich soll underschieden/un erkärt werden/die vom Tauff saget/wie der Hailig gaist mit seinen gaben vor und nach kumpt/un seine werck laistet/erstlich durch den glaube der laer* (n.p., [1526]) (hereafter referred to as *Wie die Gschrifft*). The treatise numbers 21 pages including the title page. We list here only a few concepts which recur in Christoph's later work: (1) the statement contained in the title that the Spirit is received before or after baptism, (2) the idea that "Crysam/Saltz/Kot/Teufelausstreybung/von der gfatterschaft" are misuses, "so auss der Römischen Kirchen zu uns ist krochen," (3) the identical argument rejecting circumcision, (4) the claim that babies were now baptised before they had totally emerged from their mother's womb, (5) the distinction between John the Baptist's baptism unto repentance and that of Christ in the Spirit, and (6) the differentiation between New and Old Testament.

43. *Wie die Gschrifft,* sig. B iv v.-C r.: "Unnd zuletst durch die Propheten gar abgeschafft, und für ain untüchtig ding gehalten."

44. Only Ulrich Bergfried has analysed its contents in some detail. *Verantwortung als theologisches Problem im Täufertum des 16. Jahrhunderts* (Wuppertal, 1938). See also Clasen's comments in *Wiedertäufer im Herzogtum Württemberg,* p. 6, n. 29, and *Anabaptism; a Social History,* pp. 354, 356.

45. Eleutherobios, *Vom warhafftigen Tauf,* sig. A iii v.-A iv v. It is possible that Freisleben's description of the historical evolution of pedobaptism depended on other sources familiar to early Anabaptists. An Anabaptist named Erhard Pilraust, arrested in Müntzer's old parish of Allstedt in the fall of 1532, related that a stranger had read from "A book of creation or kings" how the custom of pedobaptism evolved gradually. First, all persons twelve years of age and over were granted baptism. Then exceptions were made for the weak and dying under that age. Eventually it became customary to baptise all children. Wappler, *Die Täuferbewegung in Thüringen,* pp. 345, 347.

46. Eleutherobios, *Vom warhafftigen Tauf,* sig. B r.

47. *Ibid.*, sig. A iv v.-B v.
48. *Ibid.*, sig. C ii v.-C iv v.
49. *Ibid.*, sig. D r.-D ii v. and sig. B iii r.
50. *Ibid.*, sig. A ii r.-A iii r.
51. *Ibid.*, sig. B iv r.-C v.; see also C ii v.
52. *Ibid.*, sig. C ii v., D iii v.
53. There is also a very strong emphasis on discipleship and church discipline in Christoph's tract. The brotherhood of true believers is explicitly compared with a monastic order. There is even a hint at communalism. *Ibid.*, sig. B iv r.-v.
54. See letter of April 3 in L. K. Enthoven, ed., *Briefe an Desiderius Erasmus von Rotterdam* (Strassburg, 1906), pp. 117-119.
55. Kenneth Davis, "Erasmus as a Progenitor of Anabaptist Theology and Piety," *MQR*, XLVIII (1973), pp. 163-178.
56. Gustav Bossert, "Christoph Eleutherobios oder Freisleben. Der frühere Täufer, später Syndikus der Wiener Universität und bischöflicher Offizial," *Jahrbuch der Gesellschaft f. d. Geschichte d. Protestantismus in Oesterreich*, XXIX (1908), p. 1.
57. Bucer's *Nachlass* contained a letter by Christoph addressed to Schwenckfeld. Unfortunately this document has not survived. *TA: Elsass*, I, pp. 151, 528.
58. Bossert, "Zwei Linzer Reformationsschriftsteller," p. 137. The play was entitled *Ain Kurtzweylig unnd nit minder nutzlich Spyl des Plantisch Stichus genant, zu Teutsch gebracht gereymt und gehalten zu Ingolstatt.* It was printed by Ulhart in 1539.
59. Eder, *Das Land ob der Enns vor der Glaubenspaltung*, p. 407.
60. Paul Burckhardt, *Die Basler Täufer: Ein Beitrag zur Schweizerischen Reformationsgeschichte* (Basel, 1898), pp. 53-54; Gustav Bossert, "Kleine Mittheilungen," *Jahrbuch d. Gesellschaft f. d. Geschichte d. Protestantismus in Oesterreich*, XIII (1892), p. 56.
61. *ME*, II, p. 184.
62. Gäbler, "Uebersetzung des Freisleben," pp. 72-73.
63. For the full title of the tract see *Ibid.*, pp. 71-75; Schottenloher, *Ulhart*, p. 89.
64. *Ain Kurtzweyligs und Lustigs Spil, von der Weissheit unnd Narrheit darin kain unzucht, sonder vil guter leer und lächerliche schwänk begriffen sind* (Augsburg: Ulhart, 1550). I obtained a photocopy of the rare booklet from the British Museum.
65. Schottenloher, *Ulhart*, p. 87; *Ein schöns Gesprech zwischen Aim Edelman und seinem Knecht vom Apostolischen Tauff und die gehorsam der Oberkait belangend. Und wie der Knecht sich durch den Edelman unnd sein Pfarherren mit hailiger Schrifft weysen lasst* (n.p., n.d. [c. 1532]).
66. Schottenloher, *Ulhart*, p. 87.
67. *Aufdeckung der Babylonischen Hurn und Antichrists alten unnd newen gehaimnuss und grewl. Auch vom sig, frid und herrschung warhaffter Christen, unnd wie sy der Oberkait gehorsam, das creutz on aufrhur und gegenwer mit Christo inn gedult und liebe tragen zum preiss Gottes und allen frumen und Gottsuchenden zu dienst, stercke und besserung an tag gebracht (n.p. [c. 1530]) (hereafter Aufdeckung der Babylonischen Hurn).* A microfilm copy is found at the Mennonite Historical Library, Goshen. The tract is reproduced in Hans Hillerbrand, "An Early Anabaptist Treatise on the Christian and the State," *MQR*, XXXII (1958) (hereafter "Early Anabaptist Treatise"). pp. 34-47.
68. Hillerbrand, "Early Anabaptist Treatise," p. 29.
69. The title page of Sattler's work carries the same ornamentation.
70. *Aufdeckung der Babylonischen Hurn*, sig. A iv r.-B r.
71. *Ibid.*, sig. B iii v.
72. *Ibid.*, sig. C v. See Stayer's excellent discussion of the subject. *Anabaptists and the Sword*, pp. 170-172.
73. Wiedemann, "Die Wiedertäufergemeinde in Passau," p. 268.
74. *TA: Oesterreich*, I, pp. 123-128. Brandhuber himself appears in the confessions as

"schneyder von sanct Niclas."

75. This is an inference from Steffan Zerer's confession. *TA: Oesterreich*, I, p. 125. For the events in Freistadt see above, pp. 141-142.

76. Jacob Storger from Koburg testified years later that he had been baptised by Brandhuber in Wels sometime in 1529. Wappler, *Die Täuferbewegung in Thüringen*, pp. 159, 425-426.

77. The *Hutterite Chronicle* suggests that the other seventy prisoners were executed also. *TA: Glaubenszeugnisse*, I, pp. 136-137. Beck, however, believed that many of these recanted. *Die Geschichtsbücher der Wiedertäufer in Oesterreich-Ungarn*, p. 88, n. 1. *TA: Oesterreich*, 1, pp. 207-210; Nicoladoni, *Bünderlin*, pp. 213-216.

78. Beck, *Die Geschichtsbücher der Wiedertäufer in Oesterreich-Ungarn*, pp. 88-89.

79. *TA: Glaubenszeugnisse*, I, pp. 137-143.

80. The latter had been Müller's conclusion. *TA: Glaubenszeugnisse*, I, p. 143, n. 2.

81. Freisleben: "Ir Lothischen geet auss von Sodoma und Gomorra. Gen. 19." Eleutherobios, *Vom warhafftigen Tauf*, sig. D iii v. Brandhuber: ". . . und geet aus ir Lotischen von Sodoma und Gomorra, damit ir nit sambt ir verderbt und irer bösen werken tailhaftig werdent." *TA: Glaubenszeugnisse*, I, p. 143.

82. *TA: Glaubenszeugnisse*, I, pp. 137-138, 140.

83. *Ibid.*, p. 139. See above p. 64.

84. *TA: Glaubenszeugnisse*, I, pp. 139-140.

85. Only one statement appears to make the contrast between the "inner" and "outer word" in terms reminiscent of Hut, Denck, and Müntzer. *TA: Glaubenszeugnisse*, I, p. 139: "Lieben brüeder, merkent, so euch alle geschrift umbstossen wirt, geet in abgrund eures herzen, merkent, was uns die kraft des heiligen geists leernet und zuesagt. . . ."

86. *Ibid.*, p. 142.

Chapter VII. The Emergence of the "Homeless Minds": Hans Bünderlin and Christian Entfelder

1. See Gerhard Steupen's letter to Bucer and the reply by Bucer, *TA: Elsass*, I, pp. 283-284, 330.

2. This point was first made by Nicoladoni, who maintained that Bünderlin was a student of Denck, blending ideas from German mysticism, the Jewish Cabala, and other Neoplatonic sources into a humanistic *Weltanschauung*. Nicoladoni, *Bünderlin*, pp. 134, 139, 156. Similar observations are found in Alfred Hegler, *Geist und Schrift bei Sebastian Franck*, p. 273, and *Beiträge zur Geschichte der Mystik in der Reformationszeit* (Berlin, 1906), pp. 67-68; Eberhard Teufel, "Bünderlin," *Neue Deutsche Biography*, II (1955), p. 740; Christian Neff, *ME*, I, pp. 469-470.

3. Claude Foster, "Hans Denck and Johannes Buenderlin: A Comparative Study," *MQR*, XXXIX (1965), p. 116.

4. That Franck was an avid student of Bünderlin is clear from his letter to Johann Campanus; *TA: Elsass*, I, pp. 317-320.

5. Ulrich Gäbler, "Zum Problem des Spiritualismus im 16. Jahrhundert. Das Glaubensverständnis bei Johannes Bünderlin von Linz," *TZ*, XXIX (1973) (hereafter "Problem des Spiritualismus"), pp. 334-336.

6. The major proponent of this thesis was Kiwiet, *Pilgram Marbeck*, pp. 49-50.

7. A similar suggestion was made by William Klassen, "Pilgram Marbeck in Recent Research," *MQR*, XXXII (1958), p. 217.

8. Groundbreaking work on Bünderlin was done by Gustav Bossert, "Hans Bünderlins Vorgeschichte," *Jahrbuch d. Gesellschaft f. d. Geschichte d. Protestantismus in Oesterreich*, XI (1890), "Noch einmal Hans Bünderlin," *Jahrbuch d. Gesellschaft f. d. Geschichte d. Protestantismus in Oesterreich*, XV (1894), and "Zwei Linzer Reformationsschriftsteller."

9. Klassen, "Michael Gaismair, Rebel and Reformer," pp. 50, 53-54.

Notes   225

10. Nicoladoni was unaware that the Hans Vischer appearing in Anabaptist documents was identical with Bünderlin. Jäkel followed Nicoladoni. Jäkel, "Geschichte der
Wiedertäufer," pp. 58-59.
11. TA: Elsass, I, pp. 229, 232.
12. See the confessions of Hans Stiglitz, Jr., and Hermann Keull. Nicoladoni,
Bünderlin, pp, 189, 201, 207.
13. Christian Neff, ME, I, p. 469. Williams somewhat illogically had Bünderlin
baptised twice, once by Denck and once by Hut. The Radical Reformation, pp. 156, 167.
14. This emerges again from his confession given in Strassburg. Even though some of
the Nicolsburg Articles reflect ideas propagated by Bünderlin, the suggestion that he was
present at the disputation between Hut and Hubmaier must remain speculative. Neff,
ME, I, p. 469; Williams, The Radical Reformation, p. 178.
15. His activities came to the attention of the authorities sometime in March. TA:
Elsass, I, pp. 71-72.
16. The split took place during March 1528, a time when Bünderlin was no longer in
Linz and probably in Nicolsburg. Zeman, Anabaptists and Czech Brethren, pp. 192, 233,
n. 244.
17. The dispute has been recorded in Zieglschmid, Die älteste Chronik der Hutterischen Brüder, pp. 52-54, 86-88.
18. This is borne out by the independent research of Zeman. He noticed a decisive
change in Anabaptist attitudes in Moravia during the latter part of 1528, reflected in the
negotiations between the Anabaptists in the area and the Unitas Fratrum. During the
early negotiations the Anabaptists agreed to a compromise permitting both adult and infant baptism. Later they opted for adult baptism only. Zeman concluded rightly that the
early spokesmen for the Anabaptist cause represented a more liberal and spiritualistic
position. Anabaptists and Czech Brethren, pp. 240-241.
19. Meyer was specifically mentioned in Hätzer's farewell letter to Capito. TA:
Elsass, I, pp. 71-72.
20. Ibid., p. 234.
21. Ibid., p. 138; see above, p. 133.
22. TA: Elsass, I, pp. 184-186.
23. Ibid.
24. Ibid., pp. 185-186. Meyer was still holding private studies as late as 1533. The notorious Claus Frey and his illegitimate wife, Elisabeth Pfersfelder, were among those attending.
25. Ibid., pp. 187-192, 194-218, 241-246, 249-250.
26. Ibid., p. 155: "Nennen sich den geist gottes und die andern, so jrer sect nit
anhangen, das stinckened fleisch." Ibid., p. 236. According to Meyer's own statement he
and his followers aimed at a via media between Catholicism and Lutheranism. Christoph
Freisleben made a similar claim in his treatise of early 1528.
27. One of the meetings was held at Claus Bruchen's house. Bruchen was a sympathetic acquaintance of Marpeck and the employer of Sigmund Bosch, one of the
contributors to Das Kunstbuch. TA: Elsass, I, p. 230; see also Fast, "Marbeck und
Täufertum," p. 234.
28. Also implicated were a convert of Hans Römer and one person from as far away as
Holland. The rest came primarily from South German and Austrian territory. TA: Elsass,
I, p. 229.
29. He was still alive in 1539. Gäbler, "Problem des Spiritualismus," p. 335.
30. They were printed by Balthasar Beck. The titles and a description of their content
are found in Nicoladoni, Bünderlin, pp. 132, 138, 144, 153; see also Gäbler, "Problem des
Spiritualismus," p. 335, n. 7. I was able to use a microfilm copy (Mennonite Historical Library, Goshen) of the Sammelband found in the Landesbibliothek Dresden.
31. The full title read: Erklärung durch vergleichung der Biblischen geschrifft, das

der wassertauff sampt andern eusserlichen gebreůchen, in der Apostolischen kirchen geůbet. On Gottes befelch und zeůgniss der geschrifft, von etlichen diser zeit, wider eefert [eingefůhrt] wirt. Sintemalen der Antichrist dieselben all, zehand nach der Apostel abgang verwůst hat. Welche Verwůstung dann biss an das ende bleibt (n.p., 1530) (hereafter referred to as *Erklārung*). Because of the difficulty of following the original signatures on microfilm I am using the pagination found on the top of each page of the microfilm copy.

32. Bünderlin, *Erklārung*, p. 459.

33. In general, Bünderlin echoed all the arguments against the *Evangelischen* first registered by Müntzer and repeated by early South German Anabaptists. *Ausz was Ursach sich Gott in die nyder gelassen unnd in Christo vermenschet ist, durch welchen, und wie er des menschens fall in jm selbs durch den gesandten Messiah verstůnet, und widerpracht hat* (Strassburg, 1529) (hereafter referred to as *Ursach*), pp. 23-24, 39, 70-71, 74; *Ein gemeyne Berechnung uber der heyligen schrifft innhalt, in derselben natůrlichen verstand (mit anzeygung jres missuerstands grund unnd ursprung) eynzuleyten, durch etlicher puncten gegensatz erklārung, dabey man die anderen, so vilfāltig in der schrifft verfasst seind, auch abnemen mag* (Strassburg, 1529) (hereafter referred to as *Berechnung*), pp. 159, 168, 204.

34. Bünderlin, *Ursach*, pp. 76-77, 121 and *Berechnung*, p. 287.

35. Bünderlin held to progressive revelation. Each new revelation was intended to wean man further from the material and external. *Berechnung*, pp. 179, 212-215.

36. Although Bünderlin drew a clear dispensational distinction between Old and New Testament, an analysis of his understanding of "law" indicates that he did not contrast the two dispensations in terms of law and gospel. The real essence of the law had always been spiritual. It was not abolished but its true nature more perfectly revealed. *Berechnung*, pp. 192, 211, 270, 278, 298-299, 304, 334 and *Ursach*, pp. 36-37, 41-43, 78.

37. Bünderlin, *Erklārung*, pp. 409-410, 414, 418, 448, 544. Bünderlin had earlier voiced a similar argument against the Lutherans, whose insistence on the letter he described as belonging to the age of the external law. *Ursach*, p. 123.

38. This is illustrated in (1) his fondness for apocryphal texts in particular about the Maccabean struggle, (2) his repeated references to the apocalyptic Elijah who would butcher the servants of Antichrist (however, Bünderlin appears to have understood this as a spiritual slaying) and (3) references to an expected conversion of Israel, which was also part of the apocalyptic tradition. Bünderlin, *Ursach*, pp. 88-89 and *Erklārung*, pp. 392, 446.

39. Bünderlin, *Berechnung*, p. 357; also p. 282.

40. Bünderlin speaks of Satan as the collective soul of the host of Antichrist. *Ibid.*, pp. 202-204.

41. Foster has already drawn attention to Bünderlin's agreement with Denck on these issues. "Hans Denck and Johannes Buenderlin," pp. 119-121, 124.

42. Bünderlin, *Erklārung*, p. 368: ". . . darinn das geheimnuss Gottes vollendet soll werden, Apoc. X. das dann allein dem end, und nit dem anfang zugehoret, in dem es alles zusamen fleusst, unnd alles widerumb geistlich wirt, wie Gott ist. . . ." See also *Ursach*, p. 105, and *Berechnung*, p. 238.

43. These were the divine attributes already used by Denck, Haug, Hut, and, as we will see, again by Entfelder.

44. Bünderlin, *Berechnung*, pp. 143, 145.

45. Bünderlin, *Ursach*, p. 7 and *Berechnung*, pp. 177, 227, 247.

46. We made similar observations regarding Denck and others. Bünderlin, *Ursach*, pp. 8-10 and *Berechnung*, pp. 142-144, 154-155, 169, 228, 297; compare also Foster, "Hans Denck and Johannes Buenderlin," pp. 120-121.

47. Bünderlin, *Berechnung*, pp. 184, 244, 336, 350-352 and *Ursach*, pp. 8-10, 110.

48. Bünderlin, *Berechnung*, pp. 340-348, and *Erklārung*, p. 400.

49. He speaks of them as "pigs and dogs" rummaging through the Scripture. In another place he describes them as "monkeys and birds" flinging themselves into a "glue tree." Bünderlin, *Berechnung*, pp. 134, 137-138, 185, 316.

50. Bünderlin, *Erklärung*, p. 444. Hut had given a similar explanation at his trial.

51. Bünderlin, *Berechnung*, p. 173, and *Erklärung*, p. 382.

52. Bünderlin, *Berechnung*, p. 139; see also pp. 209-210, 354, and *Ursach*, pp. 11-13.

53. Bünderlin, *Berechnung*, pp. 150, 172, 183 and *Ursach*, pp. 15, 43-44. For Bünderlin's understanding of faith see Gäbler, "Problem des Spiritualismus," pp. 339-344.

54. Bünderlin, *Berechnung*, pp. 157, 182, 187, 197; *Ursach*, pp. 2, 48-49, 129-132 and *Erklärung*, p. 388. Here the concept of *Widerspruch* found in Müntzer, Denck, and Hut reappears.

55. Bünderlin, *Berechnung*, pp. 358-359.

56. Bünderlin, *Berechnung*, p. 338: ". . . wie er dann alle sichtbare creature unserthalben also gemacht hat, die nicht allein gott an jm nit hat, sonder gerad das gegentheyl ist . . . dz wir dan durch die umbstend der geschopff und zeugnuss des gewissens wissen müssen, das er ist, und wir nicht allein auss und in jm seind, sondern alles guts von jn entphahen. . . ." See also pp. 141, 336 and *Erklärung*, pp. 363-364. Bünderlin was here moving back to the more traditional understanding of the witness of creation.

57. Bünderlin, *Ursach*, p. 102; *Erklärung*, p. 376.

58. Bünderlin, *Erklärung*, p. 386.

59. Bünderlin, *Erklärung*, p. 245; *Ursach*, pp. 8,13; *Berechnung*, pp.153,160,333,355.

60. Bünderlin, *Ursach*, pp. 45, 90 and *Erklärung*, p. 395. In this regard Bünderlin had earlier criticized the Waldensians because they considered themselves alone to be God's chosen. *Berechnung*, pp. 201-202.

61. For details of Marpeck's response see William Klassen, "Pilgram Marpeck's Two Books of 1531," *MQR*, XXXIII (1959), pp. 18-30, and *Covenant and Community* (Grand Rapids, Michigan, 1968), pp. 37, 40-41. Another document that may reflect the resulting controversy is the anonymous "Täuferbekenntnis" published by Hans Hillerbrand, *ARG*, L (1959), pp. 41-50.

62. A similar observation was made by William Klassen, "Pilgram Marpeck in Recent Research," p. 219.

63. Horst Penner, "Christian Entfelder. Ein mährischer Täuferprediger und herzoglicher Rat am Hofe Albrechts von Preussen." *MGB*, XXIII (1966) (hereafter referred to as "Entfelder"), p. 19.

64. *TA: Hubmaier*, p. 348; Bergsten, *Hubmaier: Stellung*, p. 427; Zeman, *Anabaptists and Czech Brethren*, p. 230.

65. Paul Tschackert, ed., *Urkundenbuch zur Reformationsgeschichte des Herzogthums Preussen*, I (Osnabrück: Otto Zeller, 1965), reprint of 1890 edition, pp. 324-325.

66. He left Moravia because of persecution. Three Anabaptists of his district had been burned. Williams, *The Radical Reformation*, p. 267.

67. Williams suggested that the two were associated in Strassburg. *Ibid.*

68. It has been variously speculated that he returned to Moravia or visited the Netherlands. It is also possible that he remained in South Germany. Penner, "Entfelder," pp. 19-20; *TA: Elsass*, II, pp. 381-382.

69. Penner, "Entfelder," pp. 20-22.

70. *Corpus Schwenckfeldianorum*, VIII, pp. 423-424.

71. *Corpus Schwenckfeldianorum*, XVII, pp. 213-232.

72. This observation was made by Zeman, *Anabaptists and Czech Brethren*, p. 233, n.243; Williams, *The Radical Reformation*, p. 453.

73. *Von den manigfaltigen im glauben Zerspaltungen, dise jar erstanden. Inn sonderhait von der Tauffspaltung und jrem urtail, Ain bedacht* (Strassburg, 1530) (hereafter referred to as *Zerspaltungen*). The tract was also published by Ulhart in

Augsburg. I used a Strassburg copy found in the Mennonite Historical Library, Goshen. *Von warer Gotseligkait, wie der mensch allhie in diser zeyt dartzu kommen mag, ain kurze, aber gar nutzliche betrachtung* (Strassburg, 1530) (hereafter referred to as *Gotseligkait*). This tract was written and published a few months after *Zerspaltungen*. It found its way into *Das Kunstbuch*. I obtained a microfilm copy from the Amsterdam Doopsgezinde Archief, Amsterdam University Library.

Von Gottes und Christi Jesu unnsers Herren erkandtnuss, ain bedacht, Allen schulern des hailigen gaysts weiter zebedencken aufgezaichnet mit freyen urthail (hereafter referred to as *Erkandtnuss*). While neither the date, place, nor publisher appears on the booklet, we can assume that it was published in 1533 and probably also printed in Strassburg. Entfelder comments that he had written *Zerspaltungen* three years earlier (sig. C v v.). I obtained a microfilm copy from the Amsterdam Doopsgezinde Archief, Amsterdam University Library.

74. Entfelder, *Zerspaltungen*, sig. C viii r.: "Wa aber die personen so befelch hetten, weck genomen werde . . . so befelhen sy es Gott, . . . Ey so lass auch die weil tauf und nachtmal im gaist bleiben, es hafft wa Got wölle." See also sig. C vii r.

75. *Ibid.*, sig. E v v.-E vi r.: " . . . der Johannes zuvor muss da sein." Also sig. D iii r.-D viii v.

76. *Ibid.*, sig. E ii r.-v. Entfelder here echoed Müntzer, Hut, and Bünderlin.

77. *Ibid.*, sig. E viii r.

78. This is an inference from Pilgram Marpeck's trip to Moravia to obtain baptismal authority in 1532. Scharnschlager who remained behind refused to baptise because he did not possess the proper authority. *TA: Baden und Pfalz*, pp. 419-425; *TA: Elsass*, I, p. 583, n. 1.

79. Entfelder, *Zerspaltungen*, sig. B vii r.; also sig. A iii v.-C v v, E viii r.

80. This anti-intellectualism went so far that Entfelder had his *Erkandtnuss* read to an illiterate who was, however, well seasoned in spiritual matters and could affirm the truthfulness of his writings. *Erkandtnuss*, sig. C vi v.

81. *Ibid.*, table of contents.

82. *Ibid.*, sig. A iii r.: "Gott ist aber gut, und das gut solt aussgebraittet werden, ye weyter ye besser . . . darumb musste die beschaffung himels und erden, der sichtbarn und unsichtbarn creature beschehen, darzu drang Gott auss liebe, sein aigne gute."

83. For this reason the universe was symbolized by the perfect circle. Entfelder, *Erkandtnuss*, sig. A iii r.; see also sig. C v v.

84. *Ibid.*, sig. A iii v.

85. *Ibid.*, sig. A iii v.: "Wolte aber Gott, den menschen nit vergebens erschaffen haben, so musste der unzertailige Got sich selbst, in die tail darstellen, doch on verletzung der gentze, damit den zertailte mensch, doch durch tail, widerub in dz ainig wurde gepracht. . . ."

86. Entfelder rejects explicitly the traditional division of God, the Trinity, into three persons, although he would not quibble over words. The kingdom of God consisted not of words. *Erkandtnuss*, sig. B r.

87. *Ibid.*, sig A iv r.-v.; also sig. A vii v.

88. *Ibid.*, sig. A iii v.: " . . . auss dem wesen wesentlich, doch nit abtailig von jm. . . ."

89. *Ibid.*, sig. A v r. This was a favourite medieval analogy.

90. *Ibid.*, sig. A vi v.

91. *Ibid.*, sig. A vii v.

92. *Ibid.*, sig. A vii v.

93. *Ibid.*, sig. A vii r.

94. *Ibid.*, sig. A v r. The "wider bringung des zertailten menschen, in das gantze" was to proceed to a point where "das zerthailt vergeh, und das allain gut in Gott, auch in menschen, sey unvermischt allain das gute." See also sig. B r.

95. *Ibid.*, sig. B r.-v. Hut had earlier shown a similar fondness for these labels.

96. *Ibid.*, sig. B v v.-r.
97. Entfelder, *Zerspaltungen*, sig. D ii r.
98. Entfelder, *Gotseligkait*, sig. A v v.
99. *Ibid.*, sig. A ii r.-v., A iii r., A v r. *Das Kunstbuch*, pp. 392, 394-395.
100. Entfelder describes this symbolically as the perfect and undivided circle, projecting into the divided circle. *Erkandtnuss*, sig. A v v. This was a favourite image of Nicholas Cusanus, used in reference to the incarnation of Christ.
101. Entfelder, *Gotseligkait*, sig. A iii v.; *Das Kunstbuch*, p. 393: "...spaziert on underlass hyn und wider jn ausserlichen gegenwürffen...."
102. Entfelder, *Gotseligkait*, sig. A iv r.
103. *Ibid.*, sig. A vi r.; *Das Kunstbuch*, p. 396.
104. Entfelder, *Zerspaltungen*, sig. B v., B ii r.
105. Entfelder, *Erkandtnuss*, sig. B vi v.
106. *Ibid.*, sig. B ii r.
107. *Ibid.*, sig. B vii r.
108. Entfelder, *Gotseligkait*, sig. A vii r.; *Das Kunstbuch*, p. 398.
109. Entfelder, *Gotseligkait*, sig. A viii v.; *Das Kunstbuch*, p. 398.
110. Entfelder, *Gotseligkait*, sig. A vi r.
111. Entfelder, *Erkandtnuss*, sig. B vii r.
112. Entfelder's association of faith with the painful first movement of purification is reminiscent of Müntzer. *Erkandtnuss*, sig. B vii r.
113. *Ibid.*, sig. B vii v.
114. Entfelder, *Gotseligkait*, sig. A v v.
115. Entfelder, *Zerspaltungen*, sig. A vii r.
116. *Ibid.*, sig. B vii v.; also A v v. Entfelder compares the literalist hermeneutic to a bird leaving his "nest der gelassenheit" without feathers.
117. Entfelder, *Zerspaltungen*, sig. A vi r., also A vii r.; and *Erkandtnuss*, sig. C v v.: "Das treffenlichst, vor andern, aller zerspaltunge, diser zeyt hauptstuck, ist dz schriftlich wort, und der Historische bevelch Gottes...."
118. Entfelder, *Zerspaltungen*, sig. A vii v.-r.
119. *Ibid.*, sig. A viii r.
120. Entfelder, *Erkandtnuss*, sig. B v r., C ii v., C v r.
121. *Ibid.*, sig. C vi r.
122. Entfelder, *Zerspaltungen*, sig. A vi r.-v.
123. Entfelder, *Erkandtnuss*, sig. C r.
124. *Ibid.*, sig. C ii r.
125. Entfelder, *Gotseligkait*, sig. A viii v.; *Das Kunstbuch*, p. 399.
126. Entfelder, *Zerspaltungen*, sig. C iv r., D ii v., D iii r.
127. Entfelder, *Erkandtnuss*, sig. A v v.
128. Entfelder, *Gotseligkait*, sig. A v v.; *Das Kunstbuch*, pp. 397-398.
129. Entfelder, *Erkandtnuss*, sig. A v v. -A vi v.: "den Lustgarten gottliches wesens."
130. *Ibid.*, sig. A viii r.-v.
131. *Ibid.*, sig. B vi r. See also B iii r.-v.
132. *Ibid.*, sig. A viii v.
133. *Ibid.*, sig. B v.
134. *Ibid.*, sig. A v., C v v.
135. Entfelder, *Zerspaltungen*, sig. B iii r., C ii r., C vii r,-v.

BIBLIOGRAPHY

Reference Works

Friedmann, Robert (ed.). *Die Schriften der Huterischen Täufergemeinschaften. Gesamtkatalog Ihrer Manuskriptbücher, Ihrer Schreiber und Ihrer Literatur 1529-1667.* Vienna: Hermann Böhlaus Nachfolger, 1965.
Hege, Christian, and Neff, Christian (eds.). *Mennonitisches Lexikon.* 3 vols. Frankfurt-Weierhof, 1913-1958.
Hillerbrand, Hans. *A Bibliography of Anabaptism, 1520-1630.* Elkhart, Indiana, 1962.
Schottenloher, Karl. *Bibliographie zur Deutschen Geschichte im Zeitalter der Glaubensspaltung, 1517-1585.* 6 vols. Leipzig, 1939.
The Mennonite Encyclopedia. Edited by Harold Bender and Henry Smith. 4 vols. Scottdale, Pennsylvania, 1955-59.

Unpublished Sources

Primary

Ansbacher Religions Akten., XXXIX. Staatsarchiv Nürnberg.
Bossert, Gustav, Sr. Collection of the Täuferakten of the cities of Esslingen and Ulm. Generallandesarchiv Karlsruhe.
Braitmichel Kodex (Epistelnbuch). A sixteenth-century collection of pamphlets and letters including letters by Kaspar Braitmichel. A photocopy at the Mennonite Historical Library, Goshen, and a microfilm copy at the University of Waterloo Library.
Das Kunstbuch. Edited by Georg Maler. Sixteenth-century manuscript collection of Anabaptist tracts and letters at the Bürgerbibliothek in Bern, Switzerland; Typescript copy at the Mennonite Historical Library, Goshen.
Seebass, Gottfried. "Müntzers Erbe: Werk, Leben und Theologie des Hans Hut (gestorben 1527)" Appendix. Habilitationsschrift, Friedrich-Alexander University, Erlangen, 1972.
Wiedertäuferakten, 1527-1533. Stadtarchiv Augsburg.
Zorns Chronik. Continued by J. S. Meirner. Handwritten copy at the Stadtarchiv Worms.

Secondary

Beachy, Alvin. "The Concept of Grace in the Radical Reformation." Unpublished ThD thesis, Harvard University,1960.
Born, G. "Geist, Wissen und Bildung bei Thomas Müntzer und Valentin Icklsamer." Unpublished dissertation, Friedrich-Alexander University, Erlangen, 1952.
Förschner, Franz. "Concordia, Urgestalt und Sinnbild in der Geschichtsdeutung des Joachim von Fiore. Eine Studie zum Symbolismus des Mittelalters." Unpublished PhD dissertation, Albert-Ludwig University, Freiburg, 1970.
Gerhard Werthan. "Zur Geschichte der Augsburger Täufer im 16. Jahrhundert." Wissenschaftliche Prüfung für das Lehramt an Gymnasien, University of Munich, 1972.

Goldbach, Günther. "Hans Denck und Thomas Müntzer—ein Vergleich ihrer wesentlichen theologischen Auffassungen. Eine Untersuchung zur Morphologie der Randströmung der Reformation." Unpublished DTh dissertation, University of Hamburg, 1969.

Hege, Albrecht. "Hans Denck, 1495-1527." Unpublished DTh dissertation, Eberhard-Karls University, Tübingen, 1942.

Kiwiet, Jan. "Hans Denck and His Teaching (ca. 1500-1527)." Unpublished BD thesis, Baptist Theological Seminary, Rüschlikon, Zürich, 1954.

Klaassen, Walter. "Word, Spirit, and Scripture in Early Anabaptist Thought." Unpublished PhD dissertation, University of Oxford, 1960.

——————————. "Michael Gaismair. Rebel and Reformer." Unpublished manuscript. Conrad Grebel College, University of Waterloo, Ontario.

Klassen, Herbert. "Some Aspects of the Teaching of Hans Hut. A Study of their Origins in South Germany and their Influence on the Anabaptist movement." Unpublished MA thesis, University of British Columbia, 1958.

Meissner, Erich. "Die Rechtssprechung über die Wiedertäufer und die antitäuferische Publizistik." Unpublished PhD dissertation, Georg-August University, Göttingen, 1921.

Neuser, Wilhelm. "Hans Hut. Leben und Wirken bis zum Nicolsburger Religionsgespräch." Unpublished PhD dissertation, University of Bonn, 1913.

Seebass, Gottfried. "Müntzers Erbe. Werk, Leben und Theologie des Hans Hut (gestorben 1527)." Habilitationsschrift, Friedrich-Alexander University, Erlangen, 1972.

Stayer, James. "Reublin and Brötli: The Revolutionary Beginnings of Swiss Anabaptism." Paper presented at Colloque sur les debuts et les caracteristiques de l'anabaptisme au XVIe siecle, Strassburg, February 1975.

Stoesz, Willis, "At the Foundation of Anabaptism: A Study of Thomas Müntzer, Hans Denck and Hans Hut." Unpublished PhD dissertation, Union Theological Seminary and Columbia University, 1964.

Uhland, Friedwart. "Täufertum und Obrigkeit in Augsburg im 16. Jahrhundert." Unpublished PhD dissertation, Eberhard-Karls University, Tübingen, 1972.

Windhorst, Christof "Anfänge und Aspekte der Theologie Hubmaiers zwischen Tradition und Reformation." Unpublished PhD dissertation, Heidelberg, 1974.

——————————. "Initial Stages and Aspects in the Theology of Balthasar Hubmaier." Paper presented at Colloque sur les debuts et les caracteristiques de l'anabaptisme au XVIe siecle. Strassburg, February 1975.

Published Sources
Primary

Aufdeckung der Babylonischen Hurn und Antichrists alten unnd newen gehaimnuss und grewel. Auch vom sig, frid und herrschung warhaffter Christen, unnd wie sy der Oberkait gehorsamen, das creutz on aufrhur und gegenwer mit Christo inn geduld und liebe tragen zum preiss Gottes und allen frumen und Gottsuchenden zu dienst, stercke und besserung an tag gebracht. N.p., [ca. 1530].

Bader, Johann *Brüderliche warnung für dem newen Abgöttischen orden der Widertäuffer,* N.p., 1527.

Beck, Joseph (ed.). *Die Geschichtsbücher der Wiedertäufer in Oesterreich-Ungarn, 1526-1785.* Vienna: Carl Gerolds Sohn, 1883.

Berbig, Georg. "Die Wiedertäufer im Amt Königsberg i. Fr. 1527/1528," *Deutsche Zeitschrift für Kirchenrecht,* XXXV (1903).

——————————. "Die Wiedertäuferei im Ortslande zu Franken, im Zusammenhang mit dem Bauernkrieg," *Deutsche Zeitschrift für Kirchenrecht,* XLIV (1912).

Bossert, Gustav, Sr. "Augustin Bader von Augsburg, der Prophet und König, und seine Genossen, nach den Prozessakten von 1530." *Archiv für Reformationsgeschichte,* X and XI (1912/13, 1914).

Bossert, Gustav, Sr., and Bossert, Gustav, Jr. (eds.). *Herzogtum Württemberg. Quellen zur Geschichte der Wiedertäufer.* Vol. I. *Quellen und Forschungen zur Reformationsgeschichte.* Vol. XII. Leipzig: M. Heinius Nachfolger, Eger, and Sievers, 1930.

Bucer, Martin. *Martin Bucers Deutsche Schriften.* Vol. II. Edited by Robert Stupperich. Gütersloh: Gütersloher Verlagshaus Gerd Mohn, 1962.

Bullinger, Heinrich. *Der Widertoufferen Vrsprung, fürgang, Secten, wäsen, fürnemme und gemeine jrer leer Artickel, ouch jre gründ, vnnd warummb sy sich absünderind unnd ein eigne kirchen anrichtind, mit widerlegung und antwort uff alle jre gründ und artikkel sampt Christenlichen bericht und vermanen, dass sy jres irrthumbs und absünderens abstandind und sich mit der kirchen Christi vereinigind, abgeteilt in VI. bücher.* Zürich: Christoph Froschauer, 1561.

Bünderlin, Hans. *Ausz was Ursach sich Gott in die nyder gelassen unnd in Christo vermenschet ist, durch welchen, und wie er des menschens fall in jm selbs durch den gesandten Messiah versünet, und widerpracht hat.* Strassburg, 1529.

——————————. *Ein gemeyne Berechnung uber der heyligen schrifft innhalt, in derselben natürlichen verstand (mit anzeygung jres missuerstands grund unnd ursprung) eynzuleyten, durch etlicher puncten gegensatz erklärung, dabey man die anderen, so vilfältig in der schrifft verfasst seind auch abnemen mag.* Strassburg, 1529.

——————————. *Erklärung durch vergleichung der Biblischen geschrifft, das der wassertauff sampt andern eusserlichen gebreüchen, in der Apostolischen kirchen geübet. On Gottes befelch und zeügniss der geschrifft, von etlichen diser zeit, wider eefert [eingeführt] wirt. Sintemalen der Antichirst dieselben all, zehand nach der Apostel abgang verwüst hat. Welche Verwüstung dann biss an das ende bleibt.* N.p., 1530

Cochlaeus, "Articule aliquot a Jacobo Kautio Oecolamadiano, ad populum nuper Wormaciae aediti, portim a Lutheranis, portim a Johanne Cochlaeo doctore praestantissimo reprobati (MDXXVII)." German microfilm copy at the Stadtbibliothek Frankfurt.

Dachser, Jacob, *Ein Göttlich und gründtlich offenbarung: von den warhafftigen widertauffern: mit Götliche warhait angezaigt.* Augsburg: [Ulhart], 1527.

Denck, Hans. *Hans Denck: Schriften.* Edited by Georg Baring and Walter

Fellmann. *Quellen zur Geschichte der Täufer*. Vol. VI; *Quellen und Forschungen zur Reformationsgeschichte*. Vol. XXIV. Gütersloh: C. Bertelsmann Verlag, 1959-1960.

Ein schöns Gesprech zwischen Aim Edelman und seinem Knecht vom Apostolischen Tauff und die gehorsam der Oberkait belangend. Und wie der Knecht sich durch den Edelman unnd sein Pfarherren mit hailiger Schrifft weysen lasst. N.p. [ca. 1532].

Eleutherobios [Freisleben], Christoph. *Vom warhafftigen Tauf Joannis Christi und der Aposteln, Wenn und wie der kindertauff angefangen und eingerissen hat. Item Wie alle widerreden der Widerchristen wider den Tauff sollen verantwortet werden*. [Worms: Peter Schöffer, 1528.]

Entfelder, Christian. *Von warer Gotseligkayt, wie der mensch alhie in diser zeyt dartzu kommen mag, ain kurze, aber gar nutzliche betrachtung*. Strassburg, 1530.

_____. *Von den manigfaltigen im glauben Zerspaltungen, dise jar erstanden. Inn sonderhait von der Tauffspaltung und jrem urtail, Ain Bedacht*. Strassburg, 1530.

_____. *Von Gottes und Christi Jesus unnsers Herren erkandtnuss, ain bedacht, Allen schulern des hailigen gaysts weiter zebedencken aufgezaichnet mit freyem urthail*. [Strassburg, 1533].

Enthoven, L. K. (ed.). *Briefe an Desiderius Erasmus von Rotterdam*. Strassburg: J. H. Heitz, 1906.

Fabri, Johann, *Ursach warumb der wiederteuffer patron unnd erster Anfenger Doctor Balthasar Hubmeyer zu Wienn auff den zehnten tag Martij Anno 1528 verbrennet sey*. Vienna, 1528.

Fast, Heinold (ed.). *Der linke Flügel der Reformation: Glaubenszeugnisse der Täufer, Spiritualisten, Schwärmer und Antitrinitarier*. Bremen: Carl Schünemann Verlag, 1962.

_____. *Ostschweiz. Quellen zur Geschichte der Täufer in der Schweiz*. Vol. II. Zürich: S. Hirzel Verlag, 1973.

Freisleben, Christoph. *Ain Kurtzweylig unnd nit minder nutzlich Spyl des Plantisch Stichus genant, zu Teutsch gebracht gereymt und gehalten zu Ingolstatt*. Augsburg: Phillip Ulhart, 1539.

Freisleben, Leonhard. *Ain Kurtzweyligs und Lustigs Spil, von der Weissheit unnd Narrheit darin kain unzucht, sonder vil guter leer und lächerliche schwänk begriffen sind*. Augsburg: Ulhart, 1550.

Gelbert, J. P. *Magister Johann Baders Leben und Schriften; Nikolaus Thomae und seine Briefe*. Neustadt a.H.: G. Witters Buchhandlung, 1868.

Getrewe Christliche und nutzliche Warnung etlicher oebrigkait die dass Euangelion zu Predigen zulassen und befelhen, und straffen doch desselben volziehung. N.p., 1525.

Haug, Jörg. *Ain Christliche Ordenung, aines warhafftigen Christen. zu verantwurtten, die ankunfft seines Glaubens. Jörg Haugk, von Juchsen 1. Petri 3. Seit allzeyt beraidt zu verantworten dem der grundt fordert, der Hoffnung die in euch ist, unnd das mit Sefftmutigkeit und Forcht*. Nicolsburg: Simprecht Sorg genannt Froschauer, 1526.

Hergott, Hans. *Von der newen wandlung eynes Christlichen Lebens. Hütt dich Teuffel. Die Hell wirdt zurbrechen*. Leipzig: Michael Blum, 1526 or 1527, in Götze, A., and Schmitt, L. E. (eds.). *Flugschriften der Reformationszeit 20. Aus dem sozialischen und politischen Kampf. Neudrucke Deutscher Literaturwerke des 16. und 17. Jahrhunderts.* Halle/Saale: Max Niemeyer Verlag, 1953, pp. 46-64.

Hillerbrand, Hans. "An Early Anabaptist Treatise on the Christian and the State," *Mennonite Quarterly Review*, XXXII (1958).

───────────. "Ein Täuferbekenntnis aus dem 16. Jahrhundert," *Archiv für Reformationsgeschichte*, L (1959).

Hubmaier, Balthasar. *Balthasar Hubmaier: Schriften.* Edited by Torsten Bergsten and Gunnar Westin. *Quellen und Forschungen zur Reformationsgeschichte.* Vol. XXIX. Gütersloh: Gerd Mohn, 1962.

(Hut, Hans). *Ain Christliche Unterrichtung, wie die Götlich geschrifft vergleycht und geurtaylt soll werden, auss krafft der hayligen drey anigkait, unnd zeugknuss d' drey tayl des Christenlich glaubens, sampt jren verstand, bissher noch nye erschynen, so kurtz und gründlich. Drey seind die zeugen im hymel der Vater, das Wort, und der hailig gayst. 1. Joan 5.* N.p., Johannes Landtsperger, [1527], *Mittheilung aus dem Antiquariate.* Vols. III and IV. Berlin: S. Calvary and Company, 1869.

Jörg, Edmund. *Deutschland in der Revolutions-Periode von 1522-1526.* Freiburg im Breisgau: Herdersche Verlaghandlung, 1851.

Keller, Ludwig. "Sebastian Francks Aufzeichnungen über Joh. Denck (1527) aus dem Jahre 1531," *Monatshefte der Comenius-Gesellschaft*, X (1901.).

Kessler, Johannes. *Sabbata: St. Galler Reformationschronik 1523-1539.* Edited by Traugott Schiess. *Schriften des Vereins für Reformationsgeschichte.* Vol. XXVIII (1911).

Knaake, J. K. (ed.). "Von der Nachfolgung des willigen Sterbens Jesu Christi," *Johannes Staupitzens sämtlichen Werken.* Vol. I. Potsdam, 1867.

Krebs, Manfred (ed.). *Baden und Pfalz. Quellen zur Geschichte der Täufer. Vol. IV. Quellen und Forschungen zur Reformationsgeschichte.* Vol. XXII. Gütersloh: Gütersloher Verlagshaus Gerd Mohn, 1951.

───────────, and Rott, Hans Georg (eds.). *Elsass, Part I: Stadt Strassburg, 1522-1532. Quellen zur Geschichte der Täufer.* Vol. VII *Quellen und Forschungen zur Reformationsgeschichte.* Vol. XXVI. Gütersloh: Gütersloher Verlagshaus Gerd Mohn, 1959.

───────────. *Elsass, Part II: Stadt Strassburg, 1533-1535. Quellen zur Geschichte der Täufer.* Vol. VIII: *Quellen und Forschungen zur Reformationsgeschichte.* Vol. XXVII. Gütersloh: Gütersloher Verlagshaus Gerd Mohn, 1959.

Langenmantel, Hans. *Ain kurtzer anzayg, wie Do. Martin Luther ain zeyt her, hatt etliche schriften lassen aussgeen, vom Sacrament, die doch stracks wider ainander, wie wirt dan sein, und seiner anhenger Reych bestehen.* Augsburg, 1527.

Mecenseffy, Grete (ed.). *Oesterreich, Part I. Quellen zur Geschichte der Täufer.* Vol. XI. *Quellen und Forschungen zur Reformationsgeschichte.* Vol. XXXI. Gütersloh: Gütersloher Verlagshaus Gerd Mohn, 1964.

───────────. *Oesterreich, Part II. Quellen zur Geschichte der Täufer.* Vol. XIII. *Quellen und Forschungen zur Reformationsgeschichte.* Vol. XLI. Gütersloh: Gütersloher Verlagshaus, 1972.

Menius, Justus. *Der Widdertauffer lere und geheimnis/ aus heiliger schrifft widderlegt/ Mit einer schönen Vorrede Martini Luther.* Wittenberg: Nickel Schirlentz, 1530.

Meyer, Christian. "Zur Geschichte der Wiedertäufer in Oberschwaben." Part I: "Die Anfänge des Wiedertäufertums in Augsburg." *Zeitschrift des historischen Vereins für Schwaben und Neuburg,* I (1874).

Müller, Lydia (ed.). *Glaubenszeugnisse oberdeutscher Taufgesinnter.* Vol. I. *Quellen und Forschungen zur Reformationsgeschichte.* Vol. XX. Leipzig: M. Heinius Nachfolger, 1938.

Müntzer, Thomas. *Thomas Müntzer. Schriften und Briefe.* Edited by Günther Franz. *Quellen und Forschungen zur Reformationsgeschichte.* Vol. XXXIII. Gütersloh: Gütersloher Verlagshaus Gerd Mohn, 1968.

Nestler, Hermann. *Die Wiedertäuferbewegung in Regensburg. Ein Ausschnitt aus der Regensburger Reformationsgeschichte.* Regensburg, 1929.

Nicoladoni, Alexander. *Johannes Bünderlin von Linz und die oberösterreichischen Täufergemeinden in den Jahren 1525-1531.* Berlin: R. Gärtners Verlag, 1893.

Oecolampadius, Johannes. *Briefe und Akten zum Leben Oekolampads.* Vol. I and II. Edited by Ernst Stähelin. Leipzig. M. Heinius Nachfolger, Eger, and Sievers, 1927/43.

_____. *Das theologische Lebenswerk Johannes Oekolampads.* Edited by Ernst Stähelin, Leipzig: M. Heinius Nachfolger, Eger, and Sievers, 1939.

[Osiander, Andreas]. *Grundtliche untterrichtung eins erbern Rats der Stadt Nürmberg welcher gestalt ire Pfarrher und Prediger in den Stetten und auff dem Land das volck wider etliche verfürische lere der Widertauffer in jren predigen auss heyliger Göttlicher schrifft zum getreülichsten ermanen unnd unterrichten sollen.* Nuremberg: Jobst Gutknecht [1528].

Pfeifer, Gerald (ed.). *Quellen und Forschungen zur Nürnberger Reformationsgeschichte.* Nuremberg: Selbstverlag des Stadtrats, 1959.

Pfeiffer, Franz (ed.). *Meister Eckhart.* Vol. II: *Deutsche Mystiker des vierzehnten Jahrhunderts.* Aalen: Scienta Verlag, 1962.

Quint, Josef (ed. and trans.). *Meister Eckharts Predigten.* Vols. I - V. Stuttgart: W. Kohlhammer Verlag, 1958.

Rappolt, Wolfgang. *Eyn kurtze Epistel An die vom Elpogen.* Zwickau: Jörg Gästel, 1525.

Reinhardt, Martin. *Underrichte wie sich ein frumer Christ bey den Papistischen Messen, so yetz noch vil gehalten werden (wenn er sich mit gutten fug nit absundern kan) halten sol, das er sich nit verstünde, und die zeit unnütz verliere.* N.p., 1524.

_____. *Anzaygung wie die gefallene Christenhait widerbracht müg werdn in jren ersten standt in wolchem sie von Christo unnd seyne Aposteln erstlich gepflantzt unnd auff gebawet ist. Vor hundert jaren beschriben unnd yetzt aller erst gefunden und durch den druck an tag geben.* N.p., 1524.

Rhegius, Urbanus. *Wider den newen Taufforden. Notwendige Warnungen an alle Christgleubige. Durch die diener des Euangelii zu Augspurg.* Augsburg: A. Weyssenhorn, 1527.

——————————. *Ein Sendbrieff Hans huthen etwa ains furnemen Vorsteers im wiedertaufforden verantwort.* Augsburg: A. Weyssenhorn, 1528.

——————————. *Zwen wunderseltzsam sendbrieff zweyer Widertauffer an ire Rotten gen Augsburg gesandt. Verantwurtung aller irrthum diser obgenannten brieff durch Urbanum Rhegium.* Augsburg: A. Weyssenhorn, 1528.

Röhrich, Timothy. "Zur Geschichte der strassburgischen Wiedertäufer in den Jahren 1527 bis 1543," *Zeitschrift für die historische Theologie,* XXX (1860).

Roth, Friedrich. "Zur Geschichte der Wiedertäufer in Oberschwaben". Part II: "Zur Lebensgeschichte Eitelhans Langenmantels von Augsburg". *Zeitschrift des historischen Vereins für Schwaben und Neuburg,* XXVII (1900).

——————————. "Zur Geschichte der Wiedertäufer in Oberschwaben." Part III: "Der Höhepunkt der Bewegung in Augsburg und der Niedergang im Jahre 1528." *Zeitschrift des historischen Vereins für Schwaben und Neuburg,* XXXVIII (1901).

Saint Augustine. *The City of God.* Edited by Vernon Rourke. Abridged edition, New York: Doubleday and Company, 1958.

Salminger, Sigmund. *Ausz was grund die lieb entspringt, und was grosser krafft sy hab, und wie nutz sy sey, den innerlichen menschen zu Reformieren, dass der eüsserlich sterb.* Augsburg: Philip Ulhart [ca. 1526].

——————————. *Zwen Sendbrief von der Liebe Gottes durch Georgen Preinig vor jaren weber zu Augspurg geschriben.* Augsburg: [Ulhart], 1527.

——————————. *Guldin Schatz. Hauptschrift und Handzeugger, den Inhalt der gantzen Bibel, in sich schliessende. Auch all unsers glaubens und thuns, grüntliche zeügnuss, in 547. Titel und puncten gestelt und absolviert.* Strassburg: Sigmund Bosch, 1540.

[Sattler, Michael]. *Wie die Gschrifft verstendigklich soll underschieden/ und erklärt werden/ die vom Tauff saget/ wie der Hailig gaist mit seinen gaben vor und nach kumpt/ und seine werck laistet/ erstlich durch den glauben der laer.* N.p. [ca. 1526].

Schornbaum, Karl [ed.]. *Markgraftum Brandenburg: Bayern,* Part I. *Quellen zur Geschichte der Wiedertäufer.* Vol. XVI. Leipzig: M. Heinius Nachfolger, 1934.

——————————. *Markgraftum Brandenburg: Bayern,* Part II. *Quellen zur Geschichte der Täufer.* Vol. V. *Quellen und Forschungen zur Reformationsgeschichte.* Vol. XXIII. Gütersloh: Gütersloher Verlagshaus Gerd Mohn, 1951.

Schwenckfeld, Caspar, *Corpus Schwenckfeldianorum.* Edited by Chester Hartranft, *et. al.* Vol. XIV. Leipzig: Breitkopf and Härtle, 1936.

Seypel, Joachim (ed.). *Texte deutscher Mystik des 16. Jahrhunderts Unruhe und Stillstand.* Göttingen: Vandenhoeck und Ruprecht, 1963.

Stähelin, Ernst. *Briefe und Akten zum Leben Oekolampads.* 2 vols. Leipzig: M. Heinius, 1927/34.

Tauleri, D. Johann. *Nachfolgung des Armen Lebens Christi, in zwey Theile abgeteilet: Deren der Erste sagt viele Unterschiede der wahren Armuth,*

Der Andere lehret, wie man soll kommen zu einem vollkommenen Leben. Halle: Verlegung des Hallischen Waysenhauses, 1720.

Theologia Germanica. Translated by Susanna Winkworth. Introduced by Joseph Bernhart. New York: Belgrave Press, 1949.

Tschackert, Paul. *Urkundenbuch zur Reformationsgeschichte des Herzogthums Preussen.* Reprint; Vol. I. Osnabrück: Otto Zeller, 1965.

Vetter, Ferdinand. *Die Predigten Taulers.* Dublin, Zürich: Weidmann, 1968.

Vogel, Wolfgang. *Ayn trostlicher sendbrieff unnd Christliche ermanung zum Euangelio an ain Erbarm Radt und gantze gemayn zu Bopfingen, und an alle die, so vom Euangelio unnd wort Gottes abgefallen seynd.* Nuremberg, 1526. Copy at Stadbibliothek Nürnberg.

Wackernagel, Philip. *Das Deutsche Kirchenlied.* Vols. I-V. Reprint of 1864-77. Hildesheim: G. Olms, 1964.

Wappler, Paul. *Die Täuferbewegung in Thüringen von 1526-1584.* Jena: Verlag von Gustav Fischer, 1913.

Wenger, John. "Two Early Anabaptists Tracts," *Mennonite Quarterly Review,* XXII (1948).

Williams, George, and Mergal, Angel (trans. and eds.). *Spiritual and Anabaptist Writers. The Library of Christian Classics.* Vol. XXV. Philadelphia: The Fortress Press, 1957.

Williger, J. N. E. *Newe zeittung von den widderteuffern und yhrer Sect, Newlich erwachsen yhm stifft zu Saltzburg, und an andern enden. Mehr mit dreytzehen unchristlichen Artickel unter yhn die do zu Augspurg fur unchristlich verworffen, sind, do fur sich ein yder frommer Christ wol hüten mag, domit er geferlickeit des leibs und der seel empfliehen muge, derlich hernach angezeyget.* Salzburg, 1527.

Winkworth, Susanna. *The History and Life of the Reverend Doctor John Tauler with Twenty-five of His Sermons.* London: Smith, Elder and Company, 1857.

Zieglschmid, "Unpublished sixteenth century letters of the Hutterian Brethren," *Mennonite Quarterly Review,* XV (1941).

——————————. *Die älteste Chronik der Hutterischen Brüder (Ein Sprachdenkmal aus frühneudeutscher Zeit).* Ithaca, New York: Cayugan Press, 1946.

Zwingli, Ulrich. *Huldreich Zwinglis sämtliche Werke.* Edited by Emil Egli, *et al.* Vol. VIII. Leipzig: Verlag von M. Heinius Nachfolger, 1905.

Secondary

Armour, Rollin. *Anabaptist Baptism.* Scottdale, Pennsylvania: Herald Press, 1966.

Barge, Hermann. "Die gedruckten Schriften des evangelischen Predigers Jacob Strauss," *Archiv für Reformationsgeschichte,* XXXII (1935).

——————————. *Jacob Strauss. Ein Kämpfer für das Evangelium im Tirol, Thüringen und Süddeutschland.* Leipzig: M. Heinius, 1937.

Baring, Georg. "Die 'Wormser Propheten'. Eine vor-Lutherische evangelische Prophetenübersetzung aus dem Jahre 1527," *Deutsches Bibel-Archiv Hamburg,* III (1933).

——————————. "Hans Denck und Thomas Müntzer in Nürnberg

1524," *Archiv für Reformationsgeschichte*, L (1959).

_____. "Luther und die 'Theologia Deutsch' in der neusten Forschung," *Theologische Zeitschrift*, XXIII (1967).

Bauer, Günther. *Anfänge täuferischer Gemeindebildungen in Franken*. Nuremberg: Selbstverlag des Vereins für bayerische Kirchengeschichte, 1966.

Bauman, Clarence. *Gewaltlosigkeit im Täufertum*. Leiden: E. J. Brill, 1968.

Beachy, Alvin. "The Grace of God in Christ as Understood by Five Major Anabaptist Writers," *Mennonite Quarterly Review*, XXXVII (1963).

Bender, Harold. "The Zwickau Prophets, Thomas Müntzer and the Anabaptists," *Mennonite Quarterly Review*, XXVII (1953).

Bergdolt, Johannes. *Die freie Reichsstadt Windsheim im Zeitalter der Reformation*. Vol. V *Quellen und Forschunen zur Bayerischen Kirchengeschichte*.

Bergfried, Ulrich. *Verantwortung als theologisches Problem im Täufertum des 16 Jahrhunderts*. Wuppertal: Martini and Grüttelfien, 1938.

Bergsten, Torsten. *Balthasar Hubmaier: Seine Stellung zur Reformation und Täufertum 1521-28*. Kassel: J. G. Oncken Verlag, 1961.

Blanke, Fritz. *Aus der Welt der Reformation*. Zürich/Stuttgart: Zwingli Verlag, 1960.

Boerlag, Coba. *De Geestverwantschap van Hans Denck en de Middeleeuwsche Mystieken*, Amsterdam: Proefschrift, 1921.

Boos, Heinrich. *Geschichte der rheinischen Städtekultur von ihren Anfängen bis zur Gegenwart mit besonderer Berücksichtigung der Stadt Worms*, Vol. IV. 2nd ed. Berlin: Verlag Stargart, 1901.

Bornkamm, Heinrich. *Mystik, Spiritualismus und die Anfänge des Pietismus*. Giessen: Verlag Alfred Töpelmann, 1926.

Bossert, Gustav. "Hans Bünderlins Vorgeschichte," *Jahrbuch der Gesellschaft für die Geschichte des Protestantismus in Oesterreich*, XI (1890).

_____. "Kleine Mitteilungen," *Jahrbuch der Gesellschaft für die Geschichte des Protestantismus in Oesterreich*, XIII (1892).

_____. "Noch einmal Hans Bünderlin," *Jahrbuch der Gesellschaft für die Geschichte des Protestantismus in Oesterreich*, XV (1894).

_____. "Zwei Linzer Reformationsschriftsteller," *Jahrbuch der Gesellschaft für die Geschichte des Protestantismus in Oesterreich*, XXI 1900).

_____. "Christoph Eleutherobius oder Freisleben. Der frühere Täufer, später Syndikus der Wiener Universität und bischöflicher Offizial," *Jahrbuch der Gesellschaft für die Geschichte des Protestantismus in Oesterreich*, XXIX (1908).

Braaten, Carl. "Theologie der Revolution," *Luther. Monatshefte*, V (1968).

Brandi, Karl. *The Emperor Charles V*. London: Jonathan Cape, 1967.

Bucholtz, F. B. von. *Geschichte der Regierung Ferdinand des Ersten*. Vol. II. Vienna, 1831.

Burckhardt, Paul. *Die Basler Täfer: Ein Beitrag zur Schweizerischen Reformationsgeschichte*. Basel, 1898.

Cantimori, Delig. *Italienische Haeretiker der Spätrenaissance*. Translated by Werner Kaege. Basel: Benno and Schwabe Verlag, 1949.

Clasen, Claus-Peter. "Medieval Heresies in the Reformation," *Church History*, XXXII (1963).

——————————. "Nuernberg in the History of Anabaptism," *Mennonite Quarterly Review*, XXIX (1965).

——————————. *Die Wiedertäufer im Herzogtum Württemberg und in benachbarten Herrschaften*. Stuttgart: W. Kohlhammer, 1965.

——————————. *Anabaptism; a Social History, 1525-1618; Switzerland, Austria, Moravia, South and Central Germany*. Ithaca, New York: Cornell University Press, 1972.

Clemen, Otto. "Die Elbogener Kirchenordnung von 1522," *Zeitschrift für Kirchengeschichte*, XXVI (1905).

Cohn, Norman. *The Pursuit of the Millennium*. New York: Harper and Row, 1961.

Copleston, Frederick. *History of Philosophy*. Vol. III: *Late Medieval and Renaissance Philosophy*. Part I: *Ockham to the Speculative Mystics*. New York: Image Books, 1963.

Cramer, S. "Die geschichtliche und religiöse Bedeutung Hans Dencks und der Täufer," *Protestantische Kirchenzeitung für das evangelische Deutschland*, XXX (1883).

Davis, Kenneth. "Erasmus as a Progenitor of Anabaptist Theology and Piety," *Mennonite Quarterly Review*, XLVII (1973).

——————————. *Anabaptism and Asceticism. A Study in Intellectual Origins*. Scottdale, Pennsylvania: Herald Press, 1974.

Deppermann, Klaus. "Die Strassburger Reformatoren und die Krise des oberdeutschen Täufertums im Jahr 1527," *Mennonitische Geschichtsblätter*, XXX (1973).

——————————. and Yoder, John, "Ein Briefwechsel über die Bedeutung des Schleitheimer Bekenntnisses," *Mennonitische Geschichtsblätter* XXX (1973).

Döllinger, J. *Die Reformation, ihre innere Entwicklung und ihre Wirkungen*. Vol. I. Regensburg: Verlag von Joseph Manz, 1846.

Eder, Karl. *Das Land ob der Enns vor der Glaubenspaltung. Studien zur Reformationsgeschichte Oberösterreichs*. Vol. I. Vienna, 1933.

——————————. *Glaubensspaltung und Landestände in Oesterreich ob der Enns 1525-1602. Studien zur Reformationsgeschichte Oberösterreichs*. Vol. II. Vienna, 1936.

Engelhardt, Adolf. *Die Reformation in Nürnberg*. Vol. II. Nuremberg: J. L. Schrag, 1937.

Fast, Heinold. "Pilgram Marbeck und das oberdeutsche Täufertum. Ein neuer Handschriftenfund," *Archiv für Reformationsgeschichte*, XLVII (1956).

——————————. "Hans Krüsis Büchlein über Glauben und Taufe; ein Täuferdruck von 1525," *Zwingliana*, XI (1962).

——————————. "Reformation durch Provokation. Predigtstörung in den ersten Jahren der Reformation in der Schweiz," *Umstrittenes Täufertum 1525-1975. Neue Forschungen*. Edited by Hans-Jürgen Goertz. Göttingen: Vandenhoeck and Ruprecht, 1975.

Fellmann, Walter. "Theological Views of Hans Denck." Translated by Walter Klaassen. *Mennonite Life*, XVIII (1963).

——————————. "Martin Bucer und Hans Denck," *Mennonitische Geschichtsblätter*, XXIII (1966).

Foster, Claude, "Hans Denck and Johannes Buenderlin; A Comparative Study," *Mennonite Quarterly Review*, XXXIX (1965).

Friedmann, Robert. "Concerning the True Soldier of Christ. A Hitherto Unknown tract of the Philippite Brethren in Moravia," *Mennonite Quarterly Review*, V (1931).

―――――――――. "Eine dogmatische Hauptschrift der hutterischen Täufergemeinschaften in Mähren," *Archiv für Reformationsgeschichte*, XXIX (1932).

―――――――――. "Anabaptism and Protestantism," *Mennonite Quarterly Review*, XXIV (1950).

―――――――――. "Anabaptism in the Inn Valley," *Mennonite Life*, XV (1960).

―――――――――. "A Hutterite Book of Medieval Origin," *Mennonite Quarterly Review*, XXX (1965).

―――――――――. "Die Nikolsburger Artikel von 1527," *Jahrbuch der Gesellschaft für die Geschichte des Protestantismus in Oesterreich*, LXXXII (1966).

―――――――――. "The Nicolsburg Articles, a Problem of Early Anabaptist History," *Church History*, XXXVI (1967).

―――――――――. Review of Rollin Armour's *Anabaptist Baptism*, *Archiv für Reformationsgeschichte*, LX (1970).

―――――――――. *The Theology of Anbaptism: An Interpretation.* Scottdale, Pennsylvania: Herald Press, 1973.

Friesen, Abraham. "Thomas Müntzer and the Old Testament," *Mennonite Quarterly Review*. XLVII (1973).

Gäbler, Ulrich. "Eine unbeachtete Uebersetzung des Leonhard Freisleben genannt Eleutherobius," *Archiv für Reformationsgeschichte*, LXI (1970).

―――――――――. "Zum Problem des Spiritualismus im 16. Jahrhundert. Das Glaubensverständnis bei Johannes Bünderlin von Linz," *Theologische Zeitschrift*, XXIX (1973).

Goertz, Hans-Jürgen. *Innere und Äussere Ordnung in der Theologie Thomas Müntzers, Leiden:* E. J. Brill, 1967.

―――――――――. "Die Taufe im Täufertum." *Mennonitische Geschichtsblätter*, XXVII (1970).

―――――――――. "Der Mystiker mit dem Hammer," *Kerygma und Dogma*, XX (1974).

Goeters, Gerhard. *Ludwig Hätzer (ca. 1500 bis 1529): Spiritualist und Antitrinitarier. Eine Randfigur der frühen Täuferbewegung.* Gütersloh: C. Bertelmann Verlag, 1957.

Gritsch, Eric. "Thomas Müntzer and the Origins of Protestant Spiritualism," *Mennonite Quarterly Review*, XXXVII (1963).

―――――――――. *Reformer Without a Church.* Philadelphia: Fortress Press, 1967.

Grundmann, Herbert. *Studien Über Joachim von Fiore.* Reprint of 1927. Darmstadt: Wissenschaftliche Buchgesellschaft, 1966.

Güss, Ernst. *Die Kurpfälzische Regierung und das Täufertum bis zum Dreissigjährigen Krieg.* Stuttgart: Veröffentlichung der Kommission für geschichtliche Landeskunde in Baden-Württemberg, 1960.

Haake, G. *Hans Denck, ein Vorläufer der neueren Theologie: 1495-1527.* Norden, 1897.

Haas, Martin. "Der Weg der Täufer in die Absonderung," *Umstrittenes Täufertum 1525-1975; Neue Forschungen.* Edited by Hans-Jürgen Goertz. Göttingen: Vandenhoeck and Ruprecht, 1975.

Hägglund, Bengt. *The Background of Luther's Doctrine of Justification in Late Medieval Theology.* Philadelphia: Fortress Press, 1971.

Hall, Thor. "Possibilities of Erasmian Influence on Denck and Hubmaier in Their Views on the Freedom of the Will," *Mennonite Quarterly Review,* XXXV (1961).

Heberle, Diakonus, "Johann Denck und sein Büchlein vom Gesetz," *Theologische Studien und Kritiken,* XXIV (1851).

Hege, Christian. *Die Täufer in der Kurpfalz. Ein Beitrag zur badisch-pfälizischen Reformationsgeschichte.* Frankfurt: Hermann Minjon, 1908.

Hegler, Alfred. *Geist und Schrift bei Sebastian Franck. Eine Studie zur Geschichte des Spiritualismus in der Reformationszeit.* Freiburg: Mohr Verlag, 1892.

——————————. *Beiträge zur Geschichte der Mystik in der Reformationszeit.* Berlin: Schwetschke und Sohn, 1906.

Hein, Gerhard. "Die Täuferbewegung im Mittel-Rheinischen Raum von der Reformation bis zum Dreissigjährigen Krieg," *Ebernburg-Hefte,* XL (1972-73).

Hick, John. *Evil and the God of Love.* London: Fontana Library, 1968.

Hillerbrand, Hans. "Anabaptism and the Reformation: Another Look," *Church History,* XXIX (1960).

Hinrichs, Carl. *Luther und Müntzer; ihre Auseinandersetzung über Obrigkeit und Widerstandsrecht.* Berlin: Walter de Gruyter and Company, 1952.

Holl, Karl. "Luther und die Schwärmer," *Gesammelte Aufsätze zur Kirchengeschichte,* Vol. I. Tübingen: Mohr Verlag, 1932.

Ihringer, Bernhard. *Der Schuldbegriff bei den Mystikern der Reformationszeit.* Bern: Verlag Franke, 1912.

Iserloh, Erwin. "Luther und die Mystik." *The Church, Mysticism, Sanctification and the Natural in Luther's Thought.* Edited by Ivar Asheim. Philadelphia: Fortress Press, 1967.

Jäckel, Joseph. "Zur Geschichte der Wiedertäufer in Oberösterreich und speciell in Freistadt. Mit einer Einleitung über Entstehung und Wesen des Täuferthums überhaupt," *Bericht über das Museum Francisco-Carolinium Linz,* XLVII (1889).

Kamp, August. *Die Psalmendichtung des Jacob Dachser.* Griefswald: Buchdruckerei Hans Adler, 1931.

Keller, Ludwig. *Johann von Staupitz und die Anfänge der Reformation.* Reprint of 1888. Nieuwkoop: B. De Graaf, 1967.

——————————. *Ein Apostel der Wiedertäufer.* Leipzig: Verlag von S. Hirzel, 1882.

Kiwiet, Jan. *Pilgram Marbeck: Ein Führer in der Täuferbewegung der Reformationszeit.* 2nd ed. Kassel: Oncken Verlag, 1958.

Klaassen, Walter. "Hans Hut and Thomas Müntzer," *Baptist Quarterly,* XIX (1962).

_____. "The Nature of the Anabaptist Protest," Mennonite Quarterly Review, XLV (1971).

Klassen, Herbert. "Ambrosius Spittelmayr: His Life and Teachings," *Mennonite Quarterly Review*, XXXII (1958).

_____. "The Life and Teachings of Hans Hut," *Mennonite Quarterly Review*, XXXII (1958).

Klassen, William. "Pilgram Marbeck in Recent Research," *Mennonite Quarterly Review*, XXXII (1958).

_____. "Pilgram Marbeck's Two Books of 1531," *Mennonite Quarterly Review*, XXXIII (1959).

_____. "Was Hans Denck a Universalist?" *Mennonite Quarterly Review*, XXXIX (1965).

_____. *Covenant and Community*. Grand Rapids, Michigan: W. B. Eerdman Publishing Company, 1968.

Kohls, H. "Die Judenfrage in Hessen während der Reformationszeit," *Jahrbuch der hessischen kirchengeschichtlichen Vereinigungen*, XXI (1970).

Kolde, Theodor. "Zum Prozess des Johann Denck und der 'drei gottlosen Maler' von Nürnberg," *Kirchengeschichtliche Studien*. Dedicated to Hermann Reuter. Leipzig, 1888.

_____. "Hans Denck und die 'gottlosen Maler' in Nürnberg," *Beiträge zur bayerischen Kirchengeschichte*, VIII (1902).

List, Günther. *Chiliastische Utopie und Radikale Reformation. Die Erneuerung der Idee vom Tausendjährigen Reich im 16. Jahrhundert*. Munich: Wilhelm Fink Verlag, 1973.

Lortz, Joseph. *The Reformation in Germany*. Translated by Ronald Walls. 2 vols. London, 1968.

Loserth, Johann. "Der Anabaptismus in Tirol. Von Seinen Anfängen bis zum Tode Jakob Huters (1526-1536), *Archiv für österreichische Geschichte*, LXXVIII (1892).

Maron, Gottfried. "Thomas Müntzer als Theologe des Gerichts. Das 'Urteil'— ein Schlüsselbegriff seines Denkens," *Zeitschrift für Kirchengeschichte*, LXXXIII (1972).

Mecenseffy, Grete, "Die Herkunft des oberösterreichischen Täufertums," *Archiv für Reformationsgeschichte*, XLVII, 1956.

Moeller, Bernd. "Piety in Germany around 1500." Translated by Joyce Irwin. *The Reformation in Medieval Perspective*. Edited by Steven Ozment. Chicago: Quadrangle Books, 1971.

Müller, Lydia. *Der Kommunismus der mährischen Wiedertäufer*. Leipzig: M. Heinius Nachfolger, Eger, and Sievers, 1927.

Naumann, Leopold. *Deutsche Mystik*. Leipzig: Verlag von Quelle and Meyer, 1925.

Neff, Christian. "Zur Haakeschen Schrift: Hans Denck, ein Vorläufer der Neueren Theologie," *Mennonitische Blätter*, XLV (1898).

Neumann, Gerhard. "Eschatologische und chiliastische Gedanken in der Reformationszeit, besonders bei den Täufern," *Die Welt als Geschichte*, XIX (1959).

Nicoladoni, Alexander. *Johannes Bünderlin von Linz und die oberösterreichischen Täufergemeinden in den Jahren 1525-1531*. Berlin: R. Gärtners

Verlag, 1893.

Nipperdey, Thomas. "Theologie und Revolution bei Thomas Müntzer," *Archiv für Reformationsgeschichte*, LIV (1963).

Obermann, Heiko. "Simul Gemitus et Raptus," *The Church, Mysticism, Sanctification and the Natural in Luther's Thought*. Edited by Ivar Asheim. Philadelphia: Fortress Press, 1967.

————————. *The Harvest of Medieval Theology* Revised ed. Grand Rapids, Michigan: W. B. Eerdman Publishing Company, 1967.

Oyer, John S. *Lutheran Reformers Against Anabaptists: Luther, Melanchthon and Menius and the Anabaptists of Central Germany*. The Hague: Martinus Nijhoff, 1964.

Ozment, Steven. *Homo Spiritualis. A Comparative Study of the Anthropology of Johannes Tauler, Jean Gerson and Martin Luther (1509-16) in the Context of their Theological Thought*. Leiden: E. J. Brill, 1969.

————————— (ed.). *The Reformation in Medieval Perspective*. Chicago: Quadrangle Books, 1971.

————————. *Mysticism and Dissent: Religious Ideology and Social Protest in the Sixteenth Century*. New Haven and London: Yale University Press, 1973.

————————. "Mysticism, Nominalism and Dissent," *Pursuit of Holiness*. Edited by Heiko Oberman & C.E.Trinkaus. Leiden:E.J.Brill, 1973.

Packull, Werner. "Denck's Alleged Baptism by Hubmaier. Its Significance for the Origin of South German-Austrian Anabaptism," *Mennonite Quarterly Review*, XLVII (1973).

————————. "Gottfried Seebass on Hans Hut: A Discussion," *Mennonite Quarterly Review*, XLIX (1975).

————————. "Zur Entwicklung des süddeutschen Täufertums," *Umstrittenes Täufertum 1525-1975. Neue Forschungen*. Edited by Hans-Jürgen Goertz. Göttingen: Vandenhoeck and Ruprecht, 1975.

————————; Stayer, James; and Deppermann, Klaus. "From Monogenesis to Polygenesis: The Historical Discussion of Anabaptist Origins," *Mennonite Quarterly Review*, XLIX (1975).

Penner, Horst. "Christian Entfelder. Ein mährischer Täuferprediger und herzoglicher Rat am Hofe Albrechts von Preussen," *Mennonitische Geschichtsblätter*, XXIII (1966).

Pieper, Josef. *Scholasticism: Personalities and Problems of Medieval Philosophy*. Pantheon Books, 1960.

Pleuser, Christine. *Die Benennung und der Begriff des Leidens bei J. Tauler*. Berlin: Erich Schmidt Verlag, 1967.

Prenter, Regin. *Spiritus Creator*. Translated by John Jensen. Philadelphia: Fortress Press, 1953.

————————. *Luther's Theology of the Cross*. Philadelphia: Fortress Press, 1971.

Quiring, Horst. "Luther und die Mystik," *Zeitschrift für Systematische Theologie*, XIII (1936).

Radlkofer, Max. "Jacob Dachser und Sigmund Salminger," *Beiträge für bayerischen Kirchengeschichte*, VI (1900).

Raupach, Bernard. *Presbyterologia Austriaca*. Vol. II. Hamburg, 1741.

Reeves, Marjorie. *The Influence of Prophecy in the Later Middle Ages.* Oxford: Clarendon Press, 1969.

——————————, and Hirsch-Reich, Beatrice. *The Figurae of Joachim of Fiore.* Oxford: Clarendon Press, 1972.

Rischar, Klaus. "DerMissionar Eucharius Binder und sein Mitarbeiter Joachim März," *Mennonitische Geschichtsblätter,*XXV (1968).

Rössler, Hans. "Wiedertäufer in und aus München 1527-1528," *Oberbayerisches Archiv,* LXXXV (1962).

Roth, Friedrich. "Johann Schilling, der Barfüssermönch und der Aufstand im Jahre 1524," *Zeitschrift des historischen Vereins für Schwaben und Neuburg,* VI (1879).

——————————. *Augsburgs Reformationsgeschichte.*Vol. I. Munich: Theodor Ackermann, 1881.

——————————. *Die Einführung der Reformation in Nürnberg.* Würzburg: A. Stubers, 1885.

——————————. *Augsburgs Reformationsgeschichte 1517-1530.* Vol. I. 2nd ed. Munich: Theodor Ackermann, 1901.

——————————. "Der Meistersinger Georg Breuning und die religiöse Bewegung der Waldenser und Täufer im 15. und 16. Jahrhundert," *Monatshefte der Comensius Gesellschaft,* XIII (1904).

Ruh, Kurt. "Die trinitarische Spekulation in deutscher Mystik und Scholastik," *Zeitschrift für deutsche Philologie,* LXII (1953).

Rupp, Gordon. "Thomas Müntzer, Hans Hut and the 'Gospel of all Creatures,' " *Bulletin of the John Rylands Library,* XLIII (1961).

——————————. *Patterns of Reformation.* London: Epworth Press, 1969.

——————————. "Protestant Spirituality in the First Age of the Reformation," *Popular Belief and Practice.* Edited by G. J. Cuming and D. Baker. Cambridge University Press, 1972.

Saalfeld, Hans. "Jakob Dachser. Priester, Wiedertäufer, evangelischer Pfarrer," *Zeitschrift für bayerische Kirchengeschichte,* XXXI (1962).

Schäufele, Wolfgang. *Das missionarische Bewusstsein und Wirken der Täufer: Dargestellt nach oberdeutschen Quellen.*Neukirchen: Neukirchner Verlag, 1966.

Scheel, Otto. "Taulers Mystik und Luthers reformatorische Entdeckung," *Festgabe für Julius Kafton.* Tübingen: Mohr Verlag, 1920.

Schmid, Hans-Dieter. "Das Hutsche Täufertum. Ein Beitrag zur Charakterisierung einer täuferischen Richtung aus der Frühzeit der Täuferbewegung," *Historische Jahrbuch,* XCI (1971).

——————————. *Täufertum und Obrigkeit in Nürnberg.* Erlangen: Dissertation-Druckerei Hogel, 1972.

Schnaufer, Christian and Haffner, H. *Beiträge zur Geschichte der Esslinger Reformation* Esslingen am Neckar: Otto Bechtle, 1932.

Scholem, Gershom. *Major Trends in Jewish Mysticism.* New York: Schocken Books, 1967.

Schottenloher, Karl. *Phillip Ulhart: ein Augsburger Winkeldrucker und Helfershelfer der 'Schwärmer' und 'Wiedertäufer' (1523-1529).* Reprint of 1921 edition. Nieuwkoop: B. De Graaf, 1967.

Schwab, Paul. "Augsburg and the early Anabaptists," *Reformation Studies; Essays in Honour of Roland H. Bainton.* Edited by Franklin H. Littell. Richmond, Virginia: John Knox Press, 1962.

Schwindt, Adolf. *Hans Denck, ein Vorkämpfer undogmatischen Christentums, 1495-1527.* Habertshof: Neuwerkverlag Schlüchtern, 1924.

Seebass, Gottfried. "Die Reformation in Nürnberg," *Mitteilung des Vereins für Geschichte der Stadt Nürnberg,* LV (1967-68).

_____. *Das Reformatorische Werk des Andreas Osiander.* Nuremberg: Selbstverlag des Vereins für bayerische Kirchengeschichte, 1967.

_____. "Zwei Briefe von Andreas Osiander," *Mitteilung des Vereins für Geschichte der Stadt Nürnberg,* LVII (1970).

_____. "Apologia Reformationis. Eine bisher unbekannte Verteidigungsschrift Nürnbergs aus dem Jahre 1528," *Zeitschrift für bayerische Kirchengeschichte,* XXXIX (1970).

_____. "Bauernkrieg und Täufertum in Franken," *Zeitschrift für Kirchengeschichte,* LXXXV (1974).

_____. "Das Zeichen der Erwählten. Zum Verständnis der Taufe bei Hans Hut," *Umstrittenes Täufertum 1525-1975. Neue Forschungen.* Edited by Hans-Jürgen Goertz. Göttingen: Vandenhoeck and Ruprecht, 1975.

Seifert, Wolfgang. *Synagogue and Church in the Middle Ages: Two Symbols in Art and Literature.* New York: Ungar Publishing Company, 1970.

Seubert, Josef. *Untersuchung zur Geschichte der Reformation in der ehemaligen freien Reichsstadt Dinkelsbühl.* Hamburg: Mathiesen Verlag, 1971.

Sider, Ronald, *Andreas Bodenstein von Karlstadt. The Development of His Thought 1517-1525.* Leiden: E. J. Brill, 1974.

Siedel, Gottlob. *Die Mystik Taulers.* Leipzig: Hinrichsche Buchhandlung, 1921.

Smucker, Donovan. "The Theological Triumph of the Early Anabaptist Mennonites: The Rediscovery of Biblical Theology in Paradox," *Mennonite Quarterly Review,* XIX (1945).

Stadelmann, Rudolf von. *Vom Geist des Ausgehenden Mittelalters: Studien zur Geschichte der Weltanschauung von Nicolaus Cusanus bis Sebastian Franck.* Halle/Saale: Max Niemeyer Verlag, 1929.

Stähelin, Ernst. *Das theologische Lebenswerk Johannes Oekolampads.* Leipzig, 1939.

Stayer, James. "Hans Hut's Doctrine on the Sword: An Attempted Solution," *Mennonite Quarterly Review,* XXXIX (1965).

_____. "Eine fanatische Täuferbewegung in Esslingen und Reutlingen," *Blätter für württembergische Kirchengeschichte,* LXVIII/ LXIX (1968/69).

_____. *Anabaptists and the Sword.* Lawrence, Kansas: Coronado Press, 1972.

_____; Packull, Werner; and Deppermann, Klaus. "From Monogenesis to Polygenesis: The Historical Discussion of Anabaptist Origins," *Mennonite Quarterly Review,* XLIX (1975).

_____. "Die Anfänge des schweizerischen Täufertums im reformierten Kongregationalismus," *Umstrittenes Täufertum 1525-1975.*

Neue Forschungen. Edited by Hans-Jürgen Goertz. Göttingen: Vandenhoeck and Ruprecht, 1975.

Steinmetz, David. "Scholasticism and Radical Reform; Nominalist Motifs in the Theology of Balthasar Hubmaier," *Mennonite Quarterly Review*, XL (1971).

——————————. *Reformers in the Wings.* Philadelphie: Fortress Press, 1971.

Teufel, Eberhard. "Bünderlin," *Neue Deutsche Biographie*, II (1955).

Thurmann, Philoon. "Hans Greiffenberger and the Reformation in Nuernberg," *Mennonite Quarterly Review*, XXXVI (1962).

Troeltsch, Ernst. *Die Soziallehren der Christlichen Kirchen und Gruppen.* Tübingen: Mohr Verlag, 1912.

Vittali, Otto. *Die Theologie des Wiedertäufers Hans Denck.* Offenburg, 1932.

Vogelsang, Erich. "Weltbild und Kreuzestheologie in den Höllenfartsstreitigkeiten der Reformationszeit," *Archiv für Reformationsgeschichte,* XXXVII (1940).

Weiss, Konrad. "Die Seelenmetaphysik des Meister Eckhart," *Zeitschrift für Kirchengeschichte,* LII (1933).

Widmoser, Eduard. "Das Tiroler Täufertum," *Tiroler Heimat. Jahrbuch für Geschichte und Volkskunde,* XV (1951).

Wiedemann, Hans. "Die Wiedertäufergemeinde in Passau 1527-1535," *Ostbayrische Grenzmarken: Passauer Jahrbuch für Geschichte, Kunst und Volkskunde,* VI (1962/63).

Williams, George. "Popularized German Mysticism as a Factor in the Rise of Anabaptist Communism," *Glaube, Geist, Geschichte: Festschrift für Ernst Benz.* Edited by Gerhard Müller and Winfried Zeller. Marburg, 1967.

——————————. *The Radical Reformation.* Philadelphia: Westminster Press, 1962.

——————————. "Sanctification in the Testimony of Several So-called Schwärmer," *The Church, Mysticism, Sanctification and the Natural in Luther's Thought.* Edited by Ivar Asheim. Philadelphia: Fortress Press, 1967.

Windhorst, Christof. "Wort und Geist: Zur Frage des Spiritualismus bei Balthasar Hubmaier im Vergleich zu Zwingli und Luther," *Mennonitische Geschichtsblätter,* XXXI (1974).

Wiswedel, Wilhelm. *Bilder und Führergestalten aus dem Täufertum.* Vols. I and II. Kassel: J. G. Oncken Nachfolger, 1928.

——————————. "Gabriel Ascherham und die nach ihm benannte Bewegung," *Archiv für Reformationsgeschichte,* XXXIV (1937).

Wolfart, K. "Beiträge zur Augsburger Reformationsgeschichte. Part III: Caspar Schwenckfeld und Bonifacius Wolfart," *Beiträge zur bayerischen Kirchengeschichte,* VIII (1902).

Yoder, John. "The Hermeneutics of the Anabaptists," *Mennonite Quarterly Review,* XLI (1967).

Zeman, Jarold. *The Anabaptists and the Czech Brethren in Moravia. A Study of Origin and Contacts.* The Hague: Mouton, 1969.

Zschäbitz, Gerhard. *Zur mitteldeutschen Wiedertäuferbewegung nach dem grossen Bauernkrieg.* Berlin: Rutten and Loening, 1958.

Zur Mühlen, Karl Heinz. *Nos Extra Nos. Luthers Theologie zwischen Mystik und Scholastik.* Tübingen: J.C.B. Mohr, 1972.

INDEX

Werner O. Packull was born July 14, 1941, in East Prussia, Germany. He is presently an assistant professor at Renison College, University of Waterloo, Ontario, Canada.

He received his BA at the University of Guelph in 1969, his MA at the University of Waterloo in 1970, and his PhD at Queen's University in 1974. He was granted a Canada Council Doctoral Fellowship for 1970-74 and The Swiss Ambassador Award at the University of Guelph in 1969.

Dr. Packull's writing has appeared in the *Mennonite Quarterly*

Review and in *Umstrittenes Täufertum 1525-1975: Neue Forschungen*, edited by Hans-Jürgen Goertz. He is a member of the American Society for Reformation Research, Mennonitischer Geschichtsverein, and of the supporting faculty of the Consortium in Reformation History of University of Guelph and University of Waterloo.

Dr. Packull and his wife are the parents of two children.